MONETARY THEORY, POLICY, AND FINANCIAL MARKETS

MONETARY THEORY, POLICY, AND FINANCIAL MARKETS

William R. Hosek
Professor of Economics
Whittemore School of Business and Economics
University of New Hampshire

Frank Zahn
School of Business and Economics
Madison College
and
Bowling Green State University

McGraw-Hill Book Company
New York   St. Louis   San Francisco   Auckland   Bogotá   Düsseldorf   Johannesburg
London   Madrid   Mexico   Montreal   New Delhi   Panama   Paris   São Paulo   Singapore
Sydney   Tokyo   Toronto

To
Jeanette
Sibyl
Marissa
and
Roberta
David
Deborah

**MONETARY
THEORY,
POLICY,
AND
FINANCIAL
MARKETS**

1 2 3 4 5 6 7 8 9 0 DODO 7 8 3 2 1 0 9 8 7 6

This book was set in Optima by Textbook Services, Inc.
The editors were J. S. Dietrich and Annette Hall;
the designer was Jo Jones;
the production supervisor was Leroy A. Young.
The drawings were done by ANCO/Boston.
R. R. Donnelley & Sons Company was printer and binder.

Library of Congress Cataloging in Publication Data

Hosek, William R
    Monetary theory, policy, and financial markets.

    1. Money. 2. Monetary policy. 3. Money—Mathematical models. 4. Finance. I. Zahn, Frank,
date   joint author. II. Title.
HG221.H83   332.4   76-22724
ISBN 0-07-030436-X

CONTENTS

PART FOUR MONETARY POLICY

PREFACE

This book is designed for use in a one-quarter or one-semester course in monetary economics which is offered in undergraduate business administration and economics programs. While the approach used in presenting the material is mostly verbal and nontechnical, the book provides a thorough analysis of all substantive theoretical, empirical, and policy issues. Students who have completed a principles of economics course and who have little or no background in mathematics will be able to understand the material.

Two main features distinguish this book from others. First, in addition to the traditional IS-LM framework for monetary analysis, a financial market model is provided so that students can understand more clearly the mechanism by which monetary (and fiscal) policy is transmitted to the real (goods and services) sector of the economy. Recent developments in macroeconomic theory and econometric model building indicate that if the impact of monetary policy on the economy is to be understood, it must be discussed in the broader context of the financial system. Money and the banking system play a central role in the financial system. But to appreciate fully this role, it must be analyzed in relation to the whole system. Second, emphasis is placed on utilizing economic theory to understand the impact of monetary policy on the economy. Consequently, the theory is developed before the policy is discussed rather than the other way around. About one-third of this book is a discussion of foreign and domestic policy goals, modes of policy implementation, and constraints on policy. Moreover, policy is not discussed in a vacuum. References are made to the performance of the United States economy throughout the book.

The book is divided into four parts. Part One defines money and explains its role in facilitating the flow of goods and services in the economy. In addition, money's role in facilitating the flow of loanable funds in financial markets is explained. Part Two provides a detailed analysis of the money market, including the money creation process and theories of money supply and demand. Differences between the monetarist and Keynesian approaches to money demand are carefully identified. Part Three discusses the models that are used for monetary analysis. Actually the models are not completely distinguishable, since their theoretical content overlaps. However, each provides its own unique perspective and helps to acquaint the student with the breadth and diversity of thinking in monetary economics. The models include the IS-LM model, a financial market model we call the LB-LM model, portfolio balance models, econometric models, and disequilibrium models. Part Four uses the analytical tools developed in the first three parts to discuss the problems toward which monetary policy is directed. These include inflation, unemployment, balance of payments, and economic growth. Throughout the policy discussions, issues of the Keynesian-monetarist controversy are carefully explained.

We are indebted to more people than can be acknowledged in a preface. However, there are those whose special contributions must be mentioned. Among these are J. Stephen Dietrich, economics and finance editor of McGraw-Hill, David Vroorman, Karen Johnson, Jerry Hollenhorst, Charles J. Ellard, W. Douglas Morgan, Thomas F. Cargill, Bernard Gauci, V. Michael Hartman, Rodger Trenary, Patrick O'Brien, Heidimarie Sherman, and Donald Sternitzke, who provided valuable comments during the preparation of the manuscript. Very special thanks go to James R. Ostas, who read the final manuscript and provided many substantive comments on the material. Finally, thanks go to Kris Carmichael, Linda Fitzgerald, Cindy McElhiney, and Dolores Reynolds, who typed the drafts of the manuscript. The sole responsibility for any shortcomings and errors in the book is the authors'.

William R. Hosek

Frank Zahn

MONETARY THEORY, POLICY, AND FINANCIAL MARKETS

ONE

MONEY AND ITS PLACE IN THE ECONOMY

INTRODUCTION

This book is about money, that mysterious good that has been described by some as the "root of all evil" (actually the adage is "The Love of money is the root of all evil") and by others as the "great wheel of circulation." However, in discussing money, we shall be a little less romantic and somewhat more concrete. Money is an important element in economic affairs, and consequently we shall be interested in learning what money is, why people hold money, how money affects the economy, and what role the government plays in regulating the amount of money in the economy. Toward that end it will first be necessary to settle on a definition of money. That is the function of this chapter.

1.1 THEORETICAL DEFINITION OF MONEY

In the popular mind money is often confused with wealth and income. As we shall see later in the book, depending on the assumptions made, money is part of total wealth, but money and income are conceptually different things. We often say that we work to "make money" when we are actually earning income. There are relationships between the two; however, they are different concepts. Income represents a flow of resources over time. For example, I receive income for my labor services which may be used to purchase $200 worth of goods and services per week. Money, on the other hand, is the total amount or stock of a particular asset or group of assets at a point in time.

Money is normally used to facilitate the financing or payment of income. For example, I could receive my salary income in the form of jewelry ($200 worth per week if the above rate applies). However, to get the goods and services I ultimately desire, such as food, clothing, and housing, I would have to convert my income into those commodities. Under normal circumstances, it would not be a simple matter for me to convert jewelry into food, clothing, and housing. There is, however, an asset that is easily convertible into the ultimate goods and services I desire. There is an asset that people are willing to accept in exchange for any good and with which they are willing to make payment for any good. The asset is called *money*. Thus, the property that distinguishes money from all other goods is the fact that money is a universally accepted *medium of exchange*. This is perhaps its most important function, for without money, exchange of goods and services would be more complicated and difficult. Where exchange is restricted or made more difficult, people become worse off.

The use of money is not confined to its function as a medium of exchange. Since money is convertible into goods and services, command over such goods and services can be stored up by storing up money. Thus, money is useful as a convenient *store of value*. Its convenience follows from the fact that money is nonbulky and lightweight, it is easily divisible into small units, and it is nonperishable. Moreover, the costs of storage are low (although not zero, as we shall see in a later chapter). Real goods, of course, may be used as a store of value. However, their use in this capacity does not exhibit the same level of convenience as the use of money does.

A third function of money follows from its general acceptance as a medium of exchange. If money is readily convertible into all kinds of goods and services, then the prices of all goods and services may be stated in terms of money rather than in terms of each other. Money provides a quick and efficient method of calculating exchange ratios of goods and services. To illustrate, suppose we had an economy with only three goods and no money, and suppose the three goods were horses, footballs, and beer. Admittedly it would be a strange economy, but after all, this is only an illustration. In order for exchange to take place in this three-commodity world, six separate prices must be known: (1) the price of horses in terms of footballs, (2) the price of horses in terms of beer, (3) the price of footballs in terms of horses, (4) the price of footballs in terms of beer, (5) the price of beer in terms of horses, and (6) the price of beer in terms of footballs.

When money is introduced, the price of every commodity can be expressed in terms of money. In the three-commodity world with money, there would be only three prices. Given the money prices of beer, horses, and footballs, one could quickly calculate the exchange ratios among the commodities, if desired. Thus money serves as a *unit of account* and thereby saves considerable bookkeeping and confusion.

Of course not all transactions are made with a provision for immediate payment. Often goods are purchased with the provision that payment is to be made at some time in the future. Money serves as a unit of account in this case also, both for the payment of the purchase price (the principal of the loan) and for the amount of interest, if any.

Although the functions of money can be readily identified, the identification of those specific things in the real world that serve as money is not as simple. Consequently, considerable controversy has been generated in empirical studies over the "true" definition of money. Were the only function of money its use as a medium of exchange, the identification of money would be relatively easy. In the United States economy today only two assets are generally accepted as exchange media. These are currency holdings of the nonbank public and demand deposits of the nonbank public.* Currency includes both paper money and coin, and demand deposits are primarily checking account balances at commercial banks. No other assets in the United States economy are as widely accepted in payment for goods and services as these. The sum of these two assets constitutes the conventional, or narrow, definition of money, currently referred to as M_1.

However, we noted that money does perform other functions. From the standpoint of the empirical definition of money, the most important other function is money's service as a store of value. In recognition of this function, other definitions of money have been developed. These other definitions include, in addition to currency and demand deposits, financial assets that are stores of value and that are very close to being a medium of exchange in the sense that they can be easily and quickly converted into currency or demand deposits. Thus a second definition of money adds time deposits at commercial banks to M_1. This definition of money is popularly called M_2. Beyond that, there is a third definition, M_3, which adds to M_2 deposits at mutual savings banks and savings and loan associations (and, since 1975, credit union shares).†

Nonbank public is a term used to identify the private sector exclusive of commercial banks.

†For the precise definitions, see "Revision of Money Stock Measures and Member Bank Reserves and Deposits," *Federal Reserve Bulletin,* December 1974, pp. 817–827. Current Federal Reserve practice excludes United States government demand deposits and interbank deposits from the definition of money.

Further definitions of money are possible, since any asset can serve as a store of value. However, the distinguishing feature which enables an asset to be included in the definition of money is the extent to which that asset can be easily and quickly converted into M_1. The ability to be converted into M_1 is called *liquidity*. The more liquid an asset, the lower the cost of converting it into M_1. The broader definitions of money add to M_1 those assets that are "highly" liquid. For example, time deposits of commercial banks are included in the M_2 definition of money because, in general, their conversion costs per dollar are lower than those of other assets such as stocks, bonds, and real estate.

How liquid must an asset be before it is included in a definition of money? That depends on the interpretation of the person defining money, and this interpretation varies from person to person. That is why we have many definitions of money. For all practical purposes, however, the above three definitions are the most widely used.

Table 1.1 lists the three measures of money for the years 1960 through 1975. Their growth rates are also shown in the table. One of the purposes of studying money and banking is to learn what the relationship is between changes in money and changes in the level of economic activity. If the three measures of money shown in Table 1.1 all changed at the same rate, it would not make much difference which definition of money we adopted. However, an exami-

Table 1.1
Measures of the Money Stock and Their Growth Rates: 1960–1975

	M_1		M_2		M_3	
Year	Level (billions)	Annual Percentage Change	Level (billions)	Annual Percentage Change	Level (billions)	Annual Percentage Change
1960	$144.2	0.5	$217.1	2.9	$ 314.4	5.0
1961	148.7	3.1	228.6	5.2	336.5	7.0
1962	150.9	1.5	242.8	6.2	362.9	7.8
1963	156.5	3.7	258.9	6.6	393.2	8.3
1964	163.7	4.6	277.1	7.0	426.3	8.4
1965	171.3	4.6	301.4	8.7	462.7	8.5
1966	175.4	2.4	317.8	5.4	485.2	4.8
1967	186.9	6.5	349.7	10.0	532.8	9.8
1968	201.5	7.8	382.4	9.3	577.1	8.3
1969	208.6	3.5	392.1	2.5	593.8	2.8
1970	221.2	6.0	425.2	8.4	641.2	7.9
1971	235.2	6.3	473.0	11.2	726.9	13.3
1972	255.7	8.7	525.5	11.1	822.4	13.1
1973	271.5	6.1	572.2	8.9	895.3	8.8
1974	283.6	4.4	613.8	7.2	955.0	6.6
1975 (est.)	296.3	4.4	667.5	8.7	1,046.7	9.6

Source: Economic Reports of the President.

nation of the growth rates indicates distinct differences among the three measures. Consequently we shall have to settle on a single definition of money for use in the rest of the book. We will do this after we examine some of the empirical studies that bear on the definition problem.

1.2 EMPIRICAL DEFINITION OF MONEY

It might be expected that the use of different definitions of money would create some confusion in the literature on monetary theory and policy. Policy makers seeking advice from economists about the proper conduct of monetary policy often must first determine how those economists define money.* Further, empirical conclusions about the effect of money on the economy depend in part on the definition of money used by the investigator. To help us understand the problems involved, it is appropriate that we examine some of the attempts to discover or determine empirically the "correct" definition of money.

The preceding section should provide some ideas for a further examination of the issue. Consider the relationship between money and income. Money is the economy's medium of exchange. As such, the demand for money to use in conducting transactions should depend in part on the level of income. Presumably, as an individual's income rises, he or she will make more purchases or transactions than before. Thus a greater quantity of money will be needed or demanded to carry out the increased number of transactions. If this relationship is stable, there should be a strong relationship between income and the correct definition of money and a weak relationship between income and the incorrect definition of money.

The relationship between money and income may also be viewed from another perspective. We will discover later that the quantity of money may be an important determinant of income. Changes in the amount of money in the economy will produce changes in financial and other markets that will ultimately lead to changes in the economy's level of income. Again, the implication is that money and income are positively or directly related.

If we do accept, on such grounds, the statement that money and income are closely related, it follows that the "best" definition of money is the one that correlates most closely with income. The danger with this approach is that it tends to assume the conclusion. Perhaps our theories are wrong. Perhaps money and income are really unrelated. If so, we shall be in error if we define money as that asset which correlates most closely with income. If we adopt that definition, we will be unable to test the role of income in money demand and the causal influence of changes in money on income.

---

*For example, see the questions asked by Senator William Proxmire in Committee on Banking, Housing and Urban Affairs Hearings, *Monetary Policy Oversight,* U.S. Senate, 1975.

However, this approach has been used by some writers * Their results, taken together, do not provide a solid basis for selecting any particular set of assets and calling it money. The statistical results indicate that all three of the most important definitions of money are closely related to income. The differences are too small to be significant.

The earlier discussion suggests an alternative approach to the definition of money. Money is a medium of exchange, and only currency and demand deposits fulfill that function. However, money is also a store of value, and other assets such as savings accounts, stocks, bonds, and real estate are substitutes for currency and demand deposits as a store of value. Suppose we assume that the store of value function of money is very important, perhaps even more important than the medium of exchange function. Then if we include currency and demand deposits in the definition of money, we should also include those other assets that substitute very closely for the value storage function of currency and demand deposits.

Thus, a second approach to the definition problem would attempt to measure the degree of substitutability between various financial assets and M_1. Assets that are sufficiently close substitutes for M_1 would be counted as money. The most common approach measuring the degree of substitutability is to estimate the relative responsiveness of M_1 to changes in the yields or interest rates on potential substitutes. A single number measure of such responsiveness is the *cross elasticity*, which is the percentage change in M_1 divided by the percentage change in the yield on the substitute asset.

For example, suppose a 10 percent *increase* in the interest rate on ordinary savings accounts induces people to *reduce* their holdings of M_1 by shifting 5 percent of those holdings into their savings accounts. The cross elasticity between M_1 and savings accounts is

$$\frac{\text{Percent change in } M_1}{\text{Percent change in savings account yield}} = \frac{-5\%}{10\%}$$
$$= -0.5$$

If M_1 and savings accounts were not substitutes at all, a change in the interest rate on savings accounts would induce no change in M_1. In that case the cross elasticity would be zero. The opposite occurs when two goods are perfect substitutes. In that case the cross elasticity tends toward minus infinity.

In one study, Tong Hun Lee found the cross elasticity of M_1 with respect to

---

*A representative sample would include M. Friedman and D. Meiselman, "The Relative Stability of Monetary Velocity and the Investment Multiplier in the United States, 1897–1958," in Commission on Money and Credit, *Stabilization Policies* (Englewood Cliffs, N. J.: Prentice-Hall, 1963); D. Hulett, "More on an Empirical Definition of Money: Note," *American Economic Review,* June 1971, pp. 462–468; G. G. Kaufman, "More on an Empirical Definition of Money," *American Economic Review,* March 1969, pp. 78–87; and R. H. Timberlake and J. Fortson, "Time Deposits in the Definition of Money," *American Economic Review,* March 1967, pp. 190–194.

the yield on savings and loan association shares to be -0.408 and with respect to the yield on commercial bank time deposits to be -0.106.* This would imply that savings and loan association shares are closer substitutes for M_1 than are commercial bank time deposits, although the degree of substitutability in either case is not very high.†

If the degree of substitutability is less than perfect, money measures such as M_2 and M_3, which simply add the relevant time and savings deposits to M_1, may be faulty as empirical counterparts of the money we think of in theory. Consequently, some writers have suggested that money be defined as a weighted average of money-type assets where the weights reflect the degree of substitutability between M_1 and the substitute asset. Perfect substitutes receive weights of unity (1), and imperfect substitutes receive smaller (but positive) weights.

This approach was taken recently by V. Karuppan Chetty.‡ Chetty estimated the relevant weights for M_1, commercial bank time deposits T, mutual savings bank deposits MS, and savings and loan association shares SL. The weights reflect the extent to which T, MS, and SL exhibit the "moneyness" that M_1 exhibits. The resulting definition of money is

$$M = M_1 + T + 0.880 MS + 0.615 SL$$

Thus T has the same degree of moneyness as M_1, and mutual savings bank deposits have only 88 percent as much moneyness as M_1. However, Chetty's approach and results are still under discussion.§

Thus universal, or even near-universal, agreement on the correct definition of money simply does not exist. From the above results Lee and Chetty reach different conclusions about the relationships among M_1, time deposits, and savings and loan association shares. This reflects, in part, the different approaches taken and, in part, the inadequacy of existing statistical tools. In the course of the book we will discover many other areas of disagreement. Rather than becoming discouraged, the student should recognize that there are still many opportunities for creative work in economics. Ultimate truth still awaits discovery. However, for purposes of this book we must make a decision about the definition of money to be used.

We shall use M_1 (currency and demand deposits) as the definition of money

---

*T. H. Lee, "Alternative Interest Rates and the Demand for Money: The Empirical Evidence," *American Economic Review,* December 1967, pp. 1168–1181.

†Lee's results have not gone unchallenged. See M. J. Hamburger, "Alternative Interest Rates and the Demand for Money: Comment," *American Economic Review,* June 1969, pp. 407–412.

‡V. K. Chetty, "On Measuring the Nearness of Near-Moneys," *American Economic Review,* June 1969, pp. 270–281.

§See T. H. Lee, "On Measuring the Nearness of Near-Moneys: Comment," and L. Steinhauer and J. Chang, "Comment," *American Economic Review,* March 1972, pp. 217–225.

for two reasons. First, only M_1 fulfills all the functions of money. Second, no compelling evidence exists to support an alternative definition.

1.3 PLAN OF THE BOOK

The nation's quantity of money is a stock measured at a point in time. During a time period the stock of money is used to facilitate multiple transactions, i.e., money turns over several times. The turnover rate on all transactions in output, factor input, and financial markets is called the *transactions velocity of money*. The quantity of money times its turnover rate defines the *funds* during a time period which facilitate the flow of goods and services in output and factor input markets and financial assets in financial markets. To understand money's role in the economy and the impact of changes in the quantity of money on both output (and factor input) and financial markets, it is necessary to understand (1) the motivation for income and expenditure flows in output and factor input markets, (2) the motivation for lending and borrowing flows in financial markets, (3) the determinants of the quantity of money, and (4) the interrelationships between output and financial markets.

In Chapter 2 we begin by developing a theory of income and expenditure flows and indicate the need for a theory of financial markets in order to explain economic activity. In Chapter 3 we provide descriptive material about financial markets, institutions, and instruments. And in Chapter 4 we develop a theory of loanable funds (i.e., a flow analysis of financial markets) and indicate the need for a stock analysis of financial markets (i.e., an analysis of the money market). In Part Two we develop a theory of the money market, examining in detail the forces which shape the supply and demand for the stock of money.

In Part Three, Chapter 9 we integrate our analysis of income and expenditures (flows) with our analysis of money (stock) and examine the impact and effectiveness of policies, particularly the policies of the monetary and fiscal authorities, on output demand. In addition, we integrate our loanable funds theory with our monetary theory in order to more carefully explain the financial activity that transmits the policy changes to changes in output demand. In Chapter 10 we analyze the relationship between the money and output markets, paying particular attention to the determination of the price level. Chapter 11 is a discussion of the more recent portfolio balance models for monetary analysis. Many of the ideas developed in the first 11 chapters have been incorporated into statistical forecasting models that are useful in policy formulation because they provide quantitative estimates of the impact of monetary policy on the economy. Chapter 12 deals with a representative sample of such models. Part Three closes with a discussion in Chapter 13 of disequilibrium approaches to the analysis of financial markets, a relatively new area of investigation.

Monetary theory and policy are usually spoken of in the same breath. Since the end of World War II, the United States has sought, under statute, to use policy to stabilize the economy. Part Four, Chapters 14 through 18, deals with the goals and objectives of domestic and foreign policy, problems of policy implementation, and comparisons of monetary and fiscal policies. The book ends with a review in Chapter 19 of the history of policy in the United States.

SUMMARY NOTES

1. Money is an asset that serves as a medium of exchange, a store of value, and a unit of account.
2. Depending on the relative importance of the different functions, the empirical definition of money ranges from a narrow definition consisting of currency and demand deposits to broader definitions which add time deposits and other assets to the narrow definition.
3. Various attempts to identify the "correct" definition of money have ended in stalemate.
4. The quantity of money times its turnover rate defines the funds available for transactions in goods, factors of production, and financial assets.

DISCUSSION QUESTIONS

1. Money serves as a medium of exchange, or a means of payment. What about credit cards, money orders, and traveler's checks? Do they fulfill the functions of money? Why or why not?
2. Are checks part of the nation's money supply? Why or why not?
3. Large-denomination negotiable bonds are both a medium of exchange and a store of value. Why are they not included in the M_1 definition of money?
4. Must paper money be "backed up" by gold? Why or why not?
5. If you earn interest on your savings account and earn no interest on your checking account or on cash in your pocket, why do you maintain a checking account or cash in your pocket?
6. Try to distinguish among the money stock, total funds in the economy, loanable funds, and income.

INCOME-EXPENDITURES FLOWS

2

The economy can be described as a circular flow of income and expenditures between households, businesses, the government, and foreign economies. Money is used to implement these flows. Once we understand how planned expenditures are formulated and implemented, we are in a position to appreciate money's vital role in the economy and the way that changes in the quantity of money affect the level and composition of current output required to realize planned expenditures.

In preparation for this objective, we begin in this chapter by explaining the relationships between income and expenditures. Afterward, we develop a theory of planned expenditures. Finally, we point out the need for an analysis of financial markets in order to explain not only the level of output but the market interest rate, which is an important determinant of planned expenditures.

2.1 CIRCULAR FLOW OF INCOME AND EXPENDITURES

The Department of Commerce maintains a well-known system of social accounts called the *national income accounts.** The system provides a record of the economy's nonfinancial transactions involving currently produced goods and services. It shows how current income receipts of each sector of the economy (the household, business, government, and international sectors) are allocated to current consumption, saving, and taxes, and then are used to realize plans for current consumption (including consumer durables), investment (excluding financial investment), government, and net foreign (excluding financial investment) expenditures.

Each sector's current income, expenditures, and saving for a specific time period are recorded in its current account statement. An example of a summary of a sector's current account which is general enough to apply to any sector is given below:

**Summary of a Sector's Current Account
Statement for Fourth Quarter 19___**

(In billions of dollars)

Transaction Category	Uses	Sources
Current Income		195
Current Expenditures	75	
Saving	120	
Total	195	195

The summary statement shows that the sector's current income from other sectors in the economy is $195 billion. Each sector's sources of income will vary. For example, government sources include taxes from households and businesses; business sources include sales revenue from government and households; household sources include wages and salaries from business and government.

The summary statement also shows that the sector's income was used to purchase $75 billion of goods and services from other sectors. Each sector makes different uses of funds. For example, government purchases include goods and services from business and labor services from households; business purchases include intermediate goods from other businesses, labor services from households, and police protection from government; household purchases include goods and services from business and recreation park services from government.

It is important to note that one sector's current expenditures are another sector's sources of income. For example, business sales revenues (a source) are

---

*An excellent discussion of national income and other economic accounts is S. Rosen, *National Income and Other Social Accounts* (New York: Holt, 1972).

household payments for business products (a use), and government taxes (a source) are business and household payments for government services (a use). Thus the current income and expenditures accounts of all sectors are interrelated.

Finally, the summary statement above shows that current income exceeds current expenditures by $120 billion. This sector enjoys a surplus in its current account. That is, saving is positive. If saving were negative (if dissaving took place), the sector would be incurring a deficit in its current account. Saving is the balancing entry in the current account statement. That is, saving ensures that each sector's current account balances so that uses equal sources. Household saving is called *personal saving*. Business saving is called *retained earnings*. Government saving is called a *budget surplus* (or, if it is negative, a *budget deficit*). The saving of surplus sectors that is made available in financial markets provides a source of funds for use by deficit sectors that wish to spend more than their income.

The national income accounts divide the economy into four sectors: the household sector, the business sector, the government sector, and the international—or rest of the world—sector. However, in this chapter we shall confine our discussion to a closed economy, i.e., one consisting of only the first three sectors. The household sector is usually a surplus sector, since its expenditures are usually less than its income. The business sector is normally a deficit sector, since it generally spends more than its net income.* Finally, the government sector, especially in recent years, is a deficit sector, since its tax receipts are generally less than its expenditures.

The three sectors, together with those flows, are shown in Figure 2.1. All the flows shown in the diagram are flows of dollars; flows of currently produced goods and services move in the opposite direction. The household sector supplies factor services, such as labor, capital, and land, to the business sector. The business sector uses those services to produce final goods and services, which are sold in the output market. In return for supplying factor services, the household sector receives income from the business sector in the form of wages and salaries, rent, interest, and profits. A portion of that income is diverted to the government sector in the form of taxes, which becomes the income of the government sector. The business sector receives income in the form of total sales of the goods and services it has produced. For purposes of simplification we assume that the total income received by the business sector is paid out to the factors of production supplied by the household sector. Thus saving of the business sector is zero.

On the expenditures side, the household sector takes its disposable (after-

---

*We use *net income* here to describe what the business sector retains after the factors of production, taxes, and dividends are paid. The remainder is undistributed profits and depreciation. (The national income accounts normally call this *gross business saving*.) This is usually insufficient to cover gross expenditures on capital goods, and so the business sector is a deficit sector.

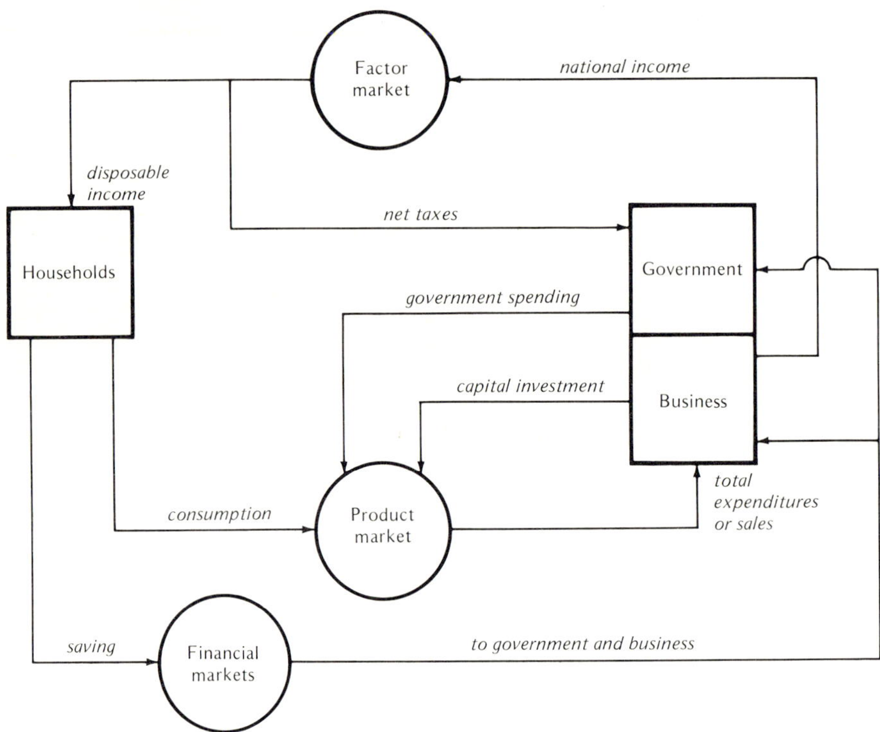

Figure 2.1

Circular flow of income and expenditure.

tax) income and splits it between expenditures on goods and services (consumption) sold in the output market and household saving, which flows through the financial markets to the government and business sectors. The government sector purchases goods and services in the output market, and these may include such items as military aircraft, highways, and office buildings. The government also makes payments that are not in return for current production. These include welfare payments, college scholarships, and Social Security payments. These payments, known as *transfer payments,* become income to the household sector even though they are not received in return for factor services. It will simplify our analysis if we subtract transfer payments from taxes and call the result *net taxes.* If we interpret transfers this way, government expenditures include only expenditures on currently produced output.

The business sector also makes expenditures in the output market. These expenditures are called *capital investment* and involve the purchase of producer or capital goods. Capital goods, such as machinery and factories, are goods that are used in the production of other goods and services. We will distinguish expenditures on capital goods from purchases of stocks and bonds by calling the former *capital investment* and the latter *financial investment.*

To the extent that government expenditures on goods and services exceed the net tax receipts of the government, the government will need to borrow additional funds in the financial markets. Also, since we have assumed that the saving of the business sector is zero, the funds that it spends on capital equipment must be obtained by borrowing in the financial markets. Thus, in this simple framework, the flow through the financial markets is primarily from the household sector to the government and business sectors.

The flows shown in Figure 2.1 suggest certain useful accounting definitions. First, actual expenditures EXP in the output market are identical to the sum of the three classes of expenditures in that market: consumption C, government spending on goods and services G, and capital investment expenditures I.

$$EXP \equiv C + I + G \tag{2.1}$$

Second, disposable income Y_D received by the household sector is defined as the difference between national income Y paid out by the business sector and net taxes T deducted by the government sector,

$$Y_D \equiv Y - T \tag{2.2}$$

Third, by definition, the disposable income received by the household sector is split between expenditures on consumer goods, or consumption, and saving S.

$$Y_D \equiv C + S \tag{2.3}$$

The above relationships can be combined to yield a fourth. If we equate (2.2) and (2.3),

$$\begin{aligned} Y - T &\equiv C + S \\ Y &\equiv C + S + T \end{aligned} \tag{2.4}$$

or

And fifth, the sum of actual expenditures is identical to national income in the sense that what has been sold in the output market must have been purchased, so that

$$Y \equiv EXP \tag{2.5}$$

or, by (2.4) and (2.1),

$$C + S + T \equiv C + I + G \tag{2.6}$$

or

$$S \equiv I + (G - T) \tag{2.7}$$

where saving is identical to the actual capital investment of the business sector plus the difference between actual government expenditures and net taxes, i.e., the actual government deficit.

This is the place to mention that terms such as national income and output are generic terms used to identify the aggregate production of goods and services in the current accounting period and the income that flows from such production. From time to time we shall need to refer to actual data contained in the national income accounts in connection with either examples drawn from the real world or the results of empirical studies. In such cases output will generally be measured by gross national product in constant dollars (*real GNP*). Once in a while nominal national income is used, and for that we will use *nominal GNP* (GNP in current dollars). Generally we will use lowercase letters to denote real values and capital letters to denote nominal values. For example, y is output or real income and Y is nominal income. Note that if P is the price level, then $Y = Py$.

We will have occasion to use different values of variables in different examples. Different values of endogenous variables will be identified by different numerical subscripts. The higher the subscript, the higher the value of the variable. Thus for output, an endogenous variable, y_2 is greater than y_1.

Different values of exogenous variables are identified by different numbers of overbars. The more overbars, the greater the value of the variable. Thus for real government spending, an exogenous variable, $\bar{\bar{g}}$ is greater than $\bar{g}$.

Functional relationships will be denoted by a capital letter with one or more primes ('). The capital letter generally corresponds to the letter used for the variable the function explains. For example, C' would be the consumption function (the function that explains real consumption c). If in a particular example, the function shifts, C' would become C''.

In all cases, careful attention to the context in which the notation is used will help avoid confusion.

2.2 EXPENDITURES THEORY

Both the business and household sectors are perceived to respond to economic stimuli in determining their respective expenditures on capital investment and consumer goods. For our purposes, the behavior of the government sector will be treated as exogenous. That is, its behavior is determined by forces outside of the model.

All variables to be discussed are expressed in real terms. This means that the nominal values of expenditures are deflated by the price level, so that changes in these variables reflect changes in the quantity of goods and services purchased for any given price level.* For example, a change in real consump-

---

*Measures of the price level are the consumer price and wholesale price indices. For an explanation of the construction and interpretation of these indices, see F. Zahn, *Macroeconomic Theory and Policy* (Englewood Cliffs, N.J.: Prentice-Hall, 1975), chap. 6.

tion reflects a change in the quantity of consumer goods and services purchased for any given price level. As a consequence, the model that we shall develop in this chapter will determine the level of real income or output required to realize real expenditure plans for any given price level.

Consumption Expenditures

Planned real consumption expenditures and saving of the household sector are primarily determined by the real disposable income of that sector. Increases in real disposable income result in increases in planned real consumption and saving, and decreases in real disposable income result in decreases in planned real consumption and saving. Real disposable income, in other words, is treated as a constraint on the amount of planned real household consumption and saving. As the constraint is relaxed and real disposable income increases, the household sector will increase both its planned real consumption expenditures and its real saving. Since changes in real disposable income will be split between changes in real consumption and changes in real saving, it follows that the change in planned real consumption will be less than the change in real disposable income. Thus the ratio of changes in planned real consumption to changes in real disposable income (usually called the *marginal propensity to consume*) is positive but numerically less than 1.

Whatever part of a change in real disposable income is not consumed is saved. Therefore, the ratio of changes in real saving to changes in real disposable income (the *marginal propensity to save*) will also be positive and numerically less than 1. Since changes in real disposable income are split between changes in real saving and changes in real consumption, the sum of the marginal propensities to consume and to save must equal 1.

Figure 2.2 shows a linear consumption function and a corresponding saving function. The 45° line indicates zero real saving, or that all real disposable income is consumed. At real disposable income levels below yd_1, planned real consumption c exceeds real disposable income, so that real saving s is negative; i.e., savers consume past saving. At real disposable income levels above yd_1, planned real consumption is less than real disposable income, so that real saving is positive. The vertical axis intercept a of the consumption function indicates the positive value of planned real consumption if real disposable income were zero. It follows that real saving would be $-a$. The slope of the consumption function, $\Delta c / \Delta yd = b$, is the marginal propensity to consume, or the percentage of any change in real disposable income that is planned real consumption. It follows that the slope of the saving function, $\Delta s / \Delta yd = 1 - b$, is the marginal propensity to save, or the percent of any change in real disposable income that is real saving.

The saving and consumption functions can be expressed in terms of real national income and net taxes as well. In Eq. (2.2) disposable income is defined as

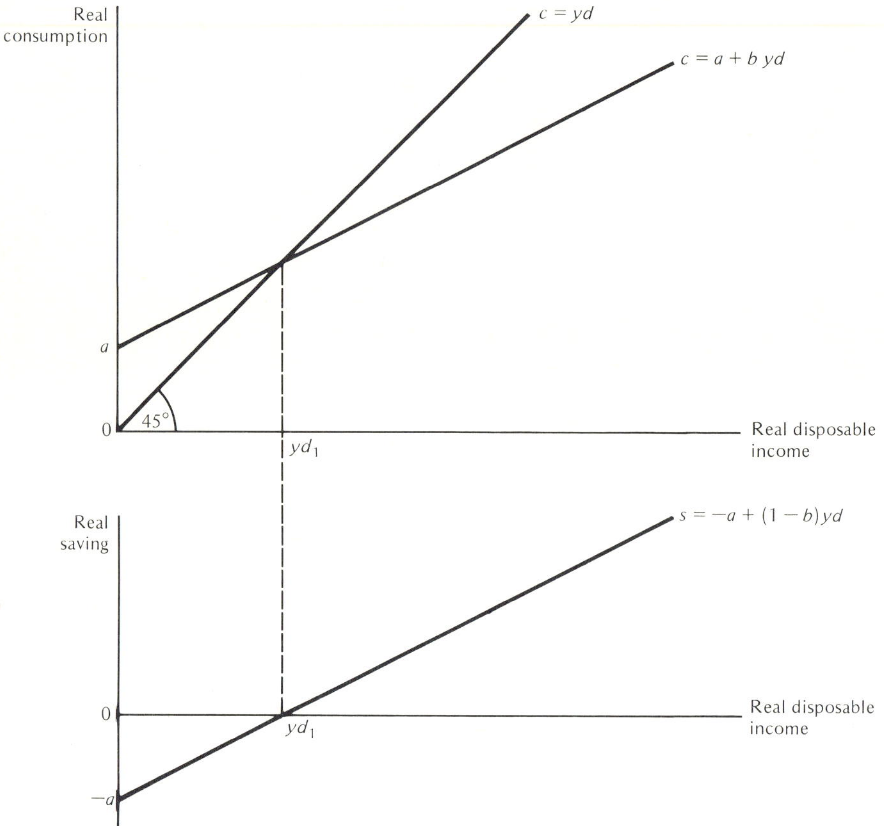

Figure 2.2

The consumption and saving functions.

the difference between national income and net taxes. By substituting this definition into the consumption and saving functions specified in Figure 2.2, we derive an expression for real saving and real consumption in terms of real national income or output and real net taxes t, as shown in Figure 2.3. The vertical axis intercept of the consumption function shows the value of planned real consumption $a - bt$ if output were zero. The vertical axis intercept of the saving function shows that if output were zero and planned real consumption $a - bt$ were positive, real saving $[-a - (1 - b)t]$ would be negative. Although the values of the intercepts differ when the saving and consumption functions are expressed in terms of output, the slopes are the same as they are when the functions are expressed in terms of real disposable income. This is true because changes in real net taxes change the level of real saving and planned real consumption for any given level of output, but not the marginal propensities to

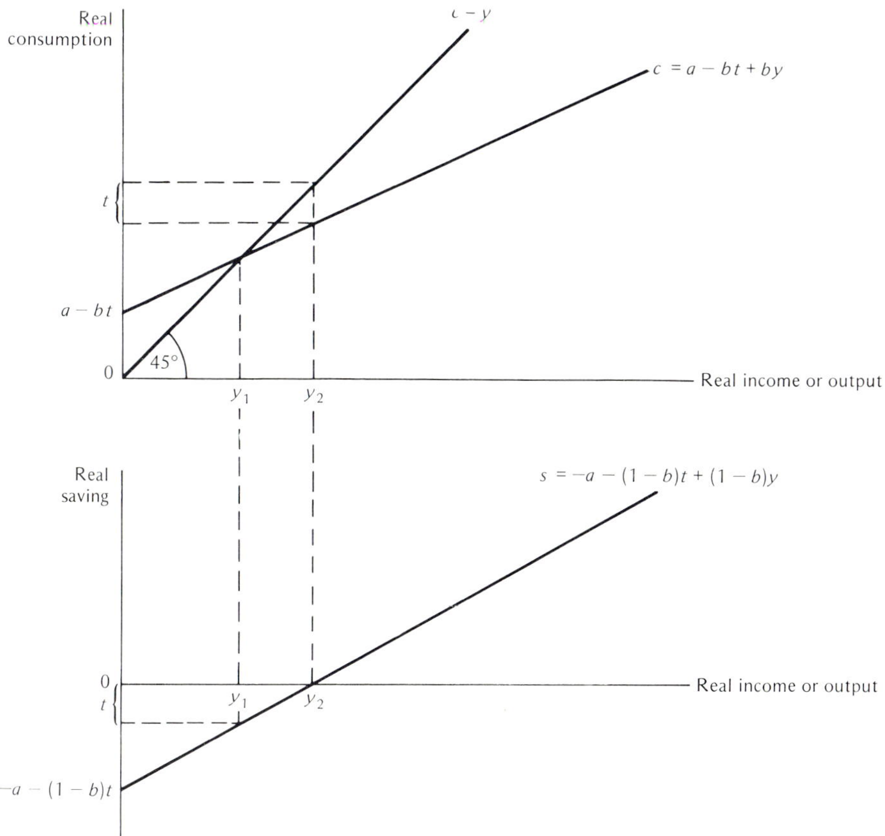

Figure 2.3
Consumption and saving functions in terms of national income and taxes.

save and consume. The impact of changes in real net taxes as a fiscal policy variable will be explained shortly.

You will notice in Figure 2.3 that when output is y_1, all output is consumed, and real saving is negative. Real saving must be negative by the amount of real net taxes. Moreover, when output is y_2, real saving is zero, and output must exceed real consumption by the amount of real net taxes.

Capital Investment Expenditures

The business sector makes expenditures on capital goods for the purpose of earning a profit. Moreover, we assume that business firms attempt to maximize profits. It follows that business firms will want to buy capital equipment in order to produce goods and services as long as the rate of return on additional capital equipment exceeds the cost of financing its purchase.* The finance costs are represented by the market rate of interest on borrowed funds. In our simplified model the business sector has no savings. Any real capital investment expenditures must be financed by borrowing in the financial markets. If the market rate of interest is less than the rate of return on the planned capital investment expenditure, the firm will borrow the funds and buy the capital equipment. If the market rate of interest exceeds the rate of return on the proposed capital expenditure, the firm will not borrow and the expenditure will not be made.† As the rate of interest falls, more projects become profitable because there will be more projects whose rates of return exceed the market interest rate. For this reason economists express planned real capital investment as a function of the market interest rate where, as shown in Figure 2.4, planned real capital investment i varies inversely with the interest rate R. For example, a decrease in the interest rate from R_2 to R_1 increases planned real capital investment from i_1 to i_2. An increase in the interest rate yields the opposite results.

---

*For a capital good with an infinite life, the rate of return is the net profit expressed as a percentage of the cost of the capital good. For example, if a capital good costing \$10,000 yields profits of \$500 per year forever, the rate of return is 500/10,000 = 5% per year. The calculation is somewhat more complex for a capital good with a finite life span.

†The same principle applies even when the firm already has the cash and is able to lend to others at the market interest rate. Can you see why?

Figure 2.4

The investment function.

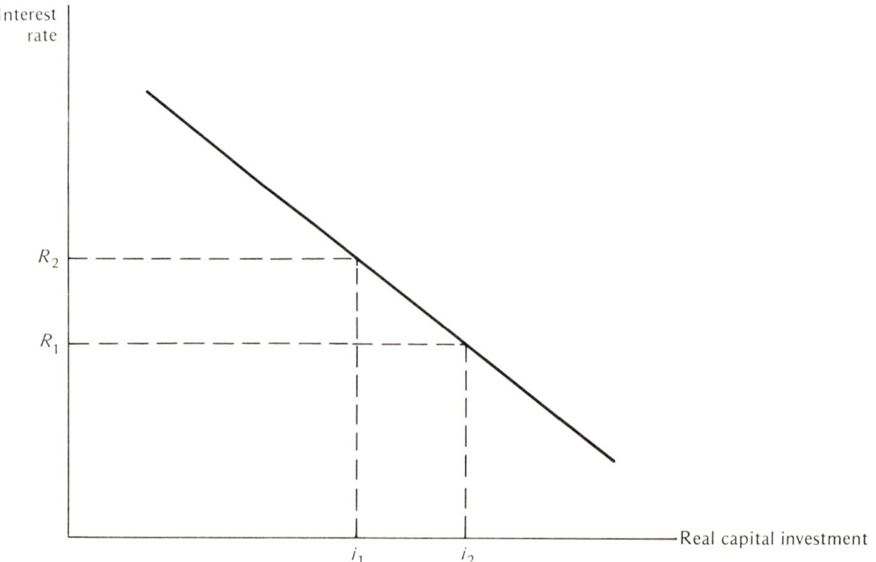

Government Expenditures

The federal government's annual budget is proposed by the President each year for congressional approval. The final draft of the budget generally represents a consensus of presidential and congressional economic objectives. It includes a list of planned expenditures and a proposal for financing these expenditures. The strategy of expenditures and finance will vary depending on the specific way in which the government wishes to affect different sectors of the economy.

Generally, expenditures are financed by several means simultaneously, namely, with profits from government businesses, taxes, increases in the money supply, and borrowing from the public. In order to put together a finance package that will achieve its objectives, the government must take into account the cash it expects to have on hand at the beginning of the budget year, profits earned during the budget year from its business operations, and expected net tax receipts during the budget year. If planned expenditures exceed cash on hand plus expected net tax receipts, the government must increase net taxes (increase taxes and/or decrease transfer payments) or increase the deficit. The ways of financing the deficit and their impact on the economy will be discussed in more detail in later chapters. For now it is important to note that in our analysis, net taxes and the deficit will be assumed to be exogenous and subject to change as the government changes its economic objectives.

Income-Expenditures Equilibrium

Equations (2.5) and (2.6) imply that output and actual real expenditures are identical, and Eq. (2.7) implies that this also means that real saving is identical to actual real capital investment plus the real government deficit. Our theory of *planned* (sometimes called *ex ante*) real expenditures should be distinguished from *actual* (sometimes called *ex post*) real expenditures. What actually takes place as described in Figure 2.1 often differs from the intentions of spenders. Of course, actual real expenditures must equal output, but these purchases may or may not have been intended. There are times when planned real expenditures may not equal output. When this occurs, the system implied by our analysis is in disequilibrium. If planned real expenditures exceed output, this means the inventories of producers of output are being depleted. Producers will respond by supplying additional output until planned real expenditures are realized. If output exceeds planned real expenditures, this means producers of output are holding excess inventories. Producers will respond by supplying less output until planned real expenditures are realized. By introducing our theory of planned real expenditures into our accounting framework, we are able to state the equilibrium condition in our analysis,

$$y = c + i + g \tag{2.8}$$

or
$$s = i + (g - t) \tag{2.9}$$

These are equilibrium conditions and not the accounting identities stated earlier. Equation (2.8) states that when output y is sufficient for the household, business, and government sectors to realize planned real expenditures $c + i + g$, the system implied by our analysis is at rest. All those who wish to sell output at the given price level can sell, and all those who wish to purchase output at the given price level can purchase. Alternatively, Eq. (2.9) states that when the real saving s of the household sector is sufficient for the business sector to realize planned real capital investment i and for the government sector to realize its planned real deficit expenditures $g - t$, the system implied by our model is at rest. Households that wish to save, save just enough income for the government and business sectors that wish to spend in excess of their income to be able to borrow at the given interest rate just enough to finance these expenditures.

Our model can be summarized by the saving function, the investment function, and the equilibrium condition just explained. Given the market rate of interest, real net taxes, and value of the real government deficit, output required to realize planned expenditures is explained or determined.

Figure 2.5 illustrates the workings of the model. The saving function S' is positively sloped because at the level of real net taxes $\bar{t}$, real saving increases as real income increases. Given the interest rate R_1 and the real government deficit $\overline{g - t}$, the expenditures function E' is horizontal because we have assumed that planned real capital investment and the real government deficit are invariant with respect to income. At output y_2, real saving s_2 equals planned real capital investment plus the real government deficit e_2. At levels of output above y_2, real saving exceeds planned real capital investment plus the real government deficit.

Figure 2.5

The expenditures model.

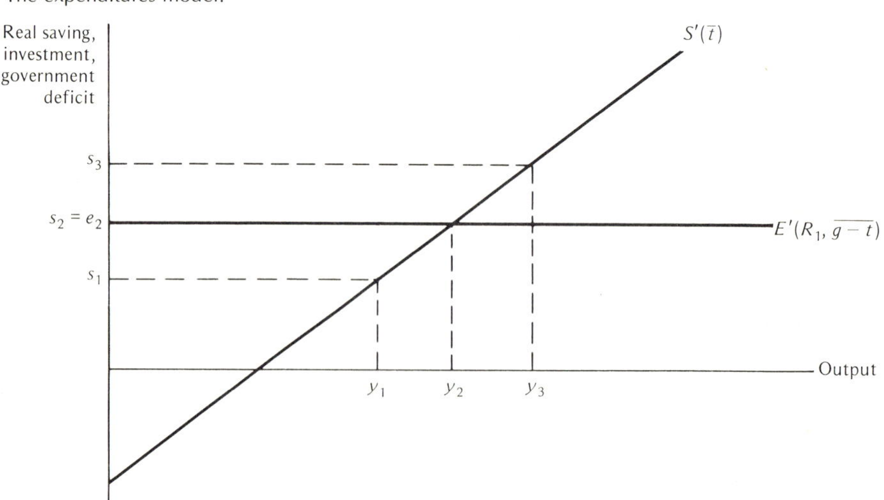

For example, at output y_3, real saving s_3 exceeds planned real capital investment plus the real government deficit e_2. This means that the business sector is
producing more goods and services than are currently being purchased. Thus,
excess inventories are accumulating. In response, businesses will cut back
production and thereby reduce output. In our example, output will fall toward
y_2. At levels of output below y_2, real saving is less than planned real capital investment plus real government deficit. For example, at output y_1, real saving s_1
is below planned real capital investment plus real government deficit e_2. This
means that the business sector is producing fewer goods and services than are
currently being purchased. Thus, desired inventories are being depleted. In response businesses will increase production. In our example, output will
increase toward y_2.

Equilibrium is displaced when there are changes in the market rate of interest and/or the components of real government deficit. The impact of these
changes will be explained once we condense our model to a form that will permit us to more easily integrate our expenditure theory with the monetary analysis which follows in later chapters.

2.3 THE IS SCHEDULE

The IS schedule shows the combinations of market interest rates and levels of
output that are able to satisfy the equilibrium condition of our expenditure
model that real saving just equals planned real capital investment plus the real
government deficit. Figure 2.6 shows the graphical derivation of the IS schedule.
Given the real government deficit $\overline{g - t}$, real net taxes $\bar{t}$, and the interest rate R_2,
the saving function S' and the expenditure function E' in the upper quadrant determine the equilibrium output y_1, and thereby real saving s_1 required to realize planned real expenditures e_1. Thus, (y_1, R_2) is a combination of output and
interest rate that satisfies the equilibrium condition of our model. If the interest
rate decreases to R_1 so that planned real capital investment increases, the expenditure curve will increase from E' to E''. As a result, output increases to y_2,
and thereby real saving increases to s_2, so that planned real capital investment
plus real government deficit e_2 can be realized. Thus, (y_2, R_1) is another combination of output and market interest rate that satisfies the equilibrium condition
that real saving equals planned real capital investment plus the real government deficit. A locus of such combinations of output levels and market interest
rates forms the IS schedule in the lower quadrant.

It is important to note that movements *along* the IS curve occur as changes in
the interest rate and output induce changes in planned real capital investment
and real saving. *Shifts* in the curve occur when non-income- or non-interest-rate-
related components of planned real expenditures change. There are two of these
components that affect the IS curve: real government expenditures and real
net taxes. Increases in real government expenditures shift the IS curve to the right,
and decreases shift the curve to the left. At given output levels, changes in real

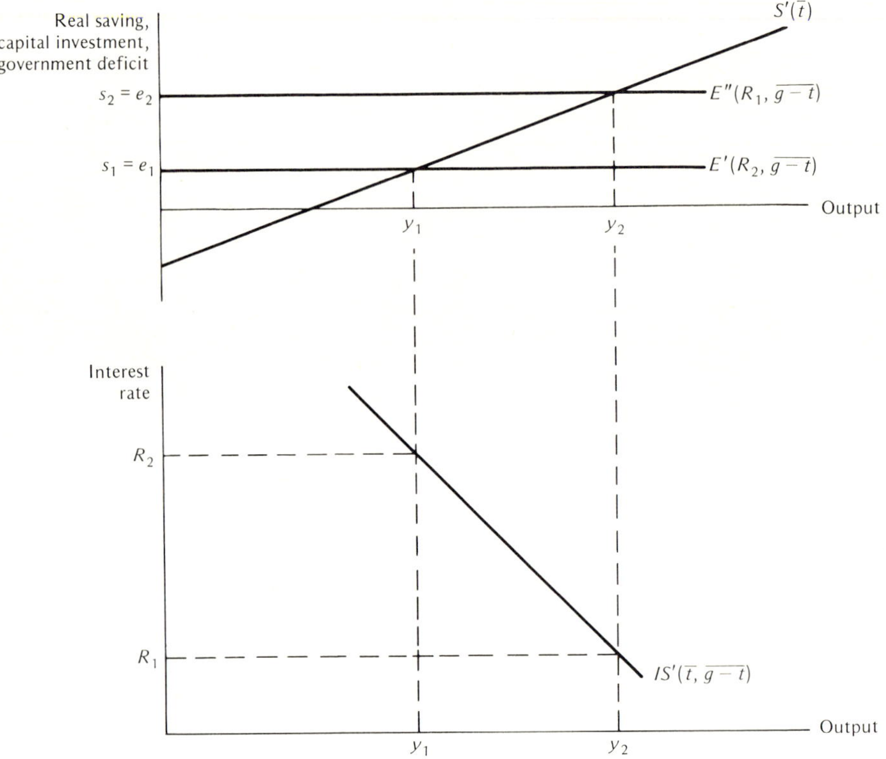

Figure 2.6
Derivation of the IS curve.

net taxes change the level of real disposable income and therefore change real consumption and real saving. The shifts are the opposite of those for changes in real government spending. Since an increase in real net taxes reduces real disposable income for every given level of output, and therefore reduces real planned consumption and real saving, such increases in real net taxes will shift the IS curve to the left. A decrease in real net taxes shifts the IS curve to the right.

Figure 2.7 illustrates two of the primary means whereby the government finances its expenditures: increases in net taxes and increases in borrowing from the public. Financing the deficit by increasing the money supply will be discussed in later chapters. For given values of real net taxes $\bar{t}$, the real government deficit $\overline{g-t}$, and the interest rate R_1, the S' saving function and E' expenditure function determine the output y_1 and real saving s_1 needed to realize intended real capital investment plus the deficit e_1. The relevant IS schedule is IS'. An increase in real net taxes from $\bar{t}$ to $\bar{t}$ shifts the saving function from S' to S''. *Given that the net tax increase is spent, so that the deficit does not change,* the IS schedule shifts from IS' to IS''. For the given interest rate, output increases

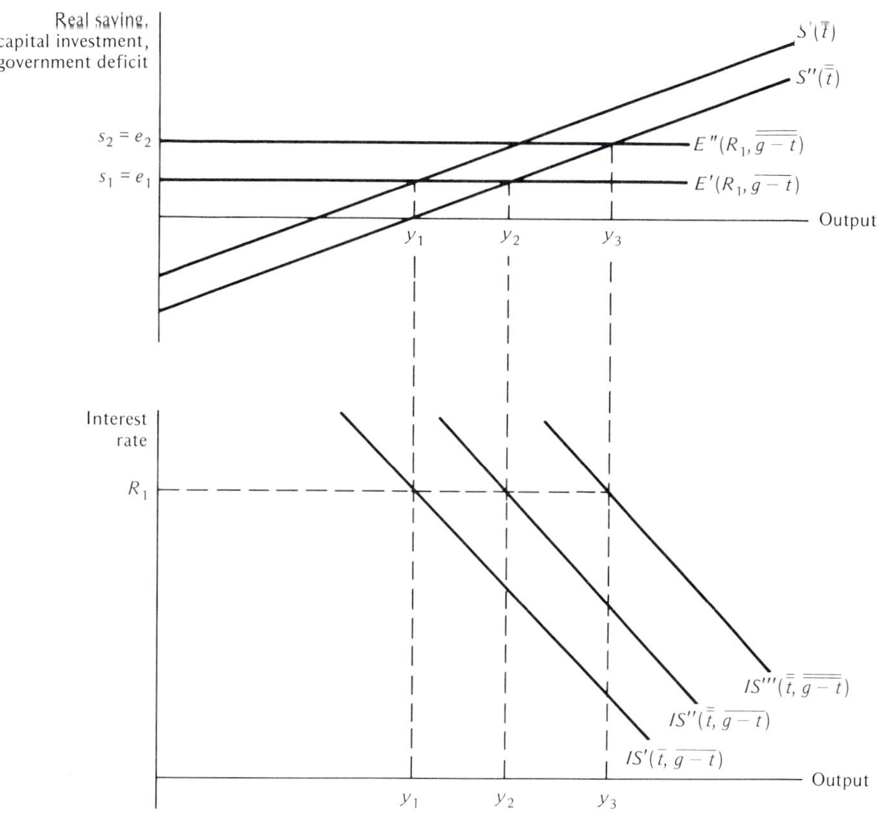

Figure 2.7

Impact of changes in real net taxes and the real government deficit on the IS schedule.

from y_1 to y_2. The increase in real net taxes and the increase in real government expenditures have a relatively small positive effect on output because only part of the amount of the net tax increase would have been spent by households if it had remained disposable income (depending on the marginal propensity to consume). But all of it is spent by the government, so that the net effect is an increase in real expenditures and thereby output.* Now suppose that the real government deficit increases from $\overline{g-t}$ to $\overline{\overline{g-t}}$ as a result of an increase in real government expenditures with no net tax increase, i.e., the increase in the deficit is financed by borrowing from the public. As a result, the expenditure function increases from E' to E''. For any given interest rate, output increases, i.e., the IS schedules shift rightward to IS'''. Given the interest rate R_1, output increases from y_2 to y_3. Decreases in the deficit yield the opposite results.

---

*An equal change in government spending and taxes is often called a *balanced-budget change*. In that case the change in output per dollar change in government spending is called the *balanced-budget multiplier*.

2.4 WHAT ABOUT FINANCIAL MARKETS?

So far, our analysis has been restricted to inflows of real income or output to and outflows of real expenditures and real saving from the various sectors of the economy. We have implicitly assumed that somehow the market rate of interest is determined in financial markets when loanable funds supplied (lending) equals loanable funds demanded (borrowing) *and* the stock of money supplied equals the stock of money demanded so that there are no further additions to holdings of money balances as a store of wealth (zero hoarding). Given the market rate of interest, we are able to determine the output required to realize planned expenditures.

But what we have implicitly assumed needs to be explicitly explained if we are to understand the financial aspects of economic activity and the role played by the money stock in the economy as well as the impact of changes in the money stock on the economy. Therefore, in the next two chapters we develop a theory of financial market flows of loanable funds.

Once we have a basic understanding of both income-expenditures flows and loanable funds flows, we will recognize that to complete our analysis of financial activity, we require an analysis of the money market. Therefore, in Part Two we will develop a theory of money that when integrated with our income-expenditures analysis explains both the interest rate and the level of output demand in the economy, and that when integrated with our loanable funds analysis explains more carefully the financial activity that underlies output demand activity. Both perspectives provide a better understanding of the role of money in the economy. As with any work of art, appreciation and understanding of this role are enhanced when the viewer has two or more perspectives.

SUMMARY NOTES

1. The national income accounts provide a record of transactions involving currently produced goods and services. For our purposes, the economy is divided into the household, business, and government sectors.
2. Planned real expenditures of the household sector depend on real disposable income, and planned real capital investment depends on the market rate of interest.
3. In equilibrium, national income and output are equal to the sum of planned government, household, and business expenditures on current output.
4. A theory of income determination may be constructed by integrating the equilibrium condition with the behavioral statements for the household and business sectors.
5. In equilibrium, planned real saving is equal to real capital investment plus the real government deficit.
6. The IS schedule shows combinations of interest rate and income that produce equilibrium in the output market.

DISCUSSION QUESTIONS

1. Figure 2.1 shows the flows of income and expenditures for an economy with institutions similar to those in the United States. Try to draw a similar circular flow diagram for a country in which the government owns all the means of production and in which private financial intermediation, which is viewed as "antisocial speculation," is illegal.

2. The discussion in the chapter makes consumption and saving depend only on disposable income, but there may be other influences. Suppose two people have the same income—$30,000 per year. Suppose one of the two already owns two houses, three cars, $10,000 worth of clothes, a boat, and much sporting equipment. The second person rents a small apartment and owns $100 worth of clothes, no cars, and no sporting equipment. Would you expect any differences in the amounts each will consume and save this year? Why?

3. We assumed that business firms will purchase capital goods up until the rate of return on new capital is equal to the interest rate on borrowed funds. We also assumed that firms have no funds of their own. Suppose we drop the latter assumption, so that firms do not have to borrow. Then firms will expand their investment spending until the rate of return is zero. True or false? Explain.

4. Suppose the marginal propensity to consume is 0.75, and net taxes are increased from $10 to $40 billion to finance government expenditures. What is the net change in output? Why?

5. Try again to distinguish among the money stock, total funds in the economy, loanable funds, income, and expenditures.

FINANCIAL MARKETS AND INSTITUTIONS

Financial markets provide the means whereby the surplus funds of savers are lent to borrowers who wish to spend in excess of their income. Financial institutions use a variety of financial instruments to meet the needs of both savers who lend and spenders who borrow. Their efforts have helped in achieving maximum economic growth and efficient allocation of wealth.

We begin this chapter by explaining the function of financial markets and the role of financial institutions which act as intermediaries for loanable funds. Afterward, we discuss the types of financial institutions and financial instruments used to facilitate the exchange of loanable funds in financial markets. Finally, we emphasize the special role played by commercial banking and the Federal Reserve in the financial system. Their special roles are the primary topics of this book.

3.1 FINANCIAL MARKETS AND INTERMEDIATION

Every society is composed of a large number of decision-making economic units. The units may be as small as a single individual or as large as a government agency. Each unit receives income from the services or goods it supplies, and each unit makes expenditures out of that income. More often than not, the expenditures and income for a given time period are not equal. If a unit spends more than it receives in income, it is called a *deficit unit,* and if its income exceeds its expenditures, it is called a *surplus unit.* Looking at the United States economy as a whole, the average household may spend between 90 and 95 percent of its annual disposable income. Consequently the typical household would be a surplus unit to the extent of 5 to 10 percent of its disposable income. On the other hand, the federal government, in the fiscal year ending June 30, 1975, spent about $43.6 billion more than it received in tax revenues. For that year the federal government was a deficit unit.

Now in order to maintain a level of expenditures that exceeds the level of income, deficit units need to obtain additional funds from other sources. Similarly, surplus units will want to use their surplus funds to earn income in the form of interest payments and dividends rather than leave those funds idle. It seems natural, therefore, that the deficit units will want to borrow from the surplus units, and the surplus units will be eager to lend to the deficit units at the appropriate rate of interest. The appropriate rate of interest falls somewhere between the maximum rate of interest the deficit unit is willing to pay for funds and the minimum rate of interest the surplus unit is willing to receive for funds. Because of the resulting lending and borrowing activity, surplus units are often called *original lenders,* and deficit units are often called *final borrowers.*

As an alternative to hoarding surplus funds, those who hold surplus funds can lend them to others by buying securities (the IOUs of others) in financial markets or by repaying debts by buying back their own securities (their own IOUs). At the same time, as an alternative to foregoing profitable capital investment opportunities, those who want to incur a deficit and spend more than their income can borrow funds in financial markets by selling their own securities (their own IOUs) or by selling their holdings of securities (the IOUs of others). Lenders benefit because they can earn interest on their surplus funds rather than simply holding them as idle balances. Borrowers benefit because they can earn a return from their capital investment which is expected to be higher than the cost of borrowing funds.

Since surplus units want to lend and deficit units want to borrow, why don't they simply get together and exchange funds at a mutually acceptable interest rate? In fact, sometimes they do, but often they do not. The reasons for their failure to deal directly with each other should be easily understood. For example, suppose the federal government wanted to deal directly with households to borrow the $43.6 billion needed to cover the 1975 deficit. Is the government going to negotiate an interest rate with every individual household? How much would it cost to find out what the acceptable interest rates are that would permit the lending and borrowing to take place? If the government wanted to borrow the money on a long-term basis and many households wanted to lend money on a short-term basis, how would this be reconciled? Such questions and problems limit the extent to which direct lending and borrowing (direct finance) can take place.

Now enter the "middleman." Suppose you decided to effect the exchange between the government and the many household surplus units. You might do this by offering to borrow funds from the household units on terms that were acceptable to them and then to lend to the government on terms acceptable to the government. What's in it for you? Recall that exchange between lenders and borrowers can take place at an interest rate that is somewhere between the maximum rate the borrower is willing to pay and the minimum the lender is willing to accept. Because the lending and borrowing preferences of the two parties may be quite different, this range of difference may be large. You will have to borrow from the surplus unit at an interest rate that is above the minimum the surplus unit is willing to accept, and you will have to lend to the deficit unit at an interest rate that is below the maximum interest rate the deficit unit is willing to pay, but you will often be able to borrow from the surplus unit at a lower interest rate than you lend to the deficit unit. The difference between the two interest rates is your profit, and the profit is your motive for engaging in this activity in the first place. By acting as a middleman between the original lender and the final borrower, you become a *financial intermediary*.

Savers who do not want to hoard all their surplus funds and who feel that long-term financial assets such as corporate bonds and mortgages are too illiquid and too risky in terms of default and capital loss can purchase the highly liquid and relatively safe time and savings deposits of financial intermediaries or institutions. These deposits are assets of depositors and liabilities of financial institutions.

Investors who wish to take advantage of profitable investment opportunities, but require external financing, can sell their securities, such as corporate bonds and mortgages, to financial institutions instead of foregoing these investment alternatives when individual savers are reluctant to lend directly.

Since 1950 the rapid growth of the United States economy has sharply increased the volume of surplus funds. Concurrently, a wide variety of financial institutions have developed to serve (for a profit) the specialized needs of both original lenders and final borrowers. Securities brokers and dealers provide efficient exchange facilities for direct finance, including important information about financial markets and the availability of funds. Financial institutions such as commercial banks, saving and loan associations, mutual saving banks, life insurance companies, pension funds, and credit unions have developed to provide indirect finance. A large portion of saving now flows through financial institutions between original lenders and final borrowers. In addition to acting as intermediaries for loanable funds, financial institutions perform additional functions which benefit the economy.

Financial institutions provide information about financial markets and financial investment alternatives. Information is costly to acquire, and therefore it neither pays the borrowers to seek out the appropriate lenders nor pays the lenders to seek out the appropriate borrowers, since that kind of search activity is not the primary function of either group. Moreover, the transaction size that lenders and borrowers seek may be different. In the example cited earlier, the federal government wished to borrow a single large sum of money, but the potential lenders were individually prepared to lend only small amounts. The role of the intermediary is to match the transaction size of the lenders and the borrowers.

Transaction size creates another problem for the original lender. Since most individual lenders purchase a relatively small number of financial assets, they stand to lose a large portion of their total assets if even one asset goes into default. In other words, a lender who has only a small amount to lend may be forced to lend the entire amount to a single borrower. The lender is forced into the proverbial position of placing all his or her eggs into a single basket. This is more risky than spreading loans over a large number of borrowers. However, having only a small surplus precludes this if the lender is to lend directly to the final borrowers. On the other hand, if the lender lends to a financial intermediary, the risk is reduced. The financial intermediary receives small loans from a large number of lenders (households) and then proceeds to diversify those funds among a large number of final borrowers (other households, the government, and business firms). That is, the institution intermediates between original lenders with preferences for relatively low risk and highly liquid financial assets (savings and time deposits) and final borrowers who want to sell relatively high risk and illiquid financial liabilities (mortgages or corporate bonds). Moreover, since financial institutions purchase a relatively large number of financial assets, any asset lost through default is a relatively small portion of total assets. Thus, due to their large size, financial institutions can diversify their asset portfolios and thereby spread the risk of lending.*

Risk is further reduced for the original lender by the fact that some institutions insure the deposits of lenders. Commercial banks and many savings and loan associations and mutual savings banks insure their deposit liabilities through the Federal Deposit Insurance Corporation.

Financial institutions bring experience and expertise to managing their asset portfolios. They are professionals in financial markets. As a result, the original lenders are likely to get higher returns than they would if they attempted to lend directly to final borrowers.

Financial institutions also provide management services that individual lenders would find very difficult and costly. For example, in mortgage lending

---

*For some illustrative examples of the way in which diversification affects risk and expected yield, see R. I. Robinson and D. Wrightsman, *Financial Markets: The Accumulation and Allocation of Wealth* (New York: McGraw-Hill, 1974), pp. 86–89.

they make property appraisals, evaluate the borrower's ability to pay, check credit references, collect monthly payments, make sure taxes and insurance are paid, and provide legal services to avoid loss through delinquency or default. They also provide refinancing to avoid losses and help investors who are temporarily having financial difficulties.

There are social benefits attached to the role played by financial intermediaries, in addition to the private benefits to lenders and borrowers outlined above. In particular, businesses tend to be deficit units because they are actively engaged in capital investment. That is, business firms buy plant and equipment, and in many cases their current expenditures on such capital exceed their current income. Without the existence of financial intermediaries, those business firms might not be able to obtain the funds to purchase capital goods, or might have to pay such high search and interest costs that many capital investment projects would not be undertaken. Without investment in capital goods, the economy's resource base cannot grow as fast as it otherwise would. In the face of a growing labor force, this means that per capita income would fall and unemployment might increase.

Financial markets provide the transmission mechanism whereby original lenders can lend surplus funds to final borrowers. The exchange of funds for financial assets takes place in financial markets directly between original lenders and final borrowers or indirectly through financial institutions. Direct finance occurs when original lenders enter financial markets and make direct purchases of the primary securities (liabilities) of final borrowers and hold them in their own asset portfolios.

Figure 3.1 illustrates the flow of funds from original lenders directly and indirectly through financial institutions to final borrowers. In exchange for funds, direct lenders and financial institutions receive primary securities such as

Figure 3.1

Direct and indirect flows of funds and financial assets in financial markets.

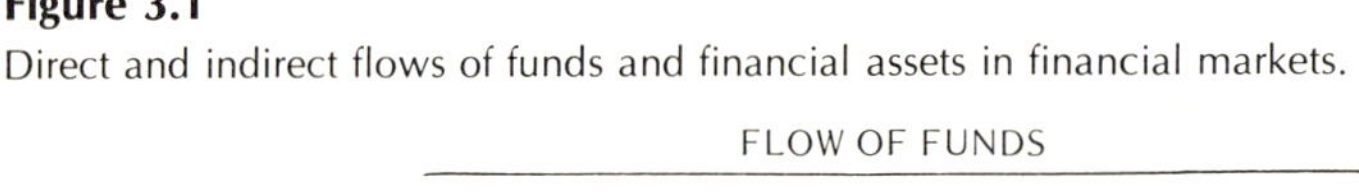

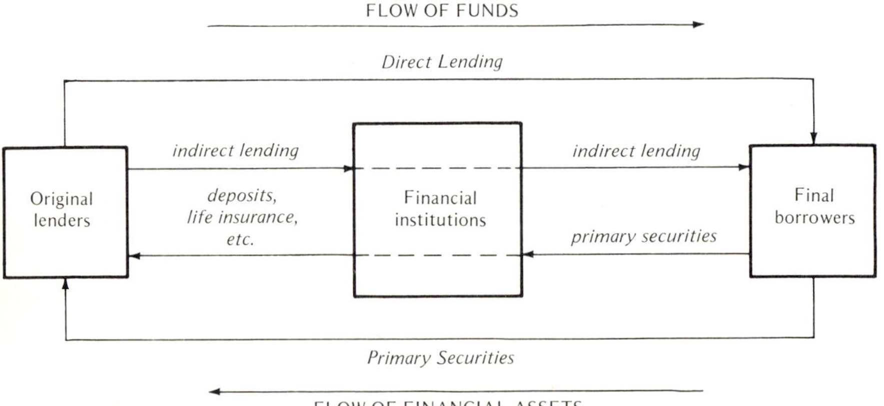

government bonds, mortgages, and corporate bonds from final borrowers. Indirect lenders receive such things as pension rights, deposits, or life insurance which are assets to original lenders and liabilities to financial institutions. Thus, the counterpart to the flow of funds in the upper part of the diagram is the flow of financial assets in the lower part of the diagram. Final borrowers and financial institutions demand loanable funds and supply financial assets; original lenders and financial institutions supply loanable funds and demand financial assets. Exchanges are facilitated with money at interest rates determined in financial markets.

Accessible, well-developed, and efficiently operated financial markets are very important in an economy that aspires to achieve its development and growth potential. If an economy is to realize its potential output, surplus funds (saving) must not remain idle. While the economy will adjust so that aggregate saving and investment are equal, their levels will be lower unless funds reach those who wish to spend in excess of their income, particularly for real investment purposes. Lower levels of spending imply lower levels of output and employment. Efficiently operating financial markets ensure that final borrowers obtain funds from original lenders so that maximum real investment expenditures and thereby maximum potential output can be realized. Although there are historical examples that can be cited which suggest that financial intermediation interfered with the efficiency of financial markets (for example, the speculative stock market booms and busts, the banking-financial crisis of the late 1800s and early 1900s, the conglomerate-merger boom of the 1960s), the weight of the evidence seems to support the proposition that financial intermediation tends to increase the efficiency of financial markets and therefore the economic welfare of the nation.

3.2 TYPES OF FINANCIAL INSTITUTIONS

Any institution that receives funds from one source in order to supply funds to another user is a financial institution or a financial intermediary. The growth and diversity of financial institutions is one of the more striking characteristics of a well-developed economy. Indeed, by strengthening the link between saving and investment, the growth of financial intermediaries makes development all the more possible. Space does not permit a discussion of all the financial intermediaries in the United States. The better-known ones, in order of size, include commercial banks, pension funds, life insurance companies, savings and loan associations, mutual savings banks, finance companies, and credit unions.*

The private institutions receive their funds from a variety of sources; the major ones are summarized in Table 3.1. Changes in the liabilities of the institutions are the most important sources and generally involve transactions with

---

*For a more detailed discussion, see R. W. Goldsmith, *Financial Institutions* (New York, Random House, 1968).

Table 3.1
Major Sources of Funds for Selected Financial Institutions
(Change in liabilities from Dec. 31, 1970, to Dec. 31, 1974, in billions)

Institution	Demand Deposits	Time Deposits	Premiums	Long- and Short-Term Debt
Commercial banks	$40.0	$193.8		
Life insurance companies			$49.4	
Savings and loan associations		96.2		
Mutual savings banks		27.1		
Finance companies				$27.3
Credit unions		12.2		

Source: *Federal Reserve Bulletins, Flow of Funds Accounts.*

original lenders. For example, changes in savings and loan shares are a major source of funds for savings and loan associations, and these changes represent a use for the surplus funds of original lenders.* Institutions may also obtain funds by selling shares of ownership or equity, but this generally is a relatively minor source. It should also be noted that the three definitions of the money supply we outlined earlier include the liabilities of certain financial intermediaries. M_1 includes the demand deposit liabilities of commercial banks; M_2 adds to that the time deposit liabilities of commercial banks; M_3 adds to that the time deposit liabilities of savings and loan associations and mutual savings banks.

The uses of these funds are reflected in changes in the asset holdings of the financial intermediaries. The major ones are shown in Table 3.2. The assets held by financial intermediaries are the debt or equity instruments of the final borrowers in society.

Thus it can be seen from the balance sheet items of the financial intermediaries that the intermediaries stand between the final borrowers and the original lenders. The assets of the intermediaries are the borrowers' liabilities, and the liabilities of the intermediary are the lenders' assets.† The intermediary offers liabilities that suit the preferences of the original lenders and accepts, as assets, those instruments that reflect the preferences of the final borrowers.

Financial institutions have much in common because their functions are similar. But there are also substantial differences among them.

Banks (commercial banks) are the only intermediary permitted to offer demand deposits. Since their sources of funds are both short- and long-term, they

---

*Deposits may be payable on demand or may require advance notice (usually at the discretion of the institution). Strictly speaking, *time deposits* applies to the time liabilities of commercial banks and includes ordinary passbook accounts and certificates of deposit. However, we will also use the term time deposits to include similar liabilities, such as savings and loan shares.

†Accounting for the exchange of financial instruments among borrowers, lenders, and financial intermediaries is accomplished by the flow of funds accounts. For details, see Chap. 4.

Table 3.2
Major Uses of Funds for Selected Financial Institutions
(Change in assets from Dec. 31, 1970, to Dec. 31, 1974, in billions)

Institution	Government Securities		Short-Term Credit			Corporate	
	U.S.	Local	Mortgages	Consumer	Business	Stock	Bonds
Commercial banks	$14.3	$32.0	$58.8	$33.9	$138.9		$ 4.8
Life insurance companies	0.3	0.4	10.9			$7.7	23.7
Savings and loan associations	13.8		99.1				
Mutual savings banks	2.0		17.5			1.7	5.8
Finance companies				14.5	12.8		
Credit unions				9.6			

Source: Federal Reserve Bulletins, Flow of Funds Accounts.

hold both long- and short-term assets. Life insurance companies acquire funds by providing protection against loss of income due to premature death or retirement; they also offer saving opportunities in the form of endowment and annuity policies. Their sources of funds are long-term, and cash outflows are predictable. Therefore, their assets are primarily long-term. Savings and loan associations and mutual savings banks are similar. They acquire funds from personal saving and purchase primarily residential mortgages. Private pension funds acquire funds from employees and employers. Since their sources of funds are long-term and cash outflows are predictable, their assets are primarily long-term. Unlike other intermediaries, mutual funds purchase primarily equity securities (corporate stocks). Finance companies specialize in loans to business firms and households. Casualty insurance companies sell protection against loss of property from fire, theft, or accident. They purchase primarily short-term and highly marketable assets because their cash outflows are less predictable. Credit unions provide saving and lending opportunities to consumers. The size and the composition of the asset portfolios of financial institutions constitute two important differences among them.*

With respect to size, the financial asset holdings of commercial banks are the largest. These banks hold over 43 percent of the total financial assets held by the 10 largest types of financial institutions. Nonbank financial institutions hold the remaining 57 percent. Of those, savings and loan associations hold 15 percent, followed closely by life insurance companies, which hold 13 percent. Private pension funds hold 6 percent, and mutual savings banks hold 6 percent. Sales and consumer finance companies, state and local government retirement

---

*See D. P. Jacobs, L. C. Farewell, and E. H. Neave, *Financial Institutions*, 5th ed. (Homewood, Ill.: Irwin, 1972).

funds, property and casualty insurance companies, credit unions, and mutual funds hold the remaining 17 percent.* Moreover, it is important to note that since 1950 the growth in nonbank financial assets has been about 500 percent, compared with 300 percent for commercial bank financial assets.

In addition to size, the composition of asset portfolios differs. One major reason for the difference is the legal restrictions imposed on financial institutions by various regulatory agencies (e.g., the Federal Reserve regulates its member banks, and the Federal Home Loan Bank regulates savings and loan associations). For example, commercial banks may not hold corporate stocks in their asset portfolios. Although all financial institutions supply loanable funds in financial markets and create a variety of credit instruments (assets to creditors and liabilities to debtors), only banks can create demand deposits. They hold a legal monopoly on demand deposits.†

Another legal restriction is the deposit rate ceilings imposed by regulatory agencies on both bank and nonbank financial institutions (savings and loan associations and mutual saving banks) that hold time and saving deposits. For example, the Federal Reserve sets the ceiling on the commercial bank deposit rate, and the Federal Home Loan Bank sets it for savings and loan associations. The deposit-rate ceiling on nonbank deposits is set higher than the deposit rate ceiling on bank deposits (by about one-quarter of 1 percent). This restriction on commercial bank competition for funds gives nonbank financial institutions an advantage in time and saving deposits.

On the other hand, the introduction of higher-yielding certificates of deposit (CD) has helped commercial banks overcome this. This is especially true in the case of large CDs (in excess of $100,000), for which there are no interest-rate ceilings at present. When these are taken into account, together with the commercial bank monopoly on demand deposits and the ability to offer "full-service banking," it is likely that the nonbank institutions' interest ceiling advantage is offset, and that both types of institutions can compete for funds on an even basis.

Commercial bank portfolios are the most diversified. As such, the creation of money involves most segments of the economy and gives the Federal Reserve (Fed) broader control over the financial system. Nonbank portfolios are specialized and provide channels through which a stimulus can be given to specific problem areas in the financial system (especially housing markets and other capital markets).‡

Banks are also required to hold reserves in the form of cash deposits with the Federal Reserve against their time and saving deposits, while nonbank reserve

---

*Estimates quoted in this section are based on data in the *Federal Reserve Bulletin,* 3d quarter 1974.

†See J. Tobin, "Commercial Banks as Creators of Money," in D. Carson (ed.), *Banking and Monetary Studies* (Homewood, Ill.: Irwin, 1963).

‡Our present system suggests that reforms are in order. But questions of inequity cannot be decided strictly in terms of equity among private institutions. If private inequities provide the best means of public control, then private welfare must give way to social welfare. It is not clear, however, that such inequities serve social welfare.

requirements are negligible.* This inequity also gives nonbank financial institutions a profit advantage over commercial banks.†

Other legal restrictions exist. Unlike banks, nonbank institutions can hold corporate securities; life insurance companies and mutual savings banks hold the major portion of outstanding corporate securities. Savings and loan associations and mutual saving banks are required to hold primarily home mortgages. Finance companies and credit unions, along with commercial banks, handle most of the consumer loans in financial markets, but savings and loan associations, life insurance companies, and mutual saving banks are prohibited from making consumer loans.

All these legal restrictions, and some other minor ones, help to explain why the composition of asset portfolios varies among financial institutions. However, the nature of the liabilities of each financial institution also plays a role. Institutions with predictable long-term commitments can afford to realize the yields on long-term financial investments in the capital market. Others, whose commitments are short-term, rely on short-term financial investment in the capital market and the money market. For example, life insurance companies have predictable long-term commitments and can afford to realize the high yield of relatively illiquid and possibly more risky long-term financial investments (corporate securities and commercial mortgages). However, fire and casualty insurance companies have less risky short-term financial assets. The commitments of other institutions fall somewhere in the middle. Commercial banks are the exception. They have both short- and long-term commitments and can become involved in both long- and short-term financial markets.

The most diversified asset portfolios are those of commercial banks. Although they are somewhat restricted in competing for time and saving deposits (when their deposit rate reaches its ceiling), they are the least restricted in terms of financial investment alternatives. The only important restriction on bank financial investments is that they cannot hold corporate equities because the stock market crash of 1929 contributed to the bank failures of the 1930s. They hold a wide variety of other financial assets, including business loans, consumer loans, mortgages, cash and reserves, United States government securities, state and local government securities, and other miscellaneous financial investments. These asset holdings are almost evenly divided among the major categories.

Nonbank assets are less diversified. Nonbank financial institutions, primarily savings and loan associations, mutual savings banks, and life insurance

---

*Nonbanks voluntarily hold the more liquid United States government securities as a reserve against unexpected deposit withdrawals.

†The President's Commission on Money and Credit in 1961 and the President's Commission on Financial Structure recommended on equity grounds that reserve requirements on all time and saving deposits be eliminated. Since reserve requirements were devised to enhance the Fed's control over the money stock and since time and saving deposits are not generally considered part of the money stock, doing away with them appears to be the logical choice.

companies, hold 80 percent of all mortgage debt outstanding (commercial banks hold the remaining 20 percent). Savings and loan associations hold primarily mortgages (85 percent of their total asset portfolio, and 80 percent of these are residential mortgages). Mutual savings banks hold primarily mortgages (70 percent of their asset portfolio, and 60 percent of these are residential mortgages) and corporate securities (20 percent of their asset portfolio). Life insurance companies hold primarily business securities (50 percent of their asset portfolio) and mortgages (35 percent of their asset portfolio, and 75 percent of these are commercial mortgages). Other financial institutions hold primarily consumer securities, government securities, and corporate securities.

3.3 TYPES OF FINANCIAL INSTRUMENTS

Financial instruments provide the means by which transactions take place between borrowers and lenders. Money, however defined, is a financial instrument, but it is only one of many types of financial instruments that are in use in the economy today. From the issuer's perspective, financial instruments may be classified as either *debt* instruments or *equity* instruments. A debt instrument is an obligation to pay a specified sum, usually with interest, at some point in the future. Most financial instruments are debt instruments. These would include mortgages, corporate bonds, government bonds, consumer and business loans from banks and finance companies, U.S. Treasury bills, negotiable certificates of deposit (CDs), and commercial paper. An equity instrument represents ownership in some ongoing enterprise. Government bonds are debt instruments; corporate stocks are equities. Money is a debt instrument, but many others do exist in the economy.

Equity instruments such as common and preferred stocks permit the transfer of ownership. Stocks and long-term debt instruments (those that mature in more than one year) are often called *capital-market instruments.* Short-term debt instruments (those that mature in less than one year) are often called *money-market instruments.*

Capital-market instruments are long-term securities which are relatively illiquid (not close money substitutes) and which expose lenders to relatively higher risks (capital loss and default risks). Money-market instruments are short-term securities which are relatively liquid (close money substitutes) and risk-free.* The capital market provides a return on surplus funds and financing for long-term deficits, while the money market provides a return on temporary surplus funds and financing for temporary deficits.

The capital market consists of submarkets for stocks, mortgages, corporate bonds, municipal bonds, long-term United States government and government

---

*See W. Lindow, *Inside Money Markets* (Chicago: Random House, 1972); *Money Market Instruments* (Cleveland: Federal Reserve Bank of Cleveland, 1962).

agencies' bonds, consumer credit, and bank business loans. Corporate stocks are financed or purchased primarily by individuals (direct finance), followed way behind by financial institutions, primarily pension funds, mutual funds, and insurance companies (indirect finance). Mortgages consist of residential, commercial, and farm mortgages. Residential mortgages are financed primarily by savings and loan associations, mutual saving banks, commercial banks, and life insurance companies. Commercial mortgages are financed primarily by life insurance companies and commercial banks. Corporate bonds are financed primarily by life insurance companies, pension funds, and individuals. Municipal bonds are financed mainly by commercial banks, property and casualty insurance companies, and individuals. Long-term U.S. government and government agencies' securities are widely held.* Big purchasers are the Federal Reserve, commercial banks, and individuals. Consumer credit and bank business loans are financed primarily by commercial banks, credit unions, sales and finance companies, and private businesses (charge accounts).

The money market consists of submarkets for U.S. Treasury bills, negotiable bank certificates of deposits (CDs), commercial paper, and bankers' acceptances. In the money market, business firms, commercial banks, and others with temporary surplus funds purchase these short-term securities and earn interest. Commercial banks are very active in money markets. They buy and sell money-market securities to maintain their required reserves and desired level of excess reserves. United States Treasury bills are financed primarily by commercial banks and corporations. Commercial banks borrow from corporations by creating CDs, which tend to attract the surplus funds of corporations away from Treasury bills. Commercial paper (short-term liabilities of prime business firms and finance companies) is mainly financed by corporations. Bankers' acceptances (short-term liabilities in international transactions) are financed primarily by commercial banks. Federal funds (member bank reserves at the Fed) are financed by excess bank reserves. That is, banks with reserve deficiencies can borrow the excess reserves of other banks on a short-term basis as an alternative to borrowing from the Fed.

Newly created financial instruments are called *primary securities.* All securities are traded once in the primary market (either the capital or the money market). *Secondary securities* are resold financial instruments. Not all securities are legally negotiable and therefore not all are traded in the secondary market. However, a wide variety of money- and capital-market instruments are negotiable, and there are very active secondary markets for them.

Unfortunately the above use of the terms *capital market* and *money market* can create further confusion. Recall that we defined capital as plant and equip-

---

*Government agencies include, for example, the Federal Home Loan Banks, the Government National Mortgage Association, and the Federal Land Banks. A former government agency, the Federal National Mortgage Association, is now a private corporation. See G. F. Break, et al., *Federal Credit Agencies* (Englewood Cliffs, N.J.: Prentice-Hall, 1964).

ment. Further, our definition of money does not include all the debt instruments that are included in the "money market." Thus one must be very cautious in interpreting the meaning of such terms as capital market and money market. Careful attention to the context in which the terms money and capital are used is needed to avoid confusion.

Many of the financial instruments listed above are the obligations of final borrowers. The possible definitions of money discussed at the beginning of this book include the obligations of certain kinds of financial intermediaries. For example, money narrowly defined, M_1, includes the obligations of the Federal Reserve System (currency) and the obligations of commercial banks (demand deposits). The narrow definition of money includes the means by which transactions are effected in financial instruments as well as in real goods. For example, an original lender will transfer surplus funds to a financial intermediary by transferring either currency or demand deposit balances in exchange for something issued by that financial intermediary. A final borrower will receive currency or demand deposit balances in exchange for a debt instrument that is sold to some financial intermediary. Thus the purchase and sale of financial instruments is similar to the purchase and sale of real goods, with the exchange medium being the other side of the transaction.

Whatever the definition of money, the noncurrency components provide one means by which certain financial intermediaries obtain the funds that they lend to final borrowers.

3.4 COMMERCIAL BANKING

Commercial banks are singled out for separate treatment for at least two reasons. First, of all the intermediary liabilities shown in Table 3.1, only the demand deposit liabilities of commercial banks serve as a medium of exchange in the United States economy. Moreover, such demand deposits are a component of every definition of money discussed earlier. While certain liabilities of other financial intermediaries serve as stores of value, none serves as an exchange medium. Second, controlling commercial banking activities is the way the nation's monetary authorities attempt to regulate the quantity of money in the economy. Consequently, a closer look at commercial banks is in order.

At the end of 1975 there were 14,629 commercial banks in the United States (and almost twice as many branches). This may be contrasted with 13,472 at the end of 1960. However, in looking at the longer term, there has been virtually no change in the total number of commercial banks since the end of World War II. While the number of banks has not changed very much, individual banks have gotten considerably larger. The total assets of commercial banks grew from $257.5 billion at the end of 1960 to $958.4 billion by the end of 1975. Thus average bank size has increased rather substantially over this period of time, from $19.1 million to $65.6 million.

Table 3.3 shows the three major components of commercial bank asset port-

Table 3.3
Comparative Balance Sheet for the Commercial Banking System
(End-of-year figures, in billions)

Assets			*Liabilities and Capital*		
	1960	**1975**		**1960**	**1975**
Cash items*	$52.1	$128.3	Demand deposits:		
			U.S. government	$ 5.9	$ 3.2
Loans	117.6	542.1	Other	133.3	278.3
Investments:			Time deposits	71.6	446.8
U.S. Treasury	61.0	84.2			
Other	20.8	145.1	Interbank deposits	18.8	53.4
Other assets	6.0	58.7	Borrowings	0.1	58.1
			Other liabilities	6.8	50.1
			Capital account	21.0	68.5
Totals	$257.5	$958.4		$257.5	$958.4

*Includes vault cash, deposits with the Federal Reserve System and with other banks, and items in process of collection.
Source: Federal Reserve Bulletin.

folios, cash, loans, and investments. Cash assets consist of reserves member banks hold at district Federal Reserve Banks for check clearing and in order to satisfy legal reserve requirements, vault cash for accommodating deposit withdrawals and satisfying legal reserve requirements, deposits in other banks for check clearing and specialized needs of its customers, and cash items in process of collection through the check-clearing process. Loans are bank earning assets involving personal relationships between the bank lender and the borrower. The relationship is personal in the sense that the loans are tailored to the particular needs of consumers and involve personal evaluation of the customers' credit rating. Loans include those to business firms, farmers, consumers, borrowers who wish to purchase stocks and bonds, financial institutions, and home buyers. *Investments* are bank earning assets involving a nonpersonal relationship between the bank lender and the borrower. The relationship is nonpersonal in the sense that the borrower is well known and the loan contract is standardized and generally large denomination. Because of these properties, the contract is often marketable in secondary markets. Investments include U.S. Treasury securities (one-year maturity and more), Treasury bills (less than one-year maturity), certificates of indebtedness (like Treasury bills except that they carry a coupon rate), Treasury notes (coupon issues of one- to seven-year maturity sold to finance a budget deficit and to service the federal debt), Treasury bonds (maturity of seven years or more), and municipal securities (debts of state, city, and local governments of varying maturity).

On the other side of the balance sheet in Table 3.3, the growth in commercial bank demand deposits has accounted for much of the growth in the narrow definition of money M_1. About 88 percent of the change in M_1 from 1960 to

1975 was due to the increase in demand deposit liabilities of commercial banks.

The three major components of commercial bank liabilities are demand deposits, time deposits, and borrowings. Changes in demand deposits are the source of approximately one-third of all funds of commercial banks. Time deposits consist of passbook savings deposits (savings accounts), consumer certificates of deposit (fixed maturity and yield) with designated denominations, and negotiable certificates of deposit (CDs), which are in large denomination (usually $1 million) and purchased by large business firms and governments. Borrowings consist of those from the Federal Funds market (the market for excess bank reserves on deposit at the Fed), those from the Fed, and those from foreign banks or overseas branches of United States banks (Eurodollars).*

The remaining account shown in Table 3.3 is the capital or equity account. This represents the value of the stockholders' ownership in the bank. The value of the account is the difference between the bank's assets and its liabilities. Equity or ownership funds must be above the legally required minimum imposed by the federal or state government to protect depositors from losses on assets. This generally varies with the size of the bank and the size of the community in which the bank does business. Since in the event of liquidation the bank's creditors must be paid before the stockholders, a large capital-to-deposit ratio implies greater protection for the depositors. In the aggregate the percentage of capital has not changed much in recent years and at present is about 9 percent for all commercial banks.

Asset and liability management is geared to maximizing overall profits subject to liquidity, legal, and regulatory requirements. Legal and regulatory requirements, which are administered primarily by the Federal Reserve, will be discussed as they bear on the theoretical and policy issues discussed in the forthcoming chapters.

Commercial banks require liquidity to accommodate deposit withdrawals. Liquid assets are cash on hand and deposits at the Federal Reserve and other commercial banks. These are the primary reserves of commercial banks, although only the first two count as *legal* reserves for purposes of satisfying the reserve requirements of the Federal Reserve. Highly marketable, but not actually liquid, assets that are quickly converted at low cost into cash (Federal Funds, Treasury bills, and commercial paper) serve as secondary reserves of commercial banks.

The yield on primary reserves is zero, and the yield on secondary reserves is less than that on investments. Commercial bank strategy is to maximize overall profits by holding the minimum amount of primary and secondary reserves consistent with liquidity (or to maximize the amount of investments consistent

---

*By far the largest component is borrowing in the Federal Funds market. This source accounted for about 85 to 90 percent of total member bank borrowing during 1975, whereas borrowings from the Federal Reserve System accounted for about one-half of 1 percent.

with liquidity requirements). The asset mix depends largely on the degree of deposit variability. Deposit variability is a measure of changes in the relationship between deposit inflows and outflows. The greater the variability, the higher the probability of deposit outflows and the greater the need for liquidity that can be satisfied by primary and secondary reserves.

Asset management takes, as given, asset and liability size, the mix of deposits, and deposit variability. Liability management is based on the recognition that a large portion of sources of funds depends on interest-rate changes. By lowering (raising) interest rates on loans below (above) market rates, banks can decrease (increase) their inflow of funds.* Using this device, banks are able to smooth out deposit inflows and outflows and thereby reduce their deposit variability. Thus, they reduce the liquidity requirements and permit greater investment (profits increase). In this way liability management supplements asset management in maximizing profits.

The comparative balance sheet in Table 3.3 indicates the important changes that have taken place in commercial banks over the past 15 years. On the asset side we note that commercial banks as a group have shifted away somewhat from United States government securities as a percentage of the total portfolio. The major use of funds has been the purchase of state and local bonds and loans and securities from the private sector. On the liability side, the largest source of funds has been the growth in time deposits. Commercial banks have received \$375.2 billion (\$446.8 − \$71.6) from that source, compared with \$145.0 billion from private demand deposits. Any well-developed theory of bank portfolio management should be able to explain the relative changes in the assets held by banks. This will be dealt with in Chapter 6.

Since banks generally stand ready to accept deposits (time and demand), the relative changes in the deposit liabilities of banks are determined by the behavior of depositors. This behavior will be dealt with in Chapters 5 and 6.

3.5 FEDERAL RESERVE SYSTEM

We noted that the commercial banking system provides the main channel through which monetary policy is implemented. The responsibility for the conduct of monetary policy belongs primarily to the Federal Reserve System. Thus a brief overview of the "Fed" at this point is appropriate.†

The Federal Reserve System was established in 1913 to provide a flexible, more "elastic" currency, to supervise banking, and to provide for the discounting of commercial paper by member banks. Over the years this responsibility has been broadened by Federal Reserve interpretation to include such general-

---

*Other devices such as free checks, dishes, or free traveler's checks are also used to induce changes in deposit flows.

†An "official" analysis may be found in *The Federal Reserve System: Purposes and Functions*, 6th ed., Board of Governors of the Federal Reserve System, 1974.

ly acceptable stabilization objectives as maintaining relatively full employment and reasonable price stability while fostering sustainable economic growth. The System consists of 12 individual Federal Reserve Banks located in Boston, New York, Philadelphia, Cleveland, Richmond, Atlanta, Chicago, St. Louis, Minneapolis, Kansas City, Dallas, and San Francisco. Overall supervision is accomplished through the Board of Governors. Appointments to the Board are made by the President with Senate confirmation for a 14-year, renewable term. Barring death or resignation, a new appointment is made every two years. This means that a President would have to serve two full terms in office to appoint a majority of the Board.

The duties of the Board of Governors include supervision of the 12 Federal Reserve Banks and appointment of the presidents of those banks. Contact is maintained between the Board and the Federal Reserve districts through the Federal Advisory Council. The Council, consisting of one representative from each district, meets about four times a year with the Board and advises the Board on economic conditions and System affairs. From a policy standpoint, the most important function of the Board is its participation in the Federal Open Market Committee (FOMC). In addition to the Board of Governors, the FOMC includes five Federal Reserve Bank presidents. The president of the New York Federal Reserve Bank is a permanent member. The other four are rotated among the remaining eleven Reserve Banks.*

The FOMC conducts policy by meeting every three or four weeks. At these meetings the state of the economy is reviewed and directives are issued instructing the manager of the System's open market account to conduct transactions in United States government securities with the aim of achieving the objectives of the FOMC. The open market manager is an officer at the New York Federal Reserve Bank, where the open market trading desk is located. On the basis of the directives, the open market manager buys or sells government securities, and these purchases and sales produce changes in bank reserves and ultimately changes in the money supply through a process we shall discuss in Chapters 5 and 6. How money supply changes affect the economy is one of the topics to be dealt with in Chapters 9 and 10.

The relative importance of Federal Reserve holdings of government securities can be seen in the balance sheet in Table 3.4. Such holdings constitute nearly 80 percent of all Federal Reserve assets.

While open market operations, as determined by the FOMC, may be the most important tool of monetary policy, they are not the only tool. The Federal Reserve can also regulate the ratio of reserves to deposits (required reserve ratio) that member banks of the Federal Reserve System must maintain, as well as the interest rate (discount rate) that is charged to member banks when they borrow from the Fed and, under Regulation Q, maximum interest rates on time deposits. These tools directly affect member banks, but not all commercial

---

*For an interesting history of the FOMC, see Committee on Banking and Currency, *Federal Reserve Structure and the Development of Monetary Policy: 1915–1935,* U.S. House of Representatives, 1971.

Table 3.4
Federal Reserve System Balance Sheet as of Jan. 31, 1976
(In billions)

Assets		Liabilities and Capital	
Gold certificates	$ 11.6	Federal Reserve notes	$ 73.9
Cash	0.4	Member bank deposits	27.3
Loans and acceptances	1.2	U.S. Treasury deposits	10.1
U.S. government securities	89.9	Other deposits	0.9
Federal agency obligations	6.6		
Float	1.6	Other liabilities	1.2
Other	4.4	Capital	2.3
	$115.7		$115.7

Source: Federal Reserve Bulletin.

banks. At the end of 1975 5,800 banks, or 40 percent of all commercial banks, were member banks. However, these member banks held 76 percent of all commercial bank assets. In 1960, 46 percent of all commercial banks were member banks, and they held 84 percent of total assets. Thus membership in the Federal Reserve System involves relatively fewer banks with a relatively smaller share of total commercial bank assets. How nonmembership as well as the existence of other financial intermediaries outside of the Federal Reserve System affects monetary policy is a topic to which we shall return in Chapter 16.

In addition to regulation and monetary control, the Federal Reserve System supplies a number of services. One of the most important from the standpoint of banking operations is the provision of check-clearing services for member banks. Checks deposited in one member bank which are drawn on other member banks may be processed through the System. The appropriate Federal Reserve Bank(s) will credit the reserve account of the bank receiving the checks and charge the reserve accounts of the banks against whom the checks were drawn. Thus member bank reserve accounts (member bank deposits in Table 3.4) serve functions other than monetary control.

The mechanics by which the Federal Reserve influences the reserves of member banks and ultimately the money supply are discussed in Chapter 6. We defer until Part Four an examination of the role of the Fed in economic stabilization.

SUMMARY NOTES

1. Financial markets provide a means by which original lenders, or surplus units, may lend to final borrowers, or deficit units.

2. Financial intermediaries act as "middlemen" by providing an indirect route through which the funds of surplus units may be channeled to deficit units.

3. Financial intermediaries include commercial banks, life insurance companies, and savings and loan associations, among others; commercial banks are the largest group. Government agencies such as the Federal Reserve System and the Government National Mortgage Association are also financial intermediaries.

4. Financial instruments used to transfer funds or ownership include both capital-market instruments (long-term) and money-market instruments (short-term).

5. Commercial banks are particularly important because they are the only private institutions that issue exchange media. Moreover, monetary policy is implemented primarily through the commercial banking system.

6. The Federal Reserve System has the primary responsibility for the conduct of monetary policy.

7. The Fed consists of 12 Federal Reserve Banks supervised by a Board of Governors. Open market policy formulation is accomplished by the Federal Open Market Committee and implemented through open market operations.

8. Other policy tools include the discount rate, Regulation Q, and the required reserve ratio.

DISCUSSION QUESTIONS

1. Financial intermediaries are middlemen, and we all complain about the way in which middlemen seem to ''raise prices'' unnecessarily. If so, why don't final borrowers eliminate the middleman by performing the middleman's functions?

2. Certain nonbank financial intermediaries in Massachusetts and New Hampshire offer time and savings accounts against which checks may be drawn (called NOW accounts for Negotiable Order of Withdrawal). If this is authorized on a nationwide basis, what will be the effect on the relative growth rates of commercial banks and nonbank financial intermediaries?

3. With respect to the previous question, what is likely to be the response of commercial banks to the widespread use of NOW accounts?

LENDING-BORROWING FLOWS

In Chapter 2 (Figure 2.1), we noted the relationship of financial markets to the circular flow of income and expenditure. Chapter 3 discussed the institutions that deal, and the instruments traded, in financial markets. The picture of financial markets may be completed by constructing a model of the saving- (lending-) borrowing process. That is the purpose of this chapter.

Savings not used to increase holdings of money balances (net hoarding) or directly invested in capital goods are the loanable funds supplied (net lending) in financial markets. Suppliers exchange loanable funds for the primary securities (IOUs) of demanders who wish to borrow at the market rate of interest and spend in excess of their income. Exchange takes place in financial markets either directly between original lenders and final borrowers or indirectly through financial institutions.

In this chapter we begin by explaining the accounting framework within which a flow analysis of financial markets can be undertaken. Afterward, we develop a theory of loanable funds and explain how financial intermediation and changes in net government borrowing affect financial markets. Finally, we condense our loanable funds analysis to a form which will permit us to integrate it with our forthcoming monetary analysis.

4.1 FLOW OF LOANABLE FUNDS

The Fed has developed a system of social accounting called the *flow of funds accounts.** The system provides a record of the flow of funds, for both financial and nonfinancial transactions, among the various sectors of the economy. Although this record of nonfinancial transactions is structured differently, it is similar to the record of those transactions in the national income accounts, discussed in Chapter 2. However, unlike the national income accounts, the flow of funds accounts also record the economy's financial transactions. They show how current saving is distributed among each sector's investments. These accounts reflect the flow of loanable funds in financial markets.

The flow of loanable funds in the economy is constructed by (1) constructing each sector's balance sheet (a record of its stocks of assets, liabilities, and net worth) at two specific points (or days) in time, (2) constructing each sector's capital account (a record of its financial transactions) during a period of time by calculating the changes in the stocks in the two balance sheets, and (3) placing all the sectors' capital accounts side by side and aggregating the data.

A summary of a sector's balance sheet which is general enough to apply to all sectors is given below.

Summary of a Sector's Balance Sheet
December 31, 19—
(In billions of dollars)

Assets		Liabilities and Net Worth	
Financial assets:		Liabilities:	
Money	25	Short term	35
Nonmoney	100	Long term	75
Capital assets	700	Net worth	715
Total	825	Total	825

The summary balance sheet shows that the sector holds $700 billion in capital assets and $125 billion in financial assets. The composition of the sector's asset portfolio depends on the sector being considered. For example, business capital assets include inventories, plant, and equipment; household capital assets include residential housing. A capital asset appears only on the owner's balance sheet.

Financial assets include both money ($25 billion) and nonmoney assets ($100 billion). Nonmoney assets include corporate shares and bonds and other

---

*See *The Flow of Funds Accounts,* Board of Governors of the Federal Reserve System, February 1968, pp. 7–45. Also see L. Ritter, "The Flow of Funds Accounts: A Framework for Financial Analysis," *New York University Bulletin,* no. 52, pp. 4–36; and J. Cohen, "Copeland's Moneyflows after Twenty-five Years: A Survey," *Journal of Economic Literature,* March 1972, pp. 1–25. A more recent reference is *Introduction to Flow of Funds,* Board of Governors of the Federal Reserve System, February 1975.

debt instruments issued between and among the sectors. Since a financial asset is a claim against someone else, it appears on two balance sheets, the owner's balance sheet (as a financial asset) and the issuer's balance sheet (as a liability). This means that although no single sector's financial assets necessarily equal its liabilities, for the whole economy financial assets must equal liabilities.

The summary balance sheet above shows that the sector's liabilities are $110 billion ($35 billion in short-term debts and $75 billion in long-term debts). The composition of sector liabilities will vary. For example, household sector short-term liabilities include charge accounts at department stores, and long-term liabilities include mortgages; business liabilities include short- and long-term loans from financial institutions.

The balancing entry in the summary sheet above is net worth of $715 billion. Net worth is simply the difference between a sector's assets and its liabilities, or the difference between what a sector owns and what it owes. Since a single sector's financial assets need not equal its liabilities, a sector's capital assets need not equal its net worth. For example, a sector may have liabilities in excess of financial assets, so that capital assets exceed net worth. However, since financial assets in the whole economy equal liabilities, capital assets in the whole economy are the economy's net worth or wealth.*

By calculating changes in the stocks shown on each sector's balance sheet between two points in time, the capital account statement for each sector can be derived. The capital account records a sector's inflows (sources) and outflows (uses) of loanable funds for a specific time period. A summary of a sector's capital account statement which is general enough to apply to any sector is given below (let Δ equal a discrete change in a variable).

**Summary of a Sector's Capital Account Statement
For Fourth Quarter 19—**

(In billions of dollars)

Transaction Category	Uses	Sources
Δ Financial assets (financial investment):		
Δ Money (net hoarding)	5	
Δ Nonmoney (net lending)	115	
Δ Capital assets (capital investment)		
Δ Liabilities (net borrowing)		
Δ Net worth (saving)		120
Total	120	120

---

*At this point the student may wonder why issuing corporate shares, which represent ownership in the firm, does not add to net worth. Suppose General Motors sells $100 of new GM stock, for cash, to households. Households increase their GM holdings by $100 and reduce their cash holdings by $100. General Motors increases its cash holdings by $100 and increases its "paid-in capital" by $100. The transaction does not change real or capital assets of either GM or households. Thus for our purposes we treat the sale of stocks in the same way as we treat the sale of bonds.

The summary statement above shows that during the fourth quarter, the sector's financial assets increased by $120 billion, consisting of an increase in net hoarding of money (hoarding less dishoarding) of $5 billion and an increase in net lending of $115 billion (new purchases less sales of financial assets) by purchasing financial assets. Capital assets did not change. These uses of funds in the sector's capital account were financed with saving, so that additional liabilities or net borrowing (new loans less debt repayments) were not necessary. Just as saving (a use) of $120 billion is the balancing entry in the sector's current account statement shown in Section 2.1, saving or changes in net worth (a source) of $120 billion balances the sector's capital account.

By combining the sector's current account statement, shown in Section 2.1, and its capital account statement above, we can derive its uses and sources statement. A summary of a sector's complete uses and sources statement which is general enough to apply to any sector is given below.

A Sector's Uses and Sources of Funds Statement
For Fourth Quarter 19—
(In billions of dollars)

Transaction Category	Uses	Sources
Current income		195
Current expenditures	75	
Saving	120	
Subtotal on current account	195	195
Δ Financial assets:		
Δ Money (net hoarding)	5	
Δ Nonmoney (net lending)	115	
Δ Capital assets (capital investment)		
Δ Liabilities (net borrowing)		
Δ Net worth (saving)		120
Subtotal on capital account	120	120
Total on current and capital accounts	315	315

The statement clearly shows that since uses equal sources, both the current account and the capital account must balance. Note that the sector's saving (income less expenditures) on its current account is the same as its saving (or additions to net worth) on its capital account.

We may summarize a sector's uses of funds as current expenditures, net hoarding, net lending, and capital investment, and a sector's sources of funds as current income and net borrowing. Saving on the current account is used as a source on the capital account. Since each sector's capital account balances, each sector's capital investment plus net lending plus net hoarding must equal saving plus net borrowing. Thus, when a sector's saving exceeds capital investment, its net lending plus net hoarding exceeds net borrowing, and when a sector's capital investment exceeds saving, its net borrowing exceeds net lending plus net hoarding. A surplus sector (in which saving exceeds capital investment) will use all its surplus for lending, repaying debts, or hoarding. A deficit sector (in which capital investment exceeds saving) will finance its deficit by selling other asset holdings, borrowing, or dishoarding.

By placing the uses U and sources S statements of all sectors side by side, a flow of funds matrix for the economy can be derived. The matrix shows the financial interrelations among the household, business, and government sectors. The following is an example of the economy's flow of funds matrix which summarizes the principal transactions that describe the intersector flow of loanable funds.

The Economy's Flow of Loanable Funds Matrix
For Fourth Quarter 19—
(In billions of dollars)

| | Sectors | | | | | | All Sectors | |
| | Household | | Business | | Government | | | |
Transaction Category	U	S	U	S	U	S	U	S
Saving (Δ net worth)		120				−20		100
Capital investment (Δ real assets)			100				100	
Net borrowing (Δ liabilities)				100		20		120
Net lending (Δ nonmoney financial assets)	115		5				120	
Net hoarding (Δ money holdings)	5		−5					
Total	120	120	100	100	0	0	220	220

The transactions categories are rearranged, but they are essentially the same as those described earlier. Current income and expenditures are excluded from the matrix because funds which directly facilitate income expenditures flow are not loanable funds. However, current income and expenditures are implicitly included because their difference, saving (or dissaving), appears in the matrix.

The flow of loanable funds matrix clearly shows that although each sector's uses and sources are equal, a sector's saving may exceed (be less than) its capital investment. Consequently, net lending plus net hoarding exceeds (is less than) net borrowing by an equal amount. For example, the household sector's saving exceeds its capital investment by $120 - 0 = \$120$ billion, and net lending plus net hoarding exceeds net borrowing by an equal amount, $115 + 5 - 0 = \$120$ billion. As indicated by our numerical example, we will continue to assume for simplification purposes that the household sector is the source of all saving in the economy, and that it makes no capital investment (consumer durables are considered consumption expenditures of the household sector). Thus, the household sector's saving is allocated between net lending and net hoarding. For simplification, we assume that the net borrowing of the household sector is zero.

The business sector's capital investment is greater than its saving by $100 − 0 = $100 billion, and net borrowing is greater than net lending plus net hoarding by $100 − ($5 − $5) = $100 billion. As indicated by our numerical example, we will continue to assume for simplification purposes that the business sector has zero saving and that it must borrow and/or dishoard money balances to finance the capital investment that takes place in the economy.

The government sector's saving is less than its capital investment by −$20 = −$20 − 0 billion, and its net borrowing is greater than its net lending plus net hoarding by $20 = $20 − 0 billion. Like the business sector, the government sector is frequently a net borrower of funds. We will continue to assume for simplification purposes that the government sector is not a net lender of funds and does not invest in capital goods. Only the other sectors are net lenders, and only the business sector invests in capital goods.

In the whole economy saving equals capital investment, $100 billion = $100 billion, and therefore net borrowing equals net lending plus net hoarding, $120 = $120 + 0 billion. It also follows that total uses equal total sources, $220 billion = $220 billion for the whole economy. Since aggregate saving equals aggregate capital investment, a surplus sector like the household sector must dispose of its saving by net lending and/or net hoarding. This implies that at least one other sector, such as the business sector, invests more than it saves by net borrowing and/or net dishoarding. Thus, a surplus sector implies the existence of a deficit sector, and vice versa. As in our example, we will continue to assume that the saving of the household sector is borrowed by the business and government sectors. The business sector finances its investment by borrowing funds and by dishoarding. The government borrows to finance its deficit.

The flow of loanable funds suggests certain useful accounting definitions. First, saving TS (private saving S and the government surplus $GS = T − G$) plus actual net borrowing B (including private sector borrowing PB and government borrowing from the public GB) is identical to actual capital investment I plus net lending L plus net hoarding H (including temporary hoarding by government to finance the deficit GH and private sector hoarding PH). That is,

$$TS + B \equiv I + L + H \tag{4.1}$$

or, since
$$TS \equiv S + T − G \tag{4.2}$$

and
$$B \equiv PB + GB \tag{4.3}$$

and
$$H \equiv PH + GH \qquad\qquad (4.4)$$
then
$$S + T - G + PB + GB \equiv I + L + PH + GH \qquad\qquad (4.5)$$

Since we continue to assume that the government surplus is nonzero $(T - G = 0)$ and that government net hoarding during an accounting period is zero $(GH = 0)$, (4.5) becomes

$$S + T - G + PB + GB \equiv I + L + PH \qquad\qquad (4.6)$$

It follows that if total actual borrowing $(B \equiv PB + GB)$ is identical to actual net lending L plus private net hoarding PH,

$$B \equiv L + PH \qquad\qquad (4.7)$$
then
$$S + T - G = I \quad \text{or} \quad S = I + G - T \qquad\qquad (4.8)$$

You will notice that this identity was also derived in Chapter 2 from the national income accounts. Thus, given the assumptions we have made, the two accounting systems yield this same definition.

It also follows that if (4.8) is true by definition, then (4.7) is true by definition.

4.2 LOANABLE FUNDS THEORY

In Chapter 2 we introduced expenditure theory into the accounting definition, Eq. (2.6), and explained the behavior of the economy from the perspective of the flow of income and expenditures. Implicit in that analysis was the condition that when saving equals capital investment plus the government deficit, net borrowing equals net lending plus net hoarding.

By introducing loanable funds theory into the accounting identity, Eq. (4.7), we can develop an alternative explanation of the behavior of the economy. The alternative makes the financial aspects of macroeconomic behavior more explicit.

Both the business and household sectors are perceived to respond to economic stimuli in determining their respective borrowing, lending, and hoarding of funds. The behavior of the government sector, for our purposes, will be treated as exogenous. That is, its behavior is determined by forces outside the system implied by our model.

Loanable Funds Supply

Individuals who hold surplus funds that they do not want to use for capital investment can hoard them and/or lend them in financial markets to final borrowers by demanding additional primary securities or by depositing funds in accounts at financial institutions. The quantity supplied of loanable funds (net lending) depends on the allocation between net lending and net hoarding of saving not directly invested and on injections of new money into the system by the monetary authorities. The allocation between net lending and net hoarding of saving not directly invested depends on the rate of return from lending, i.e., the market rate of interest, and the deposit rate on close money substitutes of financial institutions, i.e., time and savings deposits.

Net lending varies directly with the market interest rate, so that net hoarding varies inversely with the market interest rate. That is, as it becomes more profitable to exchange funds in financial markets for the primary securities of final borrowers who wish to spend in excess of their income, original lenders and financial institutions will decrease net hoarding (dishoard) and increase the quantity of loanable funds supplied (net lending).

Net lending also varies directly with the deposit rate, so that net hoarding varies inversely with the deposit rate. That is, as it becomes more profitable to deposit funds in financial institutions, original lenders will reduce the more risky direct lending in financial markets and decrease their holdings of money balances by net dishoarding. The extent of net dishoarding determines the increase in net lending.*

Net lending and net hoarding vary directly with saving. Since saving varies directly with income, both net lending and net hoarding also vary directly with income. Changes in the supply of money in the system also provide additional funds in the system. The additional funds are injected into the economy through financial markets as additions to loanable funds supply. In Part Two we will explain in detail how which changes in the quantity of money occur in financial markets. But for now it is sufficient to recognize that increases (decreases) in the money stock provide more (less) loanable funds.

In fact, our analysis of the money market in Part Two will enhance our understanding of the way in which changes in both the supply of money and the deposit rate affect the loanable funds supply. Briefly, we will see that changes in those variables affect supply and demand conditions in the money market and therefore change the rate at which net hoarding takes place for any given market interest rate and level of income. Consequently, we include the deposit rate and the real value of additional money balances as determinants of loanable funds supply.

Figure 4.1 shows a loanable funds supply curve L' in real terms for given values of real income or output y_1, the deposit rate $\overline{DR}$, and the real value of additional money balances in the economy ab_1.

Changes in the market interest rate positively affect the quantity of loanable

---

*The net lending and net hoarding decision of original lenders is complicated by the existence of both direct and indirect finance between original lenders and final borrowers. For any given interest rate and level of income, an increase in the deposit rate increases the supply of loanable funds. Although original lenders will substitute deposits in financial institutions for primary securities, and thereby cause only a negligible change in the supply of loanable funds, net dishoarding will cause the supply of loanable funds to increase. In short, by increasing the deposit rate, financial institutions redirect funds away from direct finance and into indirect finance. In the process they cause net dishoarding of money balances.

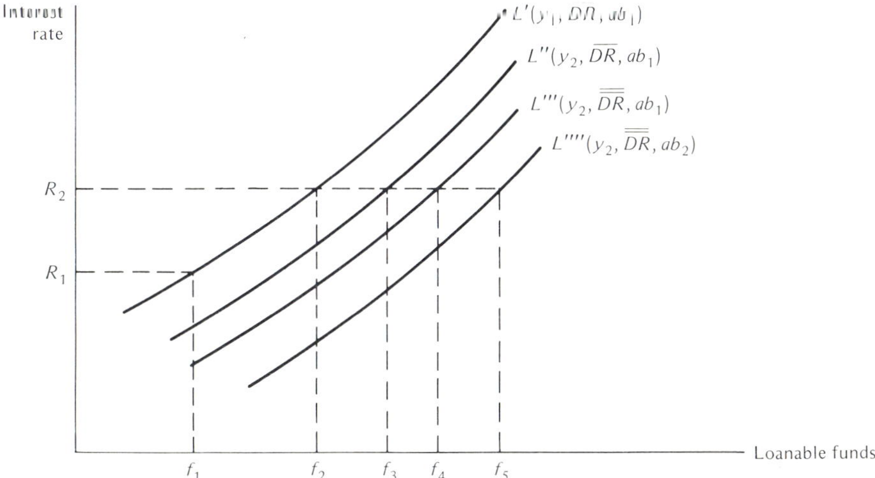

Figure 4.1

Supply of loanable funds.

funds supplied (net lending). For example, for a given level of output y_1, deposit rate $\overline{DR}$, and real value of additional money balances ab_1, an increase in the market interest rate from R_1 to R_2 increases the quantity supplied of loanable funds from f_1 to f_2 along L'. Changes in output change the capacity (real saving) for net lending and positively affect the supply of loanable funds. For example, given the deposit rate $\overline{DR}$ and the real value of additional money balances ab_1, an increase in output from y_1 to y_2 increases real saving. Sectors with surplus funds will increase the supply of loanable funds from L' to L''. For any given market interest rate, say R_2, the quantity supplied of loanable funds increases from f_2 to f_3. Changes in the deposit rate by financial institutions positively affect the supply of loanable funds. For example, given the level of output y_2 and the real value of additional money balances ab_1, an increase in the deposit rate from $\overline{DR}$ to $\overline{\overline{DR}}$ causes savers to dishoard and increases the supply of loanable funds from L'' to L'''. For any given market interest rate, say R_2, loanable funds supplied increase from f_3 to f_4. Finally, changes in the real value of money balances positively affect the supply of loanable funds. For example, given the level of output y_2 and the deposit rate $\overline{\overline{DR}}$, an increase in the real value of additional money balances from ab_1 to ab_2 shifts the loanable funds supply curve from L''' to L''''. For any given market interest rate, say R_2, the quantity of loanable funds supplied increases from f_4 to f_5.

Loanable Funds Demand

Individuals who want to spend more money than they have on hand borrow funds in financial markets by supplying additional primary securities to original lenders and/or financial institutions. The private sector's demand for loanable funds (private net borrowing) depends primarily on the cost of loanable funds, the market rate of interest.* Changes in the interest rate negatively affect the quantity of loanable funds demanded, particularly for purposes of capital investment by the business sector. For example, a decrease in the market interest rate is a decrease in the cost of borrowing, and therefore the quantity of loanable funds demanded increases. Conversely, an increase in the market interest rate decreases the quantity of loanable funds demanded.

Figure 4.2 shows a loanable funds demand curve PB' in real terms, which, according to the foregoing discussion, slopes downward. A decrease in the market interest rate from R_2 to R_1 increases the real value of the quantity of loanable funds demanded from pb_1 to pb_2.

Public sector or government real net borrowing also takes place in financial markets. Governments frequently incur a deficit and must borrow to finance it. We will assume that the government's demand for loanable funds (government net borrowing) is an exogenous variable in the market system implied in our model.

---

*Output might also be included in our analysis as a determinant of the private demand for loanable funds. For any given interest rate, changes in income positively affect the demand for loanable funds. For example, for any given interest rate an increase in income increases the demand for loanable funds, particularly for purposes of investment in consumer durables and business capital. The opposite results occur when output decreases. For simplification purposes we will not include output as a demand determinant. However, its impact should be kept in mind.

Figure 4.2

Private sector demand for loanable funds.

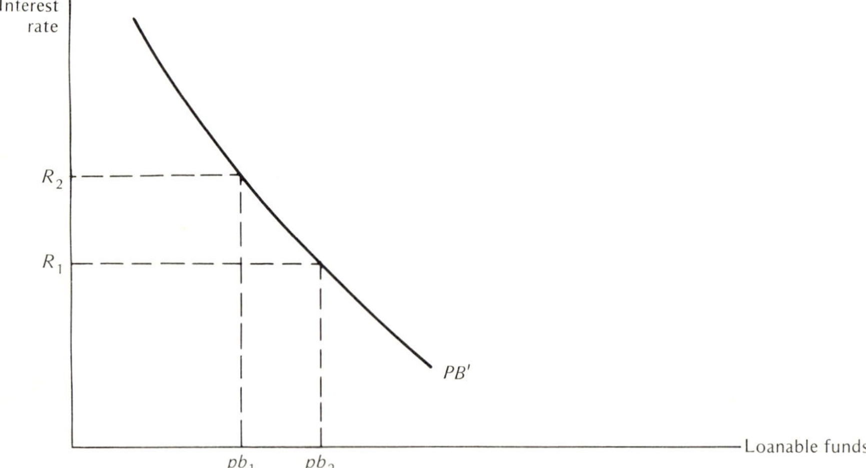

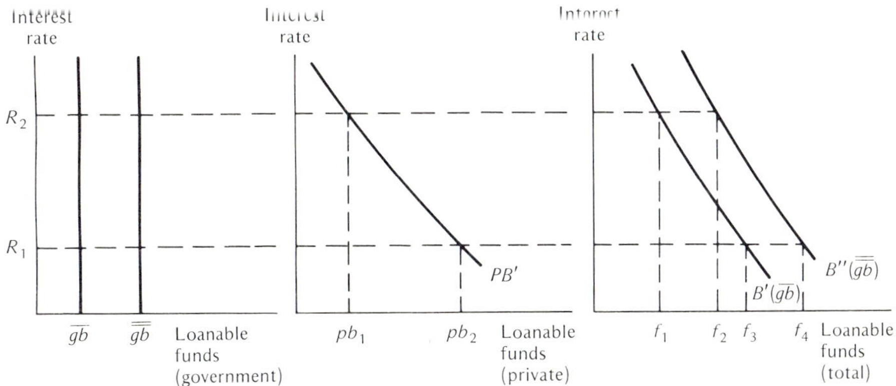

Figure 4.3
Demand for loanable funds.

Figure 4.3 derives the total demand curve for loanable funds in real terms and shows the impact of changes in government demand for loanable funds (real government net borrowing) on the total demand for loanable funds (total real net borrowing). Suppose the real value of government demand for loanable funds is $\overline{gb}$, and suppose it is invariant with respect to the market interest rate. Moreover, suppose PB' is the private sector demand curve for loanable funds in real terms. By horizontally summing the real values of the quantities of government and private demand for loanable funds at given market interest rates, we derive the total demand curve for loanable funds B'. At interest rate R_2, $\overline{gb} + pb_1 = f_1$, and at R_1, $\overline{gb} + pb_2 = f_3$. Changes in the real value of the government's demand for loanable funds positively affect the total demand for loanable funds in real terms. For example, an increase in the real value of the government demand for loanable funds from $\overline{gb}$ to $\overline{\overline{gb}}$ shifts the total demand curve rightward to B''. For any given loan rate, say R_2, the total quantity demanded increases from f_1 to f_2, where $f_2 - f_1 = \overline{\overline{gb}} - \overline{gb}$. Given the interest rate R_1, total quantity demanded increases from f_3 to f_4, where $f_4 - f_3 = \overline{\overline{gb}} - \overline{gb}$.

Loanable Funds Market Equilibrium

When the supply of loanable funds just equals the demand for loanable funds, the equilibrium values of the loan rate and the real value of the quantity of loanable funds are determined. This condition means that in real terms the amount lent is just equal to the amount borrowed, or stated differently, it means that in real terms suppliers (net lenders) supply enough funds so that demanders (net borrowers) can acquire the funds they need to realize expenditures. By implication it also means that in real terms just enough additional financial assets are being supplied for desired additional holdings of financial assets to be realized.

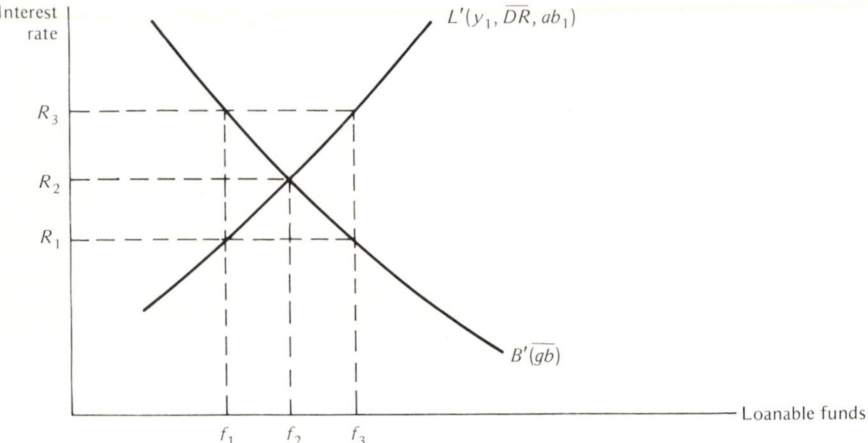

Figure 4.4
Loanable funds market equilibrium.

In Figure 4.4 we plot the loanable funds supply curve L' from Figure 4.1 and the loanable funds demand curve B' from Figure 4.3. For a given level of output y_1, deposit rate $\overline{DR}$, real value of additional money balances ab_1, and net government borrowing $\overline{gb}$, the supply of and demand for loanable funds determine the equilibrium values of the market interest rate R_2 and the real value of the quantity of loanable funds f_2 in financial markets during a specific time period. Since the exchange of funds is accomplished by the exchange of financial assets, flow equilibrium in the loanable funds market implies flow equilibrium in financial asset markets.

When the loanable funds market is in disequilibrium, adjustments will take place until equilibrium is attained.* *For any given level of output y_1, the market interest rate adjusts until equilibrium is attained.* Suppose the loan rate is R_3, where the quantity of loanable funds supplied f_3 exceeds the quantity of loanable funds demanded f_1. As the market interest rate falls toward R_2 to eliminate the excess supply, the quantity demanded of loanable funds (net borrowing) increases toward f_2. At the market interest rate R_1, excess demand equal to $f_3 - f_1$ exists in the loanable funds market. As the market interest rate rises to eliminate the excess demand, savers dishoard money balances and increase the quantity supplied of loanable funds (by net lending) toward f_2. When supply does not equal demand, the market interest rate adjusts until the supply of

---

*Since saving is allocated to net lending, net hoarding, or direct investment by savers, the percentages of saving allocated to the three alternatives must sum to 100 percent. That is, the marginal propensities to net lend, net hoard, and directly invest saving fall between 0 and 1. It follows in our model that a stable equilibrium is attainable.

loanable funds just equals the demand for loanable funds.* Only then will savers who lend and hoard and spenders who borrow be satisfied.†

4.3 THE LB SCHEDULE

A condensed version of the loanable funds market will permit us to integrate more easily our loanable funds theory with the theory of the money market in Part Three. The condensed version is called the *LB schedule*. The LB schedule is defined as the locus of points representing combinations of output level and market interest rate that satisfy the equilibrium condition for the loanable funds market.

On the right-hand side of Figure 4.5, loanable funds supply curves L' and demand curves B' determine the equilibrium values of the market interest rate R_2 and the real value of the quantity of loanable funds f_1, for a given level of output y_1, real government net borrowing $\overline{gb}$, real value of additional money balances ab_1, and deposit rate $\overline{DR}$. Thus, (y_1, R_2) represents one combination of output and market interest rate on the LB schedule, and it appears on the left-hand side of the diagram. By varying output we can derive other combinations as well. Another combination on the *LB* schedule is (y_2, R_1). Notice that the LB

---

*We do not explain here the path of disequilibrium adjustment, only the net effect of the disequilibrium adjustment that is implicit in our model.

†When our financial model is complete, we shall see that output is also an adjustment variable. Both the market interest rate and output are endogenous variables in the complete model. This means that loanable funds theory is incomplete. In technical language, there is one more endogenous variable (output) than there are equations in the loanable funds model. Until the complete model for financial analysis is developed, income is temporarily treated as an exogenous variable.

Figure 4.5

The LB schedule.

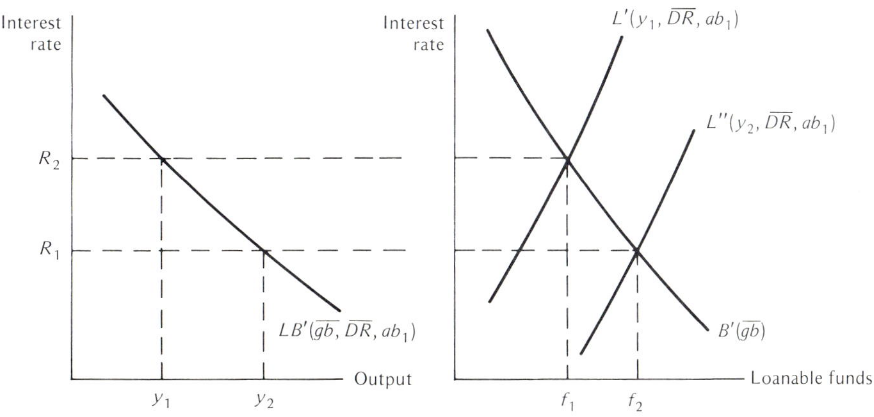

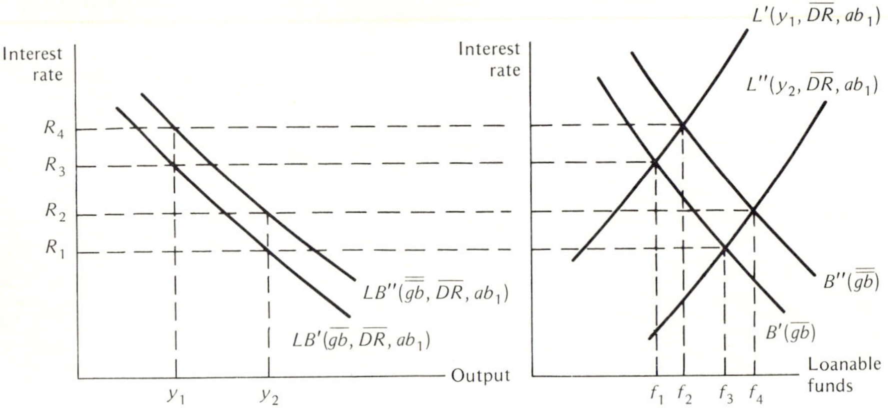

Figure 4.6
Increase in net government borrowing.

schedule shows a negative relationship between output and the market interest rate.

Changes in real government net borrowing, the deposit rate, and the real value of additional money balances shift the LB schedule. For any given level of output, the market interest rate varies directly with real government net borrowing and inversely with the deposit rate and the real value of additional money balances. Thus, increases in real government net borrowing and decreases in the deposit rate and the real value of additional money balances shift the LB schedule rightward. The opposite changes in these variables shift the LB schedule leftward.

Figure 4.6 shows the impact of an increase in real government net borrowing on the LB schedule. An increase in real government net borrowing from $\overline{gb}$ to $\overline{\overline{gb}}$ shifts the loanable funds demand curve from B' to B''. Given the level of output y_1, deposit rate $\overline{DR}$, and real value of additional money balances ab_1, the real value of the quantity of loanable funds increases from f_1 toward f_2 as the market interest rate rises from R_3 to R_4. Given the level of income y_2, deposit rate $\overline{DR}$, and real value of additional money balances ab_1, the real value of the quantity of loanable funds increases from f_3 toward f_4 as the market interest rate rises from R_1 to R_2. Thus, the LB schedule shifts rightward from LB' toward LB''.

Figure 4.7 shows the impact of an increase in the deposit rate on the LB schedule. An increase in the deposit rate from $\overline{DR}$ to $\overline{\overline{DR}}$ induces savers to dishoard by substituting the time deposit liabilities of financial institutions for money balances. Thus, the supply of loanable funds increases from L' toward L''. Given the level of output y_1, real government net borrowing $\overline{gb}$, and real value of additional money balances ab_1, the real value of the quantity of loanable funds increases from f_1 to f_2 as the market interest rate decreases from R_2 to R_1. Since these results occur for any given level of output, the LB schedule shifts leftward from LB' toward LB''.

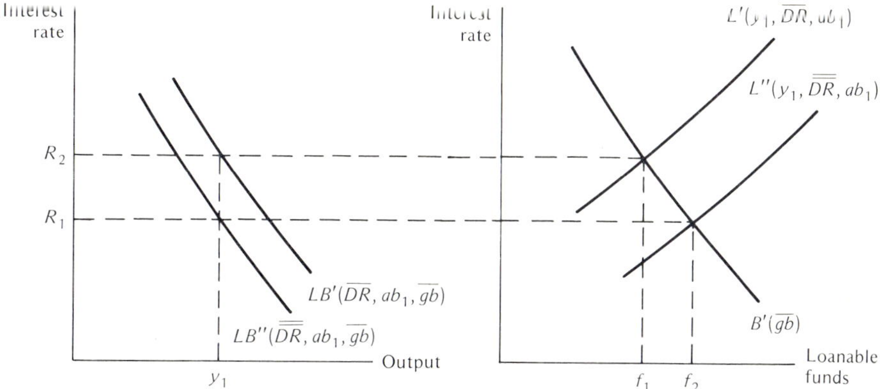

Figure 4.7

Increase in the deposit rate.

Figure 4.8 shows the impact of an increase in the real value of additional money balances on the LB schedule. An increase in the real value of additional money balances from ab_1 to ab_2 means the supply of loanable funds increases from L' to L''. Given the level of output y_1, real government net borrowing $\overline{gb}$, and deposit rate $\overline{DR}$, the real value of the quantity of loanable funds increases from f_1 to f_2 as the market interest rate decreases from R_2 to R_1. Since these results occur for any given level of output, the LB schedule shifts leftward from LB' toward LB''.

4.4 WHAT ABOUT THE MONEY MARKET?

In Chapter 2 we explained the determination of output given the market interest rate. Implicit in that analysis is the condition that when output just equals

Figure 4.8

Increase in the real value of additional money balances.

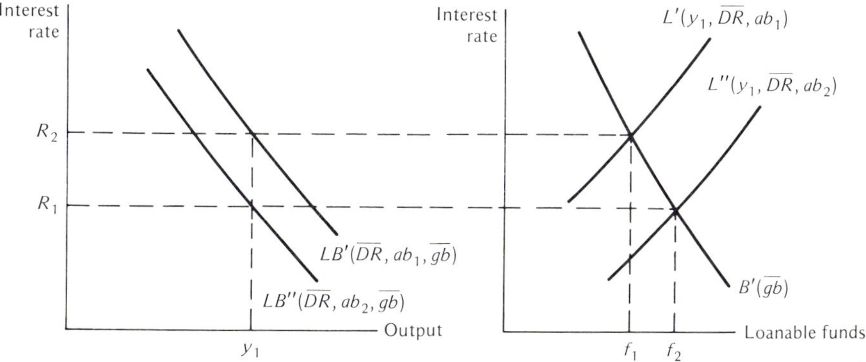

planned real expenditures, the supply of loanable funds just equals the demand for loanable funds. But these conditions hold simultaneously only if money supply just equals money demand at the current market rate of interest, so that net hoarding is zero. Put another way, if planned output and expenditures are equal, planned saving equals planned capital investment plus the government deficit. This is equivalent to saying that planned lending equals planned borrowing only if net hoarding is zero (i.e., if no saving is diverted into net hoarding).

In this chapter we explained the determination of the market rate of interest given the level of output. Implicit in our analysis is the condition that when loanable funds supply just equals loanable funds demand, planned real expenditures just equal output. But again, these conditions can hold simultaneously only if money supply just equals money demand at the current level of output, so that net hoarding is zero.

Regardless of what is made implicit and explicit in our analysis, we need an analysis of the money market in order to explain the nature of net hoarding and its determinants. More important, for our purpose, we need to explain the determination of the quantity of money in the economy as well as changes in the quantity of money if our analysis of output and financial markets is to be clearly understood. Only then will we be in a position to appreciate the impact of monetary policy on both output and financial markets.

SUMMARY NOTES

1. Financial flows are accounted for by the flow of funds accounts. The accounts show how sources of funds (mainly saving) are allocated among various uses for each sector as well as showing the transactions that take place between sectors.
2. The supply of loanable funds depends upon real income and the market interest rate.
3. The demand for loanable funds is assumed to depend on the market interest rate and planned real government net borrowing.
4. Given real income and real government net borrowing, the loanable funds market determines the market interest rate.
5. The LB schedule shows combinations of real income and market interest rate that are consistent with equilibrium in the loanable funds market.

DISCUSSION QUESTIONS

1. Question 1 in Chapter 2 asked you to trace the circular flow of income and expenditures in an economy in which private financial intermediation was illegal and the government owned all the means of production. Now construct the flow of funds matrix for such an economy.

2. The chapter pointed out that the demand for, and supply of, loanable funds is the mirror image of the supply of, and demand for, financial assets. Could we have constructed a model of the market for financial assets rather than for loanable funds? What problems would we encounter? (*Hint:* How would you measure quantity?)

3. If financial institutions were required to hold a percentage of their deposit liabilities in idle reserves, how would this affect the quantity of loanable funds flowing to final borrowers? Would the market rate of interest be lower or higher when financial institutions are required to hold reserves?

4. Suppose the loanable funds market is summarized by the following model:

$$\text{Real net lending} = \$50 + .02 + \$700R$$
$$\text{Real net borrowing} = gb - \$300R$$
$$\text{Real net lending} = \text{real net borrowing}$$

where $y = \$1,300$
$\quad gb = \$100$

Solve for the equilibrium market rate of interest and quantity of loanable funds. If output increased by $100, what would be the change in the quantity of loanable funds and the market rate of interest?

PART

TWO

ANALYSIS OF THE MONEY MARKET

THE MONEY CREATION PROCESS

The monetary authorities (the Federal Reserve and the Treasury) supply the *monetary base* (or high-powered money) used to create the country's money supply. The Fed and the Treasury directly determine the monetary base, and the Fed directly determines the reserves member banks are required to hold against their deposit liabilities. Under the fractional reserve system, changes in the monetary base and the base money multiplier precipitate changes in the money supply.

In this chapter we begin by defining the monetary base. Afterward, a naïve definition of the base money multiplier is used to explain the principles of money (demand deposit) creation by the banking system, given changes in the monetary base and/or the base money multiplier. Finally, the definition of the base money multiplier is expanded to explain how leakages of reserves, which are determined by member banks and the nonbank public, dampen the multiplier effect of the money creation process.

The seminal work appears in K. Brunner, "A Schema for the Supply Theory of Money," International Economic Review, *January 1961, pp. 79–109. For a more complete treatment, see A. E. Burger,* The Money Supply Process *(Belmont, Calif.: Wadsworth, 1971).*

5.1   THE MONETARY BASE

The base used by the banking system to create the nation's money supply can be viewed as an asset solely determined by the monetary authorities (the Fed and the Treasury) and supplied to the banking system. The sources of the base are the monetary assets of the monetary authorities. The uses of the base are primarily the monetary assets of commercial banks and the nonbank public (which are the liabilities of the monetary authorities). The size of the base is determined by the monetary authorities, while the allocation of its uses is determined primarily by commercial banks and the nonbank public.

This base, which is called the *source base,* can be calculated from data that appear on the consolidated balance sheet of the monetary authorities. The data are published in the *Federal Reserve Bulletin.**

Table 5.1 shows the calculation of the source base for January 31, 1975. On the right-hand side are the noncompeting uses (total uses less competing uses) which define the source base. Noncompeting uses are those items which are available for currency held by the nonbank public and member bank reserves held with the Fed and by member banks as vault cash. The noncompeting uses of the source base are the liabilities of the monetary authorities and assets of member banks and the nonbank public.

Three accounts make up the noncompeting uses of the source base —"member bank reserves held by the Fed," "currency held by the nonbank public," and "currency held by banks (vault cash)." Member banks are required to hold reserves with the Fed against their deposit liabilities. Although the major portion of required reserves is held with the Fed, vault cash is also counted as required reserves. Currency includes Federal Reserve currency (paper dollars) and Treasury currency and coin.

On the left-hand side of Table 5.1 are the sources of the base less competing uses. The sources of the base are the assets of the monetary authorities, and the competing uses are those uses (reserves and other deposits) derived from the sources that make these sources unavailable for currency holdings and for member bank reserves, i.e., unavailable for use in the money creation process.

"Reserve bank credits" are an important source of the base. They consist of "United States government securities" (including securities of United States government agencies such as the Federal Home Loan Bank), "loans to member banks," the "float," and "other assets." "United States government securities" reflect the government debt held in the Fed's asset portfolio. They account for roughly 80 percent of the source base. "Float" arises from the Fed's responsibility for check collection. Checks received by the Fed but not yet collected are

---

*The relevant asset accounts are shown in the *Federal Reserve Bulletin* under the heading "Member Bank Reserves, Federal Reserve Bank Credit, and Related Items." This account lists the factors supplying reserve funds (the assets of the monetary authorities) and factors absorbing reserve funds [the assets (liabilities) of commercial banks and the nonbank public (the Fed and the Treasury)], as well as those factors which both supply and absorb reserve funds (the Treasury and the Fed).

Table 5.1

The Monetary Base, Jan. 31, 1975

(In millions of dollars)

Sources Less Competing Uses			Noncompeting Uses	
Reserve Bank Credits:*		92,185	Member bank reserves	
U.S. government securities	86,134		held by Fed	28,839
Loans to member banks	103			
Float	1,466		Currency held by non-	
Other Fed assets	3,518		bank public	68,911
Gold certificates		11,635	Currency held by banks	
			(vault cash)	7,431
SDR certificates		400		
Treasury currency outstanding		9,305		
Minus competing uses:		8,344		
Treasury deposit with the Fed	3,540			
Other deposits with the Fed	1,139			
Other Fed liabilities and capital	3,415			
Treasury cash holdings	250			
Equals:			Equals:	
Source base		105,181	Source base	105,181
Less:			Less:	
Loans to member banks		103	Member bank borrowing	103
Equals:			Equals:	
Net source base or monetary base		105,078	Net source base or monetary base	105,078

*Includes $726 millon in acceptances not listed separately.
Source: Federal Reserve Bulletin, March 1975, pp. A4, A6, A12.

Fed assets which are referred to as *cash items in the process of collection.* Credits for these checks are given to banks before they are collected according to a time schedule set up by the Fed. This means that the Fed incurs a liability, referred to as *deferred-availability cash items.* The difference between the cash items in the process of collection and the deferred-availability cash items is the "float." Loans are another reserve credit item. They reflect member bank borrowing from the Fed. Member banks have the privilege (not the right) of borrowing at the Fed. At the discretion of the Fed, loans are collateralized by government securities or other eligible negotiable paper. Finally, "other assets" include the Fed's holdings of banker's acceptances, foreign exchange, and cash.

Other sources of the base are "gold certificates," "SDR certificates," and "Treasury currency outstanding." "Gold certificates" are warehouse receipts that are used to monetize the Treasury's holdings of the nation's monetary gold stock. Since January 1970 the Fed holds special drawing rights certificates (SDRs). These are issued by the Treasury to monetize the International Monetary Fund's new international reserve asset. The SDRs are warehouse receipts for the Treasury's holdings of these assets. The remaining source is "Treasury currency outstanding." It consists of coin minted by the Treasury and a very small amount of Treasury currency.

The competing uses of the source base in Table 5.1 include Treasury deposits with the Fed, foreign deposits with the Fed, and other Fed liabilities, including nonmember bank deposits with the Fed, and capital (net worth of the monetary authorities). These items are subtracted from the total uses and sources of the base because although they are derived from the sources of the base, they are not available for use in the creation of the nation's money supply.*

In Table 5.1 the amount of Fed loans to member banks (member bank borrowing at the Fed) is subtracted from the source base. The result is called the *net source base,* hereafter called the *monetary base.* The base is adjusted in this way in order to separate, in the forthcoming analysis of member bank behavior, the influence on the money supply of changes in member bank borrowing from that of changes in the base.

As you can see by examining Table 5.1, the monetary base is the same regardless of whether it is calculated from the sources less competing uses side or from the noncompeting uses side. As we will see later in our discussion of monetary policy and control over the money supply, the choice between the two methods of calculation is very important.

5.2 PRINCIPLES OF THE MONEY CREATION PROCESS

The nation's money supply MS can be expressed as a multiple m of the monetary base MB,

$$MS = m \cdot MB \tag{5.1}$$

For purposes of simplifying the essential mechanics of the money creation process, we temporarily assume that the money supply consists only of demand deposits (bank money) DD,

$$MS = DD \tag{5.2}$$

---

*Most economists argue that all bank reserves should be included in the monetary base so that the increasingly important influence of Eurodollar borrowings (borrowings on deposits denominated in United States dollars in foreign banks), time deposits, etc., can be incorporated into discussions of the money supply process. Others argue that they are not systematically related to demand deposits and adjust the base to exclude them. For a detailed discussion, see L. C. Andersen and J. L. Jordan, "The Monetary Base—Explanation and Analytical Use," *Review,* Federal Reserve Bank of St. Louis, August 1968, pp. 7–14; and L. C. Andersen, "Three Approaches to Money Stock Determination," *Review,* Federal Reserve Bank of St. Louis, October 1967, pp. 6–13.

and that the monetary base consists only of reserves RD member banks are required to hold against their demand deposit liabilities,

$$MB = RD \tag{5.3}$$

These assumptions imply that member banks hold no excess reserves, i.e., that they stay "loaned up," and that the nonbank public holds no currency or time deposits. We also assume that the member bank borrowing is zero.

By solving (5.1) for m and substituting (5.2) and (5.3) into the results, we define the base money multiplier,

$$m = \frac{MS}{MB} = \frac{DD}{RD} = \frac{1}{RD/DD} \tag{5.4}$$

Under a fractional reserve banking system, member banks are required to hold a percentage r_D of their demand deposit liabilities as reserves,

$$RD = r_D \cdot DD \tag{5.5}$$

or

$$r_D = \frac{RD}{DD} \tag{5.6}$$

The required percentage is called the *required reserve ratio* on demand deposit liabilities. By substituting (5.6) into (5.4), we can rewrite the definition of the base money multiplier as

$$m = \frac{1}{r_D} \tag{5.7}$$

under a fractional reserve banking system, since $0 < r_D < 1$, $1/r_D > 1$.

By substituting (5.7) into (5.1), we derive an expression for the money supply in terms of the required reserve ratio on demand deposits and the monetary base,*

$$MS = \frac{1}{r_D} MB \tag{5.8}$$

---

*This equation is the sum of a geometric progression where MB is progressively multiplied by $(1 + r_D)^{-1}$

$$MS = MB\,[(1 + r_D)^{-1} + (1 + r_D)^{-2} + (1 + r_D)^{-3} + \cdots + (1 + r_D)^{-n}] \tag{1}$$

We can find the sum of the series by multiplying both sides by $(1 + r_D)^{-1}$, subtracting the results from (1), and multiplying both sides of the results by $1 + r_D$. These operations yield

$$MS = \frac{1}{r_D} MB\,[1 - (1 + r_D)^{-n}] \tag{2}$$

This expression means that the reciprocal of the required reserve ratio (the base money multiplier) and the monetary base are the only determinants of the money supply. For example, if $MB = \$20$ billion and $r_D = 0.25$, so that $1/r_D = 4$, the money supply would be

$$\$80 \text{ billion} = (4)\ (\$20 \text{ billion})$$

It follows from (5.8) that for a given monetary base $MB = \overline{MB}$,

$$\Delta MS = \Delta\left(\frac{1}{r_D}\right) \overline{MB} \tag{5.9}$$

For example, if $MB = \$20$ billion and the Fed decreased r_D from 0.25 to 0.20 so that $\Delta(1/r_D) = 1$, the money supply would increase by

$$\$20 \text{ billion} = (1)\ (\$20 \text{ billion})$$

It also follows from (5.8) that for a given $r_D = \overline{r}_D$,

$$\Delta MS = \frac{1}{\overline{r}_D} \Delta MB \tag{5.10}$$

For example, if $r_D = 0.20$ so that $1/r_D = 5$ and the Fed increased the monetary base by \$10 billion, the money supply would increase by

$$\$50 \text{ billion} = (5)\ (\$10 \text{ billion})$$

Conversely, increases in r_D and decreases in MB decrease the money supply.

A numerical example that illustrates the mechanics of the money creation process that results from an increase in the monetary base is summarized in

---

As $n \to \infty$, $(1 + r_D)^n \to 0$ and $[1 - (1 + r_D)^n] \to 1$. Thus

$$MS = \frac{1}{r_D} MB \tag{3}$$

and
$$\Delta MS = \frac{1}{r_D} \Delta MB$$

Given our assumptions, (5.8) can be alternatively expressed as

$$DD = \frac{1}{r_D} RD$$

where $1/r_D$ is referred to as the *reserve-deposit multiplier*.

Table 5.2. The table shows the consolidated assets and liability accounts of all banks in a hypothetical banking system. Under the assumptions of our naïve version of the money creation process, we begin our illustration with all banks' assets ($20 billion of required reserves plus $60 billion of loans to the nonbank public plus $20 billion of other bank assets) initially equal to all banks' liabilities ($100 billion of demand deposits). We assume that net worth is zero. Given

Table 5.2
Consolidated Balance Sheet Showing the Banking System's Money Creation Process Given an Increase in the Monetary Base
(In billions of dollars)

| | | Assets | | | Liabilities |
| | Reserves | | Loans to Nonbank | Other Bank | |
Banks	Required	Excess	Public	Assets	Demand Deposits
Total for all banks	20.0	0.0	60.0	20.0	100.0
Changes by bank 1		+10.0 −10.0	+10.0	−10.0	
Subtotal for all banks	20.0	0.0	70.0	10.0	100.0
Changes by bank 2	+2.0	+10.0 −10.0	+8.0		+10.0
Subtotal for all banks	22.0	0.0	78.0	10.0	110.0
Changes by bank 3	+1.6	+8.0 −8.0	+6.4		+8.0
Subtotal for all banks	23.6	0.0	84.4	10.0	118.0
. . .		. . .			. . .
Subtotal for all banks	29.9	0.0	109.6	10.0	149.5
Changes by bank n	+0.1	+0.5 +0.5	+0.4		+0.5
Total for all banks	30.0	0.0	110.0	10.0	150.0
Total net changes	+10.0	0.0	+50.0	−10.0	+50.0

the required reserve ratio on demand deposits of 20 percent, banks hold $20 billion of reserves against $100 billion of demand deposits.

Suppose that the monetary authorities increase the monetary base by purchasing $10 billion of other bank assets from bank 1. The transaction is recorded on the consolidated balance sheet of the monetary authorities as a $10 billion increase in the appropriate asset account (a source of the monetary base) and an equal increase in the member bank reserve account (a noncompeting use of the monetary base). The corresponding entry is shown on bank 1's accounts in Table 5.2 as an asset transfer from "other bank assets" to "excess reserves." The transaction means that additional reserves of $10 billion have been injected into the banking system.

Given the assumption that banks stay "loaned up," bank 1 will lend its excess reserves of $10 billion to the nonbank public. The transaction is shown on bank 1's accounts in Table 5.2 as an asset transfer from "excess reserves" to "loans." The nonbank public borrows in order to finance its expenditures. When the borrowed funds are received by sellers, it is likely that they are not redeposited in the same bank from which they were borrowed. Rather, they will be deposited in other banks, which we will call bank 2. This transaction can be described as a $10 billion transfer of reserves from bank 1 to bank 2, where demand deposits of an equal amount are created for the nonbank public at bank 2.

However, bank 2 is required to hold only 20 percent in reserve against its demand deposit liabilities. That is, it must hold additional reserves of $0.2 \times 10 billion = $2 billion. Bank 2 will stay "loaned up" by lending the remaining $8 billion of excess reserves to the nonbank public. This transaction is shown on bank 2's accounts as an asset transfer from "excess reserves" to both "required reserves" ($2 billion) and "loans" ($8 billion).

Again assume that once the $8 billion of borrowed funds are spent, they wind up as reserves in other banks, which we will call bank 3. This transaction can be described as an $8 billion transfer of reserves from bank 2 to bank 3, where demand deposits of an equal amount are created for the nonbank public at bank 3.

However, bank 3 is required to hold additional reserves of only $0.2 \times 8 billion = $1.6 billion against its demand deposit liabilities. To stay "loaned up," it will lend the remaining $6.4 billion of excess reserves to the nonbank public. The transaction is recorded as an asset transfer from bank 3's "excess reserves" to "required reserves" ($1.6 billion) and "loans" ($6.4 billion).

The process continues as more member banks and more members of the nonbank public become involved. Given the $10 billion injection of reserves into the banking system and a required reserve ratio of 20 percent, the money supply (demand deposits) increases by a geometric progression from $100 billion to $150 billion, or since

$$\Delta MS = \frac{1}{r_D} \Delta MB$$

the money supply increases by

$$\$50 \text{ billion} = (5) (\$10 \text{ billion})$$

Notice that bank credit expands by $50 billion, and the $10 billion of reserves injected into the banking system is absorbed as required reserves. Also notice that the entries on the accounts of the banking system imply corresponding entries on the accounts of the nonbank public. The cumulative $50 billion increase in demand deposit liabilities supplied by the banking system means an equal increase in the quantity of demand deposit assets demanded by the nonbank public. In addition, the $50 billion increase in bank loans (assets of banks) means an equal increase in nonbank public borrowings (liabilities of the nonbank public).

After full adjustment each bank has realized its desired level of excess reserves (in our example the desired level is zero) and has supplied to the nonbank public the maximum amount of money (demand deposits) possible under the constraints imposed on the banking system by the magnitude of the monetary base and the reserve requirements. Thus the banking system is at rest.

A numerical example that illustrates the mechanics of the money creation process that results from a decrease in the required reserve ratio on demand deposits from 20 percent to 10 percent is summarized in Table 5.3. Under the assumptions of our naïve version of the money creation process, we begin our illustration with all banks' assets ($30 billion of required reserves plus $110 billion of loans to the nonbank public plus $10 billion of government securities) equal to all banks' liabilities ($150 billion of demand deposits). We assume that net worth is zero. Given the required reserve ratio on demand deposits of 20 percent, banks hold $30 billion of reserves against $150 of demand deposits.

If the required reserve ratio decreases from 20 percent to 10 percent, $15 billion (0.1 × $150 billion of demand deposits) of required reserves become excess reserves in the banking system. Notice that there is no change in the monetary base, but only a change in the status of reserves.

Given the assumption that banks stay "loaned up," they will lend their $15 billion of excess reserves to the nonbank public. The transaction is shown in Table 5.3 on the accounts of "all banks" as an asset transfer from "required reserves" to "excess reserves" and, once the loans are made, from "excess reserves" to "loans." The nonbank public borrows, for example, to spend on goods and services made available by sellers. When the borrowed funds are received by sellers, we will assume that they are deposited in other banks, which we will call bank 1. This transaction can be described as a $15 billion asset transfer of excess reserves of "all banks" to bank 1 where demand deposit liabilities of an equal amount are created for the nonbank public at bank 1.

Since bank 1 is required to hold only 10 percent in reserve against its demand deposit liabilities, the bank will hold 0.1 × $15 billion = $1.5 billion

Table 5.3
Consolidated Balance Sheet Showing the Banking System's Money Creation Process Given a Decrease in the Required Reserve Ratio
(In billions of dollars)

| Banks | Assets | | Loans to Nonbank Public | Other Bank Assets | Liabilities |
| | Reserves | | | | Demand Deposits |
	Required	Excess			
Total for all banks	30.0	0.0	110.0	10.0	150.0
Changes by all banks	−15.0	+15.0 −15.0	+15.0		
Subtotal for all banks	15.0	0.0	125.0	10.0	150.0
Changes by bank 1	+1.5	+15.0 −15.0	+13.5		+15.0
Subtotal for all banks	16.5	0.0	138.5	10.0	165.0
Changes by bank 2	+1.35	+13.5 −13.5	+12.15		+13.5
Subtotal for all banks	17.85	0.0	150.65	10.0	178.5
. . .		. . .			. . .
Subtotal for all banks	29.85	0.0	258.65	10.0	299.5
Changes by bank *n*	+0.15	+1.5 +1.5	+1.35		+1.5
Total for all banks	30.0	0.0	260.0	10.0	300.0
Total net changes	0.0	0.0	+150.0	0.0	+150.0

and lend out the remaining \$13.5 billion of excess reserves to the nonbank public. This transaction is shown in Table 5.3 on bank 1's accounts as an asset transfer of "excess reserves" to both "required reserves" (\$1.5 billion) and "loans" (\$13.5 billion).

Again assume that once the $13.5 billion is spent it winds up as excess reserves, where demand deposit liabilities of an equal amount are created for the nonbank public at bank 2. This transaction can be described as an asset transfer of reserves from bank 1 to bank 2.

The process continues as more banks and more members of the nonbank public become involved. Given the decrease in the required reserve ratio on demand deposits so that the base money multiplier increases from 5 to 10, the money supply (demand deposits) increases by a geometric progression from $150 billion to $300 billion, or since

$$\Delta MS = \Delta \left(\frac{1}{r_D}\right) MB^*$$

the money supply increases by

$$\$150 \text{ billion} = (5) \ (\$30 \text{ billion})$$

Notice that bank credit expands by $150 billion, and although the required reserve ratio on demand deposits is lower, the excess reserves of $15 billion are again absorbed as required reserves. Again, the entries on the accounts of the banking system imply corresponding entries on the accounts of the nonbank public. The cumulative $150 billion increase in demand deposit liabilities supplied by the banking system means an equal increase in the quantity of demand deposit assets held by the nonbank public. In addition, the $150 billion increase in bank loans (assets of banks) means an equal increase in nonbank public borrowings (liabilities of the nonbank public).

After full adjustment each bank has realized its desired level of excess reserves (in our example the desired level is zero) and has supplied to the nonbank public the maximum amount of money (demand deposits) possible under the constraints imposed by the magnitude of the monetary base and the new required reserve ratio. Thus the banking system is at rest.

By the process just explained, the banking system, stimulated by the monetary authorities and in collaboration with the nonbank public, increases the money supply, if there is either an increase in the monetary base or a decrease in the required reserve ratio. A decrease in the monetary base or an increase in the required reserve ratio yields the opposite results. Although we will drop some of our naïve assumptions in the next section of this chapter and expand the explanation of the money creation process, the principles of money creation by the banking system just explained remain the cornerstone of the money supply process.

---

*See previous footnote and exchange $1/r_D$ for MB in the calculations.

5.3 THE EXPANDED BASE MONEY MULTIPLIER

The money creation process described above shows the maximum change in the money (demand deposits) supply that is possible given either a change in the monetary base or a change in the required reserve ratio for demand deposits. It was assumed that there are no leakages of reserves from the process, that member banks hold no excess reserves, and that the nonbank public holds no currency or time deposits. Also it was assumed that member bank borrowing was zero.

A more realistic description of the money creation process relaxes these restrictive assumptions and considers the role that leakages and borrowed reserves play in the process of money creation.

As stated earlier, money consists not only of demand deposits held by banks but of currency held by the nonbank public,

$$MS = DD + C^P \tag{5.11}$$

Moreover, the monetary base consists not only of required reserves banks hold against demand deposits but also of total unborrowed reserves held at the Fed and by member banks MBR and currency held by the nonbank public,

$$MB = MBR + C^P \tag{5.12}$$

By solving (5.1) for m and substituting (5.11) and (5.12) into the results, we expand the definition of the base money multiplier to include currency held by the public and unborrowed reserves,

$$m = \frac{DD + C^P}{MBR + C^P} \tag{5.13}$$

Total unborrowed reserves is the sum of required and excess reserves $RR + ER$ less borrowed reserves BR,

$$MBR = RR + ER - BR \tag{5.14}$$

Further, we recognize that member banks are required to hold as required reserves RD, a percentage r_D of demand deposit liabilities DD,

$$RD = r_D \cdot DD \tag{5.15}$$

and as required reserves TR, a percentage r_T of time deposit liabilities TD,

$$TR = r_T \cdot TD \tag{5.16}$$

Substituting (5.14) into (5.13), we obtain

$$m = \frac{DD + C^P}{RR + ER - BR + C^P} \qquad (5.17)$$

Since total required reserves is the sum of required reserves on demand deposits and required reserves on time deposits, we can substitute (5.15) and (5.16) into (5.17):

$$m = \frac{DD + C^P}{r_D \cdot DD + r_T \cdot TD + ER - BR + C^P} \qquad (5.18)$$

Finally we can divide by DD letting $C^P/DD = c$, $TD/DD = t$, $ER/DD = e$, and $BR/DD = b$, with the following result:*

$$m = \frac{1 + c}{r_D + r_T t + e - b + c} \qquad (5.19)$$

This expanded definition of the base money multiplier includes not only the required reserve ratio on demand deposits r_D, but the required reserve ratio on time deposits r_T, nonbank public preference for currency relative to demand deposits (the currency ratio) c, nonbank public preference for time deposits relative to demand deposits (the time deposit ratio) t, member banks' excess reserve ratio e, and member banks' borrowed reserve ratio b.

By substituting (5.19) into (5.1), we express the money supply in terms of the components of the expanded base money multiplier and the monetary base,

$$MS = \frac{1 + c}{r_D + r_T t + e - b + c} \, MB \qquad (5.20)$$

This expression means that not only do r_D and MB determine the money supply, but r_T, c, t, e, and b also determine it by determining the base money multiplier. As in our earlier example, assume that $MB = \$20$ billion and $r_D = 0.20$. Further, assume that $r_T = 0.1$, $t = 0.01$, $c = 0.25$, $e = 0.01$, and $b = 0.01$. This

---

*The base money multipliers which correspond to alternative definitions of money (M_2, M_3, and so on) may be derived by the same method used to derive the base money multiplier corresponding to the M_1 definition of money. Simply begin the derivation with an alternative definiton of money. The multiplier of M_2 is

$$m = \frac{1 + c + t}{r_D + r_T t + e - b + c}$$

Similarly, the base money multiplier will vary depending on the definition of the base used in its derivation. Again, select the definition you consider appropriate and follow the same method of derivation used above.

means that the base money multiplier is

$$2.65 \simeq \frac{1 + 0.25}{0.2 + 0.1(0.01) + 0.01 - 0.01 + 0.25}$$

and the money supply is

$$\$53 \text{ billion} = (2.65)\ (\$20 \text{ billion})$$

By comparing these results with those obtained under the naïve description of the money creation process, we see that for the same values of r_D and MB, when leakages to excess reserves, currency, and time deposits and injections of borrowed reserves (a negative leakage) have occurred, the naïve version overstates the base money multiplier by $5 - 2.65 = 2.35$ and thereby the money supply by $\$100 \text{ billion} - \$53 \text{ billion} = \$47 \text{ billion}$.

Similarly, changes in the monetary base have less of an impact on the money supply in the expanded version of the money creation process because the base money multiplier is less than it is in the naïve version. The reason for the difference between the magnitudes of the naïve and expanded multiplier is that member banks hold excess reserves and borrow reserves, and the nonbank public holds time deposits and currency. These factors mean that for a given monetary base, the money supply will be less than it otherwise would be. Moreover, given a change in the monetary base, the failure of banks to lend out all excess reserves and the failure of the nonbank public to deposit all borrowed funds in demand deposits mean the money supply will not change by as much as it would otherwise. Thus, the existence of leakages means that the changes in the money supply due to changes in the monetary base or reserve requirements will be less than they would be if these leakages did not occur.

Changes in r_T, c, t, and e have the same qualitative impact on the base money multiplier and thereby on the money supply as changes in r_D. Changes in b have the opposite impact.

If r_T decreases, required reserves are freed and can be used by the banking system to supply additional bank credit. The base money multiplier increases, and thereby additional money (demand deposits) is created. Conversely, increases in r_T contract the money supply by decreasing the base money multiplier.

If member banks reduce the desired excess reserve ratio, the banking system adjusts e to its desired level by extending additional bank credit. The base money multiplier increases, and thereby additonal money (demand deposits) is created. Conversely, increases in e contract the money supply by decreasing the base money multiplier.

If the nonbank public reduces c, this provides the banking system with additional reserves that can be used to extend additional bank credit. The base money multiplier increases, and thereby additional money (demand deposits) is created. Conversely, increases in c contract the money supply by decreasing the base money multiplier.*

If member banks reduce the desired borrowed reserve ratio, the banking system adjusts b to its desired level by paying off loans from the Fed and extending less bank credit. The base money multiplier decreases, and thereby the money supply contracts. Conversely, increases in b increase the money supply by increasing the base money multiplier.

The naïve description of the money supply process indicated that whoever controls the size of the monetary base and the required reserve ratio on demand deposits controls the money supply. We will see more clearly in the next chapter that the Fed has effective control of the monetary base and the required reserve ratio on demand deposits.

The expanded description of the money creation process indicates that not only is the Fed's control over the monetary base and the required reserve ratio on demand deposits necessary to control the money supply, but control over the excess reserve ratio, the borrowed reserve ratio, the time deposit ratio, the currency ratio, and the required reserve ratio on time deposits is necessary as well. We can score another one for the Fed because it has effective control over the required reserve ratio on time deposits. However, member banks directly determine the excess reserve and borrowed reserve ratios, and the nonbank public directly determines the time deposit and currency ratios. Thus, the Fed only partially controls the money supply. After discussing the instruments by which the Fed changes the monetary base and reserve requirements in the next section, we will discuss the factors that affect member bank and nonbank public behavior in determining the excess reserve, borrowed reserve, currency, and time deposit ratios. This should give us a better understanding of the direct and indirect determinants of the money supply.

SUMMARY NOTES

1. The monetary assets of the Federal Reserve and Treasury form the base upon which the nation's money stock is built.
2. The source base consists of the monetary assets of the Federal Reserve and Treasury less certain liabilities called competing uses.
3. The monetary base is the source base less member bank borrowing from the Fed.
4. The expanded base money multiplier is determined by the required reserve ratios on demand and time deposits, the time deposit ratio, the currency ratio, the excess reserve ratio, and the borrowed reserve ratio.

---

*The currency ratio appears in both the denominator and numerator of the base money multiplier. Since the sum of the other parameters of the denominator is less than 1, increases (decreases) in the currency ratio decrease (increase) the base money multiplier.

5. The currency and time deposit ratios are determined by the preferences of the nonbank public, the excess reserve and borrowed reserve ratios are determined by the preferences of member banks, and the Federal Reserve controls the required reserve ratios and the monetary base.

DISCUSSION QUESTIONS

1. Go to the library and use the *Federal Reserve Bulletins* to calculate the expanded definition of the base money multiplier for December 31, 1974, and December 31, 1975. Do these values differ? Why?
2. Using the same *Federal Reserve Bulletins,* calculate the monetary base for the same two dates. What changes in the sources and competing uses of the monetary base account for changes in the monetary base?
3. Suppose you prefer to define money as M_2 (M_1 plus time deposits at commercial banks). Derive the base money multiplier for M_2 using the monetary base as defined in the chapter. How does your result compare with that in the footnote on page 78?
4. Show that the expanded base money multiplier becomes the naïve multiplier when the nonbank public holds no currency or time deposits and member banks neither borrow from the Fed nor hold excess reserves.
5. If new banking legislation eliminated the reserve requirements on time deposits, by how much would the money supply increase in the numerical example in Section 5.3?

MONEY SUPPLY THEORY

The instruments of monetary policy are the means whereby the monetary authorities initiate the changes in the money supply. Although the Treasury has the power to initiate changes in the money supply, the Fed is the economy's chief monetary policy maker. By using both quantitative and qualitative instruments of monetary policy, the Fed not only controls the monetary base but can both directly and indirectly change the base money multiplier. However, the Fed does not fully control the base money multiplier. The behavior of member banks and the nonbank public also exerts an important influence on it.

In this chapter we will begin by explaining the instruments of monetary policy used by the monetary authorities to initiate changes in the money supply. Afterward, theories of member bank and nonbank public behavior will be developed to provide insight into the role played by market conditions in determining changes in the money supply. Finally, the theory of money supply will be summarized along with the empirical evidence which lends support to our analysis.

6.1 INSTRUMENTS OF MONETARY POLICY

The instruments of monetary policy controlled by the Treasury are purchases and sales of gold and SDRs, changes in Treasury currency outstanding, and changes in Treasury deposits at the Fed. These operations precipitate changes in the money supply* by changing the monetary base.

The quantitative instruments of monetary policy controlled by the Fed are open market operations, which change the money supply by changing the monetary base, and discount policy and changes in reserve requirements, which change the money supply by changing the base money multiplier. The qualitative instruments of monetary policy used by the Fed to alter the allocation of reserves and deposits among commercial banks and the nonbank public are Regulation Q, selective credit controls, changes in margin requirements (for purchasing stocks and other securities), and moral suasion.

Treasury Operations

Since Treasury deposits at the Fed are a competing use of the monetary base, changes in these deposits negatively affect the monetary base. To prevent sizable variations in these deposits, the Treasury and the Fed transfer Treasury deposits between commercial banks and the Fed at a rate that stabilizes Treasury deposits at the Fed at roughly $1 billion. Variations in Treasury deposits at commercial banks due to variations in government expenditures, tax receipts, and debt repayments have no effect on the monetary base. However, these variations negatively affect bank reserves available for private demand deposits.

Changing Treasury currency outstanding is another way by which the Treasury can change the monetary base. When the Treasury mints additional coin (a source of the monetary base) and injects it into the economy, there is an increase in currency held by the nonbank public (a noncompeting use of the monetary base). Conversely, decreases in Treasury currency outstanding decrease the monetary base.

Treasury operations in gold play a unique role in changing the monetary base. Consider a Treasury purchase of gold from a foreign central bank that holds a working deposit at one of the Reserve Banks. Payment is made by an accounting transfer of funds from a Treasury deposit at the Fed to a deposit of the foreign central bank at the Fed. This is a transfer between two competing uses of the monetary base. Thus, there is no change in the monetary base. When the Treasury "monetizes" the gold by issuing gold certificates and

---

*Again see K. Brunner, "A Schema for the Supply Theory of Money," *International Economic Review,* January 1961, pp. 79–109. For a more extensive treatment, see A. E. Burger, *The Money Supply Process* (Belmont, Calif.: Wadsworth, 1971); for a survey of alternative models, see D. E. Fand, "Some Implications of Money Supply Analysis," *American Economic Review,* May 1967, pp. 380–400.

selling them to the Fed, it restores its deposits at the Fed to their former level. But still there is no change in the monetary base because both a source of the monetary base (gold certificates) and a competing use (Treasury deposits at the Fed) increase by an equal amount. However, since foreign central banks keep only working balances in Reserve Banks, they will withdraw funds acquired from the gold sales and purchase other assets, such as government securities or foreign exchange. The foreign bank's check drawn on a Reserve Bank will be deposited in a commercial bank. This leads to an increase in bank reserves (a noncompeting use of the monetary base). In this way gold purchases increase the monetary base. Treasury sales of gold have the opposite results.

Another asset bought and sold by the Treasury is the new international paper currency created by the International Monetary Fund. This asset is called special drawing rights (SDRs).* Since January 1970, the Treasury has monetized a portion of its holdings of SDRs by issuing SDR certificates and selling them to the Fed. The impact on the monetary base is the same as the impact of Treasury issuance of gold certificates.

Changes in Reserve Requirements

The Fed sets the required reserve ratios on the deposit liabilities of member banks.† Changes in the required reserve ratios negatively affect the base money multiplier and thereby the money supply. Such changes alter the status of reserves. For example, a decrease in the required reserve ratios changes the status of reserves from required to excess. As demonstrated earlier, when banks draw down these excess reserves by increasing the supply of bank credit, the supply of money increases through expansion of demand deposits. An increase in the required reserve ratios has the opposite results.

Since changing reserve requirements by a small percentage has a relatively large and abrupt impact on reserves, and therefore on the money supply, the Fed does not use this as a major monetary policy instrument. When it is used, other policy instruments (open market operations and/or discount policy) are used simultaneously to smooth out the abrupt and relatively large impact on the money supply process.

In our exposition of the money creation process, we considered only two required reserve ratios, one on demand deposit liabilities and one on time deposit liabilities. Actually there are different classifications of demand and time

---

*The value of SDRs is tied to a weighted average value of currencies of 16 major member nations of the IMF. The U.S. currency is weighted 33 percent. SDRs yield a 5 percent annual interest rate, which the IMF changes to correspond to changes in an average of short-term interest rates in major member nations. There are mandatory repurchase requirements for sales in excess of 70 percent of original allocations.

†Member banks must maintain their required reserve levels. They have one week to restore reserve deficiencies, with the option of carrying forward 2 percent of any deficiency into the next reserve-accounting week. Requirements are based on the levels of deposits two weeks before the reserve-accounting week.

deposit liabilities, and each has a different required reserve ratio. The Fed determines the classifications. Required reserve ratios on demand deposit liabilities depend on bank deposit size. The smaller the bank, the smaller the marginal required reserve ratio. Required reserve ratios on time deposits depend on the type (denomination) of time deposit liability. The larger the denomination, the larger the required reserve ratio. For example, larger-denomination certificates of deposit have larger reserve requirements than do smaller ones, and so forth down to passbook savings accounts.

Rather than complicate our analysis with additional detail, we have assumed that the required reserve ratios in the base money multiplier are weighted averages of the appropriate required reserve ratios. The ratios on demand deposits are weighted by bank size, and the ratios on time deposits are weighted by type (in dollars) of account. Although the Fed controls each ratio, it does not directly control the averages because it does not directly control the movement of funds between different sizes of banks and different types of accounts. However, changes in reserve requirements have a substantial effect on the averages. Thus, the Fed has substantial control over the required reserve ratios in the base money multiplier and can use changes in reserve requirements to affect the money supply process.

Discount Policy

Member banks have the privilege (not the right) of borrowing additional reserves on a short-term basis from the Fed. Each Federal Reserve Bank maintains a discount window where member banks may discount eligible commercial paper or obtain advances collateralized by the par value of government securities. The latter method is called the "advance technique" and is generally used.

The Fed controls the privilege of member bank borrowing at the discount window and the discount rate (the interest rate on borrowing at the Fed). The explicit cost of borrowing at the Fed is the discount rate. The total cost or *effective* discount rate is the discount rate plus the implicit cost imposed by the Fed as a condition of borrowing. The implicit cost is derived from the Fed's control over the privilege of borrowing at the discount window. Changes in the effective discount rate, whether they result from changes in the discount rate or changes in the stringency of borrowing, negatively affect member bank borrowing and thereby the base money multiplier. For example, a decrease in the effective discount rate encourages member bank borrowing at the Fed. This increases the borrowed reserve ratio and thus the multiplier. Banks can use the additional borrowed reserves to increase the supply of bank credit and thereby the supply of money. Increases in the effective discount rate discourage member bank borrowing and have the opposite results.

Banks have been reluctant to borrow from the Fed because of the Fed's close scrutiny of member banks' uses of borrowed funds. Rather, member banks have increasingly relied on the Federal Funds market (the market for excess reserves held at the Fed) to make up reserve deficiencies and, recently, to take advantage of interest-rate differentials in financial asset markets. In short, member banks have made the judgment that the Federal Funds rate is less than the effective discount rate.

Changes in the discount rate have been interpreted as a signal of the Fed's intentions regarding monetary "ease" or "tightness." An increase in the discount rate may be interpreted as a signal that the Fed intends to engage in a policy of monetary tightness, and a decrease in the discount rate may be interpreted as a signal of monetary ease. However, changes in the discount rate are open to different interpretations. If changes in the discount rate are used as an indicator of future changes in market rates, an increase in the discount rate may confirm that business activity is strong and borrowing should be undertaken before market rates rise any farther, and a decrease in the discount rate may confirm that business activity is weak and borrowing should be curtailed until market rates fall.

To avoid misinterpretation, the Fed has made few changes in the discount rate in recent years that were designed to introduce changes in policy. Rather, the Fed has relied on its control of the privilege of member bank borrowing to control member bank borrowing. Since 1973 the Fed has used changes in the discount rate primarily to encourage seasonal borrowing and to keep the discount rate in line with market interest rates. As such, discount policy discourages the use of changes in the discount rate as a signal of Fed intentions. More generally, discount policy is used to cushion the effects of changes in reserve requirements and to support open market operations. These uses of discount policy relegate it to a relatively minor role in monetary policy.

Open Market Operations

Open market operations are the buying and selling of mostly government securities (government debt) in the open market by the Fed. Fed purchases of government securities from commercial banks or the nonbank public increase the Fed's holdings of these securities (a source of the monetary base) and bank reserves (a noncompeting use of the monetary base). Bank reserves increase whether the Fed makes direct purchases from commercial banks in exchange for reserves or purchases government securities from the nonbank public, who deposit checks drawn on a Reserve Bank in commercial banks. In turn, as commercial banks increase the supply of bank credit by drawing down their excess reserves, the money supply increases.

Fed sales of government securities decrease the reserves of commercial banks whether the Fed sells directly to commercial banks or to the nonbank public, who make payments with checks drawn on commercial banks.* In

---

*Actually the Fed buys from, and sells to, dealers in United States government securities, who in turn transact with banks and the nonbank public. The effect is the same, however.

turn, as commercial banks decrease the supply of bank credit in an attempt to restore their reserve positions, the money supply decreases.

The Fed is able to purchase government securities by increasing its demand for them and thereby bidding up their price. The price increase provides inducement for commercial banks and the nonbank public to sell part of their holdings of government securities in exchange for reserves and deposits. In other words, the increase in market demand by the Fed raises the market price and causes commercial banks and the nonbank public to increase the quantity supplied in exchange for reserves and deposits. Conversely, the Fed is able to sell government securities by increasing the market supply. As the market price falls, commercial banks and the nonbank public increase the quantity demanded in exchange for reserves and deposits.

Open market policy is determined by the Federal Open Market Committee. Policy directives are sent to the manager of the Open Market Trading Desk of the Federal Reserve Bank of New York. The manager determines a trading strategy consistent with the objectives of the directives and conducts the daily operations. Changes in Fed holdings of government securities are distributed among the Federal Reserve Banks according to size.

Open market operations are the most frequently used instrument of monetary policy. They are used as a long-run policy instrument to increase the money supply at a rate judged by the Fed to be consistent with economic stabilization and growth. Since ownership of these securities is widespread and since there are strong secondary markets for them, open market operations have a pervasive impact on the economy with minimum disturbance to securities markets.

Operations aimed at long-run objectives are only a small part of total open market operations. Most operations are defensive. Their purpose is to offset undesirable changes in bank reserves (a noncompeting use of the monetary base) which occur because of changes in the competing uses of the monetary base, such as Treasury operations, changes in the float (usually due to seasonal business conditions or changes in weather conditions), or changes in foreign deposits, which are outside the direct control of the Fed. By offsetting these changes through open market operations, the Fed stabilizes short-term interest rates, the fluctuation of which creates uncertainty in financial markets. This is an important function of the Fed.*

Although a more complete analysis of monetary policy and control will be presented in Part Four, it is worthwhile at this point to mention that the Fed has effective control over the monetary base. Clearly the Treasury can change the

---

*To provide temporary reserves without signaling an overall change in policy, the Fed usually uses open market operations with a repurchase agreement. When the Fed purchases securities from dealers with a repurchase agreement, it means the Fed purchases are for temporary increases in reserves. When dealers repurchase the securities on a future date specified in the repurchase agreement, reserves are reduced. To temporarily decrease reserves, the Fed sells government securities to dealers with a repurchase agreement which requires dealers to sell the securities back to the Fed at a specified date in the future.

monetary base, but the Fed has knowledge of the Treasury's intended activities. Treasury changes in the gold stock and SDRs largely depend on changes in the balance of payments, which are known to the Fed. Information on seasonal and weather factors that influence the size of the float is also available to the Fed. Moreover, changes in other sources of the base as well as competing uses are known to the Fed. Given this body of knowledge, the Fed can use changes in its holdings of government securities, which account for roughly 80 percent of the monetary base, to control the size of the monetary base and the rate at which it is supplied. It does not follow that the Fed *will exercise this power,* only that the Fed *has the power* to determine the size of the monetary base.

Qualitative Instruments

When the Fed feels that the allocation of funds determined by market forces is inconsistent with the efficient allocation of funds (due to market imperfections) or with social priorities, qualitative instruments of monetary policy are used in an attempt to redirect funds in financial markets. Qualitative instruments include the following:

Moral Suasion   This is an attempt to obtain voluntary compliance with policy objectives by appealing to virtue, patriotism, and public spirit. These attempts have been effective in the short run, particularly during wartime when public spirit is high. But since public spirit is unequal among competitors, the Fed has found that moral suasion is most effective if it is backed up by threats of retaliation and intimidation, i.e., effective moral suasion.

Selective Credit Controls   These are an attempt to discourage the private demand for credit when interest rates and prices are rising very rapidly. During wartime the government finances its expenditures by selling government securities rather than by taxation. The wartime government expenditures result in inflation and rising interest rates, which increase the cost of financing the war. Moreover, although increases in the money supply could be used to finance the war debt, this would cause more inflation. To attempt to curb wartime rising interest rates and inflation, the Fed was empowered to impose regulations which discourage private demand for credit. For example, the Fed can impose minimum down payment requirements and a maximum term to maturity on consumer and real estate credit. Because these regulations make borrowers less able to borrow, interest rates do not increase by as much as they would otherwise. Moreover, with borrowing curtailed, private spending is curtailed as well, and inflation is not as severe. Since these controls are unpopular, they are generally used only during wartime. In fact, the Fed has not been empowered to impose such controls since 1953. More will be said about noninterest credit rationing, a market phenomenon, in Chapter 13.

Margin Requirements   These are minimum credit margins (or down payment requirements) the Fed sets on purchases of stocks and bonds or on other purchases when these items are used as collateral for loans at banks. On occasion the requirements have been set at 100 percent, but generally they are set at about 55 percent. The purpose of these requirements is to curb excessive buying on margin (or on credit). Excessive buying on margin during the 1920s drove stock and bond prices up and contributed to the price decline below the collateralized value of loans during the 1930s.

Regulation Q   This gives the Fed the authority to set ceilings on the time and savings deposit rates of commercial banks. In 1966 ceilings were set on the time and savings deposit rates of savings and loan associations and mutual savings banks by the Federal Home Loan Bank. The primary purpose of ceiling rates was originally to protect the solvency of financial institutions. Now they are used in an attempt to reduce competition between large and small banks, to reduce bank credit, and to provide additional funds in mortgage markets.

Up until the mid-1960s, deposit-rate ceilings were maintained above market interest rates, so that Regulation Q never came into play in financial markets. However, since that time Regulation Q has been used by the Fed as a major qualitative instrument of monetary policy. In the 1960s the Fed used Regulation Q in an effort to reduce inflation without the overall contraction of money supply that would be a result of using the quantitative instruments of monetary policy.

The Fed operated on the premise that if it reduced the inflow of funds into large banks relative to small banks, the supply of bank credit to large corporations (who borrow primarily from large banks) relative to small business firms (who borrow primarily from small banks) would decrease. This would reduce inflation by reducing the capital expenditures of large corporations (which were believed to have contributed in a major way to the inflation of the 1960s) relative to the expenditures of small business firms (which are not believed to be as inflationary). Also the Fed wanted to reduce the supply of bank credit relative to the supply of nonbank credit by reducing the inflow of funds into banks more than the inflow into nonbanks (savings and loan associations and mutual savings banks), who are the big suppliers of residential mortgage credit.

To accomplish these objectives, the Fed did not raise deposit-rate ceilings as market rates rose above these ceilings, and the deposit-rate ceilings of savings and loan associations and mutual savings banks were maintained at one-quarter of 1 percent above the deposit-rate ceilings of commercial banks.

The evidence suggests that the Fed's strategy was partially successful. For example, from 1967 to 1969, a period of rising interest rates, Regulation Q rates were stable. During that time, deposits at mutual savings banks and savings and loan associations rose considerably faster than time deposits at commercial banks. However, in another period, from 1973 to 1974, market rates rose relative to Regulation Q, but time deposits at commercial banks rose faster than deposits at mutual banks and savings and loan associations. Thus, the effect of Regulation Q on deposit flows is inconsistent, making Regulation Q an uncertain tool for combating inflation. One factor which is relevant at this point is the ability of financial-market participants to circumvent Regulation Q in acquiring funds. Large corporations resorted to more costly forms of borrowing. They borrowed directly in private capital markets by issuing commercial paper and using internal funds to finance capital expenditures. Banks and nonbank financial institutions used alternative (and more costly) ways of attracting funds from savers as savers began to turn away from time and savings deposits and toward direct lending (particularly by purchasing government bonds) in financial markets. Banks and nonbank financial institutions offered gifts to depositors (ballpoint pens, silverware, and dishes), free checking accounts (banks only), free safety deposit boxes, preferential treatment, and other inducements to savers of funds. Banks used alternative sources of funds, such as loans from their parent holding companies (who could issue commercial paper to finance the loan), sales of commercial paper to their parent holding companies, and loans from overseas branches (Eurodollar borrowing). Since these sources were not subject to Regulation Q, banks were able to make up much of the loss of funds resulting from Regulation Q.

The problem with the qualitative instruments of monetary policy is that they attempt to subvert self-interest rather than using it to accomplish monetary objectives. Although some short-run advantage is gained by use of these instruments, their prolonged use leads to circumvention of the original policy objective and may introduce long-term distortions into the efficient allocation of funds.*

6.2 NONBANK PUBLIC AND COMMERCIAL BANK BEHAVIOR

As long as the currency, time deposit, and excess reserve ratios are constant and the borrowed reserve ratio changes only at the initiative of the Fed, the Fed can control the money supply by using the quantitative instruments of monetary policy discussed in the last section. Also, to the extent that qualitative instruments are not circumvented, they can be used to help achieve the Fed's monetary objectives.

However, the constancy of the currency, time deposit, and excess reserve ratios and the Fed's control over the borrowed reserve ratio are based on given values of income, interest rates, and other market conditions. Any change in these determinants will cause the nonbank public and commercial banks to change the currency, time deposit, excess reserve, and borrowed reserve ratios.

If there is a stable (predictable) relationship between the currency, time deposit, excess reserve, and borrowed reserve ratios and their respective market determinants (and if their major determinants can be identified), we can build a

---

*The history of Regulation Q is summarized in C. E. Ruebling, "The Administration of Regulation Q," *Review,* Federal Reserve Bank of St. Louis, February 1970, pp. 29–41.

theory of money supply that can be used by the Fed to, first, predict the impact on the money supply of commercial bank behavior (which determines the excess reserve and borrowed reserve ratios) and nonbank public behavior (which determines the currency and time deposit ratios); and second, use changes in the monetary base (via open market operations) and changes in the base money multiplier (via changes in reserve requirements and discount policy) to offset any undesirable changes in the money supply that occur.*

Unfortunately, the empirical evidence does not consistently support the hypothesized behavior of commercial banks and the nonbank public. Except for a few variables, which include income and interest rates, many of the market forces have not yet been identified. However, in recent years economists have gained some important insight into the behavior of commercial banks and the nonbank public, and have begun to build a theory of money supply which helps us to understand the complexities of the role of commercial banks and the nonbank public in the money supply process.

Determinants of the Currency Ratio (c)

An increase in the currency ratio results from an increase in the nonbank public's preference for currency relative to demand deposits. The increase means an additional leakage of reserves to currency from the money creation process. The greater the leakage, the smaller the base money multiplier, and therefore the smaller the money supply (increase in the money supply) given the monetary base (given an increase in the monetary base). The primary determinants of the currency ratio c, which have received considerable attention, are income Y, the interest rate on interest-bearing assets, which we will call the market rate of interest R, and other market conditions X, which include the degree of public confidence in the soundness of the banking system (and the economy), the cost of holding (and transacting business with) currency relative to the cost of holding demand deposits, and the availability of nonbank consumer credit,

$$c = f(\overset{-}{Y}, \overset{+}{R}, X) \tag{6.1}$$

Both currency and demand deposits are assets, and like any other asset they are positively related to income. Although the empirical evidence is mixed, intuitively we expect demand deposits to be more responsive to changes in income than currency because as income increases the nonbank public makes greater use of demand deposits than currency. This means that the currency ratio is negatively related to income. For example, an increase in income

---

*A good summary of the problems of monetary control is found in D.I. Fand, "Some Issues in Monetary Economics," *Review*, Federal Reserve Bank of St. Louis, January 1970, pp. 10–27.

decreases the currency ratio. The decrease in the currency ratio increases the base money multiplier and thereby the money supply. A decrease in income yields the opposite results. In periods when there appears to be a positive relationship between income and the currency ratio, our negative hypothesis is not necessarily refuted. Changes in other determinants of the currency ratio may have stronger influences than changes in income on the currency ratio.*

The opportunity cost of holding either currency or demand deposits is the market rate of interest. Changes in the interest rate negatively affect holdings of currency and demand deposits. Some empirical evidence indicates that demand deposits are more responsive to changes in the interest rate than currency because demand deposits are closer substitutes with other assets than currency. This means that the currency ratio is positively related to the interest rate.† For example, an increase in the interest rate increases the currency ratio. The increase in the currency ratio decreases the base money multiplier and thereby the money supply. A decrease in the interest rate yields the opposite results.

However, other studies indicate an inverse relationship between the currency ratio and the interest rate. The inconsistency in empirical studies may be due to the fact that currency and demand deposits are almost (but not quite) perfect substitutes. Thus, the response of the currency ratio to the interest rate may be ambiguous. For our purposes we will assume that that is the case and that the currency ratio is unresponsive to the interest rate.

The other determinants of the currency ratio can be discussed and hypotheses formed about their influence on the currency ratio. However, there is little empirical evidence to support the hypotheses, primarily either because most of the variables are difficult to measure or because there are difficult statistical problems involved in estimating their impact on the currency ratio. The influences of three of these variables are briefly discussed here. First, public confidence plays an important role in determining the currency ratio. When the nonbank public loses confidence in the banking system in recessions (and particularly the Depression of the 1930s), the currency ratio rises as the nonbank public changes its preferences in favor of money in hand (currency) relative to money in banks (demand deposits). As confidence improves, preferences are reversed. Second, the cost of holding (and transacting business with) currency

---

*See P. Cagan, "Demand for Currency Relative to the Total Money Supply," *Journal of Political Economy,* August 1958, pp. 303–328; S. M. Goldfeld, *Commercial Bank Behavior and Economic Activity* (Amsterdam: North Holland, 1966); G. G. Kaufman, *The Demand for Currency,* Staff Economic Study, Board of Governors of the Federal Reserve System, 1966; W. R. Hosek, "Determinants of the Money Multiplier," *Quarterly Review of Economics and Business,* Summer 1970, pp. 37–46; A. C. Hess, "An Explanation of Short-Run Fluctuations in the Ratio of Currency to Demand Deposits," *Journal of Money, Credit and Banking,* August 1971, pp. 666–679; W. E. Becker, Jr., "A Theoretical and Statistical Analysis of the Currency–Demand Deposit Ratio for the U.S., 1952–1971," *Journal of Finance,* March 1975, pp. 57–74.

†See R. Teigen, "An Aggregated Quarterly Model of the U.S. Monetary Sector, 1953–1964," in K. Brunner (ed.), *Targets and Indicators of Monetary Policy* (San Francisco: Chandler, 1969), pp. 175–214.

relative to demand deposits is another important determinant of the currency ratio. There is no explicit cost of holding currency, but there is a service charge for holding demand deposits. Changes in the service charge negatively affect holdings of demand deposits and thereby positively influence the currency ratio. And third, increases in the availability of nonbank consumer credit, particularly by greater use of credit cards, are expected to have an important influence on the currency ratio. Greater use of credit cards means that the nonbank public requires less currency during the month and holds relatively more demand deposits, which will be drawn down to pay off bills at the end of the month. Thus, the availability of nonbank consumer credit negatively affects the currency ratio.

Determinants of the Time Deposit Ratio (t)

An increase in the time deposit ratio results from an increase in the nonbank public's preferences for time relative to demand deposits. This means an additional leakage of demand deposits to time deposits from the money creation process. The greater the leakage, the smaller the base money multiplier, and therefore the smaller the money supply (increase in the money supply) given the monetary base (given an increase in the monetary base). The determinants of the time deposit ratio t which have received considerable attention are income Y, the interest rate on time deposits R_T, and the market rate of interest R,

$$t = f(Y, \overset{+}{R_T}, \overset{-}{R}) \tag{6.2}$$

Like any other assets, time and demand deposits are positively related to income. Since time deposits are considered a luxury good and demand deposits more of a necessity, time deposits are expected to be more responsive to changes in income than demand deposits. The empirical evidence lends support to this hypothesis.* This means that income is positively related to the time deposit ratio. For example, an increase in income permits the nonbank public to purchase more luxuries, such as time deposits, relative to necessities, such as demand deposits. This increases the time deposit ratio and reduces the base money multiplier and thereby the money supply. A decrease in income yields the opposite results.

The time deposit ratio varies inversely with the cost of holding time deposits (the market rate of interest on other assets less the interest rate on time deposits) relative to the cost of holding demand deposits (the market rate of interest on other assets including time deposits plus the service charge on demand deposits). The empirical evidence supports the hypothesis that the interest rate on

---

*See R. Teigen, op. cit., pp. 212–213; and Hosek, loc. cit.

time deposits is positively related to the time deposit ratio because, as with any other asset, the interest rate on time deposits is positively related to time deposits, which is the numerator of the time deposit ratio, and the service charge is positively related to the time deposit ratio because it negatively affects demand deposits, which are the denominator of the time deposit ratio.* This means, for example, that an increase in the interest rate on time deposits or the service charge on demand deposits increases the time deposit ratio. Since the time deposit ratio is negatively related to the base money multiplier, the base money multiplier decreases. Since the base money multiplier is positively related to the money supply, money supply decreases. Thus, changes in the interest rate on time deposits negatively affect the money supply.

Moreover, since time deposits are a closer substitute for other interest-bearing assets than are demand deposits, time deposits are more responsive to changes in the market rate of interest than are demand deposits. Changes in the market interest rate change both time and demand deposits, but time deposits more than demand deposits. This means that the market rate of interest is negatively related to the time deposit ratio. Since the time deposit ratio is negatively related to the base money multiplier, and the base money multiplier is positively related to the money supply, the market rate of interest is positively related to the money supply. For example, an increase in the market rate of interest causes the nonbank public to switch out of time and demand deposits and into other assets, but out of time deposits more than demand deposits. The time deposit ratio falls; the base money multiplier, and thereby the money supply, increases.

Determinants of the Excess Reserve Ratio (e)

When member banks increase their desired level of excess reserves relative to their demand deposit liabilities, and adjust the actual to the desired level, funds are withdrawn from the money creation process, i.e., there is additional leakage of reserves to excess reserves from the money creation process. The determinants of the desired excess reserve ratio which have received considerable attention are the market rate of interest R, the effective discount rate R_D, deposit variability DV, and other market conditions Z, including the degree of bank confidence in the economy,

$$e = f(R, \overset{-}{R_D}, \overset{+}{DV}, \overset{+}{Z}) \tag{6.3}$$

The opportunity cost of holding excess reserves and demand deposits is the market rate of interest. Changes in the interest rate negatively affect bank hold-

---

*See references in previous footnote.

ings of excess reserves and nonbank public holdings of demand deposits. The empirical evidence indicates that excess reserves are more responsive to changes in the interest rate than demand deposits. This means that changes in the interest rate negatively affect the excess reserve ratio.* For example, an increase in the interest rate reduces the desired excess reserve ratio. As banks adjust the actual excess reserve ratio to its desired level, the base money multiplier increases because more reserves are being utilized by the banking system to create money. Thus, the money supply increases. A decrease in the interest rate has the opposite result.

When member banks reduce their excess reserves to take advantage of higher market rates of interest, the probability of their not being able to meet deposit withdrawals increases. This increases the probability of member bank borrowing at the Fed to make adjustments in required reserves. This means that not only the market rate of interest but the market rate relative to the effective discount rate is an important determinant of the excess reserve ratio. The effective discount rate may be viewed as a cost of borrowing to make up reserve deficiencies.

Changes in the effective discount rate, whether they are the result of changes in the discount rate itself or changes in the stringency of member bank borrowing at the Fed, positively affect the excess reserve ratio. For example, a decrease in the effective discount rate encourages member banks to reduce the desired excess reserve ratio by supplying additional bank credit (to the nonbank public or by purchasing government securities) because the penalty cost of getting caught with reserve deficiencies (the effective discount rate) is less. As banks adjust the actual excess reserve ratio to its desired level, the base money multiplier increases because more reserves are being utilized by the banking system to create money. Thus, the money supply increases. An increase in the effective discount rate yields the opposite results.

Deposit variability as a determinant of the desired excess reserve ratio is another factor which banks must take into account in responding to the uncertainty of their need for liquidity to meet deposit withdrawals and to maintain required reserves. Predictable variability is seasonal, occurring every year at the same time. Unpredictable variability shows no pattern and requires banks to hold excess reserves. The greater the degree of variability, the greater the excess reserves banks must hold relative to their demand deposit liabilities. This means that changes in deposit variability are positively related to the

---

*See D. I. Fand, "Some Implications of Money Supply Analysis," *American Economic Review*, May 1967, pp. 380–400; A. H. Meltzer, "Topics in Money: Discussion," *American Economic Review*, May 1967, pp. 426–428; A. H. Meltzer, "Controlling Money," *Review*, Federal Reserve Bank of St. Louis, May 1969, pp. 16–24; G. Morrisson, *Liquidity Preference of Commercial Banks* (Chicago: University of Chicago Press, 1962); L. C. Anderson and A. E. Burger, "Asset Management and Commercial Bank Portfolio Behavior: Theory and Practice," *Journal of Finance*, May 1969, pp. 207–222; P. A. Frost, "Banks Demand for Excess Reserves," *Journal of Political Economy*, July/August 1971, pp. 805–825. Also see references in footnote on page 92.

desired excess reserve ratio.* For example, if deposit variability increases, the desired excess reserve ratio increases. As banks adjust the actual excess reserve ratio to its desired level by decreasing the supply of bank credit, the base money multiplier and thereby the money supply decrease. A decrease in deposit variability causes the opposite results.

The final determinant of the desired excess reserve ratio that will be mentioned here is bank confidence in the economy. In times of economic crisis, such as the Depression of the 1930s, bank fears of substantial deposit withdrawals and the inability of borrowers to remain solvent cause the desired excess reserve ratio to rise. As was the case in the 1930s, the increase in the excess reserve ratio reduces the base money multiplier and thereby reduces the money supply. The fear factor is related to the uncertainty associated with deposit variability, but perhaps it should be listed separately because of its potential severity.

Determinants of the Borrowed Reserve Ratio (b)

When member banks increase their desired borrowed reserve ratio and increase the actual borrowed reserve ratio to its desired level, new reserves (obtained from the Fed) are injected into the banking system. The determinants of the desired borrowed reserve ratio which have received considerable attention are the market rate of interest and the effective discount rate,

$$b = f(\overset{+}{R}, \overset{-}{R_D}) \tag{6.4}$$

The rate of return from borrowing additional reserves and extending additional bank credit is the market rate of interest. Changes in the interest rate positively affect bank borrowing and negatively affect demand deposits. This means that changes in the interest rate positively affect the borrowed reserve ratio.† For example, an increase in the interest rate increases the desired borrowed reserve ratio. As banks adjust the actual borrowed reserve ratio to its desired level, the base money multiplier increases. Thus, the money supply increases. Actually, the act of borrowing does not imply an increase in the

---

*The greater the degree of unpredictable variability, the greater the requirements for primary reserves (vault cash and deposits at the Fed and at other banks) and secondary reserves (Federal Funds sold, short-term government securities, and other short-term private securities). The greater the liquidity associated with an asset, the lower the yield on the asset. Because of uncertainty, banks pay a price for ensuring against unexpected reserve drains. Bank asset management strategy is to maximize income by holding the minimum amount of primary and secondary reserves consistent with liquidity. In the 1960s banks recognized that by changing interest rates on certificates of deposits and Federal Funds above and below market rates, they could increase deposit inflows and increase deposit outflows, respectively. By using this device to smooth deposit inflows and outflows, deposit variability is reduced. Thus, liquidity requirements were lowered, and greater profits were possible.

†See previous reference.

money supply. But if these reserves are used to extend bank credit, the money supply increases. A decrease in the interest rate causes the opposite results.

The cost of borrowing additional reserves is the effective discount rate. An increase in the effective discount rate increases the cost of borrowing and thereby decreases the probability of borrowing for purposes of extending bank credit. This means that changes in the discount rate (relative to the market interest rate) are negatively related to the borrowed reserve ratio. For example, a decrease in the effective discount rate lowers the cost of borrowing and increases the desired borrowed reserve ratio. As banks adjust the actual borrowed reserve ratio to its desired level and use the borrowed funds to supply additional bank credit, the money supply increases. An increase in the effective discount rate yields the opposite results.

Free Reserve Ratio $(e - b)$

Instead of interpreting the impact of changes in the excess reserve ratio and borrowed reserve ratio separately, economists often combine them and use them to draw implications about the growth of the money supply. The combination is called the *free reserve ratio,* which is the difference between the excess reserve ratio and the borrowed reserve ratio.* If the free reserve ratio is positive, excess reserves are greater than borrowed reserves, and banks hold net free reserves. If the free reserve ratio is negative, excess reserves are less than borrowed reserves, and banks hold net borrowed reserves.

Decreases in the free reserve ratio increase the base money multiplier and thereby the money supply. Such decreases in the free reserve ratio occur when (1) there is an increase in the market rate of interest which increases the profitability (by increasing the return) of borrowing and reduces the profitability of holding excess reserves, and/or (2) there is a decrease in the effective discount rate which increases the profitability (by decreasing the cost) of borrowing and reduces the profitability of holding excess reserves.

Although the free reserve ratio is often used to draw implications about the growth in the money supply, it tends to obscure important behavioral aspects of bank behavior and thereby leads to erroneous forecasts of the growth in the money supply. For any given changes in the free reserve ratio, there are an infinite number of combinations of changes in the excess reserve and borrowed reserve ratios. To decide what any given change in the free reserve ratio implies about changes in the money supply requires that the theories of the excess reserve and borrowed reserve ratios be considered separately. Moreover, a distinction must be made between changes in the actual and desired free reserve ratios. If we observe an increase in the actual free reserve ratio, it does not auto-

---

*Since the denominator of both ratios is demand deposit liabilities, the net free reserve ratio embodies free reserves, where free reserves is the difference between excess and borrowed reserves.

matically imply contraction of the money supply. It may be a result of an increase in reserves in the banking system, and as banks adjust the actual free reserve ratio to its desired level, the base money multiplier will rise and increase the money supply. On the other hand it may mean a contraction in the money supply if the effective discount rate or lack of bank confidence in the economy increases the desired free reserve ratio. As banks increase the actual free reserve ratio to its desired level, the base money multiplier falls, and the money supply decreases.

Because of the problems in interpreting the free reserve ratio, many economists believe that the concept is not very useful. The impact of changes in the excess reserve and borrowed reserve ratios on the money supply should be considered separately. We have included a discussion of the free reserve ratio only because it lingers on in discussions of monetary policy.*

Federal Funds Rate

The Federal Funds market is the market for the excess reserves of member banks held at the Fed. The quantity of Federal Funds exchanged and the Federal Funds rate of interest are determined in the Federal Funds market. Changes in the Federal Funds rate are believed to exert an important influence on the money supply because such changes help to explain the mechanism whereby changes in the effective discount rate and the monetary base increase the utilization of reserves in the money creation process.

Banks borrow reserves to make up reserve deficiencies and to take advantage of interest-rate differentials in financial markets. Since banks tend to borrow at lowest cost, whether the Federal Funds rate is lower than the effective discount rate will determine whether they borrow in the Federal Funds market or from the Fed. In recent years, member banks have relied less on the Fed and more on the Federal Funds market as a source of reserves, so that they appear to have made the judgment that, on balance, the Federal Funds rate is lower than the effective discount rate.

Changes in the effective discount rate positively affect the demand for Federal Funds. An increase in the effective discount rate means that banks, following cost minimization principles, increase their demand for the relatively cheaper reserves in the Federal Funds market.† The results are an increase in the Federal Funds rate and, thereby, an increase in the quantity of Federal Funds supplied. The increase in the quantity of Federal Funds means that excess reserves of some banks are utilized by other banks in the money creation process, and the

---

*See Chapter 12 for its use in econometric forecasting models of the economy.

†Obviously, banks do not completely switch back and forth between these two means of borrowing as the discount rate changes relative to the Federal Funds rate. There are different perceptions of the effective discount rate among banks, and also there are transaction costs associated with switching that keep borrowing from both sources occurring during any given time period.

money supply increases. The opposite results occur when the effective discount rate is decreased. The positive effect of changes in the effective discount rate on the money supply, discussed here, partially offsets the negative effects on the money supply, discussed earlier.

A more important linkage role played by changes in the Federal Funds rate is relating changes in the monetary base to changes in the money supply. The Federal Funds market plays a supplemental role in transmitting changes in the monetary base to changes in the money supply. An increase in the monetary base increases the supply of Federal Funds in the Federal Funds market. As a result, the Federal Funds rate decreases, and the quantity demanded of Federal Funds increases. The increase in the quantity of Federal Funds means that the excess reserves of some banks are utilized by other banks, i.e., part of the increase in the monetary base which would increase excess reserves flows through the Federal Funds market, and greater utilization of additional reserves is achieved. The opposite results occur when the monetary base is decreased.

The Fed considers the Federal Funds rate an important target variable in its efforts to expand and contract the money supply. In later chapters we will discuss the extent to which the Fed responds to changes in the Federal Funds rate in order to control the money supply.

6.3   THE MONEY SUPPLY FUNCTION

By using the instruments of monetary policy, the Fed initiates changes in the money supply. As explained in Section 6.1 above, use of these instruments affects both the monetary base and the base money multiplier. Although the Fed has effective control over the monetary base, it does not control the base money multiplier, and therefore it does not control the money supply. Changes in the base money multiplier are also initiated by commercial banks and the nonbank public as they react to monetary policy and the market conditions discussed in Section 6.2 above.

By substituting the commercial bank and nonbank public behavioral relationships into the money supply identity (Eq. 5.20), we obtain the money supply function. The function may be expressed in a less cumbersome form by

$$MS = f(\overset{+}{R}, \overset{-}{R_D}, \overset{-}{R_T}, \overset{\pm}{Y}, \overset{-}{r_D}, \overset{-}{r_T}, \overset{+}{MB}, u) \qquad (6.5)$$

where R = market rate of interest
$\quad R_D$ = effective discount rate
$\quad R_T$ = time deposit rate
$\quad\quad Y$ = level of income
$\quad\quad r_D$ = required reserve ratio on demand deposits
$\quad\quad r_T$ = required reserve ratio on time deposits
$\quad MB$ = monetary base
$\quad\quad u$ = other market conditions

The signs of the relationships between the determinants of money supply (the independent variables on the right-hand side of the money supply function) and the money supply (the dependent variable on the left-hand side) that are implied in our analysis are shown in Eq. 6.5.

The banking system functions as a producer or creator of money. The theory which underlies the money supply is based on the behavioral assumption that banks in the banking system attempt to maximize profit subject to the cost constraints imposed by the Fed, other banks, and the nonbank public. R reflects the return from extending additional bank credit, which increases the quantity of money supplied. Changes in R positively affect the base money multiplier and thereby the money supply by influencing the time deposit, excess reserve, and borrowed reserve ratios in a manner explained in Section 6.2. R_D reflects the costs to banks of obtaining reserves, other than those obtained by changes in the monetary base, by borrowing at the Fed. The purpose is to extend additional bank credit and thereby increase the money supply. The difference between the banking system's returns and costs for a given value of the monetary base is the banking system's profit. In response to increases (decreases) in R, banks will demand additional reserves, and R_D may rise (fall), since the Fed often tends to adjust the effective discount rate to the market rate. The effects of changes in R and R_D on the money supply are opposite in sign; they tend to offset each other. Therefore, it is more appropriate to say that it is the increase (decrease) in R relative to R_D which increases (decreases) the money supply.

Changes in R_T affect the money supply by altering the preferences of the nonbank public for time relative to demand deposits. An increase (decrease) in R_T increases (decreases) the time deposit ratio, which decreases (increases) the base money multiplier and decreases (increases) the money supply. Thus, R_T and MS vary inversely.

Changes in income have a negative effect on the money supply by positively affecting the time deposit ratio (negatively affecting the base money multiplier), and they have a positive effect by negatively affecting the currency ratio (positively affecting the base money multiplier). The net effect is an empirical question, but the evidence is unclear as to whether the net effect is positive, negative, or zero. Although causality can run in both directions, traditionally income has been assumed to be money supply–determined (along with other market forces in the real and monetary sectors of the economy) rather than money supply–determining. Although the empirical evidence (cited above) on the relationship between income and the currency ratio is mixed, it clearly indicates that income is an important determinant of the time deposit ratio. However, income is generally considered a more important determinant of the level of money demand than of the relative demands for the liabilities of the Fed (currency) and banks (time and demand deposits). Generally, for this reason, the impact of changes in income on the money market is discussed within the theory of money demand rather than the theory of money supply.

Changes in the required reserve ratio negatively affect the money supply by

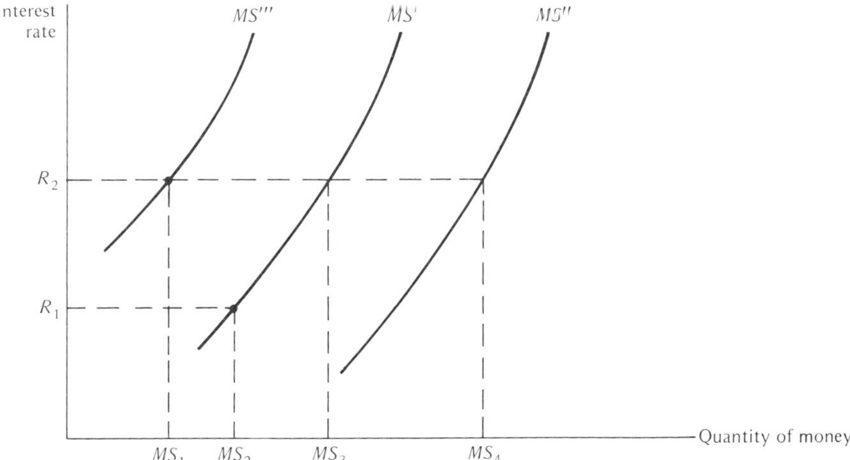

Figure 6.1

The money supply curve.

negatively affecting the base money multiplier, and changes in the monetary base positively affect the money supply. These are the two most important direct means by which the Fed influences the money supply.

Figure 6.1 shows a money supply curve MS' which indicates the positive relationship between the market rate of interest and the quantity of money supplied for a given set of values of the other variables that determine the money supply. Changes in the market rate of interest translate into movements along the money supply curve. For example, an increase in the market rate of interest from R_1 to R_2 results in an increase in the quantity of money supplied from MS_2 to MS_3, for reasons already explained. A decrease in the market rate of interest yields the opposite result.

Independent changes in the other variables which determine the money supply translate into shifts in the money supply curve. If the sign of the relationship between a determinant of the money supply and the money supply is negative, an increase (decrease) in the determinant decreases (increases) the money supply for any given market rate of interest, i.e., shifts the money supply curve leftward (rightward). If the sign is positive, an increase (decrease) in the determinant increases (decreases) the money supply for any given market rate of interest, i.e., shifts the money supply curve rightward (leftward). For example, suppose that there is an increase in the monetary base (an independent variable with a positive sign) or a decrease in the time deposit rate, the effective discount rate, or the required reserve ratios (independent variables with negative signs). For reasons already explained, the result is an increase in the money supply for any given market rate of interest, i.e., a rightward shift in the money supply curve. In Fig. 6.1 a rightward shift in the money supply curve from MS' to MS'' indicates that for any given market rate of interest, say R_2, the money supply increases, say from MS_3 to MS_4. A decrease in the monetary base or an increase in the time deposit rate, the effective discount rate, or the required reserve ratios yields the opposite results. In Fig. 6.1 a leftward shift in the money supply curve from MS' to MS''' indicates that for any given market rate of interest, say R_2, the money supply decreases, say from MS_3 to MS_1.

The available statistical techniques are simply too crude to measure the independent sensitivities or elasticities of money supply to changes in all its determinants. For example, measuring the independent interest elasticities of money supply is a particularly difficult problem. However, since changes in the market rate of interest and the other interest rates have opposite effects on the money supply, and the rates tend to move together, estimates of the interest elasticity of money supply based on the use of only the market rate of interest in the estimation process reflect the net sensitivity of the money supply to changes in all the relevant interest rates.

Because of their importance in evaluating the effectiveness of monetary policy, estimates of the monetary base and market-interest-rate elasticities of money supply have been given considerable attention. Changes in these variables can be used to explain the lion's share of changes in the money supply.

The estimates of the monetary base elasticity of money supply differ depending on the statistical technique and the definitions of the variables used in the estimation process. In order to include the impact of changes in the required reserve ratios on the money supply, economists use changes in a more inclusive concept of the monetary base to help explain changes in the money supply. This concept is called the *extended monetary base*.* It is the sum of the monetary base and a reserve adjustment which includes changes in reserves due to changes in reserve requirements and deposits subject to different reserve requirements. Estimates of the extended monetary base elasticity of the money supply range from 0.65 to 1. This means that a 1 percent increase (decrease) in the extended monetary base results in a 0.65 to 1 percent increase (decrease) in the money supply.†

There are problems with this interpretation. When estimating the money supply function, we assume that changes in the extended monetary base are in-

---

*See L. C. Andersen and J. L. Jordan, "The Monetary Base—Explanation and Analytical Use," *Review,* Federal Reserve Bank of St. Louis, August 1968, pp. 7–11.

†Some studies assume the base elasticity of money supply is 1, and others estimate it. See K. Brunner and A. H. Meltzer, "Some Further Investigations of Money Demand," *Journal of Finance,* May 1964, pp. 240–283; S. M. Goldfeld, *Commercial Bank Behavior and Economic Activity* (Amsterdam: North Holland, 1966); F. deLeeuw, "A Model of Financial Behavior," in J. S. Duesenberry et al. (eds.), *The Brookings Quarterly Econometric Model of the United States* (Chicago: Rand McNally, 1965), pp. 465–532; W. R. Hosek, "Determinants of the Money Multiplier," *Quarterly Review of Economics and Business,* Summer 1970, pp. 37–46; R. Teigen, "An Aggregated Quarterly Model of the United States Monetary Sector, 1953–1964," in K. Brunner (ed.), *Targets and Indicators of Monetary Policy* (San Francisco: Chandler, 1969), pp. 175–218 and "Demand and Supply Functions for Money in the United States, Some Structural Estimates," *Econometrica,* October 1964, pp. 476–509; F. Zahn and W. R. Hosek, "Impact of Trade Credit on the Velocity of Money and the Market Rate of Interest," *Southern Economic Journal,* October 1973, pp. 202–209.

dependent of changes in the other determinants. This is not strictly true. As we shall see in Chapter 8, changes in the extended monetary base increase the money supply and thereby lower the market rate of interest (and also the Federal Funds rate). In turn the lower market rate of interest reduces the base money multiplier and thereby reduces the money supply. Hence, changes in the extended monetary base and the interest rate are not strictly independent. However, if the market-interest-rate elasticity of the base money multiplier is small, the estimate of the extended monetary base elasticity of the money supply is reliable. The positive effect of the change in the extended monetary base and the small negative side effect through the market interest rate would suggest that the more reliable estimate of the extended monetary base elasticity is less than 1.

Estimates of market interest rate elasticities range from 0.04 to 0.66, depending on the interest rate selected and the time allowed for adjustment.* Overall, most studies indicate that the money supply is fairly insensitive to the interest rate, since most place the interest elasticity in the 0.04 to 0.22 range.

SUMMARY NOTES

1. The major quantitative instruments of the Federal Reserve in implementing monetary policy include changes in reserve requirements, the discount rate, and open market operations. Subsidiary tools include moral suasion, selective credit controls (in the past), margin requirements, and Regulation Q ceilings.
2. The currency and time deposit ratios, determined by the nonbank public, are influenced by such variables as the market interest rate, income, and the interest rate on time deposits.
3. The excess reserve and borrowed reserve ratios, determined by banks, are influenced by such variables as the market interest rate and the discount rate.
4. The Federal Funds market is a market, for excess reserves held at the Fed, in which member banks participate. Member banks often borrow in the Federal Funds market rather than at the discount window of the Federal Reserve.

DISCUSSION QUESTIONS

1. If all banks dropped out of the Federal Reserve System, would the Fed lose its power to control the money supply? Explain.
2. Enumerate possible conflicts between Fed and Treasury monetary policies.
3. Using recent issues of the *Federal Reserve Bulletin,* discuss what changes in

---

*See Robert H. Rasche, "A Review of Empirical Studies of the Money Supply Mechanism," *Review,* Federal Reserve Bank of St. Louis, July 1972, pp. 11–19.

the Federal Funds rate, free reserves, the quantity of M_1, and the monetary base indicate about Fed intentions with respect to easy or tight monetary policy in the past six months.

4. It has been suggested that banks drastically increased their desired excess reserve ratios during the 1930s because of great uncertainty about deposit withdrawals. Do you think there might be an upper limit to which banks might raise their excess reserve ratios under such conditions? What might that limit be? What effect would this have on the base money multiplier?

5. What effects would a great loss of confidence in the banking system be likely to have on the currency and time deposit ratios? Using data obtained from old *Federal Reserve Bulletins,* compute the currency and time deposit ratios for the years of the Great Depression (say, 1929 to 1934). Are your conclusions borne out by the results?

6. Using the theory developed in this chapter, explain movement along the money supply curve.

MONEY DEMAND THEORY

Conventional asset demand analysis begins at the level of individuals and explains how they allocate limited resources among various assets (real and financial) so that they maximize their economic welfare. In order to maximize economic welfare, the individual allocates income so that the rate at which one asset can be substituted for another through exchanges in the market just equals the rate at which the individual desires (is willing) to do so. This means that given tastes and preferences, the demand for an asset depends primarily on (1) relative prices (the price of an asset relative to the price of all other assets that compete for an individual's expenditures) and (2) the individual's income. The relative price variables indicate the opportunity cost of acquiring one asset in terms of the return foregone by not acquiring another asset. Income indicates the command over all assets and thereby sets an upper limit to the total amount of assets that can be purchased.

Income and relative prices play important roles in demand analysis. Income and substitution effects which operate through these variables are the two primary forces that influence the amount of any asset demanded. The substitution effect refers to the change in expenditure pattern as a result of a change in relative prices which alters the rates of exchange among assets and induces the substitution of relatively cheaper for relatively more expensive assets within the asset mix. The income effect refers to the price-induced change in real income which alters the limits of the total amount of assets that can be purchased.

By aggregating all the individual demand functions, we derive the market demand for each asset. Relative prices and income are the primary arguments in market demand functions as well. Conventional demand analysis provides us with a set of tools that can be employed to identify the principal determinants of various asset demands. However, conventional analysis was not introduced into monetary analysis until the mid 1930s, and it was not until the 1950s that money demand analysis was fully integrated into the rational choice framework of conventional demand analysis.

In Chapter 5 we explained the money creation process. The process implies that the forces of both money supply and money demand determine the equilibrium quantity of money in the economy. Considerable judgment must be used to separately identify supply and demand factors in the money market. In Chapter 6 we developed a theory of money supply, and although the relative demands for the financial liabilities of the Fed and commercial banks were identified as determinants of money supply, money demand was taken for granted.

In this chapter we will develop the theory of money demand while taking money supply for granted. We will follow the development of money demand theory as it evolved from pre-Keynesian (or classical) theories, through Keynes' money demand theory, and into the portfolio balance approach to money demand theory, an approach which treats money as an asset like any other asset and analyzes the demand for it within the framework of conventional demand theory.* Finally, we specify a money demand function which reflects the basic principles of portfolio balance theory and summarize the evidence which lends empirical support to the money demand function.

7.1 MONEY DEMAND THEORY BEFORE KEYNES

Up until the mid 1930s, conventional demand theory was considered incapable of explaining why any individual would want to hold money because it was believed that holding money yields no economic welfare. Money was considered strictly a medium of exchange which is used to facilitate market transactions. This is the feature that distinguishes money from other assets. Accordingly, the demand for holding money was ignored by monetary analysts.

Instead, monetary analysts concentrated on the demand for spending money. Professor I. Fisher, a leading exponent of this approach, did not write out his money demand function.† Instead, he examined the behavior of money and prices within the framework of his famous equation of exchange,

$$MV_T = P_T T \qquad (7.1)$$

where $M =$ the quantity of money

$\qquad V_T =$ the speed at which money is spent on all money transactions, or the *transactions velocity* of money

---

P_T = the price per transaction

T = total number of transactions involved in the exchange of both real and financial assets

The equation states that total spending MV_T equals the aggregate value of transactions $P_T T$.

If we assume that the money supply is determined by the monetary authorities and is a given datum in the analysis, and that V_T and T are independent of the money supply, the money concept in the equation of exchange may be interpreted as the quantity of money demanded MD. Given this interpretation, we can rearrange (7.1) and express the money demand function as

$$MD = \frac{T}{V_T} P_T \qquad (7.2)$$

This equation states that the demand for spending money depends on three variables, T, V_T, and P_T.

Fisher argued that the determinants of V_T are technological and institutional factors which are subject to only gradual change, so that it is roughly constant. These factors include the state of development of the banking system, frequency of receipts and payments, length of payment period, degree of synchronization of money inflows and outflows, and rapidity of communications and transportation. Fisher also argued that T is determined by the full employment of available resources (labor, capital, etc.), which is subject to only gradual change, so that it is roughly constant. Given the values of V_T and T, money demand varies directly and proportionally with the price level, where T/V_T is the factor of proportionality. That is, a given percentage increase in P_T results in an equal percentage increase in MD.

Beginning in the 1930s a small group of economists at Cambridge University in England gained prominence by taking the initial step in developing the theory of money demand within the framework of conventional demand analysis.* They focused attention on those properties of money which make it desirable as an object to hold as distinct from an object to spend. They concentrated on the relationship between money, prices, and final output (or income) rather than on the more inclusive concept of total transactions. In so doing, they opened up the possibility of viewing money as an abode of purchasing power which can be held as a medium of exchange and a store of wealth.

They restated the equation of exchange as

$$MV_Y = Py = Y \qquad (7.3)$$

where M = the quantity of money

---

*An important economist in the Cambridge school was A. C. Pigou. See his, "The Value of Money," *Quarterly Journal of Economics,* November 1917, pp. 38–65.

V_Y = the speed at which money is spent on current output, or the *income velocity* of money
P = the price per unit of output
y = real income or output
Y = nominal income or Py

The equation states that total spending on output MV_Y equals real income or output y valued at market prices P, or nominal income Y.

Notice that the Fisher and Cambridge definitions of velocity differ. In the Cambridge equation velocity is defined as the speed at which money is used to facilitate the expenditure of income on output rather than the speed at which money is used to facilitate all transactions, including transfers of capital assets which are not income-producing. Since transactions is the broader concept, the value of the transaction velocity of money is larger than the value of the income velocity of money for any given quantity of money.

Unlike Fisher, who focused attention on the speed at which money is spent, the Cambridge economists emphasized the desired ratio of money balances to income k. They attempted to explain money demand by the desired ratio, the level of current output, and the price level (or income). Although they acknowledged that output and the desired ratio need not be independent of the money supply, the main thrust of their argument permits us to make the assumption that they are independent and rewrite the equation of exchange as a money demand function,

$$MD = kPy = kY \qquad (7.4)$$

where the money concept in their equation of exchange can be interpreted as the quantity of money demanded and $k = 1/V_Y$. Although k implicitly considers the speed at which money turns over, the Cambridge formulation diverted attention from the speed of spending money to the proportion of income individuals desire to hold as money because it is an asset that serves not only as a medium of exchange, but as a store of wealth. The focus on MD suggested that money holdings yield utility like any other asset and that the demand for it is based on individual choices and decisions.

By emphasizing current output rather than total transactions and the demand for *holding* money balances, the Cambridge economists made explicit the income constraint, $Py = Y$, in their theory of money demand. This is an important step toward analyzing money demand within the framework of conventional asset demand analysis. Moreover, the Cambridge economists acknowledged that such factors as interest rates, the stock of wealth, expectations of future interest rates, and prices are determinants of money demand. However, they assumed that the influences of these variables are minimal. They assumed that k and y are determined by much the same factors as Fisher's V_T and T, so that they are roughly constant. Thus, like Fisher, the Cambridge economists concluded that money demand varies directly and proportionally with the price level.

7.2   KEYNES' LIQUIDITY PREFERENCE THEORY

J. M. Keynes extended the Cambridge theory of money demand by analyzing not only the effect of changes in income on money demand, but the effect of changes in interest rates and expectations of future changes in the interest rate on money demand.* He called the part of his theory of money demand that specified the relationship between the quantity of money demanded and interest rates *liquidity preference theory*. In so doing he took another important step toward analyzing money demand within the framework of conventional demand theory. He formulated his theory by emphasizing the motive for holding money for transactions and for precautionary and speculative purposes.

Keynes' theory of *transactions money demand* is identical in structure to the money demand theory of the Cambridge economists. Transactions balances are held as an abode of purchasing power to facilitate expenditures. Thus, transactions demand is determined primarily by the price level and quantity of output Py or income Y. Transactions balances vary directly and proportionally with income, but not necessarily with the price level or output when the economy is at less than full-employment output.† For example, if income increases, transaction requirements increase, and more money in proportion to the change in income will be held for transaction purposes. This implies that the transactions income velocity of money is constant. Keynes considered the determinants of the transactions income velocity of money to be the same institutional and technical factors referred to by the Cambridge economists.

Keynes' theory of transactions money demand emphasized the holding of money for planned transactions. But money can also be held for unplanned transactions. Keynes called money balances held for these purposes *precautionary money demand*. They are a reserve for unforeseen emergencies and opportunities for advantageous purchases. By introducing precautionary demand, Keynes divorced himself from his predecessors by assuming that decisions are made in a world of uncertainty rather than certainty. He argued that the primary determinant of precautionary money demand is the same as that of transactions money demand, namely income. Precautionary balances vary directly and proportionally with income. For example, an increase in income increases the ability and need to hold money balances for precautionary purposes. Given the precautionary income velocity, the increase in income increases the demand for precautionary balances proportionally.

Assuming that the behavior of decision makers is similar, the aggregate demand for both transactions and precautionary balances can be summarized by

$$MT = kY \tag{7.5}$$

---

*J. M. Keynes, *The General Theory of Employment, Interest and Money* (London: Harcourt, Brace and Co., 1936), chaps. 13 and 15.

†Keynes took exception to the assumption of full employment of resources made by his predecessors. If less than full-employment output increases due to an increase in the money supply or other factors such as government spending, simultaneous increases in the price level will not result in proportional increases in the quantity of money demanded. Only if full-employment output is being produced will the proportional relationship hold.

where MT is both transactions and precautionary money demand, Y is income, and k is the factor of proportionality (the reciprocal of a weighted average of the transactions and precautionary income velocities of money) relating money demand to income. Although Keynes' formulation is the same as that of the Cambridge economists, it is important to emphasize that MT does not represent total money demand. Rather, it represents only money demanded for both planned and unplanned transactions.

Like the Cambridge economists, Keynes argued that since money is an abode of purchasing power, it functions not only as a medium of exchange but also as a store of wealth. He argued that money is held to satisfy *speculative money demand* in excess of transactions and precautionary requirements depending on individual preferences for liquidity, i.e., preferences for money holdings relative to other stores of wealth such as bonds. He argued that the primary determinant of speculative balances is the interest rate on bonds. If it is assumed that bonds, other nonmoney financial assets, and money are very close substitutes for one another, changes in the rate of interest on bonds will reflect changes in other money substitutes as well.

For simplification purposes, assume that bonds are expected to yield a constant annual return (in perpetuity), so that the present value of a bond or the maximum price that bond holders are willing to pay for bonds is

$$PV = \frac{ER}{R} \qquad (7.6)$$

where PV is the present value or price of bonds, ER is the annual constant return expected from bonds, and R is the interest rate on bonds. For example, if a bond is expected to yield \$1 per annum and the interest rate is 10 percent, a person is willing to pay up to \$1/0.10 = \$10 for the bond.

As indicated by (7.6), changes in the interest rate change the price of bonds, causing capital gains or losses to bond holders. In our example above, if the interest rate falls to 5 percent, the price would rise to \$20, and the bond holder would realize a capital gain of \$20 − \$10 = \$10. Conversely, if the interest rate rises to 20 percent, the price of bonds would decrease to \$5, and the bond holder would realize a capital loss of \$10 − \$5 = \$5.

If the interest rate never changes, all wealth would be held as bonds, because unlike money, bonds yield a positive return. But the interest rate does change, and this exposes the decision maker to possible capital losses as well as capital gains. Thus, Keynes argued, the decision about whether to hold one's asset portfolio in bonds or money would be made by comparing the interest income that would be sacrificed by holding money with the expected capital gain or loss from holding bonds. The latter depends on decision makers' expectations of future changes in the interest rate (bond prices) and the degree of certainty with which those expectations are held.

Keynes assumed that each individual has certain expectations of some "nor-

mal" or permanently maintainable rate. Each individual formulates expecta
tions of changes in the future interest rate by comparing the current rate with
the normal rate. If the current rate exceeds the normal rate, individuals will expect the current rate to fall to its normal level. Since bond prices vary inversely
with bond yields, expectation of a falling interest rate means expectation of rising bond prices and thereby expectation of rising capital gains. The higher the
current rate, the greater the amount of capital gains expected because the
larger the spread between the current and normal rates, the greater the probability that the interest rate will fall (bond prices will rise) and the greater the
amount by which it can be expected to fall. Thus, the higher the current rate,
the more costly are speculative (idle) money holdings in terms of expected capital gains sacrificed as well as interest income foregone. Consequently, the
higher the current rate, the more probable it is that no money balances will be
held to satisfy speculative demand.

Conversely, if the observed rate is below the normal rate, expectations of rising interest rates and falling bond prices make money the preferred asset in
decision makers' portfolios. An individual expecting bond prices to fall at a rate
that would more than offset the interest earned would be motivated to hold
non-interest-bearing money rather than the overpriced bonds. Generally, the
lower the current rate, the closer to unanimous will be the expectation that the
interest rate will subsequently rise, imposing capital losses on bond holders.
Thus, the lower the current rate of interest, the greater the number of people
who prefer to hold money rather than bonds, and therefore the greater the
quantity of money demanded to satisfy the speculative motive.

Keynes' argument implies that every individual decides to hold all wealth
either in bonds or in speculative balances. Speculative balances are zero when
the observed rate exceeds the normal rate (by more than some critical amount),
and only bonds are held in asset portfolios. When the normal rate exceeds the
observed rate, bond holdings are zero, and only speculative balances are held
in asset portfolios. Although this either/or decision holds true for the individual,
individuals have different perceptions of the normal rate in the aggregate, and
so we observe an inverse relationship between speculative balances and the interest rate. For example, if individual A is convinced the interest rate will rise
while individual B is convinced the interest rate will fall, individual A will hold
only bonds and individual B will hold only money, so that between the two,
both bonds and money are held. The relationship can be expressed

$$MA = f(R) \tag{7.7}$$

where MA is speculative balances and R is the market rate of interest.

Combining the two components of demand in (7.5) and (7.7) gives Keynes'
total money demand function

$$MD = MT + MA = kY + f(R) \tag{7.8}$$

According to this function the quantity of money demanded varies directly and proportionally with income and inversely with the interest rate.

It should be noted that the last term in (7.8) is improperly specified. According to Keynes' discussion, the demand for speculative balances depends on the current rate of interest in relation to some expected normal rate. Thus, the latter rate properly should be included as one of the explanatory variables determining money demand. However, Keynes (and his followers) chose to treat the expected normal rate as an exogenous factor contributing to erratic shifts in the relationship between the quantity of money demanded and the current rate. It is on the basis of these volatile expectations that Keynes and his followers argued that the money demand function is highly unstable.

Keynes also mentioned in passing that there is some critical positive rate of interest so low that if the current rate were at that level, no one would expect it to go any lower and everyone would expect it to rise, i.e., expectations of bond prices would be unanimous. At this point, expected capital losses would offset interest returns, and there would be no advantage to holding bonds. Money would become a perfect substitute for bonds, and money demand would become insatiable. (Of course, the aggregate stock of money actually held is subject to the constraint imposed by its actual supply.) This is a pathological condition that Keynes called *absolute liquidity preference*.

The curve implied by Keynes' speculative demand is shown in Figure 7.1. The normal rate of interest is higher than or equal to R^* for everyone in the community. Thus, at R^* the curve flattens out and liquidity preference becomes absolute.

7.3 MONEY DEMAND THEORY AFTER KEYNES

Hicks' Analysis

Keynes' chief contribution to money demand analysis is the introduction of a variable representing the cost of holding money balances (the rate of interest) into the money demand function. This innovation permitted examination of the substitution effect on money demand of changes in relative rates of return. In giving explicit consideration to the yields on assets that compete with money, Keynes became one of the founders of the portfolio balance approach to monetary analysis, i.e., the approach that interprets money demand as part of the choice of an optimum (utility-maximizing) portfolio of assets.

At least equal recognition for originating the portfolio approach, however, should be given to J. R. Hicks, who in 1935 first suggested that money demand be treated as a problem of balance sheet equilibrium or asset choice to be analyzed along the lines of orthodox commodity demand theory.†

Hicks pointed out that if money were to be analyzed as a capital asset and not

---

†J. R. Hicks, "A Suggestion for Simplifying the Theory of Money," *Economica,* February 1935, pp. 1–19.

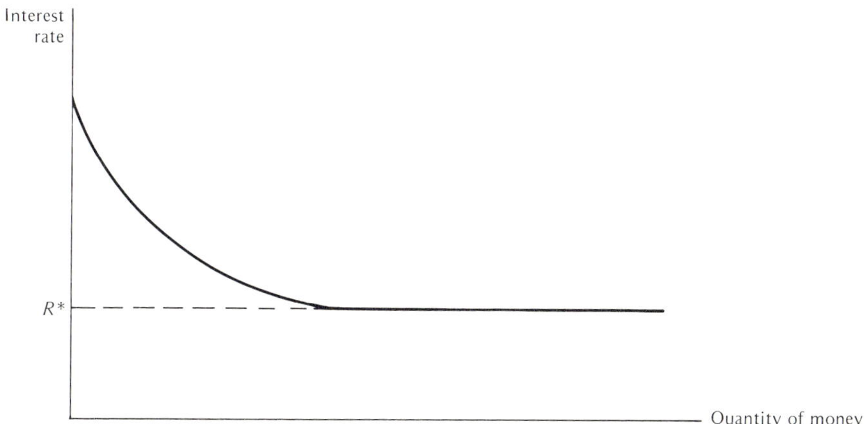

Figure 7.1

Keynes' speculative demand.

just as a mechanical medium of exchange, the money demand function would have to include, as explanatory variables, total wealth and expected rates of return on other assets. The wealth variable would represent the constraint on money holdings, since individuals could choose to hold their entire wealth portfolios in the form of money. The yield variables would represent both the opportunity costs of holding money and the portfolio-substitution effects of changes in relative rates of return. Individual portfolio optimizers would compare these yields with the imputed convenience and security yield from holding money balances in deciding whether to substitute other assets for money in their balance sheets.

Hicks' specification of wealth as the constraint variable was a significant departure from the Cambridge and Keynesian formulations, both of which used income in the money demand equation. This shift from income to wealth as the constraint variable underscored the shift from the transactions approach to the capital asset or portfolio approach in Hicks' article. Income is a magnitude that has the time dimension of a flow (an amount that occurs over an interval of time, or so much per unit of time). Wealth, on the other hand, has the time dimension of a stock (so much existing at a given point in time). The rationale for the income constraint in the Cambridge and Keynesian formulations was that money is used to finance a flow of transactions or spending that is closely related to the flow of income. Hicks' use of the wealth constraint, by contrast, called attention to the stock of money as a store of wealth, i.e., a service or utility-yielding alternative to other asset stocks.

In addition to his pioneering proposal that conventional demand analysis be applied to money in its role as a balance sheet asset, Hicks also took the initial step in extending the theory of choice or optimizing behavior to explain the demand for transactions (as distinct from specuiative or asset) balances. Prior to

Hicks, no one had attempted this. Even Keynes had limited his application of rational choice analysis to the asset component of money demand. Moreover, no one previously had provided a convincing explanation of why individuals would be willing to hold transactions balances when riskless, interest-bearing assets of virtually instantaneous redeemability (e.g., time deposits) were available. Hicks argued that transactors would sacrifice voluntarily the option of holding interest-yielding, speedily convertible assets for the option of holding money because the latter option may be less costly. In short, the existence of transactions balances could be explained as the outcome of rational, cost-minimizing behavior. More specifically, the only reason for holding transactions balances is the conversion costs (brokerage fees, effort and inconvenience, etc.) of transferring money into earning assets and vice versa. Hicks pointed out that it would not pay to get out of money into earning assets for short periods of time if the two-way conversion costs exceeded the interest income foregone by holding money balances.

Hicks' observation that the demand for transactions balances stems from cost-minimizing behavior, together with his proposal that money holdings be analyzed as a component of a portfolio of assets (or wealth), served to eliminate much of the remaining disparity between money demand theory and conventional asset demand theory. The final steps, however, were taken beginning in the 1950s by analysts working along the lines opened by Hicks and Keynes.

In fact, the portfolio balance analysis of money demand took two avenues of development. One avenue is the extension and reformulation of Keynes' motives approach to money demand theory. The principal contributions are J. Tobin's reformulation of liquidity preference theory as portfolio balance behavior toward risk and W. J. Baumol and J. Tobin's refinement of transactions money demand theory. The other avenue of development utilizes Hicks' more general capital asset approach to money demand theory. The principal contributions are M. Friedman's restatement of the quantity theory of money and K. Brunner and A. H. Meltzer's wealth adjustment approach.

Although both avenues of development (which are not strictly independent) result in the portfolio balance approach to money demand theory, there have been (and still are) substantive differences between them. These differences (which have changed from time to time) form the basis for the current Keynesian-monetarist controversy. Arguments based on the Cambridge-Keynes-Hicks-Baumol-Tobin evolutionary process are called *Keynesian,* and those based on the Cambridge-Keynes-Hicks-Friedman-Brunner-Meltzer evolutionary process are called *monetarist.* Differences between these two positions continue to haunt deliberations on monetary (and fiscal) policy.

In the next section we first explain the Keynesian development of the portfolio balance approach to money demand theory and then explain the monetarist development. Differences between the two positions will be pointed out along the way. But a complete explanation of their conflicting views on monetary (and fiscal) policy will be deferred until later chapters.

Tobin's Liquidity Preference Theory*

Tobin's portfolio balance analysis refines Keynes' liquidity preference theory. In Keynes' analysis an individual holds either all bonds or all money in an asset portfolio depending on expected changes in the market interest rate. If the market rate is expected to rise because the normal rate exceeds the current rate (by some critical amount), only money will be held, and if it is expected to fall because the current rate exceeds the normal rate, only bonds will be held. The assumption of certainty of expectations and the conclusion that either money or bonds, but not both, are held in individual asset portfolios are unrealistic. Individuals have expectations, but they are generally held with uncertainty. Moreover, asset portfolios are generally diversified, including both money and bonds.

In reformulating liquidity preference theory, Tobin initially assumed a two-asset world and assumed that an asset or wealth holder is uncertain about the future interest rate (and therefore the price of bonds) and is just as likely to overestimate the future interest rate in any given period (and the future bond price) as to underestimate it. This assumption means that expected (or average) capital gain after many similar periods is zero and that the extent of actual capital gains in any period depends on the level of uncertainty. Since money yields no explicit return, the expected return on an initial endowment of wealth is the interest income from the proportion of wealth held in the form of bonds. It follows that the expected value of wealth is the initial endowment of wealth plus expected return. Expected wealth is not the actual value of wealth at the end of any given period, but the average value of wealth after many similar periods because actual wealth is just as likely to be above its expected value in any period as below it.

Given the interest rate, expected return varies directly and proportionally with the proportion of wealth held in bonds. Since holding bonds exposes the individual to the risk of capital loss, risk also varies directly and proportionally with the proportion of wealth held in bonds. It follows that expected return varies directly and proportionally with risk. Moreover, given an initial endowment of wealth, the expected value of wealth at the end of a period varies directly and proportionally with risk. Given the level of uncertainty, holding all wealth in the form of money balances means zero risk is taken and zero return is expected at the end of the period, i.e., the expected value of wealth at the end of the period equals the initial endowment. At the other extreme for any given level of uncertainty, holding all wealth in the form of bonds means maximum risk is taken and maximum return is expected, i.e., the expected value of wealth at the end of a period increases by the expected return from bonds. Be-

---

*J. Tobin, "Liquidity Preference as Behavior towards Risk," *Review of Economics Studies*, February 1958, pp. 65–68; J. Tobin, "Money, Capital and Other Stores of Value," *American Economic Review*, May 1961, pp. 26–37. A simplified exposition of Tobin's original analysis is found in D. E. W. Laidler, *The Demand for Money: Theories and Evidence* (Scranton, Pa.: International Textbook, 1969), pp. 67–76.

tween these two extremes are combinations of expected wealth and risk and associated combinations of bonds and money balances that the wealth holder can choose for any given level of uncertainty and interest rate. The locus of these combinations is the wealth holder's opportunity constraint on the portfolio decision. For any given interest rate and level of uncertainty (associated with maximum risk), expected wealth at the end of the period varies directly and proportionally with risk. The higher the interest rate, the greater the expected wealth for any given level of risk.

Although the opportunity constraint permits us to derive the combinations of money and bonds a wealth holder is able to hold for any given interest rate and level of uncertainty, it does not permit us to derive the specific combination to be held. In order to determine this, we also need to know the wealth holder's preferences concerning certainty with zero increments in expected wealth and risk with positive increments in expected wealth.

By assuming that (1) for any given level of economic welfare (or utility) wealth holders are generally risk averters, i.e., they require greater expected wealth if additional risk is to be taken, (2) for any given level of economic welfare they are risk diversifiers, i.e., they require increasing amounts of expected wealth per unit of additional risk taken, so that both money and bonds are likely to be held, and (3) they prefer more wealth to less for any given level of risk or less risk to more for any given level of expected wealth, Tobin used indifference curves to illustrate a wealth holder's preferences or willingness to accept possible combinations of risk and expected wealth and hold associated combinations of money and bonds for given levels of expected economic welfare.

Afterward, by combining a wealth holder's preferences and opportunity constraint, Tobin was able to explain the rational wealth holder's decision to hold combinations of money and bonds in an asset portfolio which for a given interest rate and level of uncertainty maximizes expected economic welfare. As in conventional demand analysis, the rational wealth holder allocates wealth so that the rate at which one good can be substituted for another through exchange in the market just equals the rate at which the wealth holder is willing to do so. In the language of our present analysis, the wealth holder maximizes expected economic welfare from an asset portfolio by holding that combination of bonds and money for which the expected return per unit of risk the wealth holder is willing to accept (or is indifferent to) just equals the additional wealth that is expected from taking the additional risk of holding an additional bond.

Figure 7.2 illustrates Tobin's analysis. Expected wealth at the end of the period W is on the vertical axis, and portfolio risk σ is on the horizontal axis. The indifference curves I_1, I_2, and I_3 define combinations of risk and expected wealth at the end of the period which satisfy given levels of expected economic welfare. The expected economic welfare associated with I_3 is greater than that of I_2, and the expected economic welfare associated with I_2 is greater than that

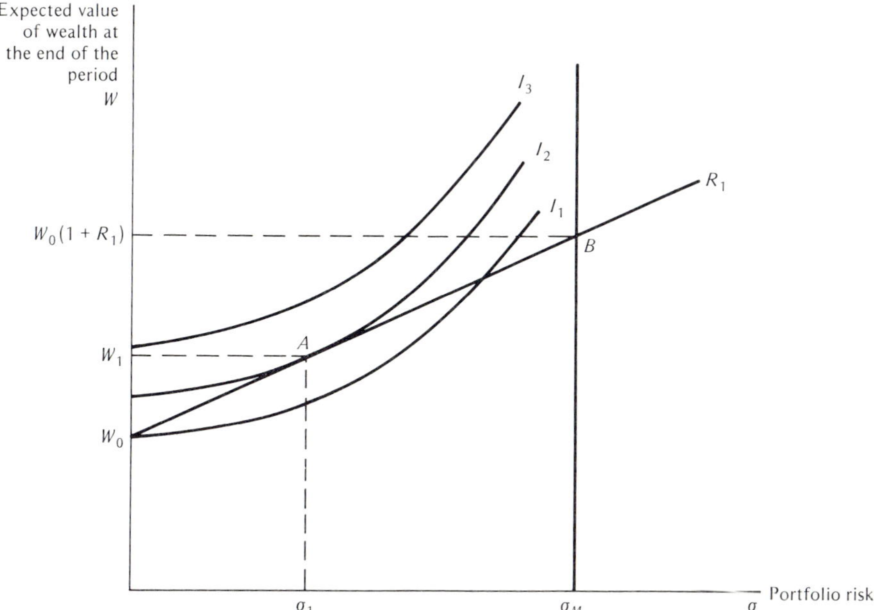

Figure 7.2

Portfolio decision as behavior toward risk.

of I_1. These levels of expected economic welfare reflect the assumption (3 above) that the wealth holder prefers more wealth to less and less risk to more. Each indifference curve reflects the assumptions (1 and 2 above) that the wealth holder is a risk averter, because they indicate a positive relationship between expected wealth and risk, and that the wealth holder is a risk diversifier, because each indifference curve is convex from below. These indifference curves are but a sample of the indifference map reflecting the wealth holder's preferences.

The opportunity constraint for the interest rate R_1, the level of risk σ_M, and initial endowment of wealth W_0 is shown by the line W_0R_1 in Figure 7.2. If only money balances are held, expected wealth at the end of our period of analysis is W_0 (the same value as the initial endowment), since zero risk is taken by holding only money balances in asset portfolio. If zero money balances are held, the expected value of wealth is $W_0(1 + R_1)$ (the maximum value of expected wealth), since maximum risk σ_M is taken by holding only bonds (point B) in asset portfolio. Combinations of risk and expected wealth along the W_0R_1 opportunity constraint show values of expected wealth and risk between the two extremes that the wealth holder is able to accept for a given interest rate R_1. The relationship is linear because increments in expected wealth are proportional to risk. Remember that expected wealth is not what the wealth holder will actually have at the end of each period, but the average wealth at the end of many similar periods. Actual wealth is just as likely to be above expected wealth at the end of any given period as below it.

Given the interest rate R_1 and level of risk σ_M, the wealth holder will maximize expected economic welfare by obtaining the highest level of expected economic welfare (indifference curve) possible given the opportunity constraint W_0R_1. In Figure 7.2, point A is a combination of expected wealth and risk the wealth holder can accept, because it lies on the opportunity constraint, and it is the combination the wealth holder is willing to accept, because it lies on the highest level of expected economic welfare possible, I_2. Thus, the wealth holder chooses σ_1 risk and expects W_1 wealth at the end of the period by holding W_0 in associated combinations of money and bonds. This combination satisfies the wealth holder's asset portfolio equilibrium condition that the rate at which the wealth holder is willing to accept additional risk for additional expected wealth at the end of the period just equals the expected return per unit of risk, i.e., the slope of the indifference curve just equals the slope of the opportunity constraint.

In Figure 7.3 another opportunity constraint line is drawn for a higher interest rate R_2 to illustrate the effects of a change in the interest rate on the portfolio decision. If the interest rate rises to $R_2 > R_1$, the opportunity constraint pivots to W_0R_2, and the individual can reach a higher level of expected economic welfare I_3 by incurring σ_2 risk and expecting greater wealth W_2 at point C. The higher level of risk is taken by holding a greater proportion of portfolio in bonds and less in money balances.

If similar behavior is assumed for all wealth holders, the aggregate quantity of money demanded varies inversely with the interest rate. Since bonds constitute the remainder of the two-asset portfolio, it follows that the quantity of bonds demanded varies directly with the interest rate. Decreases in the interest rate have the opposite results.*

In the manner just explained, Tobin reformulated Keynes' liquidity preference theory as behavior toward risk. Tobin generalized his two-asset analysis for n assets, which he believed should include money, real business capital, bonds, and other nonmoney financial assets. His definition of wealth includes only nonhuman assets and is called the *narrow definition of wealth*. Keynes set forth the principle that cost factors enter into the decision to hold speculative or asset balances, and he used the two-asset case of bonds and money to illustrate his point. Tobin extended the analysis not only by introducing uncertainty of expectations into the analysis, but by explaining liquidity preference as the result of a broader decision-making process, namely, the rational decision to

---

*Our conclusion about the inverse relationship between the interest rate and money demand holds under the reasonable assumption that the substitution effect of interest rate changes outweighs the income effect, i.e., as the interest rate rises, successive equilibria do not lie to the left of the initial equilibrium in Figure 7.3. If this is not true, the wealth holder's preferences would indicate a positive relationship between money balances and the interest rate. This outcome is unlikely, particularly in the aggregate.

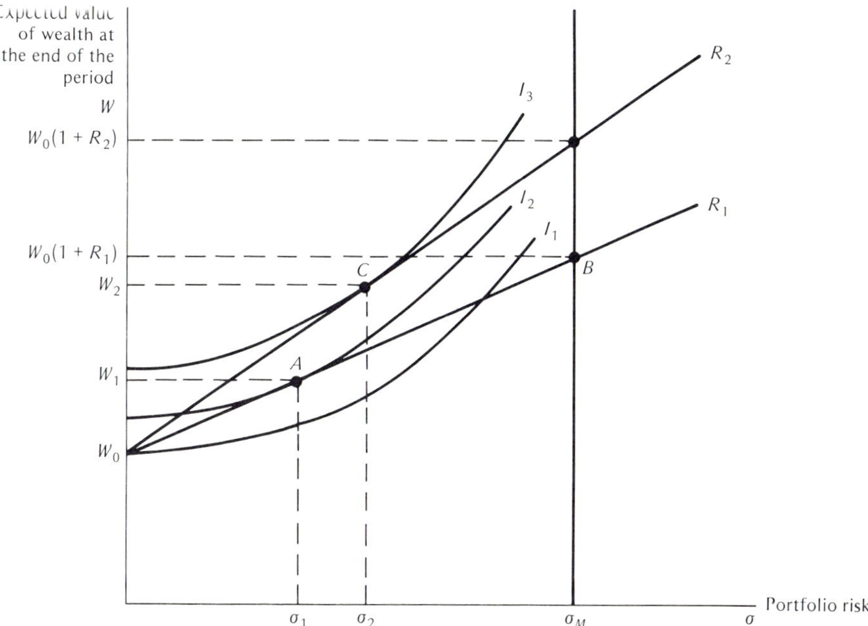

Figure 7.3

Effects of an increase in the interest rate on the portfolio decision.

hold asset money balances as a proportion of asset portfolio where more than one money substitute is available.

Baumol and Tobin's Transactions Demand Theory*

Hicks' conjecture that transactions money demand stems from cost-minimizing behavior was not supported by rigorous proof until the mid-1950s, when Baumol and later Tobin independently applied inventory management analysis to transactions money demand theory. Baumol and Tobin showed that the optimum inventory of transactions balances could be expressed in terms of the so-called lot size or square root formula of inventory theory. Their work integrates transactions money demand theory into the rational choice framework of conventional asset demand or portfolio balance theory.

Baumol and Tobin assume that the individual spends income in a steady stream during a time period. They assume for simplification purposes that to facilitate these expenditures the individual disinvests savings (e.g., sells bonds or

---

*W. J. Baumol, "The Transaction Demand for Cash: An Inventory Theoretic Approach," *Quarterly Journal of Economics,* November 1952, pp. 545–556; J. Tobin, "The Interest Elasticity of Transactions Demand for Cash," *Review of Economics and Statistics,* August 1956, pp. 241–247.

makes withdrawals from saving deposits) in order to obtain transactions money balances of a given lot size evenly spaced throughout the time period. Moreover, the individual spends these transactions balances in such a way that they are depleted at the end of each time period before replenishing them. Thus, the number of disinvestments or conversions of nonmoney assets to money during a time period is the individual's income divided by the amount of assets converted into money during each trip to the broker, Y/MT, and the average transactions balance is $MT/2$. For example, if income is \$12,000 per year and transactions balances are \$1,000, the number of disinvestments per year would be \$12,000/\$1,000 = 12, and the average holdings of transactions balances would be \$1,000/2 = \$500.

There are two types of costs associated with disinvestment: interest cost and conversion cost. If money balances were not required for transactions purposes, the individual could hold onto nonmoney assets which earn interest income. But since transactions balances are required, the individual incurs an interest opportunity cost equal to the interest rate times the individual's average holdings of transactions balances, $R(MT/2)$. In our example above, if the yearly interest rate were 8 percent, the interest opportunity cost would be $0.08(\$500) = \$40$ per year.

The other cost of disinvestment is the fixed brokerage fees and other explicit and implicit conversion costs enumerated by Hicks. This cost is the cost per unit of conversion b times the number of conversions per period, $b(Y/MT)$. In our example above, if $b = \$2$, total conversion costs would be $\$2 \cdot 12 = \$24$ per year.

The rational individual will attempt to minimize the total cost TC of meeting transactions requirements,

$$TC = R\frac{MT}{2} + b\frac{Y}{MT} \qquad (7.9)$$

by holding the cost-minimizing amount of MT. This value is derived mathematically by setting the first derivative of TC with respect to MT equal to zero and solving for MT.* These operations yield the cost-minimizing amount of transactions balances for each conversion,

$$MT = \sqrt{2bY/R} \qquad (7.10)$$

This formulation is called the *square root rule* for holding an inventory of an asset, in this case transactions money balances. Note that since average trans-

---

*We are using a method for solving (7.9) for the value of MT where TC is at a minimum. By setting

$$\frac{\partial TC}{\partial MT} = -b\frac{Y}{MT^2} + \frac{R}{2} = 0$$

and solving for MT, we get Eq. (7.10).

actions balances equal $MT/2$, the demand for average transactions balances can be obtained by dividing both sides of Eq. (7.10) by 2.

According to this formula, the average transactions balances would be directly proportional to the square root of income and the fixed cost of conversion, and inversely proportional to the square root of the opportunity cost of a money inventory, i.e., the interest rate. Thus, given the level of income, the transactions money demand depends on the relation between the yield on a nonmoney asset such as bonds and the cost of buying and selling bonds. If the latter were greater than the former, it would not pay to substitute earning assets for money. Consequently, money holdings would be relatively large. But as yields rise relative to conversion costs, it would pay to economize on transactions balances. Hence, the quantity of transactions money demanded varies inversely with the interest rate. If the income varied, however, the demand for money would vary in the same direction but less than proportionally. This implies that the more prosperous a person or firm is, the smaller will be the increase in transactions balances necessary to cover a given increase in income, i.e., there are economies of scale.

Baumol and Tobin's studies contribute to the closing of the gap between conventional demand theory and Keynesian money demand theory because they show that transactions balances, like any other asset that is held, are determined by cost or yield variables. Rational choice analysis governs the transactions money demand just as it governs speculative money balances. Although transactions balances are governed by cost minimization rather than utility maximization, both these methods are attempts at maximization of economic welfare.*

Taken together, Baumol and Tobin's transactions demand theory and Tobin's liquidity preference theory form the basis for the Keynesian portfolio balance approach to money demand theory, i.e., an approach that analyzes total money demand on the basis of rational choice within the framework of conventional asset demand analysis. The proportion of a given endowment of wealth held in money balances varies inversely with the interest rates on assets which substitute for money as a store of wealth. Moreover, money balances vary directly with income because money serves as the medium of exchange. Income is included in the Keynesian money demand function as the constraint

---

*There is also a cost associated with holding unplanned transactions or precautionary balances. See E. L. Whalen, "A Rationalization of the Precautionary Demand for Cash," *Quarterly Journal of Economics,* May 1966, pp. 314–324; and M. H. Miller and D. Orr, "A Model of the Demand for Money by Firms," *Quarterly Journal of Economics,* August 1966, pp. 413–435.

As in Baumol and Tobin's analysis, the interest rate is the interest opportunity cost of holding money balances. But there is a cost of not holding money balances, that is, a penalty associated with not being able to pay for unexpected transactions. Holding zero precautionary balances makes the probability of incurring penalty costs a maximum. Holding positive precautionary balances decreases the probability. However, interest income is foregone. The more (less) an individual holds, the less(more) the probability of penalty costs and the more (less) the interest income foregone. The demand for precautionary balances is that which minimizes the sum of these two costs. Like the Baumol and Tobin analyses, this solution implies that the quantity of precautionary money demanded varies inversely with the interest rate. Thus, not only speculative and planned transactions balances vary inversely with the interest rate, but so do unplanned transactions balances.

on the portfolio decision because income (the flow counterpart of the stock, wealth) is the relevant constraining variable on the portfolio decision in the short run where changes in stocks occur.

Gurley-Shaw Thesis

J. G. Gurley and E. S. Shaw extended the theory of portfolio balance money demand to include the relatively independent influence of financial intermediation.* Asset holders hold money in asset portfolios because of the risk associated with holding primary securities. But why would they hold any money at all when relatively safe, risk-free, highly liquid, and interest-bearing deposit liabilities (time and saving deposits) of financial institutions are available? These assets are not perfect substitutes for money because they are not acceptable as a medium of exchange. Moreover, there are the costs and inconvenience of converting them to money, i.e., the costs and inconvenience of a trip to the bank or saving and loan association. But, their "near money" properties make them the closest substitutes for money.

These deposit liabilities provide asset holders with an alternative to holding money when they are unwilling to substitute primary securities for money (direct finance) at the current market rate of interest (yield on primary securities). Instead, they can substitute the time and savings deposits of financial institutions for money (indirect finance) if the deposit rate is at least as great as the costs and inconvenience of converting these assets to money (or vice versa).

The market rate of interest varies inversely with the quantity of money demanded. The market rate is the rate charged to final borrowers of funds by either original lenders (direct finance) or financial intermediaries (indirect finance). The deposit rate is the rate charged to financial intermediaries by original lenders. For any given market rate, money demand varies inversely with the deposit rate. For example, an increase in the deposit rate induces asset holders to substitute the time and saving deposits of financial institutions for primary securities and money balances in asset portfolios. To the extent that this occurs, the quantity of money demanded decreases, and more funds are made available to borrowers in financial markets. A decrease in the deposit rate yields the opposite results.

We have singled out the deposit rate on time and savings deposits from the rates or yields on other financial assets because of its unique place in financial analysis. The market rate of interest reflects the influence of one of the market forces on the quantity of money demanded. The deposit rate reflects the influence of financial intermediation on the quantity of money demanded. Changes in the deposit rate (within the limits imposed by the Fed) change the money balances held in asset portfolios and thereby change the amount of money in fi-

---

*J.S. Gurley and E. S. Shaw, *Money in a Theory of Finance* (Washington, D. C.: The Brookings Institution, 1960).

nancial circulation by activating "idle" asset money balances. The importance of these changes in evaluating the effectiveness of monetary policy will be discussed in detail in later chapters.

Friedman's Quantity Theory of Money

Following Hicks' suggestion, M. Friedman employed the procedures of conventional asset demand theory to construct a detailed money demand function.* Like Hicks, Friedman interpreted money demand as a problem in balance sheet equilibrium or asset choice. However, unlike other monetary analysts (especially the Keynesians), he did not dichotomize money demand in terms of special motives that are satisfied by holding money balances. Instead, he treated money as an asset which, like any other asset, yields a flow of services to households and business firms that makes it desirable to hold.

Like Hicks, Friedman specified wealth as the appropriate constraint on the portfolio decision. He defined it as the present value of expected future return from both human and nonhuman wealth. Human wealth is the present value of expected labor earnings. Nonhuman wealth is money (whatever its use), the present value of nonmoney financial assets (e.g., bonds) minus liabilities, and the real assets of business firms (e.g., plant and equipment) and households (consumer durables). His definition of wealth differs substantially from that of the Keynesians, who define wealth more narrowly. Remember that Tobin's definition of wealth is only those assets which serve as stores of wealth, excluding transactions money balances, human wealth, and consumer durables. Thus, the Friedman portfolio balance approach is an analysis of the larger portfolio decisions which explain the determination of all forms of wealth simultaneously.

In a manner similar to our earlier analysis of bonds, Friedman's broadly defined wealth can be expressed

$$W = \frac{Y^P}{R} \tag{7.11}$$

where W is wealth, Y^P is expected future receipts from both human and nonhuman wealth, or what Friedman called permanent income, and R is an average of rates of return (implicit and explicit) on all wealth. Wealth varies directly with permanent income and inversely with the rate of return on wealth, which in portfolio equilibrium is the market rate of interest. Since wealth varies directly with permanent income, permanent income can be used as a surrogate

---

*M. Friedman, "The Quantity Theory of Money—A Restatement," in M. Friedman (ed.), *Studies in the Quantity Theory of Money* (Chicago: University of Chicago Press, 1957), pp. 3–21. Also see a simplified formulation in "A Theoretical Framework for Monetary Analysis," *Journal of Political Economy,* March/April 1970, pp. 193–238.

variable for wealth. Although in any given period permanent income need not equal measured income, after many similar periods measured income equals permanent income, and wealth can be expressed

$$W = \frac{Y}{R} \tag{7.12}$$

where Y is measured income. Thus, measured income is also a surrogate for wealth. However, if we used it in recessions, when $Y^P > Y$, we would underestimate wealth, and if we used it in booms, when $Y^P < Y$, we would overestimate wealth.

Friedman argues that since the measures of wealth are not reliable, permanent income can be used as the constraint on the portfolio decision and thereby money demand. Like the Keynesians, he assumes that relative prices or interest rates determine the composition of asset portfolio, but interest rates include not only explicit interest rates on components of wealth, narrowly defined, but the implicit rates of return on all components of wealth, broadly defined. Friedman also argues that money is the closest substitute for the present value of human wealth and the present value of household wealth (consumer durables), so that interest rates on other assets, such as those considered important by the Keynesians (interest rates or yields on business capital and nonmoney financial assets), help very little in explaining money demand. Since the interest rates or rate of return on the more relevant assets are not observable, nominal permanent income or real permanent income and the price level are the principal variables that explain money demand.*

In addition, Friedman was the first to argue that the opportunity cost of holding money includes not only interest return, but the depreciation cost of loss of purchasing power that results from holding money during periods of inflation. Changes in interest opportunity cost inversely affect money demand. For example, if the interest opportunity cost of money balances (e.g., the interest rate on bonds) increases, bonds will be substituted for money balances in wealth portfolios. Similarly, if the rate of increase in the price level increases, the loss in purchasing power increases, so that wealth holders will substitute other assets for money balances.

When inflation persists, so that *both* interest and depreciation costs are considered important in explaining the demand for assets, these two costs can be combined as one concept, namely, the real rate of interest. Real rates are sim-

---

*Friedman includes three interest rates in his money demand function. He argues that all types of wealth (including consumer durables) are potential substitutes for money holdings in individual balance sheets. Thus, in sharp contrast to Keynes' exposition of the relationship between money demand and a single interest rate, Friedman listed the relative yield variables entering the money demand function as including the expected rates of return on bonds, equities, and real assets. Like Tobin, Friedman increases the degree of generalization of Keynes' original effort with this step. But unlike Tobin, Friedman defines wealth in a much broader context than Keynes.

ply nominal rates less the expected rate of increase in the price level. The inclusion of the expected rate of change in the price level in the money demand function is one of Friedman's most important contributions.

Friedman includes other determinants of money demand in his analysis, including economic outlook, such as war and recession, and other institutional factors which we can consider relatively fixed or proportional to income. Unlike Tobin, who assumes that wealth can be converted to money (because Tobin defines it to include only nonhuman forms of wealth), Friedman argues that without slavery, human wealth cannot always substitute for money. Thus, he argues that the percentage ratio of nonhuman to total wealth should be included in the money demand function. As the ratio increases, nonhuman wealth (a closer substitute for money) increases relative to human wealth (a not-so-close substitute for money) in asset portfolio, so that money demand decreases. This ratio is important in the money demand function of ultimate wealth holders, but not in that of business firms, who use money balances as a capital asset. Since business firms hold only nonhuman wealth, the ratio is fixed at unity and may be left out of the money demand function. This is the only substantive variable which distinguishes the ultimate wealth holder's decision from that of the business firm.

The essential parts of Friedman's analysis which distinguish it from the Keynesian portfolio balance approach are that he does not dichotomize money demand (an assumption in Keynesian analysis which in hindsight is not necessary); he defines wealth in broader terms to include the total quantity of money, human wealth, and consumer durables; he does not consider bonds and money to be close substitutes, so interest rates have little effect on money demand; and he includes expected inflation in his money demand analysis.

Thus, Friedman asserts that money is a unique asset. Money demand varies directly with wealth (or its surrogate, permanent income). Since Friedman believes that the economic system is stable, i.e., short-run departures from full-employment output are temporary, he also concludes that given full-employment output, money demand varies directly and proportionally with the price level. In so doing Friedman does not depart from the conclusion of the classical economists. Because of the close relationship between money and the price level and thereby income (where output in the long run is determined by technological factors), there is a stable relationship between money and income. In fact, Friedman's analysis is a restatement of the quantity theory of money using the portfolio balance approach to money demand theory.

K. Brunner and A. H. Meltzer have modified Friedman's portfolio balance approach.* They insist that wealth, and not a surrogate variable, along with in-

---

*K. Brunner and A. H. Meltzer, "The Place of Financial Intermediaries in the Transmission of Monetary Policy," *American Economic Review*, May 1963, pp. 372–382; K. Brunner and A. H. Meltzer, "Money, Debt, and Economic Activity," *Journal of Political Economy*, September/October 1972, pp. 951–977; and K. Brunner and A. H. Meltzer, "Mr. Hicks and the 'Monetarists,'" *Economica*, February 1973, pp. 44–59.

terest rates provides the best explanation of money demand. Although their monetary analysis makes use of a portfolio balance approach, it is called the *wealth adjustment approach* to distinguish its conclusions from those of the Keynesians. In Chapter 11 we will provide a more detailed explanation of both the Tobin portfolio balance model for monetary analysis and Brunner-Meltzer's wealth adjustment model. The opposing views in these two models form the basis for the current Keynesian-monetarist controversy.

7.4 THE MONEY DEMAND FUNCTION

Although there are important differences between the Keynesians and the monetarists (as well as among them), they share a common ground, namely, they analyze money demand within the framework of conventional asset demand theory, i.e., portfolio balance theory. Our specification of the portfolio balance money demand function includes the principal determinants of money demand. All other determinants are assumed constant over the period of our analysis.

Relative prices of assets which serve as stores of value are the allocative variables in asset portfolios. If we assume that all stores of value are such close substitutes for money (and therefore each other) that changes in a single price or interest rate reflect changes in all others (except money's price, which is always 1, that is, a dollar always costs a dollar), we can refer to the market price or the market interest rate of assets which substitute for money as stores of value. The market rate of interest is traditionally used as a measure of the value of money in terms of money substitutes that serve as stores of value.

Because the deposit rate is not solely determined by market forces in the portfolio adjustment process, but rather by financial institutions within legal limits, we include the deposit rate as an independent explanatory variable in our money demand function. Thus, the market rate of interest becomes a measure of the value of money in terms of all other stores of value except the time and savings deposits of financial institutions, while the deposit rate is a measure of the value of money in terms of time and savings deposits. The singling out of the deposit rate will permit us to more carefully analyze the impact of financial intermediation on the economy in later chapters.

Moreover, since money serves as a medium of exchange, the price of money relative to the price of current output is a measure of the value of money in terms of current output. The price of money is 1, so that the reciprocal of the price of current output is the value of money in terms of current output.

Another factor which measures the value of money is the rate of change in the price level, or the inflation rate. The value of money varies inversely with the inflation rate, so that money demand varies inversely with the inflation rate. When inflation is severe, economists speak of the real rate of interest as the more realistic measure of the "rental" value of money. The real rate is the nominal rate less the inflation rate, or the nominal interest opportunity cost of holding money less the cost of holding money due to erosion of purchasing power. For now, we will assume that the inflation rate is minimal. But the impact of this variable on money demand will become an important part of our analysis of inflation in later chapters.

Wealth, expected wealth, measured income, and permanent income have been suggested as constraints on the size of asset portfolios. If we assume that expected wealth is actual wealth after many similar periods of analysis and that expected or permanent income is actual or measured income after many similar periods, measured income after many similar periods is a constraint on the flow or change in the stock of wealth, and actual wealth after many similar periods is a constraint on the stock or absolute amount of wealth. Since our treatment of money demand in this section separates the price level from output (the product of which is income), output or real income is the appropriate flow constraint on money demand, and real wealth is the appropriate stock constraint.

The preference for output in the money demand function is based on the medium of exchange function of money. The volume of money transactions for which money is required is tied not only to the interest rate and price level, but to output as well. Thus, money demand is logically constrained by output. Use of real wealth in the money demand function is based on the larger function of money, including not only the medium of exchange function, but the store of wealth function. Although money demand is constrained by output in the short run, the absolute amount of money demanded is constrained by the amount of real wealth in the long run.

Since these arguments are not mutually exclusive, both output and real wealth could be included in the money demand function if they were largely independent explanatory variables. However, they are not independent variables. As pointed out earlier by (7.12), nominal wealth can be defined in terms of income, and therefore real wealth can be defined in terms of output (or real income). For any given rate of interest, changes in output have a unit impact on real wealth, so that output and real wealth are interchangeable in the money demand function. Changes in one variable reflect changes in the other. For this reason, monetary analysts use either real wealth or output in the money demand function, but not both.

In formalizing our portfolio balance money demand function, we will use output as the constraining variable, primarily because we will be interested in analyzing the impact of changes in the money stock on changes in output, the price level, and the interest rate and, in turn, their impact on money demand. Also the impact of changes in real wealth is introduced through the real sector analysis which follows in Chapter 9.

Our money demand function can be expressed

$$MD = f(R,\ 1/P,\ y,\ DR) \qquad\qquad (7.13)$$

where MD is the quantity of nominal money balances demanded, R is the market rate of interest, $1/P$ is the price of money relative to the price of current output, y is current output, and DR is the deposit rate. We have included in our function the principal determinants of money demand. All other determinants can be considered fixed during the period of our analysis.

The quantity of money demanded varies inversely with the value of money in terms of alternatives. That is, money demand varies inversely with the market interest rate, the deposit rate, and the reciprocal of the price level (or directly with the price level). Money demand varies directly with output. Figure 7.4 illustrates these qualitative results. The money demand curve MD' shows the inverse relationship between money demand and the interest rate for given values of the price level P_1, output y_1, and deposit rate $\overline{DR}$.

Suppose, for example, that in Figure 7.4 a decrease in the interest rate from R_2 to R_1 lowers the opportunity cost of holding money and increases the price of money substitutes. The result is an increase in the quantity of money demanded from MD_1 to MD_2. Increases in interest rates cause the opposite results.

Now suppose that in Figure 7.4 the price level increases from P_1 to P_2, so that the money demand curve increases from MD' to MD''. This means that for any given interest rate, say R_1, more money is required to purchase a given level of current output y_1, so that the quantity of money demanded increases from MD_2 to MD_3. Decreases in the price level yield the opposite results.

Figure 7.4

The money demand curve.

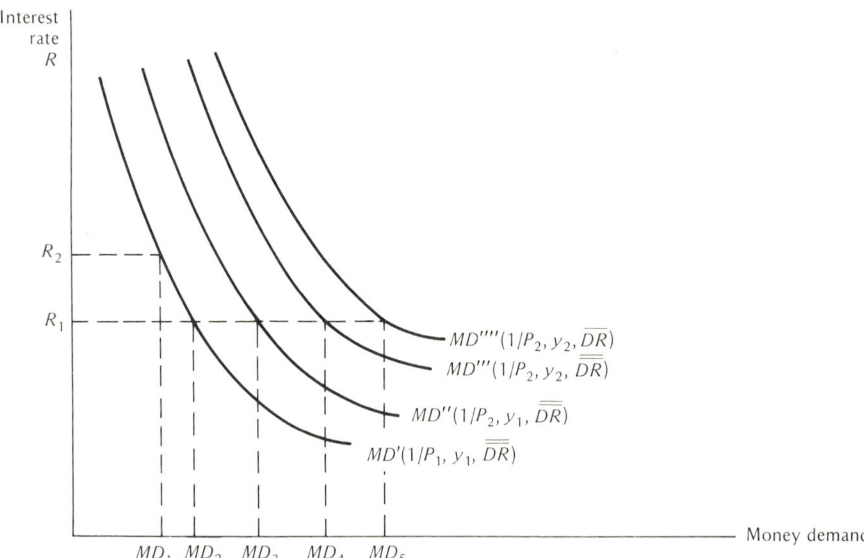

Now suppose, for example, that output increases from y_1 to y_2, so that the size of the increment in asset portfolios, including money, increases and the money demand curve in Figure 7.4 increases from MD'' to MD'''. For any given interest rate, say R_1, the quantity of money demanded increases from MD_3 to MD_4. Decreases in output cause the opposite results.

Now suppose, for example, that in Figure 7.4 financial institutions decrease the deposit rate from $\overline{\overline{DR}}$ to $\overline{DR}$, so that the money demand curve increases from MD''' to MD''''. For any given market rate of interest, say R_1, the quantity of money demanded will increase from MD_4 to MD_5 as asset holders substitute money balances for time and savings deposits. Increases in the deposit rate yield the opposite results.

The empirical evidence which lends support to the portfolio balance money demand function is varied. But it does suggest that interest rates, prices, and output (or real wealth) are statistically significant determinants of money demand. Most studies assume that the price level elasticity of money demand is unity. Other studies actually estimate it and find that it is not significantly different from unity. This means that a 1 percent increase in only the price level (the interest rate and output remain unchanged) reduces the value of money by 1 percent and thereby increases the quantity of money demanded to purchase a given amount of output. Given that the price level elasticity of money demand is 1, the following summary and discussion of the interest rate, output, and real wealth elasticities of nominal money balances is applicable.

Because of the statistical problems involved, portfolio balance analysts have used only one interest rate when estimating the money demand function. The estimates of the interest elasticity of money demand are numerous and will not be summarized here.* However, taken together they indicate that although money demand is sensitive to changes in the observed interest rates on money substitutes (particularly nonmoney financial assets), it is interest-inelastic in most cases. Both short- and long-term interest rates on bonds have been used. Most estimates fall in the lower range, between -0.1 and -1.15. This means that a 1 percent decrease in the interest rate results in a 0.1 to 1.15 percent increase in money demand.

The evidence suggests that the estimates of the interest elasticity of money demand vary depending on the definition of money. The narrow definition of money (currency and demand deposits of the nonbank public) gives estimates that are larger than those when the broad definition of money (the narrow definition plus time deposits at commercial banks) is used. This is not surprising. Narrow money yields no explicit return, but time deposits earn interest income. When interest rates (including the time deposit rate) increase, the demand for

---

*See a summary of the interest elasticities of money demand in D. Laidler, *The Demand for Money: Theories and Evidence* (Scranton, Pa.: International Textbook, 1969), pp. 91–98. Alternatively, see F. R. Glahe, *Macroeconomics: Theory and Policy* (New York: Harcourt, Brace, 1973), pp. 276–277.

narrow money falls, but the demand for time deposits may even increase. These two opposing results mean that broadly defined money responds less to interest rate changes than narrow money.

Use of long-term rates gives higher interest elasticities than short-term rates because variations in long-term rates are smaller. Also, annual data yield higher interest elasticities than quarterly data because in the short run full adjustment in money holdings to the interest-rate change may not have had time to take place.

Estimates of the real wealth and output elasticities of money demand are approximately unity.* That is, a 1 percent increase in real wealth or output increases the quantity of money demanded by 1 percent. The exception is the output or real permanent income elasticity of 1.8 obtained by Friedman.† On the basis of this estimate, he argues that money is a luxury good, the demand for which varies more than proportionally with real permanent income. However, his results are based on his use of broadly defined money. When narrowly defined money is used, the real permanent income elasticity of money demand is closer to unity.

Although the conceptual problem is solved by using either real wealth or output in the money demand function, because of imprecision of data gathering, preferences might be based on which does the best job of statistically explaining money demand. Several studies indicate that real wealth (including human and nonhuman factors) performs better than output in predicting long-run money demand. Since money demand is a stock, this result is not surprising. Output is a short-run constraint on asset portfolios as changes in stock occur, and real wealth is a constraint on the extent of the changes (flows) in the long run, i.e., a constraint on the levels of stocks. Since we will engage primarily in short-run analysis in forthcoming chapters, we will use output as a constraint variable.

SUMMARY NOTES

1. Pre-Keynesian money demand theory was based primarily on money's role as a medium of exchange. Irving Fisher, for example, concentrated his analysis on the transactions velocity of money.

---

*Meltzer, op. cit.; K. Brunner and A. H. Meltzer, "Predicting Velocity: Implications for Theory and Policy," *Journal of Finance,* May 1963, pp. 319–354; A. H. Meltzer, "The Demand for Money: The Evidence from the Time Series," *Journal of Political Economy,* June 1963, pp. 219–246; D. Laidler, "Some Evidence on the Demand for Money," *Journal of Political Economy,* February 1966, pp. 55–68; and G. Chow, "On the Long-Run and Short-Run Demand for Money," *Journal of Political Economy,* April 1966, pp. 111–131. Also see F. deLeeuw, "A Model of Financial Behavior," *The Brookings Quarterly Econometric Model of the United States* (Chicago: Rand McNally, 1965), chap. 13, p. 470.

†M. Friedman, "The Demand for Money: Some Theoretical and Empirical Results," *Journal of Political Economy,* August 1959, pp. 327–351.

2. Beginning with the Cambridge school, emphasis began to shift toward the determinants of the demand for money to hold.

3. Keynes used elements of the Cambridge tradition together with his own theory of liquidity preference. Liquidity preference made the interest rate, as well as income, a determinant of money demand.

4. Hicks treated the demand for money as a problem of balance sheet equilibrium and asset choice, which is the starting point for modern portfolio choice theory. Tobin further elaborated on portfolio theory using Keynes' liquidity preference as a starting point.

5. Other modifications of Keynesian analysis include the application of optimal inventory theory to the transactions demand for money.

6. Gurley and Shaw examined the substitute relationships between money and the liabilities of nonbank financial intermediaries. These relationships contain important implications for the effectiveness of monetary policy.

7. The quantity theory, in the context of a portfolio balance approach, has been substantially revived by Friedman and Brunner and Meltzer. Major emphasis has been placed on the role of wealth or wealth proxies as determinants of money demand.

8. Empirical evidence supports the role of the market interest rate, income, and/or wealth in money demand.

DISCUSSION QUESTIONS

1. If money demand were not responsive to changes in the interest rate, would there be any substantial difference between Keynes' theory of money demand and that of Fisher or the Cambridge economists? Explain.

2. What has happened to precautionary money demand as a result of the increases in the availability of all types of credit and near money since World War II? Explain.

3. What is the present value of a bond expected to yield a return of $10 per year forever with an interest rate of 6 percent? If the bond cost $25, would you buy it? Why or why not?

4. What would happen to the composition of asset portfolios given an increase in the level of uncertainty?

5. If banking laws were changed tomorrow so that the time and savings deposits of all financial intermediaries would become demand deposits and all financial intermediaries would become banks, what would be the significance of the Gurley-Shaw thesis?

6. Explain the effects of inflation on asset and transactions money balances.

7. How does Friedman's quantity theory of money differ from the quantity theory of the Cambridge economists?

THE MONEY MARKET

The previous three chapters were devoted to an exploration of the determinants of the money supply and money demand. It is now time to tie the two concepts together.

Suppliers (sellers) and demanders (buyers) of assets (or wealth) come together in asset markets to exchange all forms of wealth at market prices or interest rates. The money market is an important asset market because, like any other asset, money is a form of wealth, and because it facilitates not only exchanges of all other assets, but exchanges of output and factor inputs as well. For these reasons we must clearly understand the way in which the money market operates.

In this chapter we begin by analyzing the money market on the basis of the theories of money supply and money demand that were developed in the preceding chapters. Both equilibrium and disequilibrium aspects of the money market are explained. Afterward, a condensed version of the money market, the LM schedule, will be derived so that in the next chapter we can more easily interrelate money market activity with the activities of the output market. Moreover, we will be able to interrelate more easily the money market (a stock analysis of financial markets) with the loanable funds market (a flow analysis of financial markets).

8.1 MONEY-MARKET EQUILIBRIUM

The money supply function

$$MS = f(R, MB) \tag{8.1}$$

and the money demand function

$$MD = f(R, 1/P, y, DR) \tag{8.2}$$

that were developed in the two preceding chapters, along with the equilibrium condition that money supply equals money demand,

$$MS = MD \tag{8.3}$$

make up our money market model. The model determines the equilibrium values of the market interest rate and the quantity of money for given values of the price level, output, deposit rate, and monetary base.

Figure 8.1 shows a money supply curve MS' for a given monetary base $\overline{MB}$, and a money demand curve MD' for given values of the price level P_1, output y_1, and deposit rate $\overline{DR}$, that determine the equilibrium values of the interest rate R_2, and the quantity of money M_2. Only at equilibrium is the quantity of money supplied sufficient for money demanders to realize desired holdings of

Figure 8.1

Money-market equilibrium.

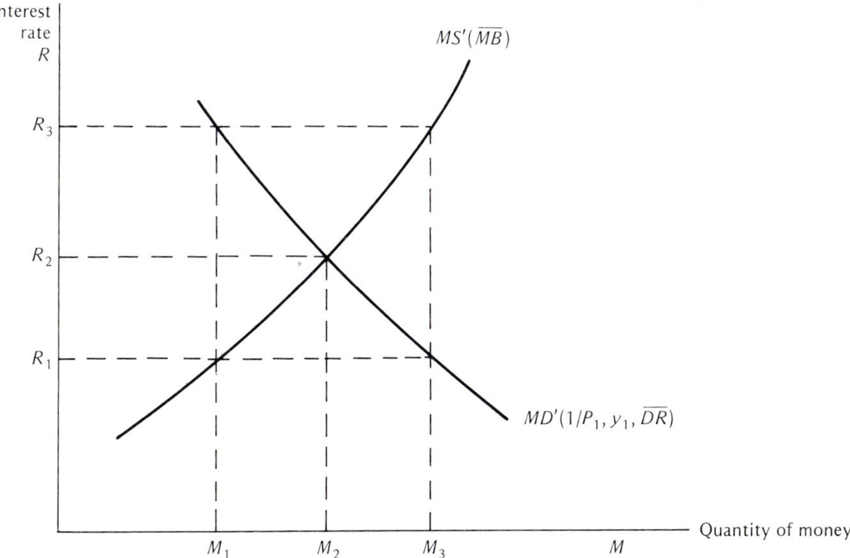

money balances. At higher interest rates, say R_3, the quantity of money supplied exceeds the quantity of money demanded, $M_3 - M_1$, i.e., individuals hold more money balances than they desire to hold. At lower interest rates, say R_1, the quantity of money demanded exceeds the quantity of money supplied, $M_3 - M_1$, i.e., individuals hold less money balances than they desire to hold. Under either of these disequilibrium conditions, market forces come into play and adjust the interest rate to R_2 and the quantity of money to M_2.

An explanation of the adjustment process is a part of the analysis of the effects that changes in the monetary base, the price level, output, and the deposit rate have on the money market. An explanation of the effects of such changes on the money market is our next undertaking.

8.2 DISEQUILIBRIUM ADJUSTMENT

Effects of Changes in the Price Level

Consider, for example, the effect of an increase in the price level on the money market for given values of output, deposit rate, and monetary base. The increase in the price level reduces the value of money in terms of output. In order to purchase the given level of output, individuals increase their demand for money and reduce their demand for other assets that substitute for money in asset portfolios. As a result, the price of money substitutes decreases and the market interest rate rises. The increase in the interest rate increases the quantity of money supplied as the banking system and the nonbank public interact in the money creation process described earlier. After full adjustment, the interest rate is higher and the quantity of money in the system is greater than before. Decreases in the price level yield the opposite results.

Figure 8.2 illustrates the qualitative results of an increase in the price level on the money market. The initial equilibrium values of the interest rate R_1 and the quantity of money M_1 are determined by the money supply curve MS' and money demand curve MD' for given values of the price level P_1, output y_1, the deposit rate $\overline{DR}$, and the monetary base $\overline{MB}$. Suppose the price level increases from P_1 to P_2, so that the money demand curve increases from MD' to MD''. At the initial interest rate R_1 there is excess demand for money balances, $M_3 - M_1$, because individuals require more money to purchase the given level of output. In order to obtain the money balances required, individuals offer for sale holdings of nonmoney assets. The interest rate rises (price of nonmoney assets falls). With the higher interest rate, the banking system interacts with the nonbank public to increase the quantity of money supplied to M_2. The new equilibrium interest rate, R_2, permits M_2 desired money balances to be realized.*

---

*It is worth mentioning at this point that the effect of an increase in the price level on the money market just explained is based on the actual price level. If decisions are based on the expected or forecasted price level, then the extent of the forecast error will determine the extent of the impact on money demand. We will consider this possibility more carefully in a later chapter on inflation.

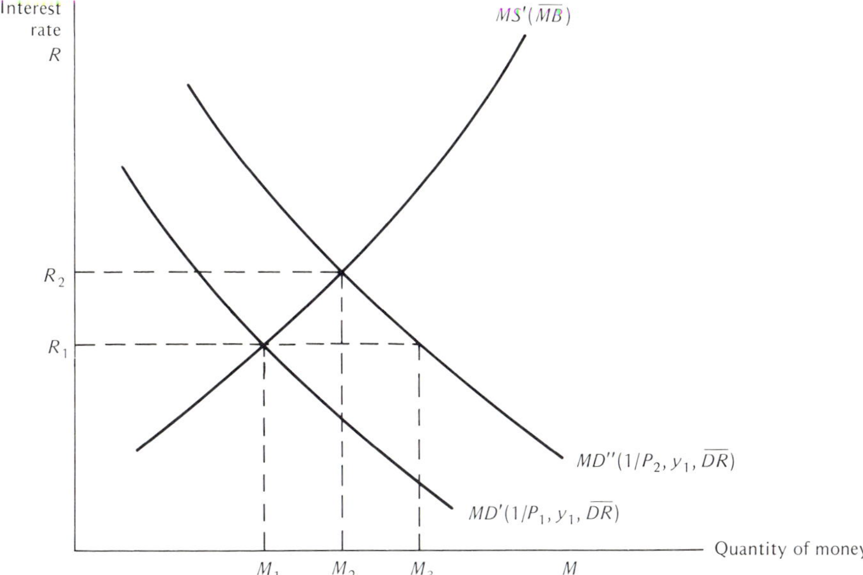

Figure 8.2
Effects of an increase in the price level on the money market.

Effects of Changes in Output

Consider, for example, the effect of an increase in output on the money market for given values of the price level, the deposit rate, and the monetary base. In order to purchase the higher level of output, individuals increase their demand for money and reduce their demand for money substitutes in asset portfolios. As a result, the price of money substitutes decreases, and the market rate of interest rises. The increase in the interest rate increases the quantity of money supplied as the banking system interacts with the nonbank public in the money creation process. After full adjustment the interest rate is higher, and the quantity of money in the system is greater than before. Decreases in output yield the opposite results.

Figure 8.3 illustrates the qualitative results of an increase in output on the money market. The initial equilibrium values of the interest rate R_1 and the quantity of money M_1 that are determined by the money supply curve MS' and money demand curve MD' for given values of the price level P_1, output y_1, deposit rate $\overline{DR}$, and monetary base $\overline{MB}$. An increase in output from y_1 to y_2 increases the money demand curve from MD' to MD''. At the initial interest rate R_1, there is an excess demand for money, $M_3 - M_1$, because individuals require more money to purchase the additional output. In order to acquire the additional money, individuals offer for sale holdings of nonmoney assets. The interest rate rises (the price of nonmoney assets rises). With the higher interest rate, the banking system interacts with the nonbank public to increase the quantity of money supplied to M_2. The new equilibrium interest rate, R_2, permits M_2 desired money balances to be realized.

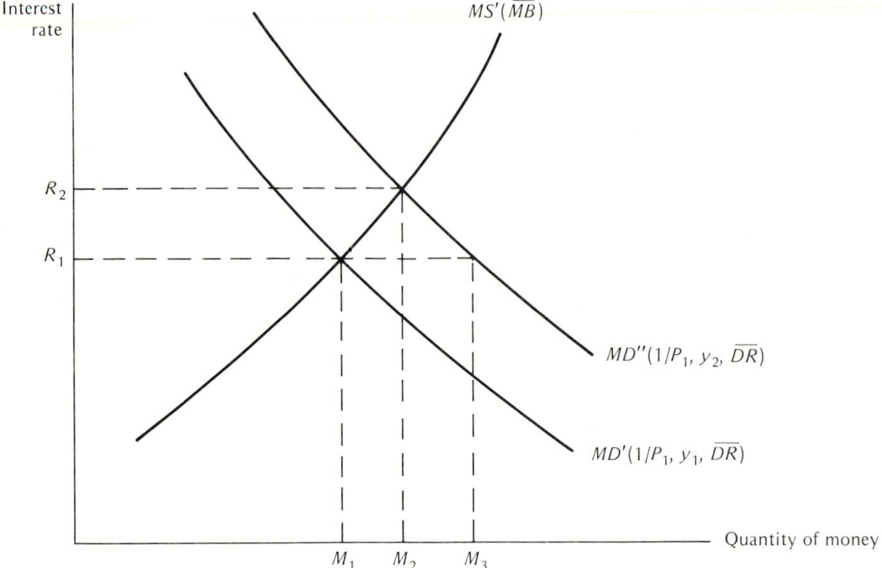

Figure 8.3

Effects of an increase in output on the money market.

Effects of Changes in the Deposit Rate

Consider, for example, the effect of an increase in the deposit rate on the money market for given values of the price level, output, and monetary base. When financial institutions raise the deposit rate in order to induce savers to purchase more of their time and savings deposits, the demand for those money substitutes increases, and the demand for money balances decreases. It is less profitable to hold money balances than substitutes because relative prices change in favor of time and savings deposits. The decrease in the demand reduces the market rate of interest. The decrease in the interest rate decreases the quantity of money supplied. After full adjustment the interest rate is lower, and the quantity of money supplied is less than before. Decreases in the deposit rate yield the opposite results.

Clearly, the market situation after final adjustment is satisfactory to financial institutions as long as the new equilibrium market interest rate (return) at least exceeds the higher deposit rate (cost) by the other marginal costs of financial intermediation plus an acceptable profit margin.

Figure 8.4 illustrates the effects of an increase in the deposit rate on the money market. The initial equilibrium values of the market interest rate R_2, and the quantity of money M_3 are determined by the money supply curve MS' and the money demand curve MD', for given values of the price level P_1, output y_1, deposit rate $\overline{DR}$, and monetary base $\overline{MB}$. An increase in the deposit rate from $\overline{DR}$ to $\overline{\overline{DR}}$ induces savers to substitute time and saving deposits for money bal-

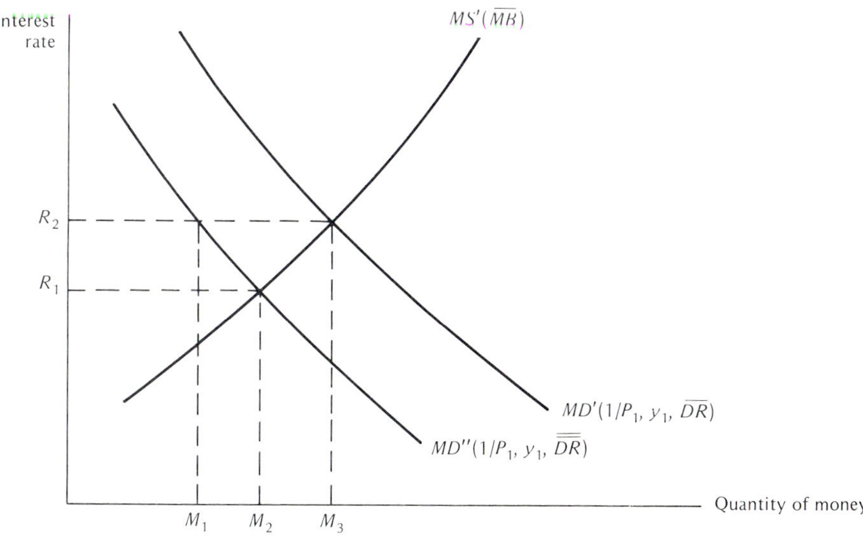

Figure 8.4

Effects of an increase in the deposit rate on the money market.

ances, so that the money demand curve decreases from MD' to MD''. At the initial interest rate R_2, excess money balances are held in asset portfolios, $M_3 - M_1$. As the interest rate falls to eliminate the excess, the banking system and the nonbank public interact to contract the quantity of money supplied. Adjustment continues until the interest rate decreases to R_1 and the quantity of money decreases to M_2.

Effects of Changes in the Monetary Base

Consider, for example, the effect of an increase in the monetary base on the money market for given values of the price level, output, and deposit rate. More specifically, suppose that the Fed increases its demand for government bonds in the open market. As a result, the price of government bonds (a money substitute) increases, and the market interest rate falls as the quantity supplied increases. Fed purchases increase the monetary base (new reserves in the banking system). The lower interest rate increases the quantity of money demanded, as the bank system increases the money supply. After full adjustment the interest rate is lower (given that output and the price level remain fixed) and the quantity of money is greater than before. Decreases in the monetary base yield the opposite results.

Figure 8.5 illustrates the effects of an increase in the monetary base on the money market. The initial equilibrium values of the interest rate R_2 and the quantity of money M_1 are determined by the money supply curve MS' and the money demand curve MD', for given values of the price level P_1, output y_1, the

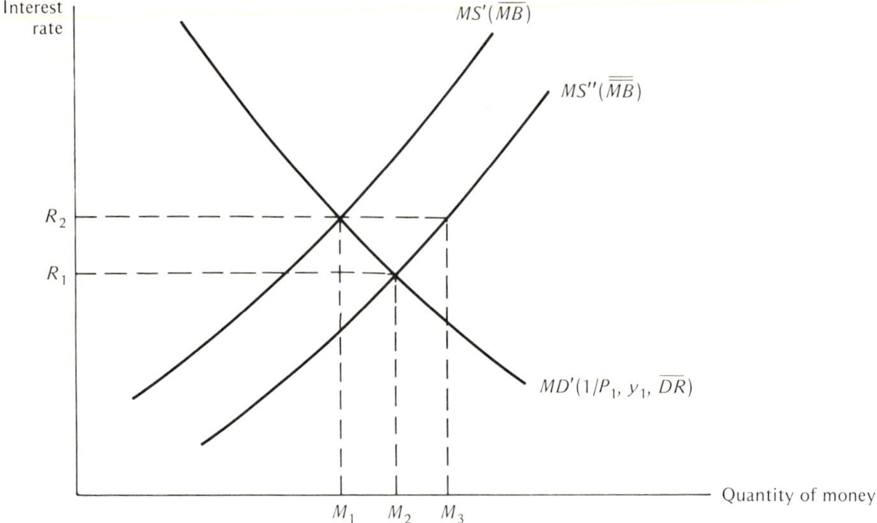

Figure 8.5

Effects of an increase in the monetary base on the money market.

deposit rate $\overline{DR}$, and the monetary base $\overline{MB}$. The Fed purchases of government bonds in the open market increase the monetary base from $\overline{MB}$ to $\overline{\overline{MB}}$, so that the money supply curve increases from MS' to MS''. At the initial interest rate R_2, there is an excess money supply, $M_3 - M_1$. As the interest rate falls to eliminate the excess supply, the nonbank public increases the quantity of money demanded, and banks respond by making loans until the actual excess reserve ratio is at its desired level. Money-market adjustment is the interaction between money suppliers-lenders and money demanders-borrowers that creates additional money in the system. Adjustment continues until the interest rate decreases to R_1 and the quantity of money increases to M_2.

So far we have assumed that changes in the price level, output, deposit rate, and monetary base are independent. And we will continue to think of them that way until we have a model of the economy sufficiently developed to explain their interdependence. In the next chapter we shall see that changes in the monetary base and deposit rate change not only the interest rate and quantity of money in the money market but the price level and output in the output market, and in turn, these changes have feedback effects on money demand in the money market.

8.3 THE LM SCHEDULE

In order for us to more easily interrelate our analysis of the money market with an analysis of the real sector of the economy, we will derive a condensed version of the money market. The condensed version is called the *LM schedule*.

The LM schedule is a locus of possible combinations of interest rates and

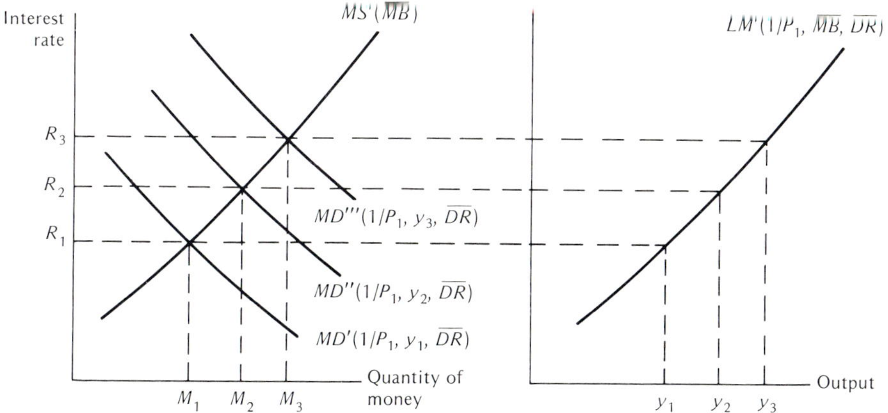

Figure 8.6

The derivation of the LM curve.

levels of output which satisfy the money-market equilibrium condition. The left-hand quadrant of Figure 8.6 represents the money market for a given monetary base $\overline{MB}$, price level P_1, and deposit rate $\overline{DR}$. Varying the level of output from y_1 to y_2 to y_3 shifts the money demand curve from MD' to MD'' to MD''', and we determine the corresponding interest rates R_1, R_2, and R_3 that satisfy the money-market equilibrium condition. The locus of such combinations forms the LM' schedule in the right-hand quadrant.

Changes in the market interest rate and output result in movement along the LM schedule. Changes in the price level, the deposit rate, and the monetary base result in shifts in the LM schedule. Changes in the price level and the deposit rate shift the LM schedule by changing money demand, and changes in the monetary base shift the LM schedule by changing money supply.

Figure 8.7 illustrates the effects of changes in the money demand variables

Figure 8.7

Effects of an increase in the price level and the deposit rate on the LM schedule.

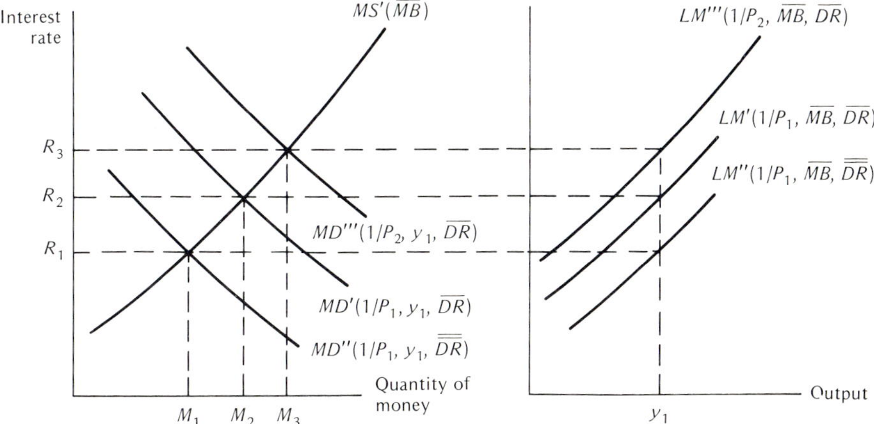

on the LM schedule. Suppose the MS' and MD' curves determine the initial equilibrium values of the interest rate R_2 and quantity of money M_2 for given values of output y_1, the price level P_1, the deposit rate $\overline{DR}$, and the monetary base $\overline{MB}$. Now suppose that the deposit rate increases from $\overline{DR}$ to $\overline{\overline{DR}}$, so that the money demand curve decreases from MD' to MD''. For reasons stated earlier, the results are a decrease in the interest rate from R_2 to R_1 and a decrease in the quantity of money from M_2 to M_1. As shown in the right-hand quadrant, this means that given the level of output y_1, the interest rate is less than before, $R_1 < R_2$. This qualitative result holds for any given level of output, so that an increase in only the deposit rate translates into a rightward shift in the LM schedule from LM' to LM''. Decreases in the deposit rate yield the opposite result. Now suppose that given our initial state of the money market, the price level increases from P_1 to P_2, so that in Figure 8.7 the money demand curve increases from MD' to MD'''. For reasons stated earlier, the results are an increase in the interest rate from R_2 to R_3 and an increase in the quantity of money from M_2 to M_3. This qualitative result holds true for any given level of output, so that the LM schedule shifts leftward from LM' to LM'''.

Figure 8.8 illustrates the effects of changes in the monetary base on the LM schedule. Suppose that the MS' and MD' curves determine the initial equilibrium values of the interest rate R_2 and quantity of money M_1 for given values of output y_1, the price level P_1, the deposit rate $\overline{DR}$, and the monetary base $\overline{MB}$. Now suppose that the monetary base increases from $\overline{MB}$ to $\overline{\overline{MB}}$, so that the money supply curve increases from MS' to MS''. For reasons stated earlier, the interest rate falls from R_2 to R_1, and the quantity of money increases from M_1 to M_2. Since this qualitative result holds for any given level of output, the LM schedule shifts rightward from LM' to LM''. Decreases in the monetary base yield the opposite results.

Figure 8.8

Effects of an increase in the monetary base on the LM schedule.

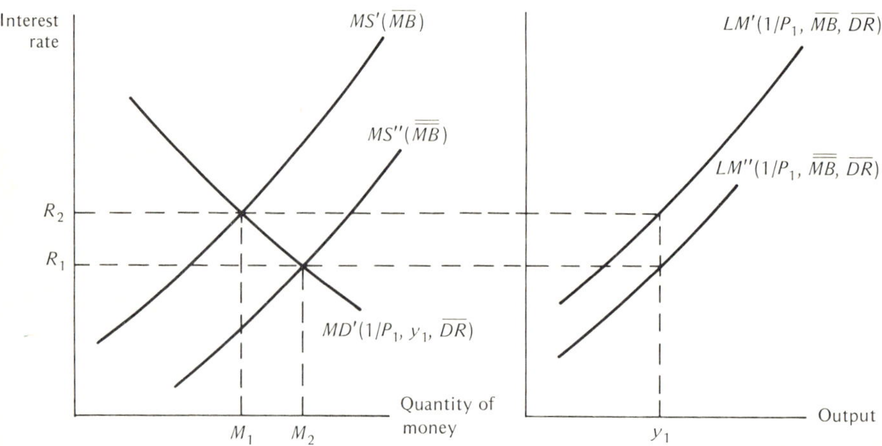

Now that we have a better understanding of how the money market operates when changes in the price level, the deposit rate, output, and the monetary base occur, we must recognize that our money-market model is limited in scope. That is, the model is capable of determining only the market interest rate and the quantity of money that will prevail in the market once full adjustment is complete. It tells us nothing about the determination of the price level, output, and the flows of funds in financial markets. By bringing our earlier analysis of expenditures (Chapter 2) and loanable funds (Chapter 4) together with our analysis of the money market, we will be able to expand the scope of our analysis and examine both the impact of monetary (and intermediary) policy on the money, loanable funds, and output markets simultaneously, and the impact of fiscal and business management policies on these markets as well. Once we have built the basic theoretical structure(s) for the analysis in the next two chapters, the rest of the book will refine our understanding of monetary theory and policy.

SUMMARY NOTES

1. Money-market equilibrium occurs when the quantity of money demanded and the quantity of money supplied are equal.
2. Given the price level, output, the deposit rate, and the monetary base, the money market determines the market interest rate and the equilibrium quantity of money.
3. Adjustment in the money market takes place as the interest rate rises in response to excess money demand and falls in response to excess money supply.
4. The interest rate increases, *ceteris paribus,* as a result of an increase in the price level or output, and falls, *ceteris paribus,* as a result of an increase in the deposit rate or the monetary base.
5. The LM curve shows interest-rate and output combinations that are consistent with equilibrium in the money market.
6. An increase in the price level shifts the LM schedule to the left, and an increase in the deposit rate or the monetary base shifts the LM schedule to the right.

DISCUSSION QUESTIONS

1. In Chapter 7 we report the interest elasticity of money demand. Explain why this elasticity is important in determining the impact of expansionary monetary policy on the money market.
2. In Chapter 6 we report the interest elasticity of money supply. Explain why this elasticity is important in determining the impact of changes in output, the price level, and the deposit rate on the money markets.
3. Show that the more interest-elastic the money supply and demand curves, the more interest-elastic the LM schedule.

4. Explain how the response of the banks and the nonbank public to an increase in money demand by an increase in output increases the quantity of money supplied.

5. Explain why theories of both money supply and demand are required to explain the money creation process.

PART

THREE

MODELS FOR MONETARY ANALYSIS

OUTPUT DEMAND MODEL

By integrating the expenditure theory developed in Chapter 2 and the monetary theory developed in Part Two, we formulate the traditional IS-LM model which can be used to explain the determination of output demand. Changes in the monetary base, the deposit rate, and the real government deficit (changes in real government spending and/or real net taxes) precipitate changes in output demand for any given price level.

Before planned expenditures can be realized, they must be financed. In our analysis the household sector finances its expenditures with its current income. However, the business and government sectors finance their expenditures by borrowing in loanable funds markets. This process was explained in Chapter 4. By integrating loanable funds theory and monetary theory, we formulate the LB-LM model, which can be used to more completely explain the financial activity that underlies the IS-LM analysis of output demand.

In this chapter we begin by using the IS-LM analysis to analyze the impact of policy on output demand. Next, we use the LB-LM model to analyze the financial activity which underlies the impact of policy on output demand. And finally, we explain differences among interest rates on financial assets with emphasis on their term structure.

9.1 IS-LM MODEL

By bringing together the IS schedule developed in Chapter 2 and the LM schedule developed in the previous chapter, we form the basis for an analysis of output demand. In Figure 9.1 the IS' and LM' schedules determine the equilibrium values of the interest rate R_1 and the output y_1 required to realize intended expenditures, or what is traditionally called the quantity of output demanded y_1, for given values of the price level P_1, the real government deficit $\overline{g-t}$, real net taxes $\bar{t}$, the deposit rate $\overline{DR}$, and the monetary base $\overline{MB}$. The IS-LM equilibrium values of the interest rate and quantity of output demanded satisfy both the money-market equilibrium condition and the condition that real saving is sufficient to realize intended real capital investment plus the real government deficit. In other words, money in the system is sufficient to realize intended expenditures.

The IS-LM model determines the quantity of output demanded for any given price level. By varying the price level we can use the IS-LM model to derive the output demand curve. In the upper quadrant of Figure 9.2 the *IS'* and *LM'* schedules determine the quantity of output demanded y_2 for a given price level P_1. If the price level were P_2 so that the LM schedule were *LM''*, the quantity of output demanded would be y_1. By deriving all such price level and output combinations, we derive the output demand curve as shown in the lower quadrant. Clearly, the quantity of output demanded varies inversely with the price level. For example, an increase in the price level increases the demand for money and thereby raises the interest rate. The increase in the interest rate reduces real capital investment and thereby the quantity of output demanded. The decrease in output decreases real consumption and saving. After full ad-

Figure 9.1

IS-LM equilibrium.

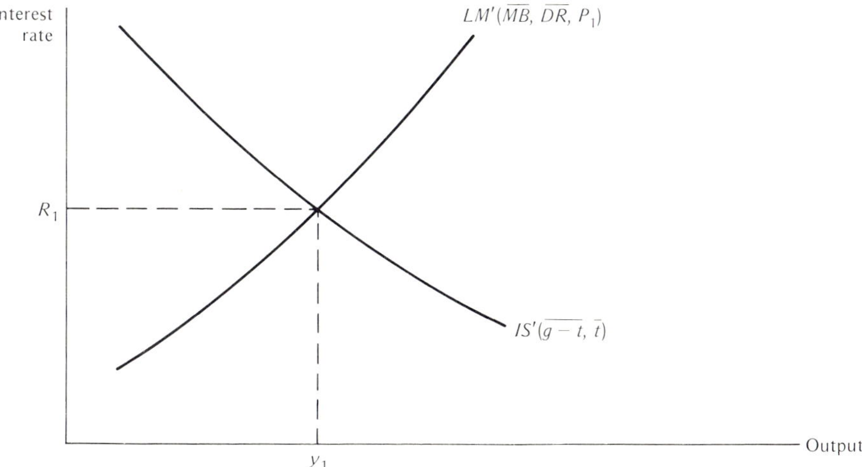

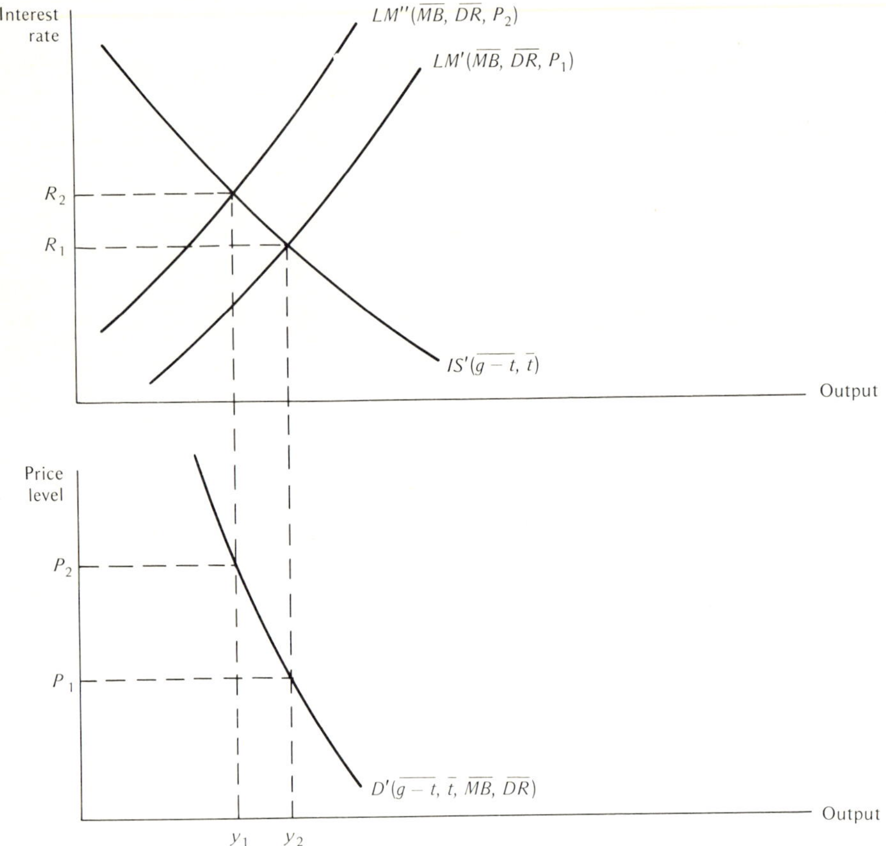

Figure 9.2

Derivation of the output demand curve.

justment, the net effects of the increase in the price level are an increase in the interest rate and quantity of money and a decrease in intended real expenditures and thereby the quantity of output demanded. A decrease in the price level yields the opposite results.

You will notice that in the derivation of the output demand curve we held the deposit rate constant at $\overline{DR}$, the monetary base constant at $\overline{MB}$, the real government deficit constant at $\overline{g-t}$, and real net taxes constant at $\bar{t}$. Only changes in the price level and corresponding changes in the quantity of output demanded are explained by movement along the output demand curve. Changes in output demand or shifts in the output demand curve are explained by changes in the deposit rate, the real government deficit, real net taxes, and the monetary base.

Changes in the real government deficit positively affect output demand for any given price level. For example, suppose the government decides to

real ne
rises, ļ
To son
goverr
hold s
which
for rea
increa
is able
tures.
ment :
funds

For
the mo
attemp
genera
additio
money
net ler
demar
ernme
spend
able ir
consu

Ho
genera
will do
As pec
still m
real sa
marke
ficient
and m
By im
ment

Ou
net go
implie
tity of
contra
borro\
and tł

Fig
rowin

increase the deficit by increasing its expenditures and financing them by borrowing in financial markets, i.e., issuing and offering for sale new government bonds. As a result, the interest rate rises, and intended real capital investment is reduced, i.e., government spending "crowds out" real capital investment. If the *crowding-out effect* is partial, the output required to realize intended real expenditures increases. After full adjustment, the net effects of the increase in the real government deficit for any given price level are an increase in the quantity of money, the interest rate, and the quantity of output demanded. A decrease in the real government deficit yields the opposite results.

Changes in real net taxes as a means of financing expenditures so that the deficit remains unchanged positively affect output demand for any given price level. For example, suppose the government increases real net taxes and spends those taxes for goods and services. The increase in net taxes reduces real consumption and real saving by the household sector. To the extent that real consumption falls, it offsets the expansionary impact of the increase in real government expenditures on output demand. However, because the increase in real government expenditures exceeds the decrease in real consumption by the decrease in real saving, the net effect of this means of financing the increase in expenditures is to increase output demand. The increase in output increases money demand and thereby the market interest rate. As a result, the quantity of money supplied increases, and real capital investment decreases. After full adjustment, the small net effects for any given price level are an increase in the interest rate, the quantity of money, and the quantity of output demanded. A decrease in real net taxes accompanied by an equal decrease in real expenditures yields the opposite results.

Changes in the deposit rate positively affect output demand for any given price level. For example, suppose financial intermediaries increase the deposit rate and not only redirect loanable funds from direct finance but induce money holders to reduce their asset or idle money balances. As a result, more money is drawn into circulation, and the market rate of interest decreases. Subsequently, intended real capital investment increases, and therefore output demand increases. Although the quantity of money supplied decreases with the interest rate, additional real expenditures are possible because formerly idle money balances are activated by the increase in the deposit rate. After full adjustment the net effects for any given price level are a decrease in the interest rate and quantity of money and an increase in the quantity of output demanded. A decrease in the deposit rate yields the opposite results.

Changes in the monetary base positively affect output demand. For example, suppose the Fed purchases government bonds in the open market and thereby increases the monetary base. As a result, the banking system holds excess reserves. This means excess (potential) money supply, so that the interest rate falls. At the lower interest rate borrowers increase the quantity of money demanded, intended real capital investment increases, and the quantity of output demanded increases. After full adjustment, the net effects of the

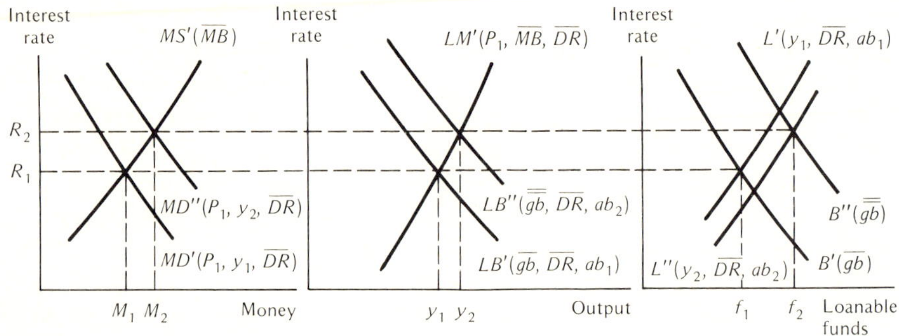

Figure 9.5
Increase in real government net borrowing.

The LM' and LB' schedules determine the initial equilibrium values of the market interest rate R_1 and level of output y_1 that are consistent with the initial equilibrium values of the quantity of loanable funds f_1 and the quantity of money M_1 for given values of the price level P_1, the monetary base $\overline{MB}$, real government net borrowing $\overline{gb}$, the deposit rate $\overline{DR}$, and the real value of additional money balances ab_1. An increase in government real net borrowing for purposes of expenditure from $\overline{gb}$ to $\overline{\overline{gb}}$ increases the demand for loanable funds from B' to B'' and thereby shifts the LB schedule from LB' toward LB''. This creates excess demand in the loanable funds market. As the market interest rate rises toward R_2 to eliminate excess demand, the quantity supplied of loanable funds increases. As real net borrowing increases, planned expenditures are realized. Output increases and shifts the loanable funds supply curve toward L''.

The increase in output also increases money demand from MD' to MD''. The increase in the market interest rate eliminates excess money demand by increasing the quantity of money supplied to M_2 and increases additional money balances from ab_1 to ab_2. Thus, the loanable funds supply curve shifts to L'', and the LB schedule shifts to LB''. After full flow adjustment, the quantity of loanable funds increases to f_2. After full stock adjustment through loanable funds market flows, the LM' and LB'' schedules show that the interest rate R_2 and level of output y_2 satisfy both money-market and loanable funds markets equilibrium conditions.

Impact of Monetary Policy

Expansionary monetary policy implemented, for example, by an increase in the monetary base increases the money supply and thereby creates an excess supply of money. As the interest rate falls, the banking system interacts with the nonbank public in the lending and borrowing activity described by the money creation process. This continues until money supply just equals money demand.

Stock adjustment in the money market implies flow adjustment in the loanable funds market. The increase in the money supply increases the real value of additional money balances created by the banking system. This increases the supply of loanable funds and thereby creates an excess supply of loanable funds. As the interest rate falls to eliminate the excess supply, the quantity demanded of loanable funds (real net borrowing) increases. As flow adjustment continues, borrowed funds are used to realize planned expenditures, and therefore output increases. The increase in output increases real saving, which further increases the supply of loanable funds This process continues until net lending just equals the net borrowing required to realize planned expenditures. After full money stock and flow of funds adjustments, the quantity of money in the system is sufficient to generate the funds required to realize planned expenditures.

Our analysis of expansionary monetary policy imposed by an increase in the monetary base indicates that its impact on the financial system implied by the model is to decrease the market interest rate and increase output, the quantity of money, and the quantity of loanable funds. Contractionary monetary policy has the opposite effects.

Figure 9.6 illustrates the impact of an increase in the monetary base. The LM' and LB' schedules determine the initial equilibrium values of the market interest rate R_2 and level of output y_1 that are consistent with the equilibrium values of the quantity of money M_1 and the quantity of loanable funds f_1 for given values of the price level P_1 the monetary base $\overline{MB}$, real government net borrowing $\overline{gb}$, the deposit rate $\overline{DR}$, and the real value of additional money balances ab_1. An increase in the monetary base increases the money supply from MS' to MS'' and thereby shifts the LM schedule from LM' to LM''. For any given

Figure 9.6

Increase in the monetary base.

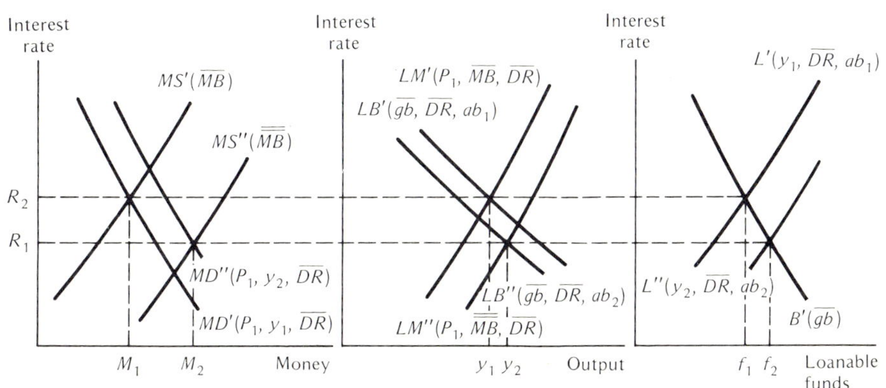

price level, the real value of additional money balances also increases from ab_1 to ab_2 and thereby increases the supply of loanable funds from L' toward L''. The LB schedule shifts from LB' to LB''. As the market interest rate falls toward R_1 to eliminate excess supply of loanable funds, the quantity demanded of loanable funds increases. As borrowed funds are used to realize planned expenditures, output increases and therefore real saving increases. Savers further increase the supply of loanable funds toward L''. After complete flow adjustment, the quantity of loanable funds is f_2. The increase in output also increases money demand from MD' toward MD''. After full stock adjustment, the quantity of money is M_2.

Impact of Financial Intermediation

An increase in the deposit rate causes savers to substitute the time and savings deposit liabilities of financial institutions for primary securities. Funds are redirected from direct finance into indirect finance. More importantly, the increase in the deposit rate causes savers to dishoard by substituting the highly liquid and relatively risk-free time and savings deposits of financial institutions for money balances. Thus, the supply of loanable funds (real net lending) increases and creates excess supply in the loanable funds market. Also, net dishoarding decreases money demand and creates excess supply in the money market. As the market rate falls, the quantity of loanable funds demanded (real net borrowing) for planned real capital investment increases, and the quantity of money supplied decreases (through a decrease in the base money multiplier). Thus, excess supplies in the loanable funds and money markets decrease. As planned real capital investment is realized, output increases. The increase in output increases both real saving and money demand. The increase in money demand reverses the decrease in money demand due to the increase in the deposit rate, so that total money demand decreases by less than it would have had there been no change in output. Savers supply surplus funds (real net lending) in loanable funds markets. Thus, the positive effect of the increase in the deposit rate on loanable funds supply is reinforced by the positive output effect.

After full adjustment of the market interest rate and level of output, loanable funds supply (real net lending) is sufficient to satisfy the demand for loanable funds (real net borrowing), and money supply is sufficient to realize money demand, so that real net hoarding is zero. By implication real saving is sufficient to realize planned real capital expenditures plus the real deficit.

This analysis of financial intermediation indicates that an increase in the deposit rate will decrease the market interest rate and increase output, the quantity of loanable funds, and the quantity of money.

Figure 9.7 illustrates the impact of changes in the deposit rate on the financial system implied by our model when all other exogenous variables remain fixed. The LB' and LM' schedules determine the initial equilibrium values of the market interest rate R_2 and level of output y_1 which are consistent with the ini-

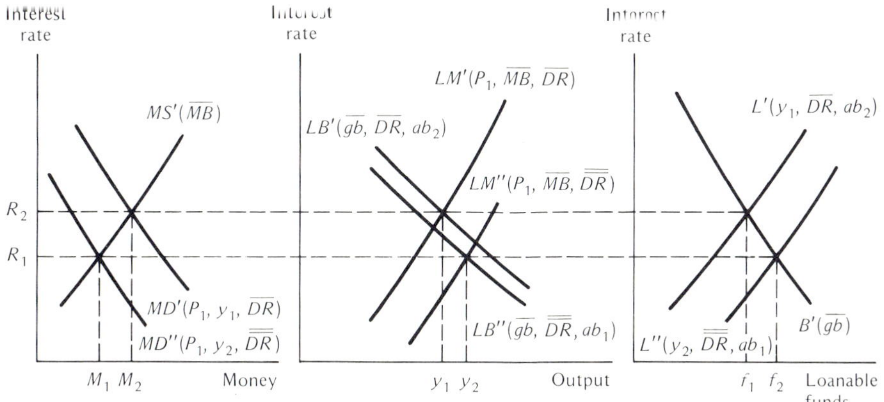

Figure 9.7
Increase in the deposit rate.

tial equilibrium values of the quantity of loanable funds f_1 and the quantity of money M_2. An increase in the deposit rate from $\overline{DR}$ to $\overline{\overline{DR}}$ causes savers to dishoard, and loanable funds supply increases from L' toward L'' and thereby shifts the LB schedule from LB' toward LB''. Moreover, money demand decreases from MD' toward MD'' and thereby shifts the LM schedule from LM' toward LM''. As the market interest rate falls toward R_1 to eliminate excess supplies in the loanable funds and money markets, the quantity of loanable funds demanded for planned real capital investment increases toward f_2 and the quantity of money supplied decreases toward M_1, and therefore the real value of additional money balances decreases from ab_2 to ab_1. As planned real capital investment is realized, output increases toward y_2. The increase in output increases money demand (or stops it from falling below MD'') and increases real saving. As savers supply additional funds (real net lending) in the loanable funds market, loanable funds supply increases further toward L''.

After full adjustment, the system implied by our model is in both flow and stock equilibrium, where the equilibrium values of the interest rate R_1, output y_2, the quantity of loanable funds f_2, and the quantity of money M_1 are determined.

A Note on the IS-LM and LB-LM Models

Clearly, the LB-LM model is an alternative to the IS-LM model. Both can be used to analyze output demand. They differ in perspective only. The former concentrates on the financial activity which constrains the plans for expenditures of the business and government sectors. The latter concentrates on output and real expenditures activity where financial activity is implicit. The LB and IS schedules differ only by the amount of real net hoarding. When money supply equals money demand, real net hoarding is zero. Thus, where the LB and LM schedules intersect, real net hoarding is zero. And when both of these conditions hold, real saving equals planned real capital investment expenditures plus the real government deficit. Thus, when LB-LM equilibrium holds, IS-LM equilibrium holds, and vice versa; or IS-LB-LM equilibrium holds after full adjustment of the system implied by each model. This simply means that after full adjustment, money, loanable funds, and output-real expenditures equilibrium conditions hold simultaneously. Money is sufficient to generate the funds required to realize planned purchases of output for any given price level.

9.3 DIFFERENCES IN INTEREST RATES

So far, we have assumed that financial assets are such close substitutes that we may speak of *the* market rate of interest. However, in actual financial markets we observe differences in the interest rates on different financial assets. Several factors account for these differences. First, interest rates vary directly with default risk. The greater the lender's perception of default risk, the higher the interest rate charged (default risk premium) to cover potential losses due to default. Long-term assets are generally associated with higher default risk than short-term assets. Second, interest rates vary inversely with the marketability of an asset. Marketability of an asset depends on the volume of exchange in secondary markets and related costs of transfer and information. The greater the volume exchanged in the secondary markets and the lower the associated costs, the greater an asset's marketability and the lower the interest rate. Short-term assets are generally more marketable than long-term assets. Third, interest rates vary directly with taxes paid on earnings from assets. Taxes vary from asset to asset, and from wealth holder to wealth holder depending on the income bracket. Because almost all long-term assets are subject to lower effective taxes, their pretax yields are lower than pretax yields on short-term assets.

A fourth difference that has been given considerable attention is *term to maturity*. Term to maturity refers to the length of time between the issuance of an asset and its maturity. The pattern of interest rates on assets with properties that are similar in all respects but term to maturity is called the *term structure of interest rates*. *Yield curves* measure term structure and show the relationship between market interest rates and term to maturity.

Figure 9.8 shows the yield curves that reflect the three basic term structures of interest rates at any point in time. Yield curve *A* indicates that long-term rates are less than short-term rates. Yield curve *B* indicates that there is no difference between short- and long-term rates. Yield curve *C* indicates that long-term rates are greater than short-term rates.

Two basic theories are used to determine the term structure of interest rates. One is called the *expectations theory*. There are two variations of this theory, namely, the *unbiased expectations theory* and the *liquidity premium theory*. The other basic theory is the *segmentation theory*.

The unbiased expectations theory is based on the argument that the long-

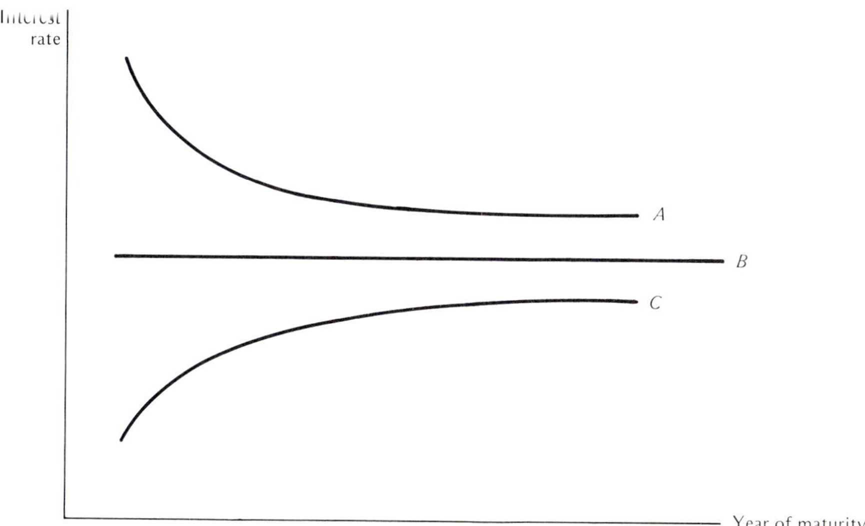

Figure 9.8

Yield curves.

term rate is the expected rate on the short-term rate. If all interest income is reinvested until the asset matures, the interest earned is viewed as the expected return on a series of consecutive short-term assets, the maturities of which sum to the maturity of the long-term asset. If transaction costs are ignored, individuals will maximize expected return on wealth portfolios without regard to the individual asset maturities. Wealth holders are indifferent to holding short- and long-term securities and consider only differences in expected rates. Thus, short- and long-term assets are substitutes, and funds flow freely between short- and long-term markets to where expected rates are higher. In the process, wealth holders alter the relative interest rates (and prices) and equalize the interest return on all assets for the same holding period.

If short-term rates are expected to be below current short-term rates, then long-term rates (averages of short-term rates) will be below current short-term rates, and the yield curve will slope downward and to the right, as shown by yield curve A in Figure 9.8. If short-term rates are expected to increase above current short-term rates, long-term rates will be above the current short-term rates, and the yield curve will slope upward and to the right, as shown by yield curve C in Figure 9.8. If short-term rates are not expected to change, the yield curve is horizontal, as shown by yield curve B in Figure 9.8.

The liquidity premium theory is the same as the unbiased expectations theory except that it postulates that a wealth holder's expectations of future interest rates are biased upward by the amount equal to the premium paid to lenders for giving up liquidity. The liquidity premium arises because lenders and borrowers have different preferences. Lenders are risk averters that prefer capital certainty, i.e., they are more concerned with recovering the purchase price of the asset at any time before maturity. Because the longer the term to maturity, the greater an asset's price fluctuation (for given changes in R), and therefore the greater the probability of loss (to which lenders are most sensitive), the longer the term to maturity the lower the capital certainty. On the other hand, borrowers are concerned more with access to a steady flow of financing at certain interest rates than with capital certainty. Thus, lenders prefer short-term lending and borrowers prefer long-term borrowing. To induce lenders to lend long-term, borrowers pay a *liquidity premium*. The liquidity premium varies directly with the capital uncertainty of lenders and therefore with term to maturity. Because of the liquidity premium, the yield curve is generally upward-sloping, differing from yield curve C in Figure 9.8 by the amount of liquidity premium, i.e., the yield curve in the liquidity premium case is more steeply sloped than the one in the unbiased expectations case by the amount of the increasing liquidity premium. Only when expected short-term rates decline by an average amount that exceeds the liquidity premium will the yield curve slope downward.

The market segmentation theory takes into account the transactions cost, i.e., the cost of search, transfer, and information, and the risks associated with forecast error in predicting interest rates. Since greater costs are associated with holding a wide variety of assets, both short- and long-term wealth holders may maximize expected return by holding assets with the same maturity (in the absence of large interest-rate differences). Thus, markets are segmented, with some wealth holders strictly in short-term markets and others strictly in long-term markets. Unlike the expectations theories, the segmentation theory states that wealth holders are sensitive to maturity and that expected interest rates are not equal, i.e., substitution of long-term and short-term assets is very limited. The yield curve reflects the segmented supplies and demands in the various markets. If demand forces dominate supply more in short-term markets than in long-term markets, interest rates will be higher for short-term assets than for long-term assets, i.e., the yield curve will be downward-sloping. Likewise, if supply forces dominate demand more in short-term markets than in long-term markets, the yield curve will be positively sloped. And if neither supply nor demand forces dominate, the yield curve will be horizontal. The important point is that unlike the expectation theories, the segmentation theory states that short- and long-term markets are unrelated, and funds do not flow through the maturity spectrum. They cannot because of segmented markets.

Near cyclical peaks (economic expansion is ending), short-term rates exceed long-term rates, i.e., the yield curve is negatively sloped. Near cyclical troughs (economic expansion is beginning), long-term rates exceed short-term rates, i.e., the yield curve is positively sloped. Midway in the cycle, the rates equal, i.e., the yield curve is horizontal. Since all three patterns of behavior are consistent with each theory, choosing among the theories is difficult. Although the unbiased expectations theory is viewed with skepticism because it ignores transactions cost and it postulates that wealth holders can and will predict short-term rates and hold the forecast without allowance for error (its expectations are held with certainty), the evidence strongly favors the expectations theories.* The evidence also suggests that a liquidity premium exists. At cyclical peaks short-term rates exceed long-term rates by less than the long-term rates exceed short-term rates at cyclical troughs. Empirical evidence also supports the segmentation theory because there are abrupt increases and declines in weekly and daily interest rates for different maturities when large new issues of assets are marketed. This suggests that funds do not flow immediately through the maturity spectrum. The mixed empirical evidence suggests that a general theory that includes parts of both expectations and segmentation theories is appropriate. There is substitution between markets, which affects relative interest rates and tends to equalize interest return. However, equalization is not complete because of differences among lenders' and borrowers' attitudes toward risk.

SUMMARY NOTES

1. The IS and LM curves, taken together, describe a model of output demand. For given values of the real government deficit, real net taxes, the monetary base, and the deposit rate, the quantity of output demanded varies inversely with the price level.
2. The interest rate and output demand are increased by an increase in the real government deficit/or a reduction in real net taxes. An increase in the monetary base or an increase in the deposit rate lowers the interest rate and increases output demand.
3. The LB and LM curves may also be used to construct a model of output demand. Unlike the IS-LM model, the LB-LM model gives explicit recognition to the role of the loanable funds market.
4. The comparative statics properties of both models are the same.
5. The term structure of interest rates shows the relationship between yield and term to maturity. Two theories of the term structure are the expectations theory and the segmentation theory.

DISCUSSION QUESTIONS

1. Using the IS-LM model, trace the effects of a decrease in the required reserve ratio for demand deposits on output demand.
2. Why do equal increases in real government spending and real net taxes have a positive impact on output demand?

---

*R. A. Kessel, *The Cyclical Behavior of the Term Structure of Interest Rates* (New York: National Bureau of Economic Research, 1965); B. G. Malkiel, *The Term Structure of Interest Rates: Expectations and Behavior Patterns* (Princeton: Princeton University Press, 1966) and *The Term Structure of Interest Rates: Theory, Empirical Evidence and Application* (New York: McCaleb-Seiler Publishing Co., 1970).

3. Using the complete LB-LM model, trace the effects of an increase in the monetary base. Now trace the effects of an increase in the monetary base in the context of the IS-LM model. Do the two results differ? Should they?

4. Using the LB-LM model as a frame of reference, describe verbally the sequence of events that results from an increase in net government borrowing (for the purpose of increasing expenditures relative to taxes).

5. Why will financing an increase in real government spending by increases in net taxes have less impact on output demand than if the expenditures are financed by borrowing in financial markets?

6. Actually real net saving, which depends positively on output and negatively on real net taxes, is the appropriate constraint on real net lending. For simplification purposes, we have used only the output argument in the net lending function. Real net taxes were assumed to be fixed. Given changes in real net taxes, the assumption would lead to inconsistency in interrelating the IS–LM and LB–LM analyses. Include real net taxes in the net lending function and examine the effects on financial markets of changes in real net taxes. Also show that the impact of such changes on output and the interest rate, given no change in the real government deficit, gives consistent results in both the IS–LM and LB–LM models.

OUTPUT MARKET MODEL

So far our analysis has assumed that the price level is exogenous. Given recurring problems with inflation, this assumption is unrealistic. By bringing together our theory of output demand and a theory of output supply, we are able to explain more completely the market rate of interest, output, the quantities of money and loanable funds, and the price level. Moreover, we are able to explain more completely the impact of monetary, fiscal, intermediary, *and* business management policies on both financial and output markets.

In this chapter we begin by developing a simplified theory of output supply. Next, we use the theories of output supply and demand to explain the determination of the price level and output in the output market. Afterward, we explain the impact of monetary, fiscal, intermediary, and business management policies on both money and output markets. Finally, we develop the arguments that are used to evaluate the effectiveness of monetary and fiscal policies on the interest rate, output, and the price level.

10.1 OUTPUT SUPPLY

In view of recent problems with inflation, the assumption that the price level is an exogenous variable in our analysis of the economy is unrealistic. In order to explain the price level, we must extend the IS-LM or output demand model to include a theory of output supply, which along with output demand determines the price level. The extension provides us with the tools that are necessary if we are to more completely analyze the relationships between the money and output markets.

Since an analysis of output supply and related factor input markets is beyond the scope of this text, we will present only a simplified theory of output supply.* We assume that output is produced in competitive markets under conditions of increasing marginal costs. Business firms maximize profit with given amounts of fixed factor inputs (capital and technology) and given factor input prices by hiring variable factor inputs (labor and raw materials) and producing the quantity of output for which the marginal cost just equals the marginal revenue (or price in competitive markets). This is the profit-maximizing position of business firms who take the output market–determined price as given. To produce less output would mean that marginal revenue would exceed marginal cost, and it would be more profitable to produce additional output. To produce more output would mean that marginal cost would exceed marginal revenue, and it would be more profitable to produce less output. Only when marginal cost equals marginal revenue are firms maximizing profit.

Given the profit-maximizing and increasing marginal cost assumptions, the quantity of output supplied varies directly with the price per unit of output for given amounts of fixed factor inputs and prices of factor inputs, i.e., the short-run output supply curve is positively sloped. Changes in the amount of fixed factor inputs and/or factor input prices change the price per unit of output supplied. Since changes in the amount of any fixed factor input (e.g., capital or land) positively affect the productivity of variable input factors per unit of output supplied, they inversely affect marginal costs (and price) per unit of output supplied for given factor input prices. For example, an increase in plant and equipment increases the productivity of labor and thereby reduces the marginal cost (and price) per unit of output supplied for given factor input prices. Also, changes in any of the given factor prices directly affect marginal cost (and price) per unit of output supplied for given amounts of factor inputs used in the production process. For example, an increase in factor input prices (such as the prices of capital, labor, or oil) increases the marginal cost per unit of output supplied for given amounts of fixed factor inputs used in the production process. Decreases in the amount of fixed factor inputs and factor prices yield the opposite results.

---

*For a more complete aggregate analysis of output supply, see F. Zahn, *Macroeconomic Theory and Policy* (Englewood Cliffs, N.J.: Prentice-Hall, 1975), chap. 7.

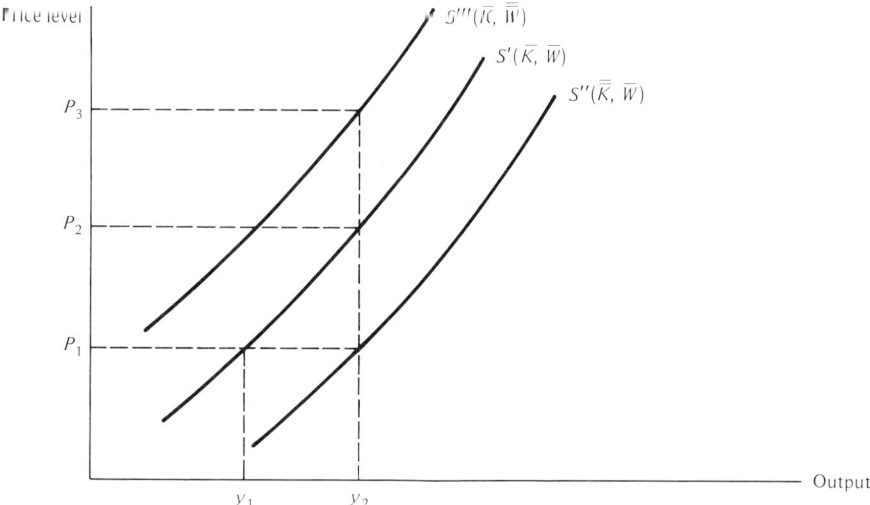

Figure 10.1

Output supply.

Figure 10.1 illustrates the qualitative results just explained. The S' output supply curve shows the positive relationship between the quantity of output supplied and the price per unit of output supplied for given amounts of fixed factor inputs $\overline{K}$ and factor input prices $\overline{W}$. An increase in the price per unit of output from P_1 to P_2 increases the quantity of output supplied from y_1 to y_2. An increase in the amounts of fixed factor inputs from $\overline{K}$ to $\overline{\overline{K}}$ reduces the price per unit of output supplied for given factor input prices $\overline{W}$, so that for any given level of output supplied, the price firms are willing to accept decreases, i.e., the output supply curve shifts rightward from S' to S''. For example, given the quantity of output supplied y_2, the price per unit of output supplied decreases from P_2 to P_1. Stated differently, given the price P_1, the quantity of output supplied increases from y_1 to y_2. An increase in the prices of factor inputs from $\overline{W}$ to $\overline{\overline{W}}$ increases the price per unit of output supplied for given amounts of fixed factor inputs $\overline{K}$, so that for any given level of output supplied, the price firms are willing to accept increases, i.e., the output supply curve shifts leftward from S' to S'''. For example, given the quantity of output supplied y_2, the price per unit of output supplied increases from P_2 to P_3.

The output supply curve is positively sloped except at the level of output associated with full employment of the factor inputs in the production process. At full-employment output the output supply curve is vertical, i.e., increases in the price per unit of output do not prompt business people to increase the quantity of output supplied. It is not that business people are unwilling to increase output. It is that they are constrained by available factor inputs. Given factor input prices and the quantity of fixed factor inputs, all available factor inputs are being employed in the production process.

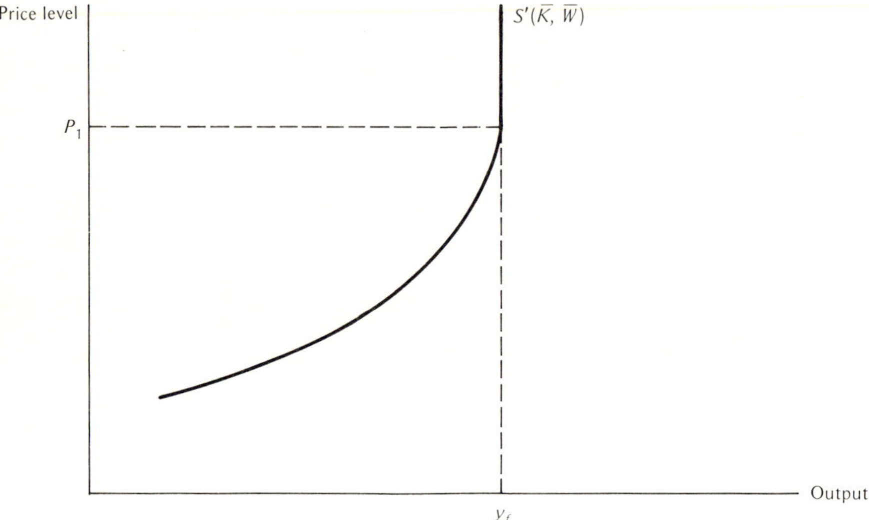

Figure 10.2
Output supply and full employment.

Figure 10.2 shows the output supply curve just explained. The quantity of output supplied below the full-employment level y_f varies directly with the price level for reasons already stated. At full employment, increases in the price level above P_1 result in negligible changes in the quantity of output supplied because resources are fully employed.

10.2 OUTPUT MARKET

By bringing together the theories of output supply and demand, we are able to explain the determination of the price level and output in the output market. Figure 10.3 shows the equilibrium values of the price level P_2 and output y_2 determined by the output supply curve S' and output demand curve D' for given values of the quantities of fixed input factors $\overline{K}$, factor input prices $\overline{W}$, the real government deficit $\overline{g-t}$, real net taxes $\overline{t}$, the deposit rate $\overline{DR}$, and the monetary base $\overline{MB}$. At (y_2, P_2) suppliers and demanders of output agree on the quantity of output to be exchanged in the market and the price level at which it is exchanged. At any other price, some who wish to buy (demanders) or some who wish to sell (suppliers) at those prices cannot. If the price level is above its equilibrium value, say $P_3 > P_2$, output supply exceeds output demand, $y_3 - y_1$. At that price level firms are producing more output than demanders are willing to purchase, and therefore firms are accumulating excess inventories. In response, firms will reduce production and lower the price level they are willing to accept in the market in order to bring actual amounts of inventories in line with desired levels. Thus, the quantity of output supplied decreases from y_3 to

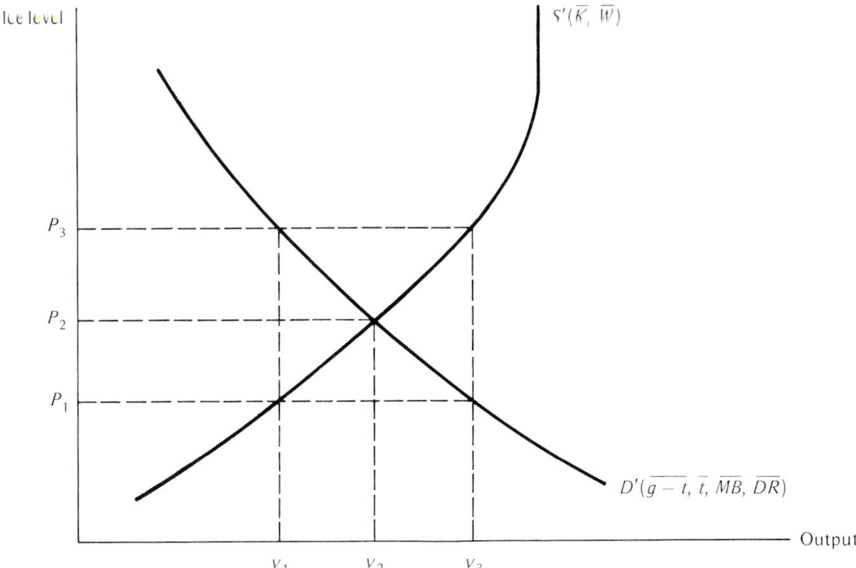

Figure 10.3
Output market equilibrium.

y_2, and the quantity demanded increases from y_1 to y_2.* If the price level is below its equilibrium value, say $P_1 < P_2$, output demand exceeds output supply, $y_3 - y_1$. At that price firms are producing less output than demanders are willing to purchase, and therefore inventories are being depleted. In response, firms will increase production to restore the desired level of inventories. Thus the price level increases from P_1 to P_2, the quantity of output supplied increases from y_1 to y_2, and the quantity demanded decreases from y_3 to y_2.†

Changes in the amount of fixed factor inputs, factor input prices, the real government deficit, real net taxes, the deposit rate, and the monetary base displace output market equilibrium and call into play market forces which affect both the price level and output. Changes in the supply variables indicate the impact that business firms and other owners of factor inputs, particularly labor, have on the output market, while changes in the demand variables indicate the impact that the fiscal authorities, financial intermediaries, and the Fed have on the output market.

In the next section of this chapter we will illustrate the impact that business firms and other owners of factor inputs, financial intermediaries, the government, and the Fed have on money and output markets.

---

*If prices are maintained and only quantity is reduced as firms reduce inventories, then output will fall from y_3 to $y_1 < y_2$.

†If prices are sticky upward, shortages will persist and less output will be supplied than the equilibrium level.

10.3 IMPACT OF POLICY

The Impact of Business Policy

Figure 10.4 illustrates the impact of the policy of business firms and other owners of factor inputs on the system implied by our output market model. For given values of the quantities of fixed factor inputs $\overline{K}$, factor input prices $\overline{W}$, real government deficit $\overline{g-t}$, real net taxes $\overline{t}$, deposit rate $\overline{DR}$, and monetary base $\overline{MB}$, it is the money supply curve MS', money demand curve MD', output demand curve D', and output supply curve S' that determine the initial equilibrium values of the interest rate R_1, price level P_1, quantity of money M_1 and output y_2. The IS-LM model links the money market to the output market through output demand.

Changes in the supply variables, either the quantity of fixed factor inputs or factor input prices, change output supply in the manner and for reasons already stated. Suppose in Figure 10.4 that factor input prices increase, e.g., wages or

Figure 10.4

Impact of business policy.

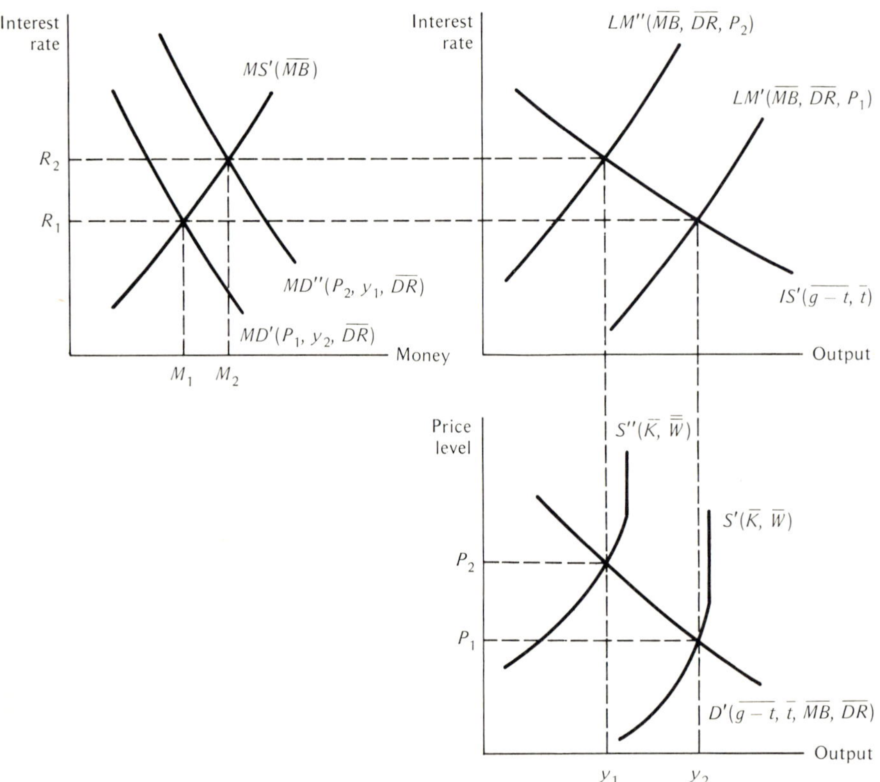

the price of oil increases, from $\overline{W}$ to $\overline{\overline{W}}$, so that business firms raise their price per unit of output supplied, i.e., the output supply curve shifts leftward from S' to S''. As a result, excess output demand is created in the output market at price P_1. As demanders bid up the price level to P_2, the quantity demanded of output decreases from y_2 to y_1. Given that the increase in the price level and decrease in output increase nominal income, the money demand curve increases from MD' to MD''. This creates excess money demand, and as demanders of money bid up the interest rate, the quantity of money supplied increases from M_1 to M_2. After full adjustment, the interest rate and price level are higher, and real saving generated by output supply and real capital investment generated by output demand are lower. Decreases in the amount of fixed factor inputs have a similar qualitative impact. Decreases in factor input prices or increases in the amount of fixed factor inputs yield the opposite results.

The Impact of Fiscal Policy

Suppose the government intends to increase its deficit by increasing its real expenditures and financing the increase in the deficit by borrowing in financial markets. By increasing the demand for loanable funds, the government creates excess demand in the loanable funds market. As a result, the market rate of interest rises. Banks increase the quantity of money supplied, and savers dishoard idle money balances and increase real net lending. Thus, the government obtains the money required to finance its intended real deficit expenditures. In turn, when intended real expenditures are realized, the demand for current output increases. As a result, the price level increases, and business firms increase the quantity of output supplied. After full adjustment in both money and output markets, the interest rate, the price level, the quantity of money, and output are higher than before. Although the increase in the deficit stimulates the economy, it does so by "crowding out" real capital investment (because the interest rate rises). Thus, fiscal policy changes the composition of output demand. In the case of expansionary fiscal policy, real consumption and real government spending substitute for real capital investment. Moreover, fiscal policy changes the composition of asset portfolios. In the case of expansionary fiscal policy, other financial assets (government bonds) substitute for money balances and real capital assets (because the interest rate rises). Contractionary fiscal policy yields the opposite results.

Figure 10.5 illustrates the impact of expansionary fiscal policy on the money and output markets. For given values of the fixed factor inputs $\overline{K}$, factor input prices $\overline{W}$, real government deficit $\overline{g - t}$, real net taxes $\overline{t}$, deposit rate $\overline{DR}$, and monetary base $\overline{MB}$, it is the money supply curve MS', money demand curve MD', output demand curve D', and output supply curve S' that determine the initial equilibrium values of the price level P_1, market interest rate R_1, quantity of money M_1, and output y_1. The IS' and LM' schedules link the money and out-

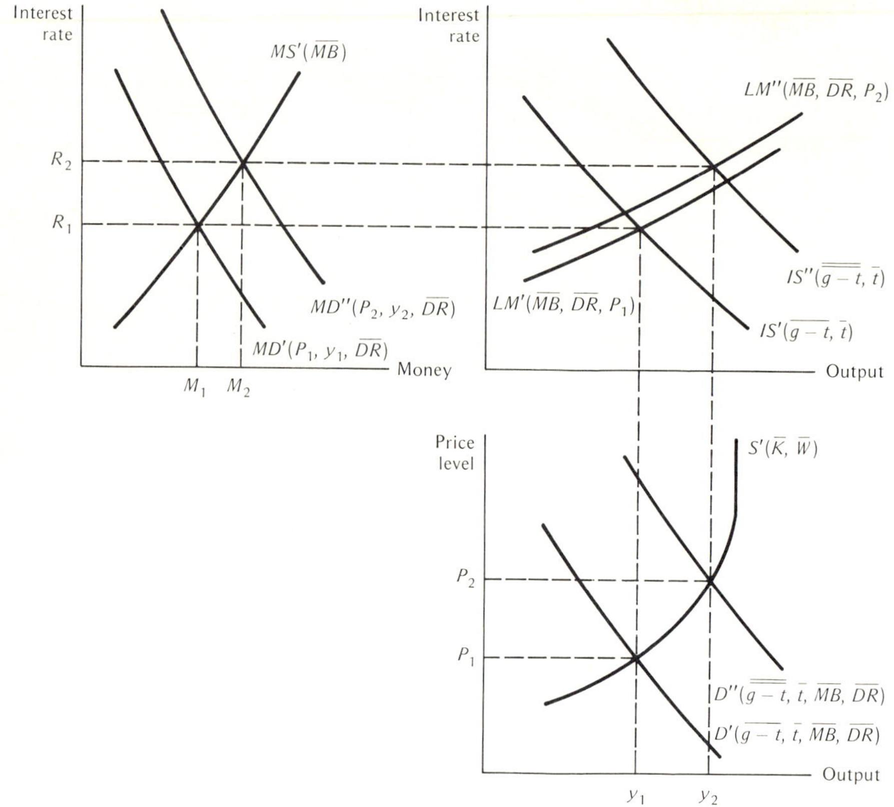

Figure 10.5
Impact of fiscal policy.

put markets. Suppose the real government deficit increases from $\overline{g-t}$ to $\overline{\overline{g-t}}$, so that the IS schedule shifts rightward from IS' to IS''. Government borrowing increases the interest rate, and asset holders substitute government bonds for money balances. Government spending increases output demand from D' to D'', and as the price level increases from P_1 to P_2, so that the LM schedule shifts leftward from LM' to LM'', business firms increase the quantity of output supplied from y_1 to y_2. The increases in the price level and output increase money demand from MD' to MD'', and the quantity of money supplied increases from M_1 to M_2 as the interest rate increases from R_1 to R_2.

Our analysis is a Keynesian explanation of the impact of fiscal policy. In general, monetarists frown on this analysis. Although they accept the initial results as essentially correct, they believe that they are only temporary. They argue that since government spending "crowds out" real capital investment, the increase in government spending does not have a permanent effect on output demand. Only changes in the fixed factor inputs (capital and technology), introduced primarily through real capital investment, can permanently change output. Thus, they view fiscal policy as a destabilizing influence on money and output markets which tends to inhibit permanent economic growth.

The Impact of Intermediary Policy

Changes in the deposit rate by financial intermediaries constitute intermediary policy in our model. Suppose, for example, financial intermediaries decide to increase the deposit rate in order to attract more funds into financial markets. Generally financial institutions increase the deposit rate following an increase in the market rate of interest due to either expansionary fiscal or contractionary monetary policy (although an increase in the interest rate could occur when factor input prices increase or the amount of fixed factor inputs decreases). The flow of funds into financial intermediaries results from reductions in holdings of money balances and primary securities (direct finance) in asset portfolios. Therefore, money demand decreases, and, as the interest rate falls, the quantity of money supplied decreases. In turn, financial intermediaries make the additional funds available in financial markets to investors, who are induced to borrow by the lower interest rate. The increase in real capital investment increases output demand, the price level, and the quantity of output supplied. After full adjustment in both money and output markets, the interest rate and quantity of money are lower and the price level and output are higher than before. Decreases in the deposit rate yield the opposite results.

The increase in the deposit rate stimulates the economy by increasing the use of existing money balances in the system, i.e., it makes existing money balances more efficient and thereby increases real capital investment. It changes the composition of asset portfolios in favor of private sector assets, and it changes the composition of output demand in favor of capital investment.

Figure 10.6 illustrates the impact of financial intermediation on the money and output markets. For given values of the monetary base $\overline{MB}$, deposit rate $\overline{DR}$, real government deficit $\overline{g-t}$, real net taxes $\bar{t}$, factor input prices $\overline{W}$, and amount of fixed factor inputs $\overline{K}$ in the production process, it is the output supply curve S', output demand curve D', money supply curve MS', and money demand curve MD' that determine the initial equilibrium values of the price level P_1, output y_1, interest rate R_1, and quantity of money M_1. An increase in the deposit rate from $\overline{DR}$ to $\overline{\overline{DR}}$ decreases the money demand curve and shifts the LM schedule rightward. The interest rate falls and increases real capital investment, so that output demand increases from D' to D''. The price level rises from P_1 to P_2, and output increases from y_1 to y_2. The increases in the price level and output have feedback effects on the money market by increasing money demand and partially offsetting the decrease in money demand due to the increase in the deposit rate. The net effect on money demand of the increase in the deposit rate is shown by a net decrease in the money demand curve from MD' to MD''. Accordingly, the net effect on the LM schedule of the increases in the price level and deposit rate is shown by a shift from LM' to LM'', which results in a decrease in the interest rate from R_2 to R_1.

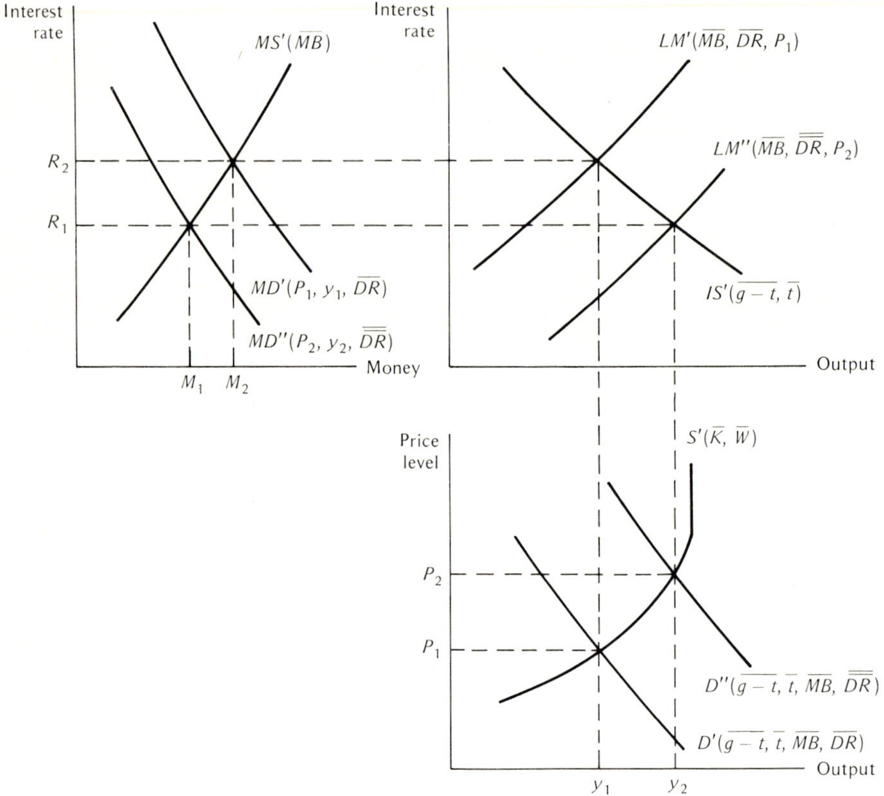

Figure 10.6

Impact of financial intermediation.

The Impact of Monetary Policy

Monetary policy is implemented primarily by changes in the monetary base. Consider, for example, an increase in the monetary base by the Fed through open market purchases of government bonds. As a result, banks find themselves with excess reserves above their desired level. As the interest rate falls to eliminate the excess, business firms increase expenditures for real capital investment. Thus, output demand increases, the price level rises, and the quantity of output supplied increases. After full adjustment, the interest rate is lower and the quantity of money, the price level, and output are higher than before. Decreases in the monetary base yield the opposite result.

Monetary policy works through the private sector to stimulate the economy. Increases in the monetary base change the composition of output in favor of real consumption and real capital investment and the composition of asset portfolios in favor of private sector assets.

Figure 10.7 illustrates the effects of an increase in the monetary base on the money and output markets. For given values of the monetary base $\overline{MB}$, deposit

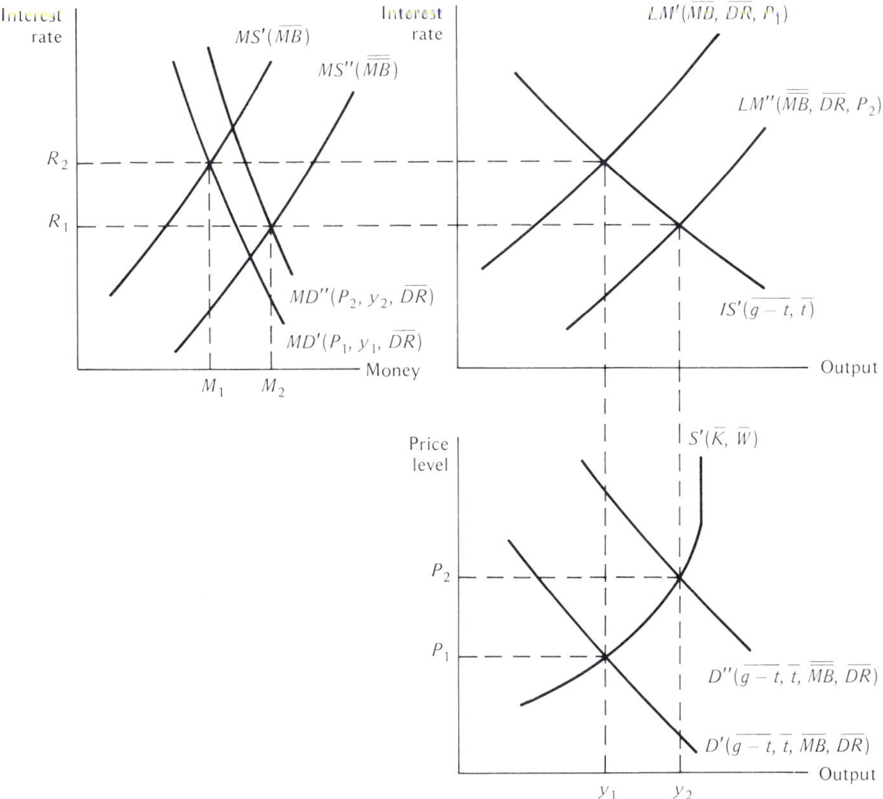

Figure 10.7

Impact of monetary policy.

rate $\overline{DR}$, real government deficit $\overline{g-t}$, real net taxes $\bar{t}$, factor input prices $\overline{W}$, and amount of fixed factor inputs $\overline{K}$, it is the money supply curve, MS', money demand curve MD', output supply curve S', and output demand curve D' that determine the initial equilibrium values of the price level P_1, output y_1, interest rate R_1, and quantity of money M_1. An increase in the monetary base increases the money supply curve from MS' to MS'' and shifts the LM schedule rightward. The interest rate falls and increases real capital investment, so that output demand increases from D' to D''. The price level increases from P_1 to P_2, and output increases from y_1 to y_2. Both of these increases feed back to the money market and increase money demand from MD' to MD''. The net impact of the increase in the monetary base and the price level on the LM schedule is to shift it rightward from LM' to LM'', so that the interest rate decreases from R_2 to R_1.

In our analysis since *both* output and price level show a net change after full adjustment, money demand does not vary directly and proportionally with the price level. We have given the Keynesian explanation of the impact of expansionary monetary policy. The monetarist approach differs. Monetarists argue that increases in the monetary base bring about proportional increases in the price level, so that although nominal income rises, real income or output remains unchanged. They contend that although the short-run influence of an increase in the money supply is to decrease the interest rate through the *liquidity effect,* monetary adjustments do not have a lasting effect on the equilibrium interest rate. Monetary adjustment has a temporary effect on the interest rate and therefore on output through an increase in real capital investment. But once output and the price level rise, the interest rate returns to its former level through the *price effect* on demand for money, and output falls back to its former level. Thus, only the price level rises in proportion to the increase in the money stock.* Moreover, they argue that the interest rate may increase beyond its former level. During periods of rising prices, lenders include a premium in the interest charged to offset the losses in purchasing power that they expect rising prices to bring about. Thus, the premium can push market interest rates above their former levels through a *price anticipation* effect.†

Monetarists get their results because they assume full employment of resources where Keynesian analysis refers to less than full employment. There are many other differences, and we will return to the issues again in a later chapter.

10.4 EFFECTIVENESS OF MONETARY AND FISCAL POLICY

The primary policy variables used to manage output demand are government spending and net taxes, and the monetary base. Changes in these variables are the primary means of implementing fiscal and monetary policies, respectively. The sensitivity of the quantity of money demanded, the quantity of money supplied, and real capital investment to changes in the interest rate and the sensitivity of output supply to changes in the price level play important roles in the evaluation of the effectiveness of output demand management.

Interest-Rate Elasticities of Money Supply and Demand

The greater the interest elasticity of money demand and/or supply, the greater the interest elasticity of the LM schedule. The more elastic the LM schedule, the greater the impact of changes in real government spending and/or real net taxes on output demand. In Figure 10.8 the *LM'* schedule is less interest-elastic than *LM"*. Suppose, for example, an increase in the real government deficit shifts

---

*W. E. Gibson, "Interest Rates and Monetary Policy," *Journal of Political Economy,* May/June 1970, pp. 431–455.

†M. Friedman, "Factors Affecting the Level of Interest Rates," *Savings and Residential Financing,* 1968 Conference Proceedings, United States Savings and Loan League, May 1968; W. P. Yohe and D. Karnosky, "Interest Rates and Price Level Changes, 1952–69," *Review,* Federal Reserve Bank of St. Louis, December 1969, p. 18.

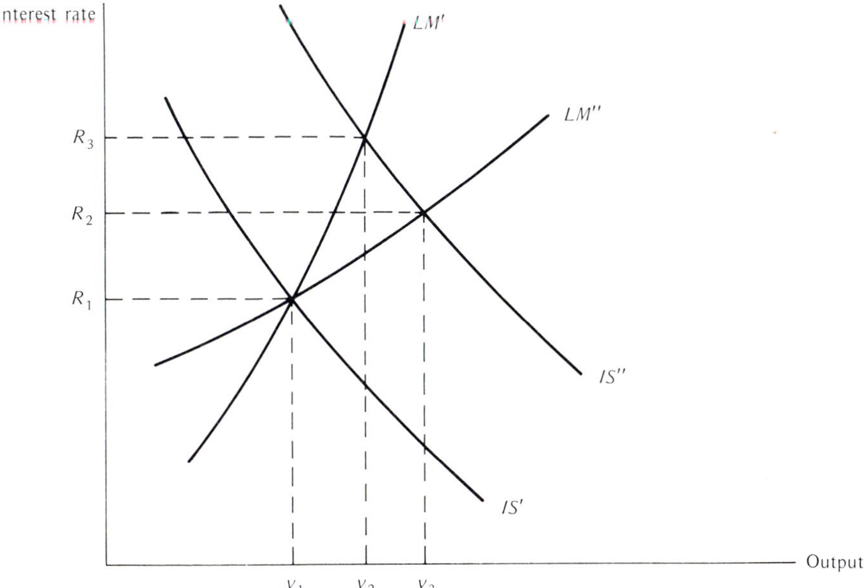

Figure 10.8
Effectiveness of fiscal policy.

the IS schedule from *IS'* to *IS"*. Clearly, the extent of the impact on the interest rate and output demand depends on the extent of the increase in the deficit, i.e., how far to the right the IS schedule shifts. But the interest elasticity of the LM schedule is important as well. Along the *LM'* schedule the interest rate increases by more and output demand by less than along the *LM"* schedule. This means that the closer money is to being a substitute for interest-bearing assets held in the asset portfolios of banks and other holders of capital and financial assets, the greater the impact of fiscal policy on output demand. The empirical evidence cited in Chapter 7 suggests that although money demand and money supply are each interest-inelastic, together they make the LM schedule somewhat less inelastic.

The extreme cases of a perfectly interest-elastic and a perfectly interest-inelastic LM schedule have been used to illustrate the relative effectiveness of monetary and fiscal policy on output demand over the business cycle. The former, called the *liquidity trap case,* was mentioned by Keynes and was made popular by the Keynesians in their efforts to discredit monetary policy. If the interest rate falls so low that asset holders hold only money balances in asset portfolios, the money demand curve becomes perfectly interest-elastic and therefore the LM schedule is perfectly interest-elastic. It was believed that this condition held in a depression and explained why increases in the monetary base which shift the LM schedule rightward would not decrease the interest rate, stimulate real capital investment, and thereby increase output demand.

Under these conditions the only solution to economic depression was thought to be an increase in the real government deficit, which directly increased output demand.

The other extreme case is called the *classical case*. If the interest rate increases so much that asset holders hold only interest-bearing assets (no idle money balances) in asset portfolios, the money demand curve becomes perfectly interest-inelastic, and therefore the LM schedule is perfectly interest-inelastic. Given this condition, changes in the deficit which shift the IS schedule would have no effect on output demand. Such changes would only change the interest rate. It is argued that this condition most closely holds in a boom economy at the peak of the business cycle. Thus, fiscal policy is ineffective, and only monetary policy can change output demand.

The two extreme cases are illustrated in Figure 10.9. Part *A* shows the liquidity trap condition. At interest rate R_1, money demand is perfectly interest-elastic, and therefore the *LM'* schedule is perfectly interest-elastic. An increase in the money supply shifts the LM schedule to *LM"*. Given the *IS'* schedule, there is no effect on output demand. All the increase in the quantity of money is held in asset portfolios. However, an increase in the real government deficit shifts the IS schedule to *IS"* and thereby increases output from y_1 to y_2. Thus, only fiscal policy is effective in changing output demand when the economy is caught in the liquidity trap.

Part *B* of Figure 10.9 shows the classical case. Above interest rate R_3, the money demand curve is perfectly interest-inelastic at the quantity of money that is held strictly for transaction requirements. The *LM'* schedule is vertical at the level of output demand y_1. An increase in the deficit which shifts the IS schedule from *IS'* to *IS"* results in no change in output demand. It remains at y_1, and only the interest rate increases to R_4. However, an increase in money supply shifts the LM schedule from *LM'* to *LM"* and increases output demand along *IS'* to y_2. Thus, only monetary policy is effective in changing output demand when the economy is caught in the classical trap.

Both of these conditions are extremes that probably have never existed. But to the extent that the initial condition of the economy leans toward one extreme or the other, monetary or fiscal policies are relatively more or less effective in changing output demand.

Interest Elasticity of Real Investment Expenditures

The greater the interest elasticity of the real capital investment demand, the greater the interest elasticity of the IS schedule. The more interest-elastic the IS schedule, the greater the impact of given changes in the monetary base. In Figure 10.10 the *IS'* schedule reflects a less interest-elastic IS schedule than *IS"*. Suppose, for example, an increase in the monetary base shifts the LM schedule from *LM'* to *LM"*. Clearly, the extent of the impact on the interest rate and output demand depends on the extent of the increase in the monetary base. But

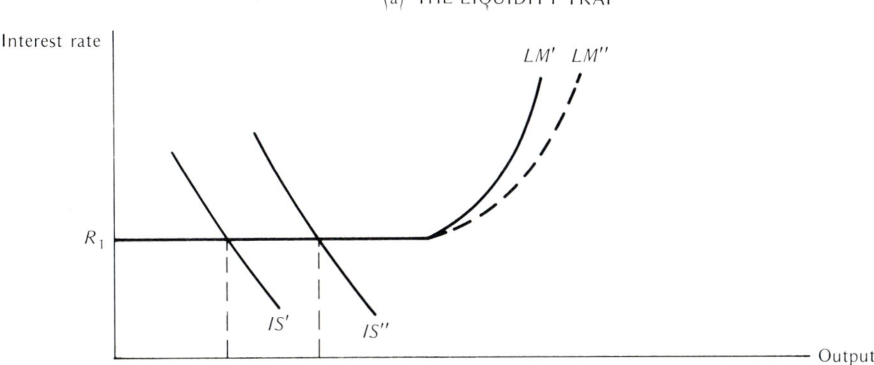

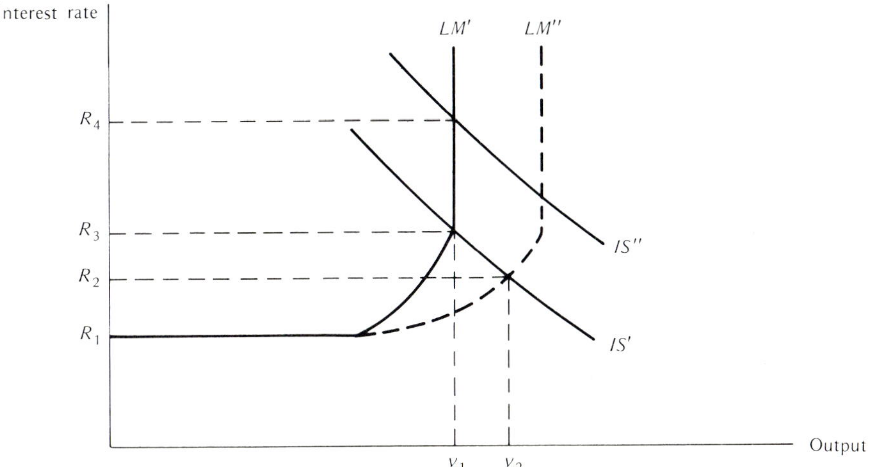

Figure 10.9

Interest elasticity extremes in the LM curve.

the interest elasticity of the IS schedule is important as well. Along the *IS'* schedule the interest rate falls by more and output increases by less than along the *IS"* schedule. The empirical evidence suggests that real capital investment (particularly in residential construction) is sensitive to changes in the interest rate, but not sufficiently so to make the IS schedule highly interest-elastic.* This result lends support to the argument that monetary policy is relatively ineffective in changing output demand.

---

*M. K. Evans, *Macroeconomic Activity: Theory Forecasting and Control* (New York: Harper and Row, 1969), pp. 133–142 and 220; and chap. 18 of this book.

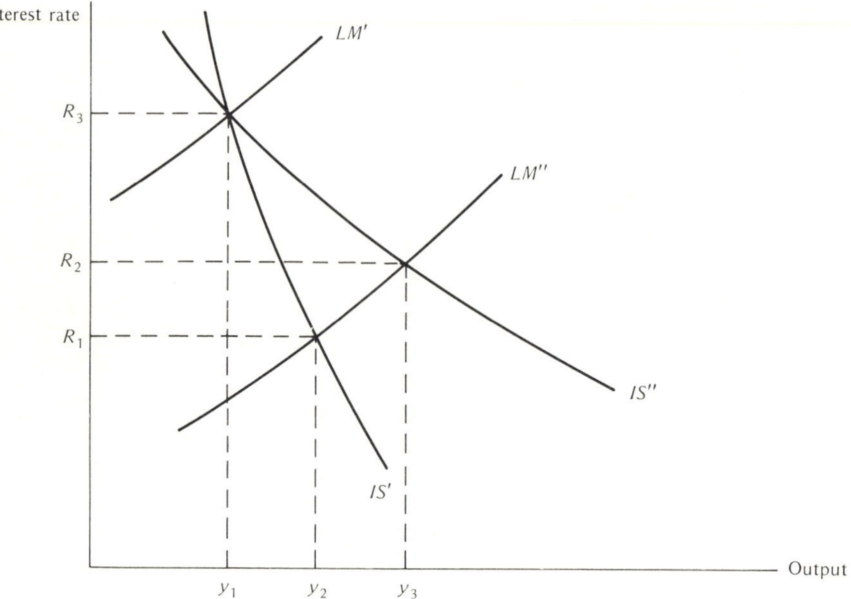

Figure 10.10

Effectiveness of monetary policy.

However, further empirical work suggests that there are other channels of monetary policy that are more important than the interest-rate effect on real capital investment. These include the direct and indirect wealth effects on real consumption.*

Wealth Effects†

The *wealth effect* is the influence of the wealth of the private sector of the economy on private sector expenditures and saving. The concept of net private wealth is often used in discussing the wealth effect because it is believed that only changes in net private wealth produce a wealth effect. Net private wealth is defined as the sum of capital assets held by the private sector and *outside* financial assets for which there is no offsetting liability in the private sector. Out-

---

*M. J. Hamburger, "Interest Rates and the Demand for Consumer Durable Goods," *American Economic Review*, December 1967, pp. 1131–1153; C. Wright, "Saving and the Rate of Interest," in A. C. Harberger and M. J. Bailey (eds.), *The Taxation of Income from Capital* (Washington, D. C. : The Brookings Institution, 1969), pp. 275–299; F. de Leeuw and E. M. Gramlich, "The Channels of Monetary Policy," *Federal Reserve Bulletin*, June 1969, pp. 472–491; F. Modigliani, "Monetary Policy and Consumption: Linkages via Interest Rate and Wealth Effects in the FMP Model," *Consumer Spending and Monetary Policy: The Linkages* (Boston: Federal Reserve Bank of Boston, 1971), pp. 9–84.

†For an excellent summary of the wealth effects of monetary and fiscal policies, see L. H. Meyer, "Wealth Effects and the Effectiveness of Monetary and Fiscal Policies," *Journal of Money, Credit and Banking*, November 1974, pp. 481–502.

side financial assets are government bonds and the monetary base. Some economists argue that certain *inside* financial assets, namely demand deposits, should be included in the definition of wealth.* They argue that demand deposits are not liabilities to banks in the usual sense of the word because there is no obligation to pay interest. Even if we consider the principal a liability, banks can attract demand deposits at zero cost and purchase other earning assets. Thus, the value of a bank to its owners increases dollar for dollar with the increase in demand deposits less reserve requirements.†

The decision to spend or save is based on the principle of maximizing expected return, in the form of either utility (for the consumer) or profit (for asset portfolio managers), subject to the constraint on available resources. Aggregate resources can be defined in real terms as the sum of current real income and real wealth (with or without inside financial assets as appropriate). Real expenditures vary directly with current real income and real wealth where the propensity to spend and save out of wealth is presumed to be small relative to the propensity to consume and save out of current income.‡

There are two types of wealth effects: *direct* wealth effects resulting from changes in wealth owned by the private sector, and *indirect* wealth effects resulting from changes in real private wealth through changes in the interest rate and the price level. To the extent that monetary and fiscal policies change wealth by direct or indirect means, they influence expenditures. We have examined to some extent the direct effects of monetary and fiscal policies on the interest rate, price level, expenditures, quantity of money, and output. Now we will go a step further and examine the subsequent wealth effects of monetary and fiscal policies. In so doing we will further evaluate the effectiveness of monetary and fiscal policies.

Given the outside definition of wealth, an open market operation yields no direct change in net wealth and therefore no wealth effect. Open market operations involve the exchange of one outside asset (the monetary base) for another (government bonds). Thus, there is no change in net wealth. Bond-financed fiscal policy directly alters the net wealth of the private sector by changing the quantity of government bonds held by the private sector. This means that private sector expenditures are directly affected. For example, expansionary policy increases the private sector's holdings of government bonds, so that expenditures increase. In summary, monetary policy yields no direct net wealth effect, whereas bond-financed fiscal policy yields a direct wealth effect which reinforces its effectiveness in either stimulating or contracting economic activity. There is one qualification to the latter: Whether or not bond-financed fiscal

---

*See B. Pesek and T. Saving, *Money, Wealth and Economic Theory* (New York: Macmillan, 1967).

†D. Patinkin, *On the Nature of the Monetary Mechanism*, Wicksell Lectures, 1967 (Stockholm: Almquist and Wicksell, 1967).

‡F. Modigliani and R. Brumberg, "Utility Analysis and the Consumption Function: An Interpretation of Cross-Section Data," in K. Kurihara (ed.), *Post Keynesian Economics* (London: Allen and Unwin, 1955).

policy yields a wealth effect depends on the extent to which the private sector takes into account the increase in future taxes required to service the debt. If the private sector discounts future taxes by creating an expected tax liability for themselves, this liability of the private sector offsets (at least partially) the additional government bonds held by the private sector. This means that the net wealth effect of bond-financed fiscal policy is at least partially offset.*

If we include demand deposits in our definition of wealth, open market operations yield a direct wealth effect because they alter the amount of demand deposits in the system. Changes in demand deposits positively affect wealth held by the private sector and thereby positively affect expenditures.

Questions about the direct wealth effect depend on the appropriate definition of wealth (inclusive or exclusive of demand deposits) and the extent to which the private sector discounts future tax liabilities. These questions lack supportive empirical evidence. In recent years, the indirect wealth effects have received considerable attention. As stated earlier, they are induced by changes in the price level and the market rate of interest.

Certain components of private wealth, namely the monetary base and government bonds, are fixed in nominal terms. For example, the currency holdings of the nonbank public are not adjusted automatically for changes in the price level. Demand deposits also fall into that category, if we choose to include them in the definition of wealth. Given fixed nominal values, the real values of government bonds, the monetary base, and demand deposits vary inversely with the price level. Therefore the stock of real wealth varies inversely with the price level. To the extent that both fiscal and monetary policy affect the price level, they indirectly affect real wealth.

Changes in the market rate of interest also produce indirect effects on real wealth. If bonds have a fixed coupon and variable price like most government and corporate bonds, the market interest rate varies inversely with the bond price as already shown in Chapter 7. This means that decreases in the interest rate result in increases in the present value of bonds and thereby real wealth.†

In the following examples we define real wealth to include demand deposits and assume that taxpayers only partially discount future tax liabilities. Then both monetary and fiscal policies have direct wealth effects on the private sector's expenditures and saving. Also, changes in the price level and the interest rate are variables which explain indirect wealth effects, where real wealth varies inversely with the price level and inversely with the interest rate. These wealth effects help to evaluate the effectiveness of monetary and fiscal policy. They can be introduced into our model by modifying our theory of real saving

---

*D. Patinkin, *On the Nature of the Monetary Mechanism*, Wicksell Lectures, 1967 (Stockholm: Almquist and Wicksell, 1967).

†If the bond has a variable coupon and fixed price, changes in the interest rate have no effect on the value of bonds and thereby real wealth.

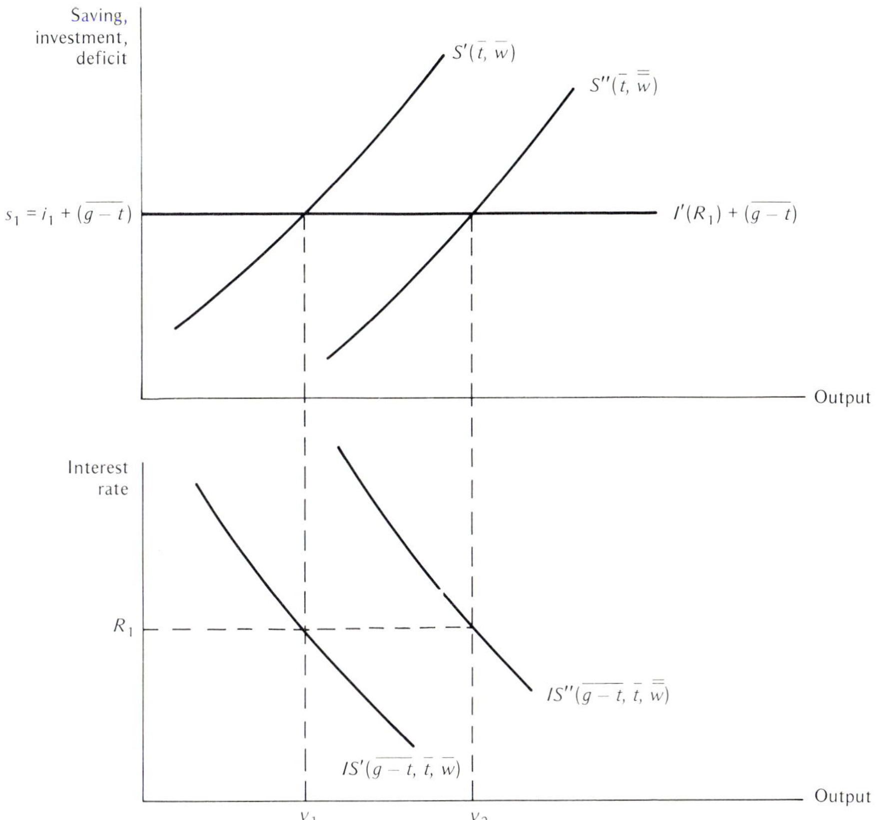

Figure 10.11
Wealth effect.

to include not only current output as a determinant but also real wealth. Real saving varies directly with current output and, because savers attempt to maintain real wealth, real saving varies inversely with real wealth.

Figure 10.11 shows the effect of a direct and/or an indirect increase in real wealth on real saving and thereby the IS schedule. An increase in real wealth from $\bar{w}$ to $\bar{\bar{w}}$ decreases the level of real saving from S' to S'', and the IS schedule increases from IS' to IS''. For any given interest rate R_1, real government deficit $\overline{g - t}$, and real net taxes $\bar{t}$, output increases from y_1 to y_2 because of the wealth effect. Decreases in real wealth yield the opposite results.

Figure 10.12 shows the impact of bond-financed fiscal policy on the interest rate, price level, and output when wealth effects are considered. The IS' and LM' schedule determines the initial equilibrium values of the interest rate R_1 and output y_1 for given values of the monetary base $\overline{MB}$, deposit rate $\overline{DR}$, real government deficit $\overline{g - t}$, real net taxes $\bar{t}$, stock of real wealth $\bar{\bar{w}}$, and price level P_1, which is determined by the output supply curve S' and output demand

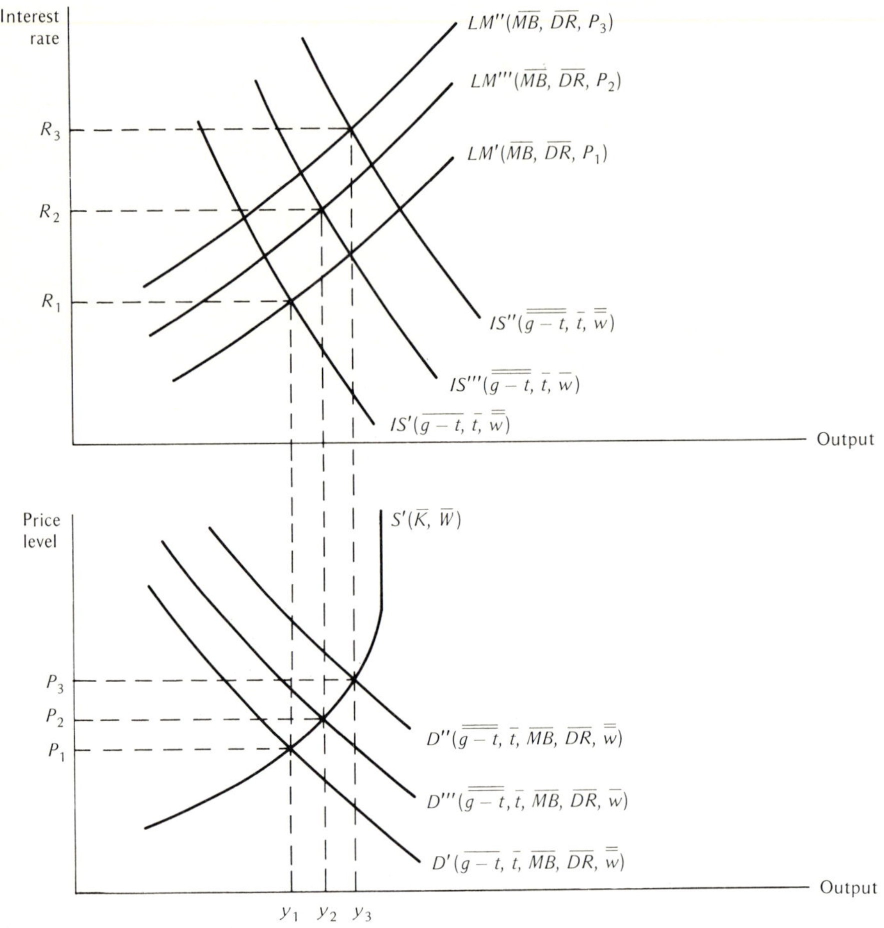

Figure 10.12

Expansionary fiscal policy and wealth effects.

curve D'. An increase in the deficit from $\overline{g-t}$ to $\overline{\overline{g-t}}$ shifts the IS schedule to IS'' and the output demand curve to D''. With no real wealth effect, the interest rate increases to R_3, output increases to y_3, and the price level increases to P_3. With a real wealth effect, real wealth increases directly because outside financial assets (government bonds) are injected into private asset portfolios. However, the increase in the price level and in the interest rate indirectly reduces real wealth. The net change in real wealth depends on whether the direct increase in real wealth outweighs the indirect decrease in real wealth through the increase in the interest rate and price level. Although the results are ambiguous, assume that the effects of the interest-rate and price-level changes dominate and that the value of real wealth decreases from $\overline{\overline{w}}$ to $\overline{w}$. Thus, savers increase their average propensity to save, i.e., increase real saving per unit of output, to restore real wealth. As a result the IS schedule shifts leftward to IS''', and the output demand curve shifts leftward to D'''. After full adjustment, the wealth effect on real expenditures and real saving lowers the interest rate to $R_2 < R_3$, output to $y_2 < y_3$, and the price level to $P_2 < P_3$. Thus, the wealth effects reduce the expansionary impact of bond-financed fiscal policy on output demand.

Figure 10.13 shows the impact that expansionary monetary policy has on the interest rate, price level, and output when wealth effects are taken into account. The IS' and LM' schedules determine the initial equilibrium values of the interest rate R_3 and output y_1 for given values of the monetary base $\overline{MB}$, the deposit rate $\overline{DR}$, the real government deficit $\overline{g-t}$, real net taxes $\overline{t}$, real wealth $\overline{w}$

Figure 10.13

Expansionary monetary policy and wealth effects.

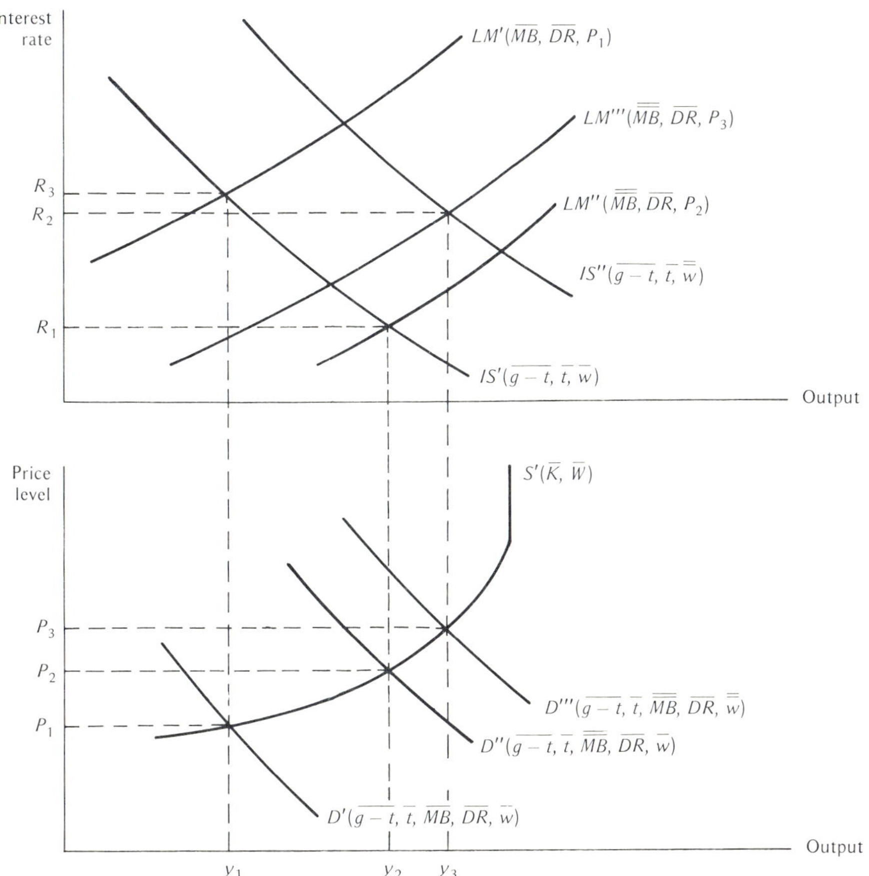

and the price level P_1, which is determined by the output supply curve S' and output demand curve D'. An increase in the monetary base from $\overline{MB}$ to $\overline{\overline{MB}}$ and a resulting increase in the price level from P_1 to P_2 shifts the LM schedule rightward from LM' to LM'' and the output demand curve from D' to D''. In addition to the increase in the price level, the interest rate falls from R_3 to R_1, and output increases from y_1 to y_2 in the absence of a wealth effect. However, if real wealth is defined to include demand deposits, real wealth directly increases, and the decrease in the interest rate indirectly increases real wealth. The price-level change indirectly decreases real wealth. Assuming that the direct and interest-rate effects outweigh the price-level effect, real wealth increases from $\overline{w}$ to $\overline{\overline{w}}$ and lowers the average propensity to save (increases the average propensity to spend). The IS schedule shifts rightward from IS' to IS'', and the output demand curve increases from D'' to D'''. As a result the price level rises to $P_3 > P_2$ so that the LM schedule shifts from LM'' to LM'''. The interest rate increases to $R_2 > R_1$, and output increases to $y_3 > y_2$. Thus, wealth effects reinforce the impact of expansionary monetary policy on output demand.

Under the assumptions made above, wealth effects are supportive of the monetarists' position that monetary policy leads to only temporary changes in the rate of interest. As indicated in Figure 10.13, the initial impact of expansionary monetary policy is to lower the interest rate. After the supportive wealth effects occur, the interest rate has a tendency to rise toward its former level. Clearly, output increases if less than full employment is assumed. However, at close to full employment of resources, output would change very little, and the primary impact of monetary policy would be to change the price level.

The wealth effects discussed are also supportive of the monetarists' position that fiscal policy has at least an ambiguous impact on output. They argue that the effects are temporary because the impact of changes in the deficit is offset by opposite changes in private spending. Wealth effects lend support to this hypothesis.

However, substantial qualifications are in order. First, the magnitude of the indirect effects depends on the extent of changes in the interest rate and price level. There will be no indirect effects if the LM and output supply curves are horizontal so that neither the interest rate nor the price level changes.

Second, the direct effect, in the case of monetary policy, depends on a definition of wealth that includes demand deposits. Agreement on that definition is by no means unanimous. Third, the same reasoning that places wealth in the saving function should also place it in the money demand function. Wealth is allocated over many assets, of which money is one. An increase in wealth should increase money demand. This would shift the LM schedule to the left.

Finally, the effects discussed here are short-run, or "first round," effects. If the government deficit is *permanent,* wealth will increase continuously, causing continuing changes in the model. Recent studies have dealt with this issue, but they are beyond the scope of this book. However, we will return to this point in Chapter 18.

The Price Elasticity of Output Supply

The extent of policy-induced changes in the interest rate, the price level, and output depends not only on the impact of policy on output demand, but on the price elasticity of output supply. The greater the price elasticity of output supply, the less the price-level increase that results from a given policy stimulus to output demand, and therefore the lower the interest rate and the greater the output. In Figure 10.14 we show two cases of the price elasticity of output supply at less than full employment of resources. The S' output supply curve in the lower quadrant reflects a less price-elastic output supply than S''. Suppose, for example, that an increase in the monetary base shifts the LM schedule in the upper quadrant rightward and the output demand curve in the lower quadrant from D' to D''. The extent of the shift in the LM schedule depends on the price

Figure 10.14

Effectiveness of demand management and the shape of the output supply curve.

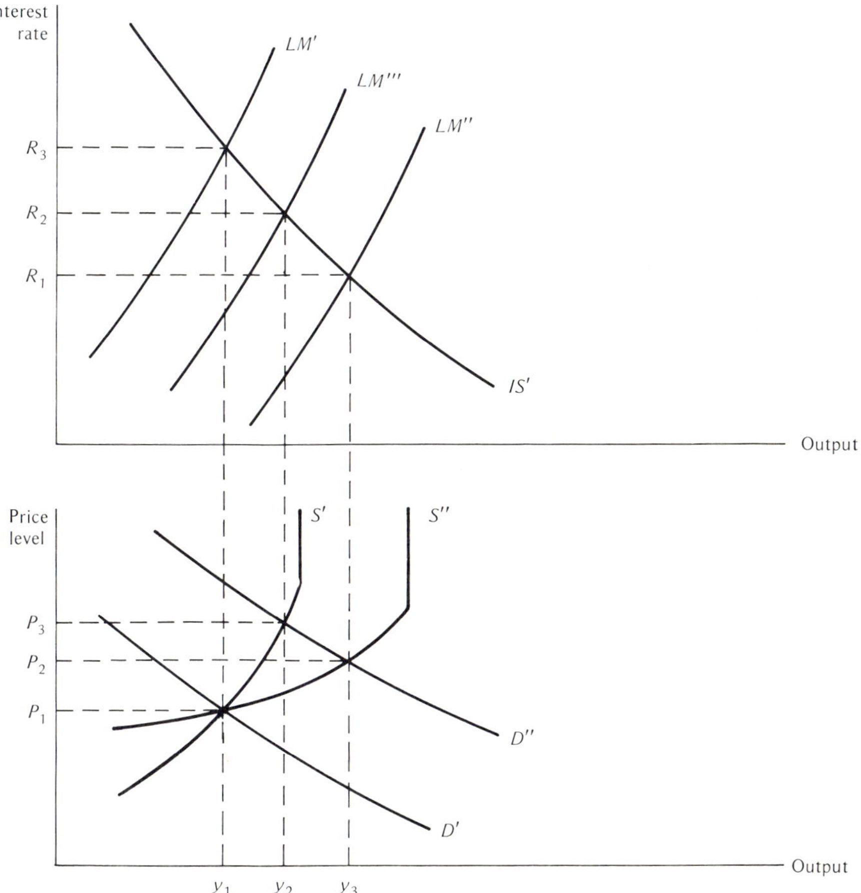

elasticity of output supply. If the output supply curve is S', the net effect of the increase in the monetary base and the price increase from P_1 to P_3 is to shift the LM schedule from LM' to LM'''. If the output supply curve is S'' so that the price increase is less, $P_2 < P_3$, the LM schedule shifts from LM' to LM''. Thus, the more price-elastic the output supply, the greater the decrease in the interest rate, the greater the increase in output, and the less the increase in the price level for a given stimulus to output demand.

Another factor that must be considered is the response of owners of factor inputs to changes in the price level. If they react to increases in the price level for output by increasing prices of factor inputs, then the extent of their responsiveness is a factor which helps to evaluate the impact of expansionary monetary and fiscal policies. Suppose, for example, in response to a policy-induced increase in the price level, laborers increase nominal wages in order to maintain at least their real wages. The result would be a decrease in output supply, i.e., a leftward shift in the output supply curve. Thus, the price level and thereby the interest rate would increase, and the policy-induced increase in output would be at least partially offset.

Keynesians argue that output supply is relatively price-elastic and that factor input prices are fixed in the short run, so that expansionary policy increases the price level by very little with substantial increases in output. Monetarists argue that in the long run factor input prices vary, so that Keynesians understate increases in the price level and overstate increases in output. Moreover, the monetarists point out that, contrary to the Keynesian cliché, in the long run we are not dead, and therefore long-run adjustments cannot be ignored.

SUMMARY NOTES

1. A theory of output supply, added to the theory of output demand, enables the full model to determine the price level as well as output and the market interest rate.
2. The quantity of output supplied is assumed to vary directly with the price level, given the stock of capital, technology, and the prices of factor inputs, as long as resources are not fully employed.
3. Decisions of business and labor affect output supply by changing the prices of factor inputs. Fiscal and monetary policies alter both the price level and output.
4. In the context of the present output market model, the relative effectiveness of fiscal and monetary policy in changing output and the price level is influenced by the interest elasticities of the IS and LM curves.
5. The influence of real wealth on real saving may be added to the output market model. When so included, the wealth effects of fiscal and monetary policy depend on the definition of wealth, the relative strengths of the direct wealth effect, the price-induced wealth effect, the interest-rate-induced

wealth effect, and the magnitudes of changes in the price level and in the interest rate.

DISCUSSION QUESTIONS

1. Using the LB-LM model, explain the impact of an increase in nominal wages on financial markets.
2. What combinations of changes in exogenous variables in our output model can produce increases in the price level, interest rates, and output?
3. Does a high and rising interest rate imply tightness of monetary policy? Explain.
4. What policy changes would you propose to curb inflation (price-level increases) and promote economic growth when prices of factor inputs are rising?
5. Monetary policy is often considered accommodative to fiscal policy. If expansionary fiscal and monetary policy go hand in hand, what factor(s) determine(s) whether the interest rate will rise substantially?

PORTFOLIO BALANCE MODELS

The IS-LM model developed in the preceding chapters is a widely used version of the framework developed by J. M. Keynes. However, alternatives to the basic Keynesian model have been developed. The Keynesian, or IS-LM, model is a general equilibrium model that determines the values of variables in the market for current output and the money market and, by implication, the loanable funds market as well. In this chapter we shall discuss two alternative general equilibrium models that go beyond the simple IS-LM model. The first model is neo-Keynesian in design and is usually called the *portfolio balance model*. The second is a monetarist model called the *wealth adjustment model*. The former is usually associated with the work of James Tobin; the latter is associated with the work of Karl Brunner and Allan Meltzer.*

The contributions these economists made to the theory of money demand were discussed in Chapter 7. But their ideas on money demand reflect only a part of their thinking about the general structure of the economy. The complete portfolio balance and wealth adjustment models contain mechanisms by which money affects the economy that go beyond the mechanisms contained in the IS-LM (or LB-LM) models. As time passes, these ideas should provide new insights.

---

*For the portfolio balance approach and applications, see J. Tobin, "Money, Capital and Other Stores of Value," American Economic Review, May 1961, pp. 26–37; J. Tobin, "A General Equilibrium Approach to Monetary Theory," Journal of Money, Credit and Banking, February 1969, pp. 15–29; and D. D. Hester and J. Tobin (eds.), Financial Markets and Economic Activity (New York: Wiley, 1967). The essentials of the wealth adjustment approach may be found in K. Brunner and A. H. Meltzer, "The Place of Financial Intermediaries in the Transmission of Monetary Policy," American Economic Review, May 1963, pp. 372–382; Brunner and Meltzer, "Money, Debt and Economic Activity," Journal of Political Economy, September/October 1972, pp. 951–977; and Brunner and Meltzer, "Mr. Hicks and the 'Monetarists,'" Economica, February 1973, pp. 44–59.

11.1 NOTES ON THE KEYNESIAN MODEL

The Keynesian models developed earlier contain four assets, government bonds, private debt (both of which are traded in the loanable funds market), capital, and money. In addition there is a market for current output, which is purchased in part by the private sector. The government sector also buys a portion of current output and may in the process run a current deficit whenever its expenditures exceed its tax receipts. When it runs a deficit, it borrows by selling bonds to the private sector or to the Federal Reserve System (through dealers in government securities). The ultimate effect of the latter action is that the deficit is financed by printing money.

Now an underlying assumption in the Keynesian model is that bonds, private debt, and capital are perfect substitutes, so that only one yield, equivalent to *the* interest rate, exists in the loanable funds market. In other words if capital, which yields a stream of production over time that can be expressed as a percentage of the price of capital, and private debt and bonds, which pay some interest rate, are perfect substitutes, the yield must be the same for all, in equilibrium. Were there a difference in yields, people would immediately switch completely to the higher-yielding asset. This would have the effect of lowering the yield on that asset and raising the yield on the alternative assets until equality was restored among the three yields. Where two or more assets are perfect substitutes, they can be considered as a single asset. Thus, for all practical purposes, our IS-LM and LB-LM models contain two existing assets, bonds and money.

The relationship between bonds and money is embodied in the LM curve, which also provides the mechanism through which monetary policy is introduced. For example, if the Federal Reserve System engages in open market purchases of government securities, it increases the private sector's holdings of money and decreases the private sector's holdings of bonds. The results of such policies within the IS-LM framework are unambiguous. If the Federal Reserve buys bonds from the private sector (and consequently increases the money holdings of the private sector), the interest rate on bonds falls, which also implies that the yields on private debt and existing capital fall, and this stimulates an increase in expenditures on newly produced capital, which results in increases in output. The magnitude of this response depends principally on the elasticity of money demand with respect to the interest rate on bonds.

Since we do live in a world of multiple interest rates, it may well be completely unrealistic to assume that private debt, bonds, and capital are perfect substitutes. The two approaches considered in this chapter distinguish between bonds and existing capital so that the effects of changes in the yield on one relative to the yield on the other can be observed.

11.2   THE PORTFOLIO BALANCE APPROACH

The Framework

The portfolio balance approach takes as its starting point the economy's capital account, which shows the distribution of asset holdings among the various elements of the private sector and the government sector (including the Federal Reserve).* The holdings are determined by examining each sector's balance sheet. To illustrate, assume that there are three sectors in the economy, the household sector, the business sector, and the government sector. Assume also that there are four assets, the existing stock of capital, money, private (interest-bearing) debt, and government bonds. Table 11.1 is a matrix showing the hypothetical holdings of these assets by each sector. Liabilities would be shown in the table as negative assets, indicated by parentheses.

The various assets are listed along the left side of the table, and the sectors together with totals are shown along the top. In the example shown, the household sector holds $50 billion of capital; the business sector, $300 billion; and the government sector, $100 billion. Note that private (interest-bearing) debt involves borrowing and lending between the two private sectors. Thus the $75 billion of private debt held by the household sector is offset by a $75 billion liability of the business sector. The total of private debt for the economy must be zero. Government bonds and the currency component of money are assets of the private sector and liabilities of the government sector.

For purposes of this illustration, the monetary authority and the government are contained in a single sector, whereas normally, in flow of funds accounting, they are kept separate. Either approach can be taken, depending on the purposes at hand. Also, for simplification we ignore the existence of all financial intermediaries. This means that the money stock is the same as currency held by the private sector and is the same as the monetary base.

In this case total private assets includes private holdings of government bonds and currency, although the total for the economy, including the government sector, is zero. Total wealth of the private sector consists of the total existing capital plus any debt of the government sector (government bonds and currency). If we include the government sector, total national wealth consists only of the existing stock of capital.

The portfolio balance approach attempts to determine the changes that take place in asset yields when the division of the capital account between the government and private sectors is changed and what implications those changes in yields have for the flow of current output.

In the short run the net worth or stock of wealth held by the private sector can be taken as given or exogenous to the private sector. For example, the

---

*"Capital account" is Tobin's term. In the flow of funds accounts discussed in Chapter 4, *changes* in assets are entries in the capital account. Tobin's analysis employs stocks. The categories, however, are similar.

Table 11.1
The Capital Account
(In billions of dollars)

Asset	Households	Business	Total Private	Government	National Totals
Capital	$ 50	$300	$350	$100	$450
Private debt	75	(75)	0	0	0
Government bonds	100	10	110	(110)	0
Money (currency)	80	40	120	(120)	0
Net worth	$305	$275	$580	$(130)	$450

Note: In the system of national income accounting currently in use, government capital is fully depreciated in the year in which it is purchased. Thus the book value of government capital is zero. However, this is an accounting decision. It should be obvious that the government owns airplanes, roads, buildings, and other pieces of capital. Therefore we have shown a positive value for government capital even though this does not conform to accounting practice.

stock of existing capital is the sum of all previous saving (equals capital investment) less depreciation. That stock can be changed only by additional saving, which takes time. Put another way, if the existing stock of capital is to increase by $20 billion, $20 billion of saving must take place over the coming year. Thus as of the moment the existing stock of capital is fixed. Total net private debt in the economy is also fixed at any point in time and is always equal to zero. The stock of government bonds and/or the stock of money held by the private sector can change with no accompanying change in any other asset only if the government runs a deficit or surplus on current account. For example, if the government runs a deficit and finances the deficit by selling bonds to the private sector, the stock of privately held government bonds will increase with no change in any of the other asset totals. The government's decisions are assumed to be exogenous to the private sector.

The *composition* of privately held wealth can also be changed by exogenous governmental action. For example, the Federal Reserve Bank can purchase today $20 billion of government bonds from the private sector in exchange for $20 billion worth of currency. This increases the private sector's holdings of money by $20 billion and decreases its holdings of government bonds by $20 billion. Total private wealth, however, remains unchanged. Thus in the short run, if we know what changes have taken place in three of the four assets, we know what change has taken place in the fourth asset because the total is fixed. In fact, since total net private debt must equal zero, if we know what changes have taken place in two of the three remaining assets, we know what change has taken place in the third. Another way of putting it is to say that considering capital, government bonds, and money, only two of the three can be independently determined by policy action.

The capital account in Tobin's framework shows only the stocks of existing assets held in the economy. It provides no information about the flow of current output. However, we can deduce what changes might take place in the flow of current output from changes that take place in the capital account. Changes in the allocation of wealth will result in changes in the relative yields of the various assets, which in turn induce changes in the spending decisions of the private sector. In order to draw these implications, we must first examine the behavior of the private sector as it relates to holdings of these various assets.

Before doing so, two points must be made. First, the analysis is confined to direct wealth effects. Indirect wealth effects are ignored. For example, if *new* government bonds are issued and the interest rate rises, no account is taken of the effect of that increased interest rate on the value of outstanding government bonds.

Second, Tobin abstracts from changes in the price level (of current output). Consequently, all nominal changes are also real changes, and there is no need to distinguish between the two.

Portfolio Balance

In order to highlight the essential features of the approach, we will treat the private sector as a single sector and not be concerned with the allocation of assets among different groups within the private sector. This means that private debt nets out and the private sector holds only three assets: existing capital, government bonds, and the currency component of money. Both bonds and currency are government debt held by the private sector; the differences between the two are that bonds pay interest and money does not, and that money serves as the medium of exchange and bonds do not.

As was discussed in Chapter 7, the demand for any given asset will vary directly with its own yield and inversely with the yield on substitutes. For example, an increase in the yield on existing capital, all other things being equal, will induce people to hold more capital, and an increase in the yield on bonds, all other things being equal, will induce people to reduce their holdings of capital and instead switch to increased holdings of bonds. For example, suppose the interest rate on government bonds falls relative to the rate of return on real estate. Some investors will sell bonds and buy real estate, lowering the price (raising the yield) of the former and raising the price (lowering the yield) of the latter until the relative yields are once again consistent with investor preferences. Thus all three assets considered here are assumed to be substitutes for one another, but not perfect substitutes. Consequently the yields may differ.

The demand for each asset is also influenced by the total stock of wealth. If the stock of wealth increases, so will the demand for each of the three assets. However, Tobin assumes that each asset responds to changes in wealth in the same way. Specifically he assumes that the elasticity of demand for each asset with respect to the stock of wealth is unitary. In other words a 10 percent increase in the stock of wealth will result in a 10 percent increase in the demand for capital, a 10 percent increase in the demand for bonds, and a 10 percent increase in the demand for money. Thus portfolio composition depends only on relative yields and is independent of the total stock of wealth. Monetary policy operates by changing the yield structure on the assets. The yield structure can be changed only by changing the relative supplies of the assets. Given Tobin's assumption about elasticities, the "balance" equations (which equate demand and supply) can be written as follows:

$$f(\overset{-}{R},\overset{+}{RK}) = \frac{K}{W} \tag{11.1}$$

$$g(\overset{+}{R},\overset{-}{RK}) = \frac{GS}{W} \tag{11.2}$$

$$h(\overset{-}{R},\overset{-}{RK}) = \frac{M}{W} \tag{11.3}$$

Each equation states that in portfolio equilibrium or balance, the demand for each asset as a percent of total wealth is equal to the percent of total wealth actually held as that asset. The yields on bonds and capital are R and RK, respectively. Capital, bonds, and money are represented by K, GS, and M, respectively; and W is total privately held wealth. Note that the demand side (the left side) of each balance equation expresses the demand for a particular asset as a percentage of total wealth. Further, since total private wealth is the sum of the existing stocks of capital, government bonds, and money, if follows that their proportions (of total wealth) must total 1.

$$\frac{K}{W} + \frac{GS}{W} + \frac{M}{W} = 1 \tag{11.4}$$

Therefore if we find values of R and RK that satisfy two of the above three balance equations, we have found values which satisfy the third. In fact the definition contained in (11.4) means that we can use any two of the three balance equations to solve for the equilibrium yields on bonds and real capital. Which two we use is purely a matter of personal preference.

In any case monetary policy will produce a change in the composition of total wealth. In response to that change the private sector will adjust its holdings of the three assets and in the process alter the structure of yields. The alteration of the structure of yields in turn affects output demand and ultimately output, the price of current output, and employment. Specifically, a fall in the yield on bonds (which is the market interest rate in this model) should stimulate capital investment for the same reason that it does in the IS-LM and LB-LM models. Similarly, a fall in the yield on existing capital makes *new* capital relatively more attractive and should therefore stimulate expenditures in that direction. What the portfolio balance model points out is that, depending on the policy change, R and RK may not change in the same direction. To illustrate, now consider two examples.*

Policy Examples

Case 1: Conventional Open Market Purchase of Government Securities from the Private Sector.   If the Federal Reserve System buys government bonds from the private sector, the effect is an equal exchange of money for bonds. Money holdings of the private sector increase, and bond holdings of the private sector decrease by the same amount. The proportion held as capital is unchanged. The composition of wealth will have changed even though its total has not.

After the purchase of bonds (which may also be called the sale of money) has occurred, at the old yield structure there will be an excess demand for bonds and an excess supply of money. The excess demand for bonds forces bond prices upward and the yield on bonds downward. Some of the excess money supply is used to buy bonds, and some of it is used to buy existing capital. How much of the excess money supply will go toward each use is determined by the preferences of money holders and the degree to which they perceive capital and bonds to be substitutes for money balances. The degree of substitutability is critical to some of the following conclusions.

It would seem that, at least initially, the effect would be to bid up the price of existing capital, thus lowering its yield along with the yield on bonds. However, that conclusion may be ambiguous. The bond rate fell initially due to the excess demand for bonds. A falling bond rate induces an increase in money demand. If money demand increases by more than the money supply initially increased, people may attempt to make up the deficiency by selling off some of their holdings of existing capital. This will cause the price of existing capital to fall and its yield to rise rather than the reverse.

Or does it? The question can be resolved by recalling the definition contained in Eq. (11.4). Since total wealth has not changed, and since there has been an equal swap of money for bonds, the ratio of capital to wealth (K/W) is *unchanged.* Therefore, in equilibrium, the demand for capital must be unchanged. Now a *fall* in the bond yield tends to *raise* the demand for capital. In order to keep the demand unchanged, this must be offset by a *fall* in the yield on capital, which tends to reduce the quantity of capital demanded. We must conclude that the open market purchase lowers both yields. The problem is illustrated in Figure 11.1.

The market for money is shown on the left side of Figure 11.1, and the market for government bonds is shown on the right side. For the sake of illustration we shall assume that bonds and capital and money and capital are very poor substitutes. This means that the demand for bonds and the demand for

---

*These two are illustrative. The student should also work through the discussion questions at the end of the chapter.

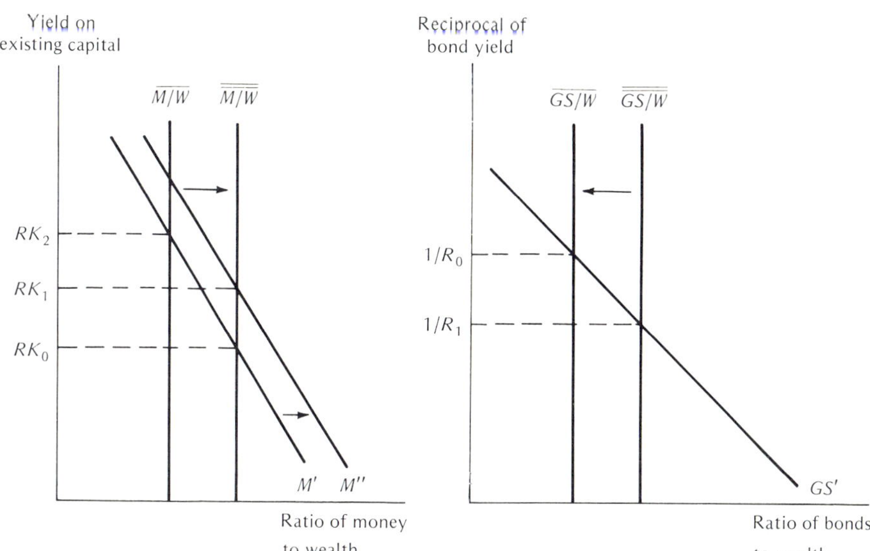

Figure 11.1

Effect of an open market purchase of government securities in the portfolio balance model.

money as a percentage of total wealth will respond only slightly to changes in the yield on real capital. We shall also assume that money and bonds are very close substitutes, so that a change in the yield on bonds will induce a fairly large change in the demand for money. In effect the assumptions state that asset holders treat financial assets as close substitutes, but treat financial assets and physical assets (capital) as poor substitutes. In terms of Figure 11.1, it means that the money demand schedule, drawn downward-sloping against the yield on capital, is fairly steep. The GS' curve on the right side of the figure will shift by a negligible amount in response to changes in the yield on capital. Note that the demand for bonds is drawn downward-sloping against the reciprocal of the yield on bonds. Since the demand for bonds varies directly with their yield, it varies inversely with the reciprocal of their yield.

The policy change under discussion shifts the money supply curve to the right from $\overline{M/W}$ to $\overline{\overline{M/W}}$ and the government bond supply curve to the left by an equal amount, from $\overline{GS/W}$ to $\overline{\overline{GS/W}}$. The initial effect is to lower the yield on bonds, raising its reciprocal from $1/R_1$ toward $1/R_0$. Under the assumption that money and bonds are very close substitutes, the money demand curve will shift to the right by a great deal, perhaps as far as M''. But according to the previous discussion, it cannot shift so far as to cause the yield on capital to exceed RK_2. Thus the new yield on capital is RK_1, which is less than or equal to RK_2. Since we have also assumed that bonds and real capital are very poor substitutes, the net decrease in the yield on capital shifts the bond demand curve to the right by a negligible amount which we have ignored in the figure.

For Tobin the crucial indicator of the stance of monetary policy is the policy's effect on the yield on existing capital. If the yield on existing capital rises (the price of capital falls) relative to the yield on new capital, the effect is contractionary because producers would prefer to buy existing capital rather than the relatively higher-priced (relatively lower-yield) currently produced capital. If the effect of policy is to lower the yield on existing capital (raise its price), the effect is expansionary because people will shift from the relatively higher-priced existing capital to the relatively lower-priced new capital. In the former case production of new capital is retarded; in the latter case it is stimulated.

Under the structure of the IS-LM or LB-LM models, we would have concluded that an open market purchase which increased the money supply and lowered the yield on bonds was expansionary. In the portfolio balance model, a normal open market purchase is also expansionary. The example considered involved changes in the supplies of only two of the three assets. Now consider the effect of changing the relative supplies of all three assets.

Case 2: The United States Treasury Retires Outstanding Bonds with Capital and Money. Monetary policy is usually implemented by the Federal Reserve System. However, Treasury actions can also produce monetary effects. Suppose in this case that the Treasury decides to retire (purchase from the private sector) some of the existing stock of government bonds. Suppose it does this by making part payment in money. The rest is paid for by transferring ownership of Hoover Dam to the private bond holders (presumably with the approval of Congress).

The effect of all this is to create, at the initial yield structure, excess demand for bonds (due to the reduction in supply) and excess supplies of money and capital. The immediate impact is to lower the yield on bonds and to raise the yield on capital. Substitution effects between bonds and capital also come into play. The increase in the yield on capital should reduce the demand for bonds, retarding or reversing the initial fall in the bond yield. The initial fall in the yield on bonds should raise the demand for capital, thus moderating the initial capital yield increase.

To make matters more complicated, consider the money market. Money, as a proportion of total wealth, has increased. Therefore money demand must also increase in order to restore equilibrium. But bond and capital yields, which are moving in opposite directions, are producing opposing effects on money demand. Final conclusions are not clear-cut. Perhaps a visual representation will help sort out the issues.

Figure 11.2 shows the markets for bonds and existing capital. The demand for bonds is plotted downward-sloping against the reciprocal of its own yield, as is the demand for capital. The actions of the Treasury serve to decrease the supply of bonds and increase the supply of existing capital held by the private sector. The yield on bonds tends to fall, and the yield on capital tends to rise.

Now continue to assume that bonds and capital are poor substitutes, as are

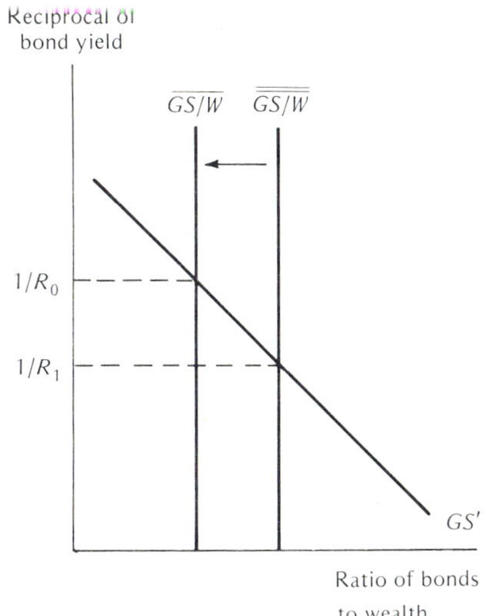

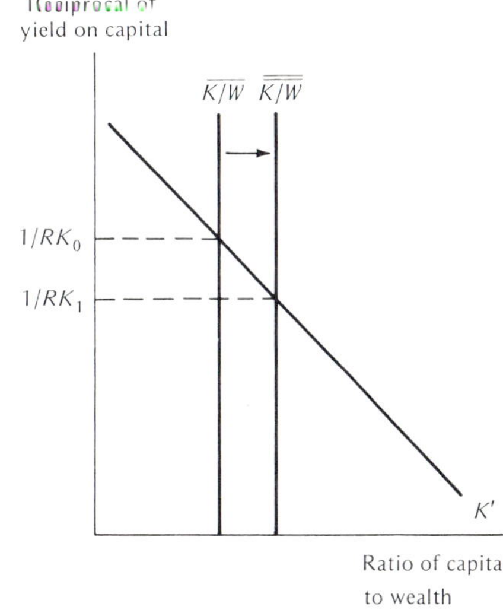

Figure 11.2
Effects of changes in capital, bonds, and money in the portfolio balance model.

capital and money. Also assume that bonds and money are good substitutes. Under these assumptions the fall in the bond yield would have little effect on the demand for capital, and the increase in the yield on capital would have little effect on the demand for bonds. Thus the demand curves in Figure 11.2 would not shift about, and we would be left with a lower bond yield and a higher capital yield. Under the same assumptions the net effect of a lower bond yield and a higher capital yield would be to increase money demand, and this would accommodate the increased money supply.

Thus the transaction results in an increased money supply and lower bond yield, which under Keynesian criteria is expansionary. However, the same transaction raises the yield on capital, which by Tobin's criterion is contractionary. The policy's effect on the market for current output is therefore ambiguous. What may have been clear-cut in the IS-LM model is not so clear-cut in the portfolio balance model. What should become clear-cut, with a little experimentation, is that the conclusions depend crucially on the assumptions made about the substitution relationships among bonds, money, and existing capital. The reader will have the opportunity to experiment by working through the exercises at the end of the chapter.

Summary

The essential feature of the portfolio balance approach is the existence of multiple assets that are less than perfect substitutes for one another. Bonds can be substituted for existing capital, capital for money, and money for bonds, so that, depending on the assumptions made about the relative degrees of substitution, various results are possible. Tobin rejects the bond yield (which some Keynesians prefer) and the money supply (which some monetarists prefer) as reliable indicators of the thrust of monetary policy.* The key indicator in this approach is the yield on existing capital. A fall in the yield on existing capital is expansionary, and a rise is contractionary.

As far as the degree of substitutability is concerned, Tobin considers bonds and money to be fairly close substitutes. The only difference between the two is that the explicit yield on money is legally fixed at zero.† They would be perfect substitutes if both paid market-determined interest rates (or both paid no interest). However, the estimated interest elasticities of money demand discussed in Chapter 7 suggest that bonds and money may not be very close substitutes.

While the portfolio balance model discusses implications for current output, prices, and employment, the real sector is not explicitly included in the model. The wealth adjustment approach, to which we now turn, does, however, explicitly treat the market for current output as part of the general model.

11.3 THE WEALTH ADJUSTMENT APPROACH

The wealth adjustment approach has many features in common with the portfolio balance model. Bonds and existing capital are assumed to be imperfect substitutes, and three asset markets are employed—the markets for money, bonds, and existing capital. However, Brunner and Meltzer also add a market for current output. There are three prices and/or yields to be determined rather than two. The wealth adjustment model determines the yield on bonds, the price of existing capital (and by implication its yield), and the price of current output.

In general the demand for each asset varies directly with that asset's yield, inversely with the yield on substitute assets, and directly with the stock of wealth. However, unlike the portfolio balance approach, Brunner and Meltzer do not assume that the demand for each asset is proportional to the stock of wealth. Thus in the wealth adjustment process, a change in total wealth may alter the yield and price structure because the demands for the individual assets will not respond in the same way.

In addition to the asset markets, the wealth adjustment model specifies a demand and supply equation for current output. Output demand principally depends on the yield on bonds, the price of and/or yield on existing capital, the price of real output, and the stock of wealth. Specifically, output demand is as-

---

*We will return to the problem of indicators of policy in Chapter 17.

†See Tobin, "A General Equilibrium Approach to Monetary Theory," *op. cit.* However, also see the comments by R. J. Barro and H. I. Grossman, "Open Market Operations and the Medium of Exchange," *Journal of Money, Credit and Banking,* May 1971, pp. 304–311.

sumed to vary inversely with the yield on bonds, inversely with the price of output, directly with the price of existing capital (or inversely with its yield), and directly with the stock of wealth. As in our output market model, government expenditures and taxes also play a role. However, we ignore those here, in the interests of simplification and because we will not experiment with fiscal policy. Output supply, on the other hand, varies directly with the price of current output and directly with the existing stock of capital. The relationships for money, bonds, and current output are summarized below.

$$MD = f(\overset{-}{R},\overset{+}{PK},\overset{+}{W}) \tag{11.5}$$

$$GSD = g(\overset{+}{R},\overset{+}{PK},\overset{+}{W}) \tag{11.6}$$

$$D = h(\overset{-}{R},\overset{+}{PK},\overset{-}{P},\overset{+}{W}) \tag{11.7}$$

$$S = j(\overset{+}{P},\overset{+}{K}) \tag{11.8}$$

Note that the equations shown here use the price of capital PK rather than its yield RK. The price of current output is P, and the demand for and supply of current output are D and S, respectively. The positive and negative signs above each equation indicate the direction of change in the dependent variable with respect to the relevant independent variable. For example, money demand varies inversely (negatively) with R and directly (positively) with PK.

Brunner and Meltzer also include anticipations about price changes and future yield on capital, and they separate wealth into its human and nonhuman components. Moreover, they make various assumptions about the speeds of adjustment in the various markets. Briefly, they assume that the prices or yields in the asset markets adjust fairly quickly, while the price of current output responds rather slowly. This means that for any given (short-run) period of time, the asset markets may reach equilibrium, but the market for current output may be in disequilibrium. The principal reason is that financial markets are more capable of rapid adjustment to equilibrium than the market for current output, which requires changes in production schedules, the hiring or firing of labor, etc.

As in the case of the portfolio balance model, the workings of the wealth adjustment model may be examined using two of the three asset markets. In the illustrations to follow we will use the money market, the bond market, and the output market.

Now consider the effect of the changes outlined in Case 2 in the previous section. The Treasury retires some outstanding bonds and pays for them partly with newly printed money and partly with existing capital. In considering the response of the various markets, for the sake of argument assume that money and existing capital are very close substitutes, so that the demand for money is very sensitive to changes in the price of capital. In fact, assume that the money market is the immediate or proximate determinant of the price of capital.*

The Treasury's transaction reduces the supply of bonds held by the private sector, increases the supply of money, and increases the supply of capital. The immediate effect is to lower the interest rate on bonds and to raise the price of capital. The price of capital increases because money holders will seek to buy existing capital with the increased money supply. But because money and capital are such close substitutes, the relative price rise necessary to clear the money market is very small.

The initial effects of the changes in asset supplies produce secondary effects. Specifically, the rise in the price of capital (which lowers its yield) increases the demand for bonds. How much, of course, depends on the degree of substitutability between bonds and capital. Nevertheless, any increase that does take place accentuates the fall in the yield on bonds. That is, a decrease in the supply of bonds coupled with an increase in demand serves to unambiguously lower the yield on bonds. A lower yield on bonds increases the demand for money. Again, how much depends on the degree of substitutability between money and bonds. If the two are poor substitutes, the increase in the demand for money will be slight. In that case, the increase in the demand for money does not produce a fall in the price of capital sufficient to offset the rise in the price of capital that was induced through the increase in the supply of money, but it does make the net increase in PK smaller than the initial change.

The net effects are a fall in the yield on bonds and a slight rise in the price of existing capital. (Given the slight change in the price of capital, the lower bond yield is likely to increase the demand for capital by more than the higher PK reduces it, thus reconciling demand for capital with the increased supply.) Changes in both these variables influence the demand for current output. Specifically, the fall in the interest rate tends to increase output demand. This is because some firms now find it profitable to sell their holdings of relatively lower-yielding government bonds in order to engage in relatively higher-yielding capital investment. Further, the higher price of existing capital makes current output relatively more attractive, increasing output demand. Thus we conclude that output demand increases.

How the increase in output demand will be distributed between a change in the quantity produced and a change in the price level is something that can only be deduced from knowledge of the output supply curve. If the economy is operating at relatively full capacity or if producers are reluctant to expand their production schedules, the increase in demand may be largely absorbed by an increase in the price of current output. On the other hand, if there is extensive unemployment or if producers anticipate future increases in demand, most of

---

*This is consistent with assumptions made in Brunner and Meltzer, ''Money, Debt and Economic Activity,'' *op. cit.*

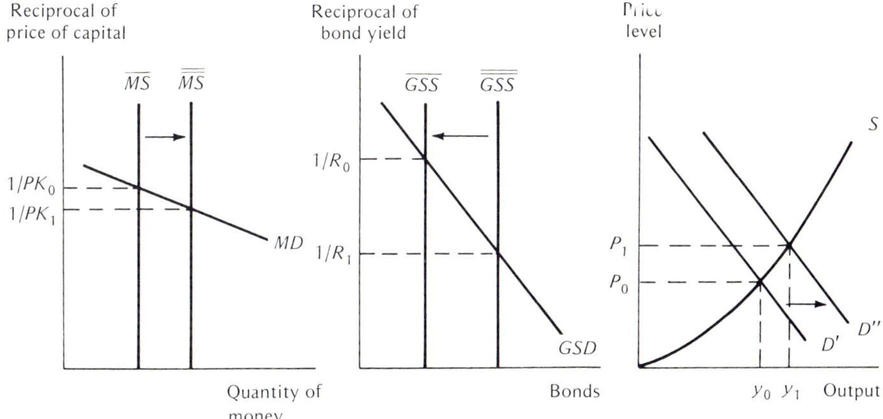

Figure 11.3

Changes in capital, bonds, and money in the wealth adjustment model.

the increase in demand may be absorbed by an increase in output, with little increase in the price level.

The process just described is illustrated in Figure 11.3. The left-hand panel in the figure shows the money market. The demand for money varies directly with the price of existing capital and therefore inversely with its reciprocal. The center panel shows the market for bonds and is drawn the same way the bond market was drawn in Figure 11.1. The right-hand panel shows the demand for and supply of current output plotted against its price. The transactions carried out by the Treasury shift the bond supply curve to the left and the money supply curve to the right. The initial effect is a fall in the yield on bonds (a rise in its reciprocal) from R_1 to R_0 and a rise in the price of capital (fall in its reciprocal). Assuming that bonds and capital are poor substitutes and that money and bonds are poor substitutes, both the bond demand curve and the money demand curve would shift to the right by small amounts. This accentuates the fall in the bond interest rate and moderates somewhat the rise in the price of existing capital.

The net increase in the price of existing capital coupled with the fall in the yield on bonds shifts the output demand curve to the right, as shown in the right-hand panel of the figure. This increase in output demand raises the price of output and the quantity of output, as shown in the figure. The distribution of change, however, is only hypothetical. It depends on the shape of the S curve and the initial position of the D curve.

Given the assumptions made about the degrees of substitution among the three assets, the transaction which increases the money supply is unmistakably expansionary insofar as the market for current output is concerned. However, different assumptions could lead to results similar to those discussed in connection with the portfolio balance model.

Compared with the standard Keynesian model (especially the IS-LM variant), both the portfolio balance and wealth adjustment models are in their infancy. A complete analysis of both models requires extensive work at an advanced level. However, the single most important feature that distinguishes both models from the IS-LM model is the separation of the market for bonds and the market for existing capital. We have been able to examine some of the implications of that separation at a highly simplified level in this chapter.

SUMMARY NOTES

1. The distinguishing feature of the portfolio balance and wealth adjustment models is the separation of the markets for existing capital and government bonds.
2. Equilibrium conditions are defined in terms of demand and supply equations for *stocks* of government bonds, existing capital, and money. The wealth adjustment model also includes a *flow* market for current output.
3. For Tobin, the effect of monetary policy is determined by its effect on the price or yield of existing capital.
4. Relative changes in the yields on bonds and existing capital depend on the degrees of substitutability among bonds, money, and existing capital.
5. Depending on the substitution assumptions made, monetary changes that yield unambiguous effects on output demand in the IS-LM model may yield ambiguous results in the portfolio balance or wealth adjustment model.

DISCUSSION QUESTIONS

1. Suppose the government increases its expenditures with no change in taxes, so that it runs a deficit. Further, suppose the Treasury finances the deficit by selling bonds to the private sector. What are the effects in the portfolio balance and wealth adjustment models? Remember to add the appropriate variables to output demand.
2. Suppose the deficit in question 1 is financed by printing new money. What are the effects in this case?
3. What common characteristics make bonds and money substitutes? Capital and money? Bonds and capital?
4. Work through Case 2 in the wealth adjustment model under the assumptions that bonds and money are close substitutes and capital and bonds are poor substitutes. How does your answer compare with the results in the portfolio balance model?

ECONOMETRIC MODELS

If anything distinguishes economics from other social sciences, it is that economic theories are capable of empirical testing and application. The theories and models discussed in the preceding chapters are highly abstract in nature. However, the variables with which they are concerned are measurable and of real world significance. Indeed, many governmental and private agencies compile data on the variables contained in those models. The existence of such data permits us to accomplish two goals. First, the data can be used to test the applicability of the various theories about the economy. Second, where theories are believed to be applicable, the data can be used in estimating the theoretical relationships. In other words, the equations of the model can be cast in quantitative form. Cast in such form, an economic model can be used for forecasting future events and for more accurately describing past events. Within economics, *econometrics* is a field whose participants are involved in converting economic theories into mathematical form and estimating the parameters of such models by various statistical techniques.

In this chapter we will examine a number of econometric models that have been constructed in the past few years. We will be primarily concerned with the financial sector of each model and the way in which financial changes are transmitted to the real sector. Thus we will be in a position to see practical applications of the theories discussed earlier in this book. We will also be able to get some idea of the magnitudes involved when changes in the financial sector influence the real sector.

The models in this chapter represent divergent viewpoints with respect to both economic theory and econometric model building. Both Keynesian and monetarist viewpoints are represented, and both large-scale and small-scale models are discussed. Before we jump right into the first model, we shall review the financial structure of the theories discussed to date and the ways in which financial changes affect the real sector.

12.1 REVIEW OF FINANCIAL STRUCTURE AND LINKAGES TO REAL SECTOR

We have up to this point examined three general models of the economy: the Keynesian model in its IS-LM and LB-LM forms, the portfolio balance model, and the wealth adjustment model. The financial sector of the Keynesian model consists of a money market and a loanable funds market. The money market was used to determine the equilibrium interest rate in the economy given the level of income, which is determined in the output market. Adjustments in the money market are made by changing conditions in the loanable funds market. In other words, attempts by business firms and individuals to increase (decrease) money holdings are accomplished by borrowing (lending) in the loanable funds market. In the process the interest rate on financial assets changes. Changes in the interest rate in turn induce changes in business sector spending on new capital goods (capital investment). A change in expenditures on newly produced capital goods is a change in output demand in the output market, which influences the equilibrium level of output and also prices and employment.

Some modifications have been made in the basic Keynesian model that do not, however, alter its basic structure. For example, the interest rate is sometimes included as a determinant of real consumption and real saving.*

Inclusion of the interest rate may affect real consumption expenditures in two ways. First, the interest rate is a measure of the price of present consumption in terms of future consumption. For example, if the interest rate is 10 percent, a dollar saved today will permit $1.10 worth of real consumption one year from now.† Put another way, at an interest rate of 10 percent, every dollar consumed today means that $1.10 worth of consumption one year from today is given up. The higher the interest rate, the higher the cost of present consumption in terms of future consumption. As the cost of present consumption increases, presumably the amount of present consumption decreases. Thus an increase in the interest rate should reduce present consumption expenditures, and a decrease should increase present consumption expenditures. Given the level of real disposable income, an increase (decrease) in real consumption decreases (increases) real saving. Thus by this effect real saving varies directly with the interest rate. This effect has been called the *substitution effect*.

However, real income has also been assumed to affect real consumption expenditures, and interest payments to the household sector constitute part of the household sector's real income. An increase in the interest rate increases the total interest payments made to the household sector and on that score should tend to increase their present consumption and saving. This effect, known as the *income effect*, tends to offset the substitution effect on consumption. The

---

*For a survey of modifications to the consumption function, see W. R. Hosek, *Macroeconomic Theory* (Homewood, Ill.: Irwin, 1975), chap. 8.

†This discussion ignores any appreciation or depreciation in the value of the dollar due to changes in the price level.

net effect of interest-rate changes on consumption is therefore ambiguous, although the relationship between the interest rate and saving is not.* In other words, an increase in the interest rate increases real consumption by the income effect and reduces it by the substitution effect. An increase in the interest rate increases real saving by *both* the income and substitution effects.

Another modification of the basic Keynesian model adds some measure of real liquid wealth or real money balances to the consumption function for reasons discussed in Chapter 10.

Inclusion of interest rates and wealth effects in the consumption function is a modification of the basic Keynesian model, not the creation of an alternative structure. The portfolio balance and wealth adjustment models, however, do substantially differ from the basic Keynesian model. In these models bonds and capital are treated as separate assets, and therefore the models must be concerned with markets for money, bonds, and capital. Changes in desired money holdings can be accomplished not only through transactions in bonds, but through transactions in capital as well. Thus attempts to adjust desired money holdings will result in alterations in the yield on bonds and the yield on capital. Changes in the yield structure in turn lead to changes in capital investment and other private spending, which ultimately lead to changes in output, prices, and employment.

All three models contain mechanisms whereby changes in output feed back to the demands for the various financial assets contained in the model, but our primary concern here is with the structure of the financial sector and the way in which changes in the financial sector are transmitted to the real sector. Having reviewed theory, we now move on to its practical application.

Figure 12.1 is a conglomeration of the many links between the financial and real sectors contained in the models discussed in the preceding chapters. Only the impulses from the financial sector to the real sector are shown. Feedback effects are left out. The figure may be compared with subsequent flowcharts for the various econometric models discussed in the chapter.

12.2 THE BROOKINGS QUARTERLY ECONOMETRIC MODEL

The Brookings model is an appropriate model to begin with because it is perhaps the ancestor of all large-scale econometric models.† The model was begun in 1961 as a joint project of economists from various universities and agencies under the supervision of the Brookings Institution. Like the other models discussed in this chapter, the Brookings model is subject to continuous

---

*Substitution and income effects of price changes generally apply to any good. Recall the application to money demand in Chapter 7.

†Like most models, the Brookings model has a number of versions. The material here is based on G. Fromm and P. Taubman, *Policy Simulations with an Econometric Model* (Washington, D. C.: The Brookings Institution, 1968); and G. Fromm, L. R. Klein, and G. R. Shink, "Short and Long Term Simulations with the Brookings Model," in B. G. Hickman (ed.), *Econometric Models of Cyclical Behavior*, vol. 1 (New York: Columbia, 1972).

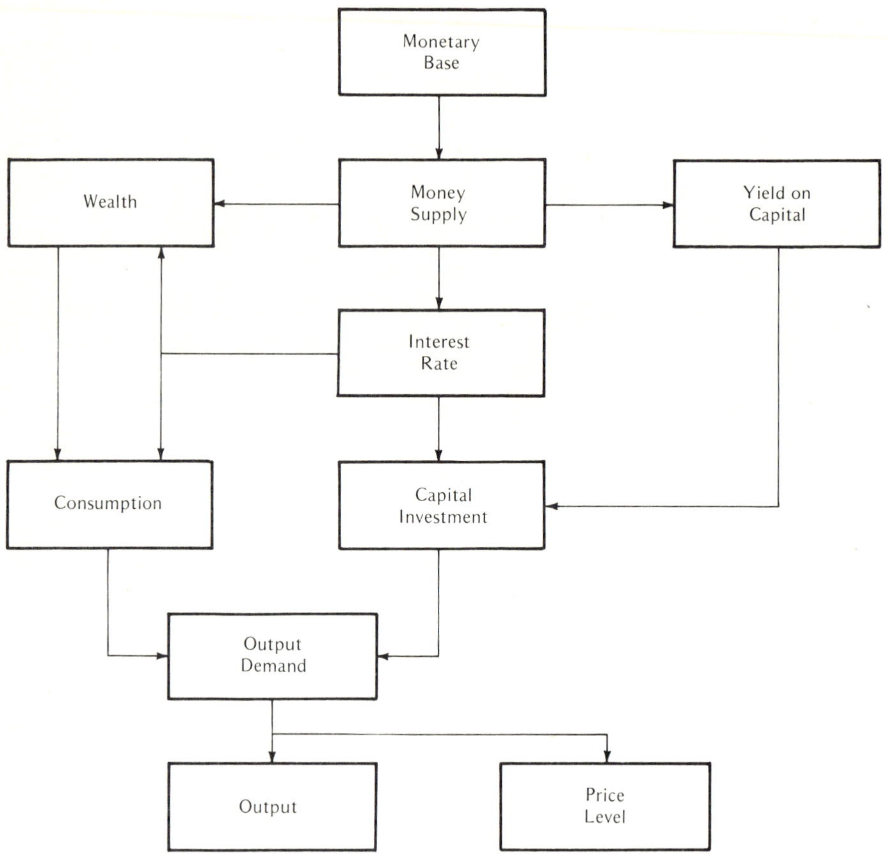

Figure 12.1

Summary of linkages between financial and real sectors.

revision and reestimation in response to advances in theory and revisions in data.

The model is huge, with the "condensed" version containing over 200 equations and variables. The financial sector alone contains two dozen equations. This represents a rather extensive disaggregation of the basic Keynesian model. Such disaggregation means that the economy can be examined in more minute detail than is possible with a quantitative version of the simple model presented in Chapters 9 and 10. However, the general features of the IS-LM model are retained in the Brookings model.

The financial sector contains equations that determine the demand for and supply of various financial assets as well as the yields on those assets. There are demand equations for money, the demand deposit component of money, and time deposits. The model includes interest rates for long- and short-term securities, time deposits, and the Federal Reserve's discount mechanism. Consistent with our discussions of money demand, the demand for money and moneylike assets in the Brookings model depends on one or more interest rates, income, and the stock of wealth. The model assumes that the wealth elasticities of the demands for financial assets are all unitary. Thus the model adopts one of the assumptions made by Tobin.

The supply side also reflects some of our discussions of the money supply process. Alterations in the demand for the components of money and for time deposits affect total required reserves of the banking system, since the required reserve ratios on time and demand deposits are different. Changes in required reserves influence the deposit expansion process in the way discussed in Chapters 4 and 5. In addition banks are assumed to adjust their ratios of free reserves to total deposits in response to short-term interest rates and the Federal Reserve's discount rate. This also is a familiar input into the money supply process.

In the Brookings model, the money market then determines a short-term interest rate which is represented by the yield on three-month U. S. Treasury bills. Separate markets for long-term securities are not included. However, it is assumed that long-term securities, time deposits, and short-term securities are imperfect but good substitutes for one another. Thus changes in the short-term rate will influence both the long-term rate and the interest rate on time deposits. The Brookings model therefore assumes that the money market determines the short-term interest rate, and then the model links the long-term rate to the short-term rate through a single equation and the interest rate on time deposits to the long-term rate through another single equation. The latter equations are called *term structure equations.**

The linkage between the financial sector and the real sector is purely Keynesian and is very much akin to the IS-LM model of Chapter 9. Changes in interest rates affect investment, but not consumption. Investment expenditures are broken into subcategories. One of these, the residential construction component, is influenced by the short-term interest rate. Another component, business expenditures on new plant and equipment, is affected by the long-term interest rate.

Figure 12.2 summarizes these relationships. Note that unborrowed reserves is the principal policy variable in the financial process. This differs from our output market model, which uses the monetary base.

The short- and long-term rates are determinants of residential housing expenditures and plant and equipment expenditures by the business sector. These two components constitute the major part of current investment expenditures, and therefore changes in them produce important changes in output. As with most econometric models, the Brookings model uses gross national product (GNP) as the measure of total output. Consistent with the IS-LM model, changes in GNP feed back to the money market as money demand responds to changes in income.

---

*The theory of the term structure of interest rates was discussed in Chapter 9. The structure used in the Brookings model reflects the expectations hypothesis.

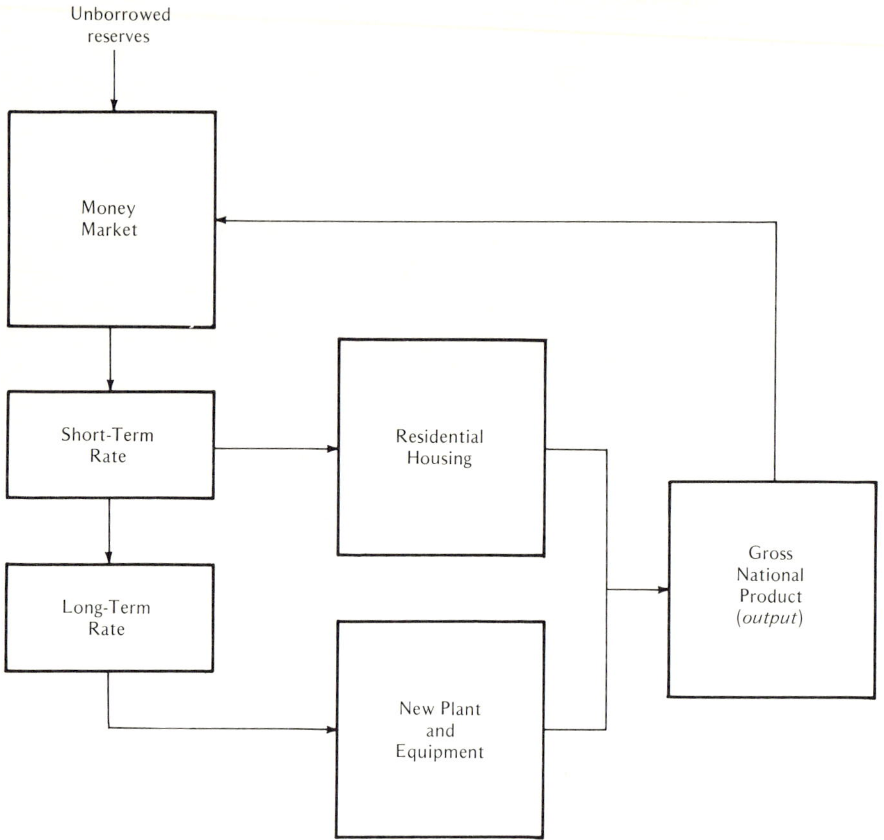

Figure 12.2

Financial linkages in the Brookings model.

In many respects then, the Brookings model is a close counterpart of the IS-LM model. The next two models are also basically Keynesian, but differ from the Brookings model in a number of important ways.

12.3 THE WHARTON QUARTERLY ECONOMETRIC FORECASTING MODEL, MARK III AND THE FRB-MIT-PENN ECONOMETRIC MODEL

The financial sectors of the Wharton and FRB-MIT-Penn (FMP) models are so similar that we will treat both in this section.* As we will see below, their major differences concern the way in which the variables determined by the financial

---

*See M. D. McCarthy, *The Wharton Quarterly Econometric Forecasting Model, Mark III* (Philadelphia: Economic Research Unit, University of Pennsylvania, 1972); F. Modigliani, "Monetary Policy and Consumption:

sector influence the real sector. The FMP model was initially developed jointly by staff economists of the Federal Reserve System and economists of the Massachusetts Institute of Technology. Subsequently the group was joined by economists of the University of Pennsylvania. The Wharton model began in 1965 as a project of the Wharton School of Finance and Commerce of the University of Pennsylvania.

Like the Brookings model, the Wharton and FMP models contain demand equations for the components of money. The demand for demand deposits depends on a short-term interest rate, the interest rate on time deposits, and the Federal Reserve's discount rate as well as on income as measured by gross national product. The demand for currency depends only on a short-term interest rate and consumption expenditures of the household sector. On the supply side, bank behavior is built into a demand equation for free reserves. Alterations in the composition of money holdings of the nonbank public affect the required reserves of the banking system. Unborrowed reserves is the principal mechanism through which the Federal Reserve System influences the supply side of the money market.* In addition to the demand for and supply of money, there are demand equations for various classes of time deposits.

The interest rate determined by the money market is the interest rate paid on three-month U. S. Treasury bills. This in turn is assumed to determine, through substitution relationships, the interest rate on four- to six-month prime commercial paper, which, together with anticipations about future price changes, determines the long-term interest rate. Various other interest rates, such as rates on time deposits and short-term business loans, are determined with similar equations. As with the Brookings model, the expectations hypothesis forms the basis for such equations. The FMP model uses the long-term rate to estimate the dividend/price ratio on corporate stocks, which in turn is used to estimate the current market value of corporate equity. We will see in a moment how this results in an important difference between the two models.

Generally for both models, the financial sector affects investment spending in the real sector through interest rates. For example, expenditures on residential construction are affected by both short- and long-term rates, and expenditures on new plant and equipment are affected by the long-term interest rate. However, the real difference between these models and the Brookings model is the way in which financial factors influence consumption expenditures.

Consumption in the Wharton model is influenced by changes in the stock of liquid assets (a component of wealth) held by the household sector and by a

---

Linkages via Interest Rate and Wealth Effects in the FMP Model," in *Consumer Spending and Monetary Policy: The Linkages* (Boston: Federal Reserve Bank of Boston, 1971); and A. Ando, F. Modigliani, and R. Rasche, "Appendix to Part I: Equations and Definitions of Variables for the FRB-MIT-Penn Econometric Model, November, 1969," in Hickman, op. cit.

*Other Federal Reserve instruments of course play a role. However, unborrowed reserves is the key instrument, and we confine our discussion to that variable.

measure of credit tightness. Liquid assets consist of money plus time deposits. Thus one of the modifications to the Keynesian model discussed earlier is included in the Wharton model. At present levels of disposable income, a $1 billion increase in liquid assets is estimated to increase total consumption expenditures by $50 million.

Credit tightness or "tight money" is measured in the Wharton model by the spread between short-term and long-term interest rates. Typically, during periods of financial stringency, the short-term rate rises relative to the long-term rate. The gap between the two rates narrows. During periods of credit ease, the spread between the two rates is observed to widen. To capture this effect, the ratio of long- to short-term interest rates is included in the consumption equation for automobiles. Thus in the Wharton model financial changes affect spending in the real sector through changes in interest rates, the stock of liquid assets, and credit tightness. Figure 12.3, which represents a composite of the Wharton and FMP models, shows these links.

Unlike the Wharton model, the FMP model includes a measure of total household wealth in the consumption equations rather than liquid assets alone. From the standpoint of the FMP model, the most important component of household wealth is the household sector's holding of corporate equities (stocks). Changes in the money market influence short- and then long-term in-

Figure 12.3

Composite financial linkages in the Wharton and FRB models.

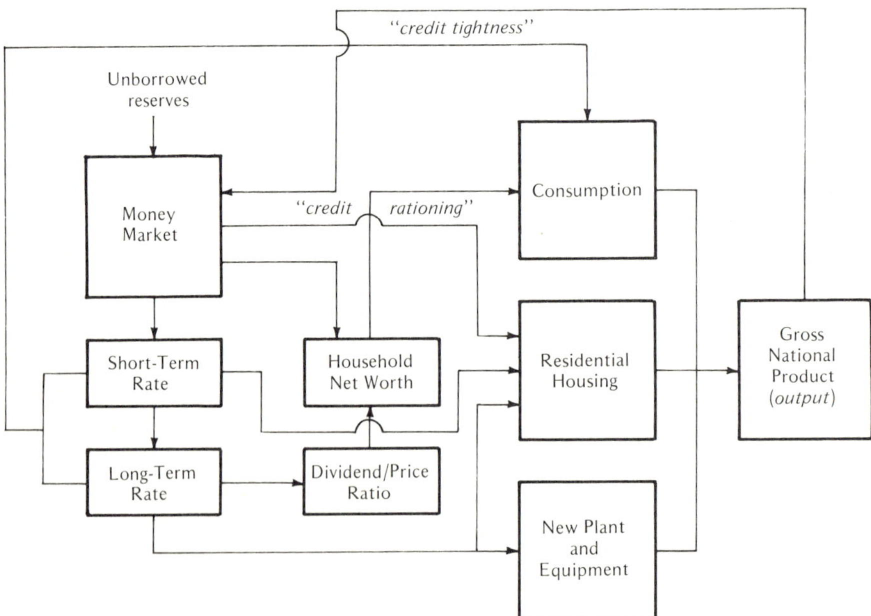

terest rates; changes in long-term interest rates in turn, through changes in the ratio of dividends to stock prices, influence the market value of corporate equity, which in turn influences consumer expenditures. Specifically, a policy that leads to a fall in the long-term interest rate leads to a fall in the ratio of dividends to stock prices and thus to an increase in the market value of corporate stocks. This constitutes an increase in the wealth holdings of the household sector, and so leads to an increase in that sector's consumption expenditures. The effect is so powerful that in the FMP model it accounts for almost half the impact of monetary policy changes.

In addition to the interest rate and wealth channels, the FMP model also contains a credit rationing channel. This channel assumes that not all credit, especially not all mortgage credit, is allocated on the basis of interest rates.* For various reasons (such as interest-rate ceilings) credit is often rationed by changing down payment terms or requirements for collateral, or by simply denying credit to the potential borrower. Thus credit ease or tightness may not always be reflected in lower or higher interest rates. The FMP model assumes that the need for such nonprice rationing becomes more intense as deposit inflows into financial institutions fall off. Therefore the extent of credit rationing is measured by deposit flows into nonbank financial institutions relative to the recent three-year history of such flows. If deposit flows exceed the past three-year average, it is assumed that financial institutions will recognize the greater availability of funds and credit will become more readily available, even though this may not be reflected in a fall in interest rates. If deposit flows fall below their most recent three-year average, the opposite is assumed. Thus, like the Wharton model, the FMP model also has three channels for monetary policy. Monetary policy affects spending in the real sector through changes in interest rates, through changes in wealth (on a somewhat broader basis than the Wharton model), and through changes in credit rationing (analogous to the credit tightness used in the Wharton model). All these channels are shown in Figure 12.3.

The wealth channel in both models represents a modification of the basic Keynesian framework and does not capture the influences outlined in the portfolio balance and wealth adjustment models. The Wharton and FMP models do not contain a market for existing capital which together with the markets for money and bonds determines relative yields, which in turn influence private spending in the market for current output (the product market). However, the models are subject to continual revision, and such channels may be incorporated at some point in the future.

It should be noted here that credit rationing was not considered in the theoretical models discussed up to this point. Credit rationing by nonprice means

---

*For a survey and critique of attempts to allow for noninterest credit rationing, see J. R. Ostas and F. Zahn, "Interest and Noninterest Credit Rationing in the Mortgage Market," *Journal of Monetary Economics,* June 1975, pp. 187–201.

occurs when the yield in a given market for funds fails to adjust completely to equate the supply of funds with the demand for funds. Thus the prevailing interest rate or yield in the market is a disequilibrium rate rather than an equilibrium rate. Our models thus far have dealt with equilibrium conditions rather than disequilibrium conditions. We will discuss the problem of disequilibrium in Chapter 13. At this point we move on to an econometric model that is quite a bit different from the preceding ones.

12.4   THE FAIR SHORT-RUN FORECASTING MODEL

The Fair econometric model differs markedly from previous models in that it contains no recognizable financial sector.* There are, however, three financial variables. These are the FHA mortgage rate, changes in private deposits in savings and loan associations, and loans to savings and loan associations by the Federal Home Loan Bank. These variables are not determined by the model in the way that financial variables are determined in the Brookings, Wharton, and FMP models. Rather, they are viewed as being exogenous to the model, determined outside its purview.

The link between the financial "sector" and the real sector is the housing market. The three financial variables, together with other exogenous variables, determine monthly housing starts. Monthly housing starts are then consolidated into quarterly figures, which together with other variables affect quarterly residential construction, a component of total investment. This in turn is one of the determinants of gross national product as shown in Figure 12.4.

Since the financial variables are exogenous, the model makes no provision for feedback from gross national product to the financial sector. There is, of course, feedback from gross national product to the consumption component of total demand, as was the case in all the previous models. The model makes the housing industry the key sector in the economy.

As it stands the model cannot be classed as either Keynesian or monetarist, although it contains some Keynesian elements. An interest rate, the FHA mortgage rate, does influence investment spending through its effect on housing starts. Yet by treating certain monetary aggregates (changes in private deposits at savings and loan associations) as exogenous, the Fair model bears some resemblance to assumptions made in the St. Louis Federal Reserve model, the monetarist model which we consider next.

12.5   THE ST. LOUIS FEDERAL RESERVE MODEL

Suppose we were to take the IS and LM curves from the Keynesian model and solve them together for the equilibrium level of output. This would be done by solving one of the two equations for the interest rate and substituting into the

---

*R. C. Fair, *A Short-Run Forecasting Model of the United States Economy* (Lexingon, Mass.: Heath Lexington Books, 1971).

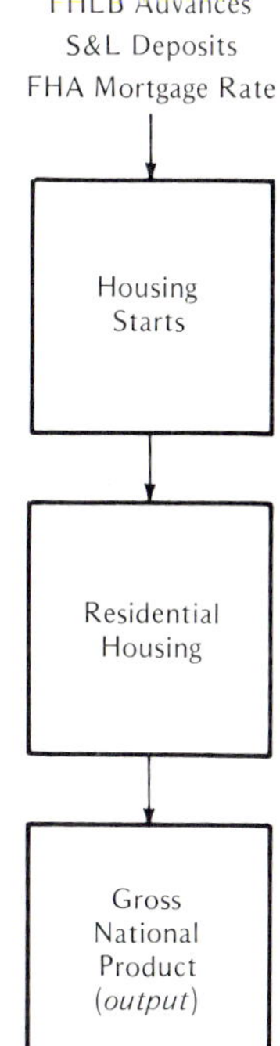

Figure 12.4

Financial linkages in the Ray C. Fair model.

other. The result would be a single equation containing four variables: output, the monetary base, real government spending, and real net taxes. By our assumptions in the IS-LM model, only output would be endogenous; the remaining variables would be policy-determined or exogenous. We could therefore solve the equation for output in terms of the monetary base, real government expenditures, and real net taxes. Had we constructed the monetary sector in such a way that the money supply was assumed to be exogenous instead of the monetary base, then the equation would express output as a function of the money supply, real government expenditures, and real net taxes. This equation would be called a *reduced-form equation* for the IS-LM system. It could be used to estimate directly the effect of changes in the money supply (or the monetary base), real government spending, and real net taxes on the level of output.

This is essentially the approach taken by the St. Louis model.* The difference between the description above and the St. Louis model is that above we started with a specified structure, the IS-LM structure, and then derived the reduced form. The impact of monetary changes on output in the reduced-form equation presumably reflects the structural mechanisms specified in the separate *IS* and

---

*See L. C. Andersen and K. M. Carlson, "A Monetarist Model for Economic Stabilization," *Review,* Federal Reserve Bank of St. Louis, April 1970, pp. 7–25. But also see L. C. Andersen, "A Monetary Model of Nominal Income Determination," *Review,* Federal Reserve Bank of St. Louis, June 1975, pp. 9–19.

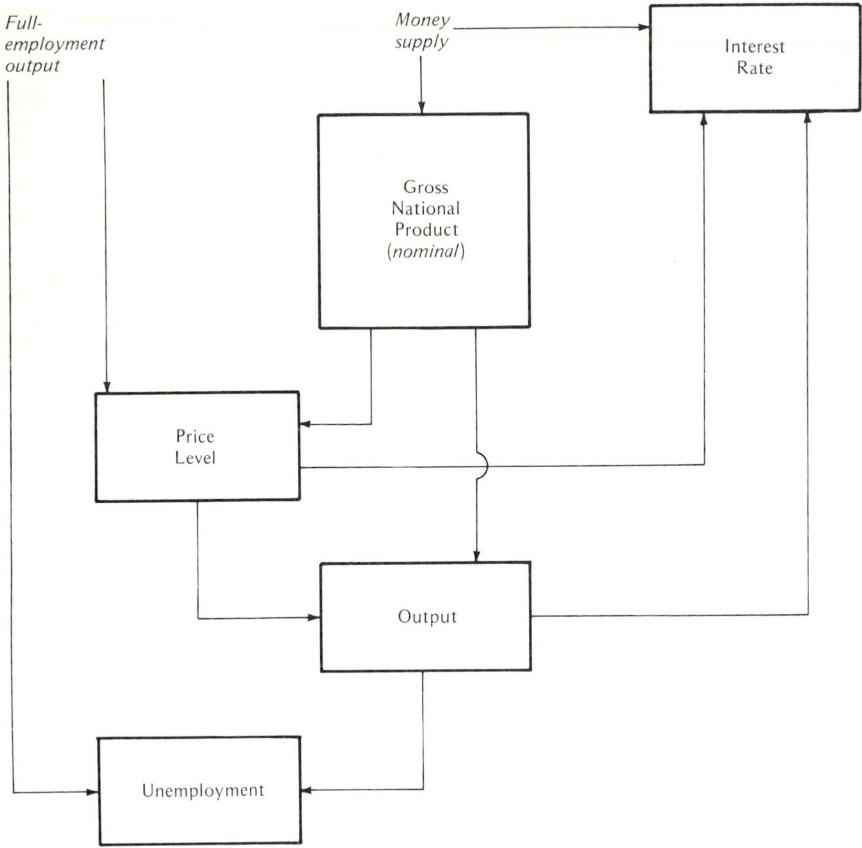

Figure 12.5

Linkages in the St. Louis model.

LM curves. However, the St. Louis approach does not specify a set of structural equations from which the reduced-form equation is derived. Rather it assumes that there are many theories of the way in which monetary factors influence gross national product and that all of these can yield a reduced form which expresses gross national product as a function of the money supply (or the monetary base) and some measure of fiscal policy. Thus we should be able to take the FMP model, which contains a variety of monetary linkages with the real sector, and derive a reduced-form equation similar to the one used in the St. Louis model. The estimated coefficient that links GNP to the money supply is a composite of all the means by which money influences gross national product. This would include the effects of interest-rate changes, wealth changes, and credit rationing. It would include those effects whether they directly impinge on consumption or on investment.

The St. Louis model then really contains no financial sector and thus bears that similarity to the Fair model. In the St. Louis model the money supply is treated as the exogenous variable. However, unlike the Fair model (and all preceding models), no linkage is specified between the money supply and gross national product. Instead monetary and fiscal policy, working through changes in the money supply and government expenditures and taxes, directly determine gross national product. An interest rate is also determined in the model, but this has no specified impact on gross national product or any of its components. Further, the model contains no feedback from either interest rates or income to the money market, since the money supply is assumed to be determined by the central bank alone. One further point is that the central equation of the St. Louis model is stated in nominal, rather than real, terms. Nominal GNP is determined by the nominal money supply (or monetary base in an alternative form) and fiscal variables in nominal form.

The flowchart in Figure 12.5 should help to clarify some of the linkages in the St. Louis model. Even though the mechanisms that transmit monetary changes to the real sector are not specified, the St. Louis model is known as a monetarist model because of the central role that the money supply plays in determining gross national product. Another feature that distinguishes the St. Louis model from its predecessors in this chapter is its small size. The St. Louis model consists of 8 equations, of which three are definitions. By comparison, the Brookings model contains over 200 equations, the Wharton and FMP models less than 100, and the Fair model about 20. The St. Louis model is less than half as large as the smallest of the other four models.

The introduction of the St. Louis model touched off a controversy over large versus small or structural versus reduced-form models among econometricians in particular and economists in general. We will touch on some of the concerns in the next section.

12.6 SOME ISSUES

A number of questions might be asked of econometric models. What do they show us about the response of the economy to changes in policy, specifically monetary policy? Are large-scale models more accurate for forecasting purposes than small, reduced-form models? Do the policy variables we use accurately measure policy changes? Are the statistical estimating techniques valid in the sense that they provide us with good estimates of the true values of the parameters of the model?

Some of these questions can be answered only by a study of econometrics and statistics. However, here we can deal with questions that relate to the effects and measurement of monetary policy. Experiments can be conducted with each model to see how the hypothetical economy represented by the model responds to a change in some policy variable if all other exogenous variables are held constant. Such an experiment is called a *simulation*. The builders of these models have in fact conducted such simulations, and we can examine their results here. The principal monetary policy variable in the Brookings,

Wharton, and FMP models is the stock of unborrowed reserves held by member banks. It is assumed that this variable can be changed by Federal Reserve open market operations. In addition, simulations have been conducted with the FMP model under the assumption that the money supply is exogenous. The results of those simulations can be compared with the St. Louis model, which treats the money supply as a major policy control variable.

The results of some of these experiments are shown in Table 12.1. Each model is characterized by lag responses in the equations of the system. For example, if a change is made that stimulates consumption expenditures, the change in consumption expenditures will not take place completely in the quarter in which the stimulus takes place. Instead the change in consumption would take place over a long period of time, as the household sector responds slowly and gradually (because of lags in multiplier rounds, lags in investment planning, etc.) to whatever stimulus had occurred. The table shows the cumulative change in gross national product that results from a sustained $1 billion increase in a policy variable. Because of the lag structure in the models, gross national product responds slowly, and it takes some time for the full change in GNP to be felt in response to the change in the policy variable. Because each model has a different lag structure, the response is faster in some models than in others.

For example, in the St. Louis model, a $1 billion increase in the money supply increases gross national product $1.2 billion in the first quarter and a total of $2.7 billion by the end of the second quarter; the total effect ($5.6 billion) is not felt until five quarters have elapsed. Thereafter no further change takes

Table 12.1
Monetary Policy Simulations: Cumulative Change in GNP
(In billions of dollars)

Model and Policy Variable*					Number of Quarters Elapsed							
	1	2	3	4	5	6	7	8	9	10	11	12
Brookings:												
Unborrowed reserves	−0.8	1.3	1.6	2.9	3.1	8.0	6.9	7.1	6.8	8.2		
FMP:												
Unborrowed reserves	0.4	1.6	4.0	7.6	11.2	15.6		29.2				81.4
Money supply	0.8	1.5	2.0	2.5	3.0	3.6		5.4				10.5
Wharton:												
Unborrowed reserves	1.0	1.8	2.5	3.2	3.6	4.2	4.8	5.3	5.8	6.2	6.5	6.7
Fair:	*not available*											
St. Louis:												
Money supply	1.2	2.7	4.2	5.2	5.6							

*All policy changes are $1 billion increases in the policy variable.

Sources: Fromm and Taubman, *op. cit.*, p. 30; Modigliani, "Monetary Policy and Consumption," *op. cit.*, pp. 46–55; McCarthy, *op. cit.*, p. 79; K. M. Carlson, "The St. Louis Equation and Monthly Data," *Review*, Federal Reserve Bank of St. Louis, January 1975, pp. 14–17.

place. The larger models respond somewhat more slowly. For example, in the FMP model a $1 billion increase in the money supply does not produce its complete impact on gross national product until approximately three years have passed. At the end of that time the response of gross national product to the $1 billion increase in the money supply is almost twice as great as it was for the St. Louis model.

Over the long run the greatest response to a change in monetary policy is shown by the FMP model. This should not be surprising, since the FMP model contains a more complete set of transmission mechanisms for monetary policy than the other large-scale models. It is clear from all the models, however, that monetary policy does produce a significant impact on the economy in the direction that we should expect from our previous theories. Simulations have also been made of changes in fiscal policy variables and comparisons made with the response of the model to changes in monetary policy. However, we will defer a comparison of the relative effects of fiscal and monetary policy to Chapter 18.

Both the large-scale and reduced-form models have been criticized on various grounds. Critics of the reduced-form models (such as the St. Louis model) have argued that those models are fraught with statistical problems because they misspecify, or fail to specify, the structure of the economy. To be valid, reduced-form estimates must be derived from a structure in which all the equations are linear (straight lines). Some of the equations in the large-scale models are nonlinear. It is not possible to estimate a linear reduced form of such models without seriously biasing the results. Indeed, the builders of the FMP model have conducted tests in which reduced-form estimates of the FMP model are made and the results compared with the whole structure.* The conclusion is that the reduced-form estimates are biased when they attempt to measure the effect of fiscal and monetary policy on gross national product.

On the other hand not everyone is happy with the large-scale models. Karl Brunner argues that the methodology used by model builders makes the large-scale models incapable of testing hypotheses about the economy.† In effect, the basic model structure is assumed to be correct, and attention is focused on refinements that give the model desirable forecasting properties. Moreover, Robert J. Gordon argues that the large-scale models are often altered without any theoretical basis for such alterations.‡ Impressive though such models may be, clearly the philosophy behind model building needs to be examined. Much work still needs to be done in converting economic theory to practical application.

---

*Modigliani, "Monetary Policy and Consumption," *op. cit.*, pp. 59–74.

†See K. Brunner's review of B. G. Hickman (ed.), *Econometric Models of Cyclical Behavior*, vols. I and II, in the *Journal of Economic Literature*, September 1973, pp. 926–933.

‡R. J. Gordon, "Discussion," in Hickman, *op. cit.*, pp. 298–310.

Another problem concerns the way in which policy changes are measured. The Brookings, Wharton, and FMP models all use unborrowed reserves as the major policy indicator. An increase in unborrowed reserves through open market purchases of government securities by the Federal Reserve system is viewed as an expansionary policy, and a contraction of unborrowed reserves as a contractionary policy. However, we know from our discussion of the sources and uses of the monetary base in Chapter 5 that total reserves or even unborrowed reserves are not independent of actions in the private sector. For example, should the nonbank public suddenly decide to increase its currency holdings, this would come at the expense of reserves. If currency holdings increase by $10 billion, reserves fall by $10 billion. Assuming no change in member bank borrowing from the Federal Reserve system, this means that unborrowed reserves would also fall by $10 billion. According to the Brookings, Wharton, and FMP models, this would be a contractionary monetary policy, even though the Federal Reserve did not engage in open market sales of government securities. In fact, in order to keep unborrowed reserves from changing at all in this example, the Federal Reserve would have to engage in $10 billion worth of open market purchases of government securities. This would increase the monetary base and so increase the money supply. Thus a policy of perceived neutrality would in fact be expansionary.

Similar arguments apply to the use of the money supply as the policy control variable. Our discussions in Chapters 5 and 6 have indicated that the money supply is jointly determined by actions of the nonbank public, banks, and the Federal Reserve system. Changes in the money supply may take place because of changes in the preferences of the nonbank public or changes in the profit-maximizing behavior of the banking system. Thus a change in the money supply may or may not indicate a policy change on the part of the Federal Reserve. We shall return to this issue in a later chapter when we discuss the problem of targets and indicators of policy.

All the models discussed thus far make use of neoclassical assumptions about the way in which markets adjust to disequilibrium. Specifically it is assumed that prices rise to clear excess demand and fall to clear excess supply. One exception was made in the case of the FMP model. It was assumed there that mortgage interest rates do not always rise sufficiently to clear excess demand in the markets for mortgage funds. Instead excess demand is reconciled with supply by nonprice or credit rationing techniques. Recently many economists have begun to devote more attention to the process of economic adjustment when prices fail to adjust in the way traditionally believed. We will deal with these "disequilibrium" approaches in the next chapter.

SUMMARY NOTES

1. Econometric models use mathematical and statistical techniques to cast theoretical models into quantitative form.

2. Monetary policy may be transmitted to the real sector through changes in interest rates, wealth, and relative asset prices.
3. The Brookings model confines the path of monetary impulses to the effect of interest-rate changes on capital investment.
4. The Wharton and FMP models make use of interest-rate, wealth, and credit availability channels.
5. The Fair and St. Louis models differ in that they contain no well-developed financial sector. The St. Louis model is a representative monetarist reduced-form model.
6. All the models indicate that financial variables exert an important influence on the economy, often with a long time lag.

DISCUSSION QUESTIONS

1. Consider the output market model of Chapter 10. If you could derive a reduced-form equation for output, what exogenous variables would it include?
2. Using the same model, derive a reduced-form equation for the price level and the interest rate. What exogenous variables are included?
3. On the basis of questions 1 and 2, what general statements can you make about reduced-form equations? How many can be derived from a given model?

DISEQUILIBRIUM MODELS

Virtually all the analysis conducted in this book thus far has been concerned with comparisons of equilibrium states in the economy. We have examined such variables as interest rates and income at one equilibrium position and then compared those values with the values taken at another position. From that analysis we drew conclusions about the effects of changes in exogenous variables on the economy. That type of analysis is call *comparative statics.*

However, markets are not always in equilibrium. In fact in the real world markets may rarely be in equilibrium. Markets are usually in disequilibrium, moving from one equilibrium position toward another. An analysis of disequilibrium states should provide the economist with at least as much useful information as an analysis of equilibrium states. Consequently a considerable portion of the literature has been devoted to an examination of the forces that operate during periods of disequilibrium. Although most of the work has focused on disequilibrium in the labor market, the approach can be used to analyze adjustment problems in the financial markets as well.

In this chapter we will examine some disequilibrium concepts and approaches with application to the financial markets. We begin here with an examination of the assumptions that form the basis for disequilibrium adjustment in conventional models.

13.1 NEOCLASSICAL MARKET ADJUSTMENT

The Keynesian model, which is the basic model used throughout most of this text, employs concepts that are traditional in neoclassical theory. In general the assumptions of the model would, under normal circumstances, lead to equilibrium states. Modifications have been made to the model to explain disequilibrium states, especially disequilibrium in the labor market. However, the underlying assumptions themselves have been subject to recent criticism. After examining the adjustment mechanisms implicit in the Keynesian model, we will consider the criticisms of those assumptions as a stepping stone to an examination of the recent approaches to disequilibrium.

The Keynesian model, as well as the Tobin and Brunner and Meltzer models discussed earlier, assumes a perfectly competitive structure in the economy. This means that any given market is characterized by large numbers of sellers and large numbers of buyers. Furthermore, it is assumed that information is perfect in the sense that all buyers and all sellers are completely aware of all relevant prices, including the prices of various factors of production. As long as information is perfect, no one seller or buyer can make a mistake about the levels and distribution of price changes. In short, the prices that sellers and buyers perceive or believe will prevail are in fact the actual prices that do prevail.

Adjustment to any exogenous change is assumed to take place through instantaneous response of the various prices. Specifically, if, in any market, the quantity demanded exceeds the quantity supplied, the price is assumed to rise until the discrepancy is resolved. Similarly, if there is excess supply (quantity supplied exceeds quantity demanded), the price is assumed to fall until the excess supply disappears.

Two pedagogical devices are often used to describe the clearing process for the various markets. The first involves the use of a hypothetical auctioneer who possesses perfect knowledge. The auctioneer knows the status of all demand curves and all supply curves for any period of time and therefore knows what set of prices will clear all markets instantaneously. The auctioneer announces that set or vector of prices, and the buyers and sellers then trade whatever quantities they desire at those equilibrium prices.

The second device makes use of a groping or searching process originated by Leon Walras.* This "tatonnement" process involves continual searching for the market clearing price. Any currently prevailing price other than the market clearing price is known as a *false price*. In the tantonnement process no trading of goods or services or financial instruments or anything else takes place at false prices. Instead the various buyers and sellers continue to search until the prices become the market clearing values, and then trade takes place all at once. One modification to the process will permit trading to take place at false prices if we include recontracting provisions so that the terms of the exchange can be adjusted if the prices at which the exchange took place are not the

---

*L. Walras, *Elements of Pure Economics,* translated by William Jaffe (Homewood, Ill.: Irwin, 1954).

market clearing prices. The final exchange or the final contract occurs at the market clearing prices.

Given that all prices are flexible in both the upward and downward directions and given that prices vary directly with excess demand, the entire price structure will move toward its equilibrium value over time. For purposes of comparative statics analysis, the adjustment time is assumed to be instantaneous. With these assumptions, persistent failure of markets to clear can only be accounted for by interferences with the market mechanism.

In the next section we will consider several types of interferences that are *imposed* on the market by external forces. These include such things as usury laws and price controls. In the following section we consider interferences that are *inherent* in the market structure.

13.2 INTERFERENCES IMPOSED ON THE MARKET STRUCTURE

The purpose of markets is to ration available supplies among competing buyers. But rationing is a term with several meanings. The most familiar refers to the process used during World War II to distribute goods in short supply. People were given ration coupons which were required in order to purchase goods in short supply. A broader meaning of rationing refers to the process for distributing all goods among competing uses. In markets where prices equalize supplies with demands for goods, the prices ration goods. Each dollar bill is a ration coupon. This is the most common type of rationing. However, when interferences exist so that prices in markets cannot adjust to eliminate shortages or excess demand, there are those who wish to purchase available supplies of goods, but are unable to do so. Thus, another type of rationing must be used to distribute goods in short supply. Types of rationing other than price rationing in goods markets are called *nonprice rationing.*

In this section we are concerned with external interferences and the resultant rationing of loanable funds in financial markets. The prices in financial markets are interest rates. However, like prices in output markets, interest rates in financial markets sometimes are not permitted to adjust to equalize supplies and demands for loanable funds (and therefore nonmoney financial assets). This means that noninterest rationing must be used to distribute funds (and therefore nonmoney financial assets) in financial markets.

Types of External Interferences

There are two major externally imposed reasons for interest rates not adjusting to equalize supplies and demands for funds. One is state usury laws, which set ceilings on the interest rates charged by lenders.* When market equilibrium

---

*J.R. Ostas, "Effects of Usury Ceilings in the Mortgage Market," *Journal of Finance,* June 1976. Regulation Q ceiling rates could also be included in this discussion. Also see N.N. Bowsher, "Usury Laws: Harmful When Effective," *Review,* Federal Reserve Bank of St. Louis, August 1974, pp. 16–23.

rates rise above ceiling rates, as they did in the 1960s and 1970s, shortages of funds are created and maintained in financial markets. Forty-five states have usury laws which affect primarily mortgage and business loan markets. While these laws were enacted to protect borrowers from "exorbitant" interest rates, they cause shortages of funds and make it necessary to distribute available funds by means of noninterest rationing.

The other major external reason for interest rates not adjusting to equalize supplies and demands in financial markets is public pressure, which makes lenders reluctant to raise interest rates immediately and too rapidly when equilibrium market rates rise. Reluctance on the part of lenders is based primarily on fear of damaging their public image and on the costs of change relative to long-run benefits. If interest rates are raised too often and/or too rapidly, lenders draw attention to their activities and run the risk of damaging their public image. That is, they encourage borrowers and legislatures to accuse them of "gouging" the public. In addition to public pressure, uncertainty about future interest rates causes lenders to be reluctant to increase interest rates to their equilibrium levels. If future rates are expected to be lower, lenders will incur costs when borrowers refinance current loans at lower interest rates in the future. Thus, the costs of refinancing could exceed the benefits of changing current interest rates.* But this is a problem of imperfect information, to which we return in the next section. Lenders' reluctance means that at current interest rates shortages of funds exist, and it is necessary for lenders to distribute available funds by means of noninterest credit rationing.

Methods of Rationing

Interest rates on consumer loans are the most sluggish in adjusting to their equilibrium levels. But demands are relatively stable and shortages are not severe, so that noninterest rationing is very slight. The primary means of noninterest rationing is raising credit standards, which means that low-income, high-risk borrowers are excluded.

Unlike the demand for consumer loans, the demand for business loans increases substantially when there are already shortages of funds. But since businesses borrow primarily from commercial banks, which can acquire funds from other sources, when interest rates rise relative to deposit rates, they are able to secure the funds they require. However, to the extent that banks do not raise interest rates to equalize supply and demand, noninterest rationing must take place. The first device used is limiting loans to present depositors who continue to have a close customer relationship. Preferences are given to larger, lower-risk businesses over smaller, high-risk businesses.

---

*J. R. Vernon, "Savings and Loan Association Response to Monetary Policies, 1953–61: A Case Study in Availability," *Southern Economic Journal,* January 1965, pp. 229–237; F. deLeeuw and E. M. Gramlich, "The Channels of Monetary Policy," *Federal Reserve Bulletin,* June 1969, pp. 472–491.

The most pronounced form of noninterest rationing occurs in mortgage markets, where supplies of funds decrease as interest rates rise relative to deposit rates paid by financial institutions to acquire funds. The supply-induced shortage as well as shortages due to increases in demand can persist for some time in mortgage markets. Mortgage lenders are so sensitive to public and government opinion that interest rates are very sluggish in adjusting to their equilibrium levels. The devices used by lenders to ration credit are to increase down payment ratios, decrease the maturity of the loan, limit loans to depositors, give preference to borrowers refinancing loans, and give preference to applicants referred by realtors who have a close relationship with the lender.

Use of noninterest credit terms instead of interest rates implies that financial markets are in disequilibrium with respect to interest rates, but are cleared (short supplies are distributed) by adjustments in noninterest credit terms. To illustrate the adjustment process which is believed to take place, particularly in mortgage markets, consider the following.*

Suppose in a expansionary period interest rates are rising rapidly because of expansionary fiscal policy and rising prices. Further, suppose that along with the resulting increase in real income, the demand for mortgage loans increases rapidly, and the supply of mortgage loans is falling because of financial disintermediation. If mortgage rates rise only slowly to their equilibrium levels because lenders are uncertain and/or fear damage to their public image, a shortage of mortgage loans persists. That is, at the current mortgage rate some borrowers cannot borrow the funds they require. Which borrowers obtain the funds they require depends on which noninterest credit terms are used to ration funds. If we assume that noninterest credit terms move together, the down payment ratio can be used as a measure of noninterest credit rationing.† When disequilibrium is created with respect to the mortgage rate and persists until the mortgage rate adjusts to its equilibrium level, the down payment ratio increases to ration available funds in short supply. The adjustment of noninterest credit terms in this manner means that all those who wish to borrow given *all* the credit terms (interest and noninterest credit terms) are able to do so. Thus, in periods of excess demand with respect to the mortgage rate, noninterest credit terms adjust to clear credit markets. This phenomenon is believed to be temporary. Once the interest rate adjusts (if possible) to equalize supply with demand, noninterest credit terms return to their former levels.

13.3 INTERFERENCES INHERENT IN THE MARKET STRUCTURE

Unlike the constraints on market adjustment discussed in the previous section, the interferences discussed in this section are part of the market structure because they depend on the behavior of market participants and/or their per-

---

* J. R. Ostas and F. Zahn, "Interest and Noninterest Credit Rationing in the Mortgage Market," *Journal of Monetary Economics,* June 1975, pp. 187–201.

†Also see the measures employed by the Wharton and FMP models discussed in Chapter 12.

ceptions about the real world. We begin with two interferences of long standing in Keynesian economics.

Interferences in the Keynesian System

While the assumption of perfect competition leads to the conclusion that all markets should clear, it is obvious that in the real world some markets do not clear, or at least clear very slowly, even when external constraints are absent. This is especially true of the labor market, where unemployment, which is an excess supply of labor, may persist for some time. Two popular reasons for persistent excess supply or unemployment in the labor market have been advanced for the Keynesian model.* The first assumes that not all prices are flexible. In particular, it assumes that the nominal wage rate, which would normally be determined in the labor market, is rigid. The second introduces into the money demand schedule a peculiar property which makes equilibrium in the output and money markets potentially inconsistent with equilibrium in the labor market.

Rigidity in the nominal wage rate is grounded in the belief that at least some workers operate under money illusion. Money illusion is present when workers believe that an increase in their nominal wage rate increases their purchasing power even when the prices of all goods and services increase by a greater percentage than the increase in the nominal wage rate. Moreover, reductions in the nominal wage rate are resisted even when such reductions would be offset by a greater decrease in prices. Thus, once a given nominal wage rate is established, it can only move in the upward direction. Decreases in output demand which lead to decreases in the quantity demanded of labor are absorbed by increases in unemployment rather than by decreases in the nominal wage rate. Money illusion, then, destroys the adjustment mechanism in the labor market when excess supply or unemployment prevails.

The second device is grounded in money holders' fear of capital risk.† If interest rates decline to a sufficiently low level (bond prices rise to a sufficiently high level), it is assumed that money holders would prefer to hold money balances rather than bonds. The reason is that bond prices cannot be expected to rise any further and must therefore decline or remain unchanged. Should bond prices decline and bond holders be forced to liquidate their bond holdings before maturity, bond holders would suffer capital losses in excess of the low interest earnings received while holding the bonds. Consequently, money demand gradually increases as the interest rate falls (bond prices increase) until the interest rate hits its assumed lower bound. Thereafter, further attempts to lower the interest rate by increasing the supply of money will be frustrated

---

*Whether Keynes would agree with these is questionable. See A. Leijonhufvud, "Keynes and the Keynesians: A Suggested Interpretation," *American Economic Review,* May 1967, pp. 401–410.

†See Chapter 7 for a more detailed discussion. Although it is developed there, the liquidity trap and its implications are worth repeating.

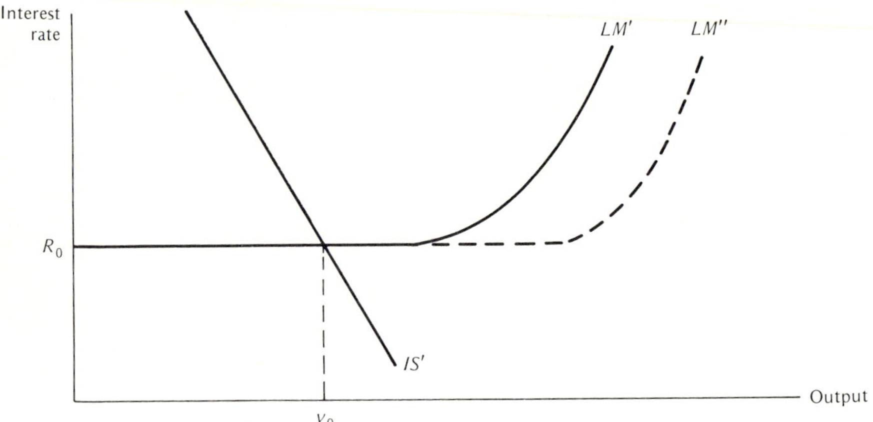

Figure 13.1

The Keynesian liquidity trap.

because money holders will accept and hold the entire increase in the supply of money and divert no additional funds into the bond market. This characteristic of money demand implies the shape to the Keynesian LM schedule shown in Figure 13.1. Equilibrium output, which is determined by the intersection of the IS' and LM' schedules, is shown at y_0. This level of output may or may not be consistent with full employment. What is more, attempts to increase output through expansionary monetary policies will be unsuccessful. If the Federal Reserve acts to increase the monetary base and thereby shift the LM' curve to the right, say to LM'', the equilibrium interest rate and output combination will not change.

Both the above devices imply conditions that seem at variance with the historical evidence under conditions of falling output demand. The rigid wage assumption implies that nominal wage rates will not fall as unemployment develops. The liquidity trap in money demand implies that once a unique low level of the interest rate is reached, a further reduction in output demand will not result in a further decline in the interest rate. That is, in the horizontal portion of the LM' curve shown in Figure 13.1, the interest rate is not changed in the face of a shift in either the IS' curve or the LM' curve. Some indication of the flexibility of nominal wage rate and interest rates is provided in Table 13.1.

The table contains two time periods. The first, from 1929 through 1938, was a period of substantial change in unemployment, which ranged from 3.2 percent of the labor force in 1929 to 24.9 percent in 1933. The second period in the table covers the years from 1970 through 1975, during which time more modest fluctuations in unemployment occurred. As an explanation of unemployment in the Great Depression, the rigid nominal wage rate hypothesis is not sufficient. As output demand fell, from 1929 to 1933, so also did the nominal wage rate, by over 20 percent. In recent years, under conditions of more modest fluctuations in output demand, the nominal wage rate continues to rise.

Two interest rates are shown in Table 13.1, a long-term interest rate and a short-term interest rate. Both rates show no tendency to settle at some minimum level in the face of changes in output demand as measured by increases or decreases in unemployment. In fact, the Federal Reserve System was successful in pushing interest rates to levels that were even lower than those for the 1930s during the years of World War II. Rather than superimposing wage and interest-rate rigidities over the model of perfect competition, recent approaches have reexamined the basic assumptions that lead to adjustment in the model of perfect competition.

Problems with the Assumptions of Perfect Competition

Suppose we drop the assumption of an all-knowing auctioneer whose function it is to announce sets of prices that will enable the markets to clear. Each buyer and each seller under conditions of perfect competition is a price taker. That is, each firm decides on the amount it will produce and offer for sale given the price, over which it has no control. Each buyer will decide on the quantity to purchase given the price, over which he or she also has no control. Suppose now that there is an exogenous decrease in the demand for the product. Under the usual adjustment assumptions, there will be an excess supply of the product,

Table 13.1
Unemployment, Wage Rates, and Interest Rates: Selected Years

Year	Unemployment Rate	Hourly Wage Rate	Commercial Paper Rate	Corporate Bond Rate
1929	3.2%	$0.56	5.85%	4.73%
1930	8.7	0.55	3.59	4.55
1931	15.9	0.51	2.64	4.58
1932	23.6	0.44	2.73	5.01
1933	24.9	0.44	1.73	4.49
1934	21.7	0.53	1.02	4.00
1935	20.1	0.54	0.75	3.60
1936	16.9	0.55	0.75	3.24
1937	14.3	0.62	0.94	3.26
1938	19.0	0.62	0.81	3.19
1970	4.9	3.36	7.72	8.04
1971	5.9	3.57	5.11	7.39
1972	5.6	3.81	4.69	7.21
1973	4.9	4.07	8.15	7.44
1974	5.6	4.40	9.87	8.57
1975	8.5	4.81	6.33	8.83

Source: *Economic Report of the President,* various years.

and this should result in a fall in the price. However, both buyers and sellers are price takers who individually have no control over the price. Consequently it is not clear who will initiate the price reduction. In fact, if the sellers continue as price takers and if they cannot sell all that they desire to sell at the current price, they will simply reduce their output. Buyers, on the other hand, will continue to buy the amount they desire to buy at the current price level. Thus producers are placed in a position of selling less than the profit-maximizing quantity given the current price.

In response to the disequilibrium state described above, we have observed not a price adjustment, but a quantity adjustment. If perfect information were available and all participants in the market were aware of the new market clearing price, instantaneous price adjustment would be possible. However, information is not perfect, and therefore false trading takes place at non–market clearing prices. Eventually, when it becomes apparent to everyone that trading is taking place at a price level that is too high for equilibrium, individual adjustments in prices will be made. However, the initial response to disequilibrium is a quantity rather than a price adjustment.

Disequilibrium analysis seeks to specify how those quantity adjustments take place, how allocation is made until a new equilibrium is reached, and how information is acquired which ultimately results in adjustments in prices.

Recent Approaches to Market Interferences and Adjustment

In order to provide a focus for the following discussion, consider the market for automobile loans.* This market is a close approximation of a perfectly competitive market, since there are many seekers of automobile loans and many institutions that supply such loans. Banks of various types as well as consumer finance companies will provide installment loans for automobiles. In order to eliminate external interferences, assume there are no usury laws or governmental pressures. Suppose that from a position of equilibrium, there is an exogenous increase in the demand for automobile loans. At the prevailing rate of interest for automobile loans, there will now be an excess demand for loans. Individual banks find that they cannot satisfy the loan demand facing them at the current interest rate. In the belief that no one single institution can by itself alter the market interest rate, the individual institutions ration the amount of loans they wish to supply at the current interest rate on the basis of the nonprice means discussed earlier.

In time, the market interest rate will rise in response to the excess demand for automobile loans. However, this will not occur until both lenders and borrowers begin to recognize that the current market interest rate is not a market

---

*A good survey of disequilibrium macroeconomics may be found in D. J. Ott, A. F. Ott, and J. H. Yoo, *Macroeconomic Theory* (New York: McGraw-Hill, 1975), chaps. 17–20.

clearing interest rate. One reason why the adjustment does not take place immediately is because lenders and borrowers do not have *perfect information* about the nature of demand and supply conditions. One reason why they do not have perfect information is that information is not a free good.* Information must be sought out and communicated to both lenders and borrowers. This requires the use of resources that could be used in other activities.

The lending institution that faces an excess demand for automobile loans employs resources in checking with other lending institutions to see whether the excess demand is localized or whether it is part of a general increase in the demand for loans. Market analysts are consulted by the lending institutions in an effort to determine whether the increase in the demand for loans is a temporary phenomenon or whether it is likely to be sustained over a longer period of time.

From the borrower's point of view, resources must also be devoted to acquiring information. A borrower who is not able to obtain a loan from a particular lending institution may not recognize that other institutions also are short of funds. Consequently the borrower may not be willing even to consider paying a higher rate of interest without checking with other lending institutions in an effort to borrow the funds at the current interest rate. It is only after spending time searching out information that the potential borrower discovers that the desired loan cannot be obtained at the current interest rate. At that time the borrower may be willing, and offer, to pay a higher rate of interest for the loan, if that will get the funds. Thus after employing various resources to seek out information, the lender feels the need to raise the interest rate and the borrower is willing to pay a higher interest rate.

How long a time period passes before both lenders and borrowers arrive at that decision depends on a weighing of relative costs and benefits. The benefit of the search activity is that the expected costs of raising the interest rate immediately are ascertained. The cost of raising the interest rate immediately if such a raise is inappropriate is the profits lost from the resulting loss of business. This cost must be weighted by the probability that an increase in the interest rate is inappropriate. An increase in the interest rate is inappropriate if the market clearing interest rate has not, in fact, risen. Information acquired through search activity enables the lender's estimate of the aforementioned probability to be adjusted toward 0 or 100 percent, depending on whether the interest-rate increase is appropriate or not. Presumably, the individual lending institution will stop searching for additional information when the marginal (or incremental) benefit derived from search is just offset by the marginal cost of the search activity. A similar argument applies to the potential borrower.

The process of acquiring information changes the perceptions of both

---

*See A. A. Alchian, "Information Costs, Pricing and Resource Unemployment," *Western Economic Journal,* June 1969, pp. 109–128.

lenders and borrowers about the appropriate set of interest rates that should prevail in the market. In fact, the state of disequilibrium may be defined as a condition in which *perceived* market clearing prices and interest rates deviate from *actual* market clearing prices and interest rates. In the case cited above, the actual market clearing interest rate is above the interest rate initially perceived by the lender. But the lender is also aware that at currently prevailing interest rates there is an excess demand for loans. Consequently the lender begins search activity in an effort to find the appropriate market clearing interest rate. As all lenders engage in this process and ultimately begin to adjust their interest rates, the perceived market clearing interest rate is brought into conformity with the actual market clearing interest rate. Once that occurs, the markets clear and there is no longer any excess demand or supply. As long as the lenders and borrowers are unaware of the appropriate market clearing interest rate, trading takes place at a false interest rate. This means that either the lender or the borrower will not be operating on the appropriate supply or demand curve. In the excess demand case just discussed, at any interest rate below the market clearing interest rate, suppliers of funds will be operating on their supply curves, but demanders will not be operating on their demand curves. At the current interest rate, borrowers will be forced to borrow less than they desire. Given the current interest rate, the amount that borrowers wish to borrow is called their *notional* demand, while the amount they are able to borrow is called their *effective* demand.

The discrepancy between notional demand and effective demand in any one market "spills over" into other markets.* For example, if seekers of automobile loans are unable to borrow the amounts they wish to borrow at current interest rates, then they will be unable to make the number of automobile purchases they wish to make in the automobile market. Thus the effective demand for automobiles will be less than the notional demand. Automobile dealers, on the other hand, will not be able to sell as much as they wish to sell at currently prevailing prices. Thus the effective supply of automobiles will be less than the notional supply. Now consider an example illustrating the implications of this *spillover effect.*

Hypothetical Adjustment in the LB-LM Model

Various equilibrium models have been used in this book. The IS-LM model determined equilibrium conditions in the product and money markets; the LB-LM model in the loanable funds and money markets; and the portfolio balance models in the bond, money, and existing capital markets. Even though we use the concept of a money market in equilibrium analysis, in reality there is no

---

*For a formal treatment, see R.J. Barro and H. I. Grossman, "A General Disequilibrium Model of Income and Employment," *American Economic Review,* March 1971, pp. 82–93.

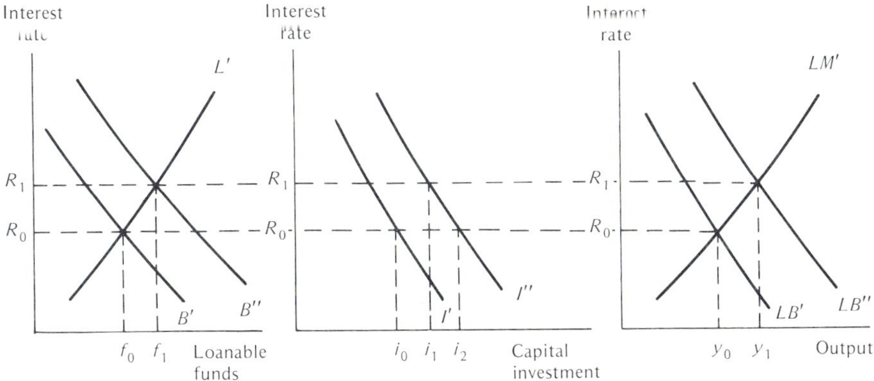

Figure 13.2
Disequilibrium in the loanable funds market.

market for money as an asset. Money is the medium of exchange. That is, it is the good that forms the other side of the transaction in the markets for financial assets, goods, and labor. Although the money-market concept is useful in determining the conditions that lead to equilibrium in the general model, changes in equilibrium conditions are best analyzed by examining the market that proximately determines the interest rate, namely, the loanable funds market.*

In the illustration below we will use the loanable funds market, which is the market in which financial assets are exchanged for money balances. Figure 13.2 shows on the left side the demand for and supply of loanable funds. The center panel shows the capital investment schedule developed in Chapter 2. The right-hand panel represents the conventional LB-LM diagram. The LB-LM curves provide a reference that shows where equilibrium takes place if all markets clear. The initial equilibrium takes place at interest rate R_0. This corresponds to the quantity of loanable funds exchanged f_0, investment i_0, and output, y_0.

Now suppose that there is a rightward shift in the capital investment schedule as a consequence of an improvement in technology that raises the productivity of new capital goods. Since the rate of return on new capital has been increased as a result, firms will demand more new capital goods at existing interest rates. The increase in intended purchases of capital goods is financed by selling additional financial assets in exchange for loanable funds. Thus the notional demand for loanable funds shifts to the right, from B' to B''. The increase in notional investment demand also shifts the LB schedule from LB' to LB''.

However, *individual* suppliers of loanable funds (purchasers of financial

---

*See D. P. Tucker, "Macroeconomic Models and the Demand for Money under Market Disequilibrium," *Journal of Money, Credit and Banking,* February 1971, pp. 57–83.

assets) will not normally be aware that there is a general increase in the demand for loanable funds. Consequently, given the current interest rate, they will continue to supply quantity f_0 of loanable funds. Allocation of the amount f_0 is accomplished not through a rising interest rate, but by means of nonprice credit rationing. The unsatisfied excess demand in the loanable funds market spills over into the market for new capital goods. Since business firms cannot obtain the funds desired, their effective demand for new capital goods is less than the notional demand. Consequently, even though there is an *intended* increase in output demand, output demand in fact does not increase.

Thus initially it appears as though the improvement in technology which raises the productivity of new capital has no effect on capital investment, output, and employment. Over time, however, as information is compiled, lenders will begin to raise the interest rate, and borrowers will become willing to pay higher interest rates. As the interest rate rises, the quantity supplied of loanable funds increases. Expanded borrowing then takes place, which leads to higher expenditures on new capital goods and ultimately increases in output demand.

As long as prices and interest rates are flexible in the long run, the final equilibrium position should be that predicted by comparative statics analysis. However, the interim process implies patterns of price and interest-rate change that the disequilibrium economists hope will conform more closely to reality than the patterns implied by comparative statics analysis. Moreover, correct specification of the process of disequilibrium will help in determining the length of the time lags that occur during the adjustment process. Aside from providing a more fruitful interpretation of real world changes, such knowledge can be useful to policy makers in the timing of policy.

There is an aside that is in order at this time. Economists in recent years have been examining something called the *efficient markets hypothesis*. Briefly stated, this hypothesis argues that financial markets (in particular) adjust very quickly to new information, so that current prices and interest rates reflect all the information possessed by market participants. Thus prices and interest rates will not display any systematic pattern over time, as they would if they gradually adjusted to new information.*

At first glance this seems inconsistent with our previous discussions of market disequilibrium. Actually it is not. Nothing in the efficient markets hypothesis says that the information contained in current prices and interest rates is correct or complete. The hypothesis only states that markets adjust very quickly to whatever information is available. Disequilibrium approaches are primarily concerned with the acquisition of correct (or market clearing) information. That process may be gradual even though the markets adjust quickly to whatever information, correct or incorrect, is available.

---

*For a practical discussion of the efficient markets hypothesis and its implications, see B. G. Malkiel, *A Random Walk down Wall Street,* college ed. rev. (New York: Norton, 1975).

Disequilibrium approaches have yet to become as widely accepted as conventional tools of analysis. This is mainly due to the fact that the development of such approaches is fairly recent. However, some applications to specific problems have been gaining acceptance. We will examine one of these applications in the next chapter when we discuss the domestic problems of inflation and unemployment which face the policy maker.

SUMMARY NOTES

1. Neoclassical market adjustment assumes the existence of perfect information. No final exchanges take place at false prices.
2. External market interferences include price controls or usury laws and public and governmental pressures that restrict price movements.
3. Where prices do not immediately clear markets, nonprice means are employed until prices adjust, if they are permitted to do so.
4. Interferences that are inherent in, or internal to, the market structure may be due to money illusion or imperfect information.
5. Discrepancies between effective and notional demand spill over into other markets, implying disequilibrium there.

DISCUSSION QUESTIONS

1. Rank the following markets in order of speed of adjustment to equilibrium: Automobiles (new), automobiles (used), corporate stocks, mortgages, apartments. What is the basis for your ranking system?
2. Considering the various types of rationing (including price) discussed in the chapter, which do you consider to be the most "equitable"? Why?
3. Different banks often charge different interest rates for automobile loans. Yet the bank with the lowest interest rate doesn't get all the business. Why?
4. Survey three or four friends and ask them the following: Base sticker price of a 1976 Mustang II, price of a 5-pound bag of Idaho potatoes, FHA mortgage rate, price of this book. Compare their answers with the correct ones. Is information perfect?

FOUR

MONETARY POLICY

POLICY GOALS: DOMESTIC

If we could single out the two most persistent economic problems facing the United States during the twentieth century, they would be inflation and unemployment. The Great Depression of the 1930s produced lasting fears that what has happened once can happen again. Massive unemployment caused such concern that following World War II, Congress passed the Employment Act of 1946, which requires the government to promote maximum employment. However, the continuing concern with unemployment diverts attention from the problem of inflation only temporarily from time to time. Although inflation is not specifically singled out as a target of government policy in the Employment Act, concern is nevertheless implied. In addition to requiring the government to promote maximum employment, the Act also requires the government to promote maximum purchasing power. Moreover, throughout the post-World War II period, the Federal Reserve System repeatedly expressed concern about inflation.

From time to time other domestic economic goals appear on the scene. For example, economic growth became a concern in the early 1960s. One of the objectives of the Kennedy administration was to "get the country moving again." Toward that end various policies were proposed that were intended to increase the growth rate of the United States economy. In the face of a rising population and a rising labor force, economic growth is necessary to maintain even a stable per capita income and a stable rate of unemployment. For per capita income to increase, the economy's potential to produce must grow faster than the population. Without economic growth, a larger slice of the economic pie for some individuals must be accompanied by a smaller slice for others.

However, growth is often treated as an intermediate target in the quest for full employment. Faster rates of economic growth permit absorption of a growing labor force, so that unemployment is held steady and possibly even reduced. The quest for growth is also subject to a certain amount of faddism. High unemployment in the early 1960s plus a desire to prevent the Soviet economy from catching up with the United States economy led to calls for higher rates of economic growth. But by the time the 1970s had arrived, policies that were originally designed to stimulate economic growth were attacked as being destructive of the environment. Some observers argue that economic growth generates pollution that will, in the long run, produce destructive effects that outweigh any of the benefits of growth.

Throughout the periods in which economic growth is alternately viewed with favor and disfavor, inflation and unemployment remain the prime targets of policy and public opinion. Considering these the primary domestic policy targets, this chapter outlines some of the possible causes of inflation and unemployment and discusses their adverse effects. The chapter concludes with the implications for policy if inflation and unemployment are to be reduced or eliminated.

14.1 THE NATURE OF INFLATION

We define inflation as a sustained increase in the general price level. Deflation then would be a continuous fall in the price level.* These changes should be distinguished from changes in relative prices. If the price of oil increases while the price of beer decreases, we can talk about neither inflation nor deflation. Those changes reflect relative increases or decreases in the supplies and demands for oil and beer. On the other hand, inflation occurs when there is a general increase in the prices of all or most products. This would reflect an increase in the demand or a decrease in the supply for all goods in general rather than a shift in preferences from one good to another or a shift in their relative supplies.

Changes across the board for all or most prices are measured through changes in a price index. A price index is a weighted average, relative to some base year, of the prices of a set of goods the index seeks to evaluate. For example, the most frequently cited index, the *Consumer Price Index*, is a weighted average of goods in a typical market basket for urban consumers. The *Wholesale Price Index* is a weighted average of prices of goods in their first transaction.† Finally, less popular but none the less important, there is the *Gross National Product Implicit Price Deflator*, or GNP deflator for short. The

---

*For a recent survey of inflation theory, see D. Laidler and M. Parkin, "Inflation: A Survey," *Economic Journal*, December 1975, pp. 741–809.

†See D. M. Beckter and M. S. Pickett, "The Wholesale and Consumer Price Indexes: What's the Connection?" *Monthly Review*, Federal Reserve Bank of Kansas City, June 1973, pp. 3–9 for a comparison.

GNP deflator is an index of prices of all final goods and services produced in the current period. Thus it is an index of the prices of the goods and services that make up the gross national product.

Although the indices measure the prices of different categories of goods, they all tend to be fairly closely correlated over time. That is, over time all three indices tend to rise and fall together. Inflation is measured by the percent change from year to year in the appropriate index. There really is no such thing as *the* rate of inflation. Rather, one can speak of the rate of inflation as measured by the Consumer Price Index or as measured by the Wholesale Price Index. Such rates of inflation are shown in Table 14.1. The table shows the average annual rates of change for the three indices over five-year periods beginning with 1945. The high rates of inflation for the 1945–1949 period reflect the aftermath of World War II. During the 1950s and early 1960s all indices display relatively modest rates of inflation. Then, beginning with the last half of the 1960s , the rates of inflation increase, reaching levels during the 1970–1974 period that are as high as they were during the immediate post-World War II period. This sharp increase in the rate of inflation, however measured, during the last decade has precipitated considerable concern on the part of policy makers and the public at large. There are, of course, a number of reasons for the concern over inflation.

The Effects of Inflation

Inflation is viewed with alarm because it is assumed that it produces adverse effects on the distribution of income, on the distribution of wealth, and on the relationship between creditors and debtors. Inflation may produce undesirable income redistributions because not everyone's source of income rises at the same rate in the face of rapidly rising prices. Many people assume that increases in prices result in increases in profits and concurrent increases in the dividends paid out of profits to the stockholders of corporations. On the other hand, because many labor contracts are adjusted only infrequently, wage

Table 14.1
Rates of Inflation: 1945–1974

	Average Annual Rates of Change		
	WPI	**CPI**	**GNP Deflator**
1945–1949	8.4%	6.4%	6.5%
1950–1954	2.5	2.5	2.5
1955–1959	1.7	1.9	2.5
1960–1964	0.1	1.2	1.4
1965–1969	2.7	3.8	3.3
1970–1974	8.6	6.1	5.8

Source: Economic Report of the President, 1975.

increases are assumed by many to lag behind increases in prices. Some individuals, especially those who are retired, live on annuities that are fixed in nominal terms. These annuities do not increase automatically when prices increase. If these assumptions are correct, an increase in prices tends to shift real resources away from those individuals living on fixed annuities and those living on wages that lag behind price changes, to those whose incomes are derived primarily from profits.

In addition to its effect on current income flows, inflation may also affect the distribution of existing wealth. The typical household may hold wealth in many forms. Real assets such as houses and automobiles are part of the stock of wealth. But financial assets are included in household wealth as well. These would include corporate stocks and bonds as well as government bonds. In the face of inflation many real assets should rise in value. Real estate values, for example, tend to rise on the average at least as fast as the rate of inflation. If investors believe that inflation leads to higher corporate profits, they will attempt to buy more corporate stock during periods of inflation, thus bidding up the price of that stock. This increases the wealth holdings of the owners of existing stocks. On the other hand, owners of bonds may be placed at a disadvantage. Bond interest payments are fixed (fixed coupon). Moreover, the maturity values of bonds are fixed in nominal terms. Any increase in the price of goods reduces the real purchasing power or the real value of bonds. Thus inflation may have the effect of reallocating real wealth from bond holders to stock holders and real asset holders.

Finally, lender-borrower or creditor-debtor relationships may be distorted as prices increase. When prices rise, loans are repaid with dollars of decreased purchasing power. For example, suppose a loan for $100 is made for a period of one year at an interest rate of 10 percent. The borrower receives $100 and at the end of the year pays the lender $110. However, if prices have risen by, say, 7 per cent during the course of the year, then each dollar repaid to the lender has been reduced in purchasing power by 7 percent. Thus in real terms it is as though the lender has received an interest rate of only 3 percent instead of 10 percent. Under such conditions inflation would shift purchasing power from the lenders to the borrowers.

However, the issue may not be that simple.* It seems reasonable to assume that if individuals expect to be hurt by inflation, they will take measures to protect themselves. If wage earners anticipate inflation, they will seek to protect themselves by demanding wage increases in excess of what they normally would demand in the absence of inflation. If retirees on Social Security expect prices to increase, they will demand that their elected representatives vote to increase Social Security payments. Similarly, lenders can protect themselves

---

*See G. L. Bach, "Inflation: Who Gains and Who Loses?" *Challenge*, July–August 1974, pp. 48–55; and E. C. Budd and D. F. Seiders, "The Impact of Inflation on the Distribution of Income and Wealth," *American Economic Review*, May 1971, pp. 128–138.

from inflation by asking for interest rates in excess of those they would desire in the absence of inflation. Moreover, if borrowers expect to benefit from inflation, they will be willing to pay higher interest rates during periods of inflation than during periods of no inflation.

Since it is reasonable to expect that individuals will so behave in the face of expected inflation, writers have tended to make a distinction between expected and unexpected inflation when they examine the effects of inflation on income and wealth distribution and on the relationships between creditors and debtors. A number of studies have concluded that the detrimental effects of inflation discussed above occur when the inflation is unexpected. However, when inflation is fully expected, the detrimental effects may not be observed. We shall return to this issue in the third section of this chapter when we consider the relationship between inflation and unemployment.

The Causes of Inflation

In individual markets we assume that prices rise in response to excess demand and fall in response to excess supply. It seems reasonable, then, that at the macroeconomic level inflation occurs when *aggregate* output demand rises relative to *aggregate* output supply, and deflation occurs when output demand falls relative to output supply. However, any theory of inflation must get at the exogenous forces that are responsible for changes in output demand relative to output supply.

In the context of the standard IS-LM model developed in earlier chapters, output demand may be altered by changes in government spending and taxes or by changes in the monetary base induced through Federal Reserve action. If fiscal or monetary policy actions result in an increase in output demand without a corresponding increase in output supply, prices will increase. This will occur principally at full employment when the quantity of output supplied cannot be increased in the face of increases in output demand. However, inflation may also occur at less than full employment if there are constraints in the economy that retard any increase in output supply (together with a decrease in unemployment) when there is an increase in total demand.

In addition to examining the exogenous causes of changes in demand relative to supply, any theory of inflation also attempts to determine the conditions under which price increases will be sustained. Consider the limiting case in which the economy is fully employed, so that the quantity of output supplied cannot be increased. An increase in output demand under such circumstances will cause the price level to rise, since the demand increase cannot be absorbed by an increase in output. The question is, "Will the price increase continue without limit or is there some self-correcting mechanism that will, over time, eliminate the excess demand?"

Suppose the increase in output demand is caused by a permanent increase in the level of government expenditure on goods and services in real terms. Assume also that taxes are held constant and that the Federal Reserve System does not change the monetary base. The increase in government expenditures adds directly to output demand. This addition is financed through borrowing by the U. S. Treasury in the financial markets. As the Treasury attempts to borrow the funds, interest rates are forced up, and this induces money holders to reduce their money balances, thereby providing the funds for the increase in government expenditures. As long as output cannot increase (or we face rising marginal costs), prices will rise. As prices rise, the demand for nominal money balances increases.

Thus two opposing factors influence the demand for money in nominal terms. A rising price level tends to increase the demand for money, and a rising interest rate tends to decrease the quantity of money demanded. In order for inflation to be sustained, the excess output demand must be maintained. That is, spending in *nominal* terms must rise as fast as the price level. It will be maintained if the increasing interest rate reduces the quantity of money demanded by more than the rising price level increases the demand for money. If that occurs, funds will continuously be made available to finance a permanently higher level of real spending (rising nominal spending). It seems doubtful that money demand could fall without limit. If it cannot, the higher level of output demand cannot be maintained, and therefore the inflation is not sustainable.

Moreover, a continuously rising interest rate is likely to induce reductions in real investment expenditures by the business sector. Such reductions in investment spending will ultimately offset the permanent increase in real government expenditures, so that output demand returns to its former level. Thus the conditions necessary for inflation to be sustained in the face of a permanent increase in output demand appear to be too extreme to be realistic.

Now consider a monetary policy–induced increase in output demand. Suppose again that output is fixed at the full-employment level. Assume that the Federal Reserve permanently increases the monetary base. This will lead to an increase in the money supply and a consequent fall in the interest rate. The fall in the interest rate in turn induces an increase in expenditures on capital goods by the business sector. Such an increase in capital goods expenditures constitutes an increase in output demand. Since the quantity of output supplied cannot increase, prices must rise. The question is, "Will they rise without limit?"

The answer is, "No!" As the price level increases, the demand for money also increases. Since the increase in the money supply was a once and for all increase, a continuously rising money demand (due to a continuously rising price level) must raise the interest rate. As the interest rate increases, investment expenditures, which had previously risen, begin to fall. They will continue to fall as long as the interest rate continues to rise. The interest rate will continue to rise as long as money demand increases, and money demand will continue to increase as long as the price level rises. Finally when the fall in investment just offsets its previous increase, output demand will have returned to its former level, and there will be no further price increases. With no further price increases, the interest rate will not rise any further, and the economy is once again in a state of zero-inflation equilibrium.

Thus neither a permanent increase in the level of real government expenditures nor a permanent increase in the monetary base is sufficient to result in sustained inflation. In fact a continuously rising level of real government expenditures may not be sufficient to sustain inflation. As before, in order for the inflation to be sustained, the continual increases in the level of real government spending must be financed by a continuously falling demand for money. The demand for money must fall so that the same quantity of output can be purchased at higher prices. Monetarists in particular tend to dismiss this possibility.

On the other hand, inflation can be sustained if there is a continual increase in the money supply brought about by a continual increase in the monetary base. Suppose an increase in government expenditures is financed by a continual increase in the money supply. Under such circumstances it is not necessary for money demand to fall, and in fact money demand can increase. Even in the absence of an increase in government expenditures, a sustained increase in the monetary base can result in a sustained rate of inflation. As long as the monetary base, and ultimately the money supply, is increased as fast as money demand increases due to rising prices, any rate of inflation can be sustained.

Thus it would appear that a *necessary* condition for sustained inflation is a continuous increase in the money supply brought about by a continuous increase in the monetary base. However, it should be pointed out that a continuous increase in the monetary base by itself may not be a *sufficient* condition to sustain inflation. If the various transmission mechanisms for monetary impulses discussed in earlier chapters are inoperative, an increase in the monetary base and subsequently the money supply will not result in an increase in output demand. If there is no increase in output demand, no excess demand, which results in rising prices, develops.

The illustration discussed above held output constant at the full-employment level. However, full employment is not a normal characteristic of the real world. Moreover, under normal conditions both output and prices respond to changes in output demand. Since unemployment can vary and since it is a target of monetary policy, we turn now to consider the nature of unemployment and some of its possible causes.

14.2 THE NATURE OF UNEMPLOYMENT

Like many other economic variables, unemployment does not have a unique definition. If you are ready, willing, and able to go to work at currently prevailing wage rates, but do not have a job, you are considered unemployed by the U.S. Bureau of Labor Statistics. The definition, however, does not distinguish between unemployment that may be voluntary and unemployment that is clearly involuntary. Some unemployment is *frictional* in the sense that job vacancies exist, but they have not been matched with the unemployed. Some frictional unemployment is voluntary because some people leave jobs to seek better jobs. During the search time they are unemployed, but this unemployment is of their own doing. Unemployment is likely to be involuntary when the number of job vacancies is less than the number of people unemployed. This type of unemployment is often called *cyclical* or *deficient demand* unemployment because expenditures on goods and services are not high enough to generate a derived demand for labor sufficient to employ all those that seek work.

However, unemployment as measured by the Bureau of Labor Statistics definition makes no distinction between frictional and cyclical, or voluntary and involuntary, unemployment. The extent of unemployment is usually measured by the unemployment rate, which is the percent of the civilian labor force that is defined as being unemployed. Table 14.2 presents average annual rates of unemployment for five-year periods beginning with 1945. Since World War II, unemployment in the United States has ranged from about 3.5 percent of the labor force to 9 percent of the labor force in 1975.

Of course the unemployment rates shown in the table represent, in effect, weighted averages of unemployment rates for various groups in the economy. There are considerable differences among different groups. For example, the teenage unemployment rate is about four times as high as the unemployment rate for those 20 years of age and over. Unemployment among blacks and other minorities is about twice as high as it is among whites. Blue-collar unemployment tends to be somewhat higher than white-collar unemployment.

The Effects of Unemployment

Like inflation, unemployment is a target of policy because it is assumed that it has adverse effects on the economy. The major problem with unemployment is that while people are unemployed, for whatever reason, they are not producing goods and services that can add to the total welfare of society. Unemployment makes the current flow of output, which is the income of soci-

Table 14.2
Rates of Unemployment: 1945–1974

Period	Average Annual Unemployment Rate
1945–1949	3.9%
1950–1954	4.0
1955–1959	5.0
1960–1964	5.7
1965–1969	3.8
1970–1974	5.4

Source: Economic Report of the President, 1975.

ety, less than it would otherwise be. This means that current consumption is smaller, current saving is smaller, and since saving adds to the stock of wealth, the stock of wealth is smaller. Computation of the exact loss due to unemployment is difficult, but Table 14.3 provides a hypothetical example.

The table covers the period from 1929 to 1941, which experienced the most massive unemployment for the United States in the twentieth century. Unemployment ranged from 3.2 percent of the labor force in 1929 to a high of 24.9 percent in 1933. Recovery after 1933 was slow, and by 1941 the unemployment rate was only down to 9.9 percent. Thereafter World War II intervened, and the unemployment rate during the war years was sufficiently low that the economy could be classified as being fully employed. The table shows the actual levels of output for those years (GNP in real terms) and actual real saving that took place for each year. Each year's saving represents the addition during that year to the economy's stock of wealth. Thus over the period of time shown in the table, the accumulated savings of $244.9 billion represents the increase in the economy's wealth for that period of time. The last two columns in the table show hypothetical figures for GNP and saving under the assumption that the unemployment rate was 3.2 percent throughout the entire period. If the hy-

Table 14.3
Hypothetical Full Employment GNP and Saving: 1929–1941
(1958 dollars in billions)

Year	Unemployment Rate	Actual GNP	Actual Saving*	Hypothetical GNP†	Hypothetical Saving‡
1929	3.2%	$203.6	$32.2	$203.6	$32.2
1930	8.7	183.5	23.9	194.2	25.3
1931	15.9	169.3	11.2	193.9	12.8
1932	23.6	144.2	2.0	181.2	2.5
1933	24.9	141.5	2.3	180.7	2.9
1934	21.7	154.3	7.6	189.3	9.3
1935	20.1	169.5	15.5	203.9	18.6
1936	16.9	193.0	16.8	223.6	19.5
1937	14.3	203.2	26.7	228.6	30.0
1938	19.0	192.9	15.9	229.1	18.9
1939	17.2	209.4	20.4	243.5	23.7
1940	14.6	227.2	31.0	256.4	35.0
1941	9.9	263.7	39.4	282.6	42.2
Accumulated savings			$244.9		$272.9

*Gross private saving plus government surplus or deficit (−).

†Computed under the assumption that 3.2 percent unemployment is "full" employment.

‡Computed using the actual saving rate for each year.

Source: Economic Report of the President, various years.

pothetical saving rate (percent of GNP that was saved) had been the same as in the actual case, total accumulated savings for the period would have been $272.9 billion. Thus by the end of the period the economy's stock of wealth was $28 billion smaller than it would have been had unemployment been maintained at 3.2 percent.

As large as the discrepancy may be between the actual and hypothetical figures, Table 14.3 probably understates the loss of income, saving, and wealth due to the unemployment of that period. Capital also becomes unemployed during such periods, as firms operate considerably below full capacity. Were we to make some adjustment to allow for full employment of capital, the hypothetical GNP and saving figures shown in the table would be higher.

In addition to the loss in production due to unemployment, other costs may also be levied upon society. For example, individuals engage in crime when the expected opportunity cost of crime is less than the expected benefits. One major element of opportunity cost is the income foregone while the individual serves time in prison. However, when an individual becomes unemployed and is forced to live on unemployment benefits or welfare, the income foregone while serving a prison term is considerably lower. A reduction in expected opportunity costs relative to the expected benefits of crime should induce an increase in crime. In the face of an increase in crime, society must devote additional resources to crime prevention and punishment, which resources cannot then be used for other purposes. It is not surprising that unemployment has become a major target of both monetary and fiscal policy.

The Causes of Unemployment

The causes of unemployment are somewhat varied. Frictional unemployment arises partly because markets do not operate under conditions of perfect knowledge. Individuals seeking better jobs may be forced to quit their present positions because they are unable to acquire information about alternative job opportunities while working full time. They therefore elect to become unemployed from their present positions and become self-employed in seeking information about potential new positions. Since self-employment in that sense is not considered employment by the Bureau of Labor Statistics, these individuals are counted as unemployed. In fact, not only does lack of information contribute to frictional unemployment, but faulty information may have the same effect. An individual working in Bowling Green, Ohio, for example, may believe that there are many job opportunities in his or her line of work in California. Given the relative desirability of living in Bowling Green, Ohio, compared with living in California, the individual may elect to quit the Bowling Green, Ohio, job and move to California. Upon arriving in California, the individual discovers that the job opportunities in the field are not so extensive. Thus the person is unemployed for a longer period of time than originally anticipated.

Stickiness in the nominal wage rate may contribute to involuntary unemployment. For example, a firm may face a decline in the demand for its product. If the firm is not in a perfectly competitive industry, it will be able on its own to reduce the price of its product in order to continue to maximize profits. The firm will also want to reduce the wage rate of its employees in order to continue to maximize profits. However, custom or union pressures may prevent the firm from reducing the nominal wage rate, at least in the short run. Under such circumstances the firm is forced to lay off more employees than otherwise would be the case.

Moreover, the employees themselves may be unwilling to accept a cut in the nominal wage rate. If a cut does take place, some of them may quit, believing that comparable jobs exist elsewhere at the higher wage rate. Thus unemployment under conditions of falling demand may contain a mixture of voluntary and involuntary elements.

Stickiness in nominal wage rates may arise for reasons other than union pressure, custom, or an unwillingness of employees to accept wage cuts. In seeking a wage increase, an employee may wish to cover increases in the cost of living plus merit increases that the job warrants. If productivity increases justify increases in the real wage rate, then nominal wages must increase by the amount of increase in productivity plus any increases in prices. For example, if productivity is increasing at 3 percent per year and prices are rising at 4 percent per year, an employee must have a 7 percent per year increase in the nominal wage rate if the real wage rate is to increase by 3 percent per year. However, information about rates of inflation may be just as faulty as information about job opportunities. In the example just cited, an employee who believes that the rate of inflation is 5 percent rather than 4 percent will seek a nominal wage rate increase of 8 percent rather than 7 percent. Thus the real wage rate will rise faster than increases in productivity. Under such circumstances the profit-maximizing employer will reduce the amount of labor employed, thus increasing unemployment. In fact, inflation, whether expected or actual, and unemployment are linked through the decision-making processes of employers and employees. In the next section we will examine two competing views of the relationship between unemployment and inflation.

14.3 THE UNEMPLOYMENT-INFLATION DILEMMA: ALTERNATIVE VIEWS

For two decades economists have been greatly concerned with the relationship between inflation and unemployment and the problem of choice that this relationship forces upon the policymaker. Theoretical and empirical results have tended to jell around two views of the inflation-unemployment relationship. The oldest is the *trade-off view*, which essentially argues that there is a stable trade-off between the rate of unemployment and the rate of inflation. The second view, which has developed more recently, can be termed the *long-run equilibrium view*. Essentially this approach argues that any trade-off between unemployment and inflation can only be observed in the short run, and that in the long run, when equilibrium is established, no trade-off exists. Because the issue is crucial to the decisions that must be made by policy makers, we now devote some time to each view.

The Trade-Off View

The trade-off view argues that there is a more or less stable inverse relationship between inflation and unemployment that, because of its nature, presents a dilemma for the policy makers. Policies designed to combat inflation will also increase unemployment, and policies designed to combat unemployment will also increase inflation. Thus full employment is purchased at the expense of higher inflation, and price stability is purchased at the expense of higher unemployment.

One line of reasoning for the trade-off view proceeds as follows: Assume there is an exogenous increase in output demand. Producers find that they can sell more than they are currently producing at existing prices, as evidenced by the fact that their inventories are drawn down. They attempt to expand output by employing additional labor. However, slack in the labor markets, or unemployment, is not uniform across different types of occupations. Moreover, some industries are characterized by monopolistic and monopsonistic structures. This means that as output is expanded and firms attempt to hire more labor, some industries run into bottlenecks caused either by a lack of trained labor suitable for those industries or by restrictions imposed by union practice. The result is that wages are bid up in some industries even before full employment is reached across the economy. Producers, in an attempt to continue to maximize profits in the face of increasing marginal costs, raise the prices of their products. As the economy approaches full employment, the upward pressure on wages and prices becomes more severe. Thus increasing employment or falling unemployment is accompanied by higher rates of inflation. The reverse occurs in the face of a fall in output demand.

No causal relationship between inflation and unemployment is implied in the analysis. Whatever changes take place in unemployment and inflation occur because output demand is either increasing or decreasing. The consequence of an increase in output demand is lower unemployment and higher inflation, and the consequence of a decrease in output demand is higher unemployment and lower inflation. The geometrical representation of the relationship is usually called the *Phillips curve.**

An empirical representation of the Phillips curve is shown in Figure 14.1, using unemployment and inflation data for the 1960s. The scatter of points in the figure indicates an inverse relationship between the rate of inflation and the

---

*A. W. Phillips, "The Relationship between Unemployment and the Rate of Change of Money Wage Rates in the United Kingdom, 1862–1957," *Economica*, November 1958, pp. 283–299.

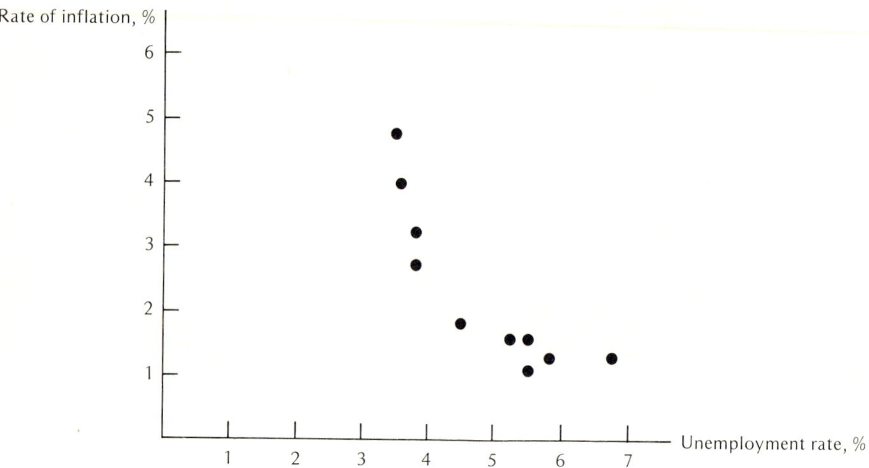

Figure 14.1

Unemployment and inflation: 1960–1969. (*Source: Economic Report of the President,* 1975.) Inflation rate is the percentage change in the GNP deflator.

Figure 14.2

Unemployment and inflation: 1955–1975. (*Source: Economic Report of the President,* various issues.) Inflation rate is the percentage change in the GNP deflator.

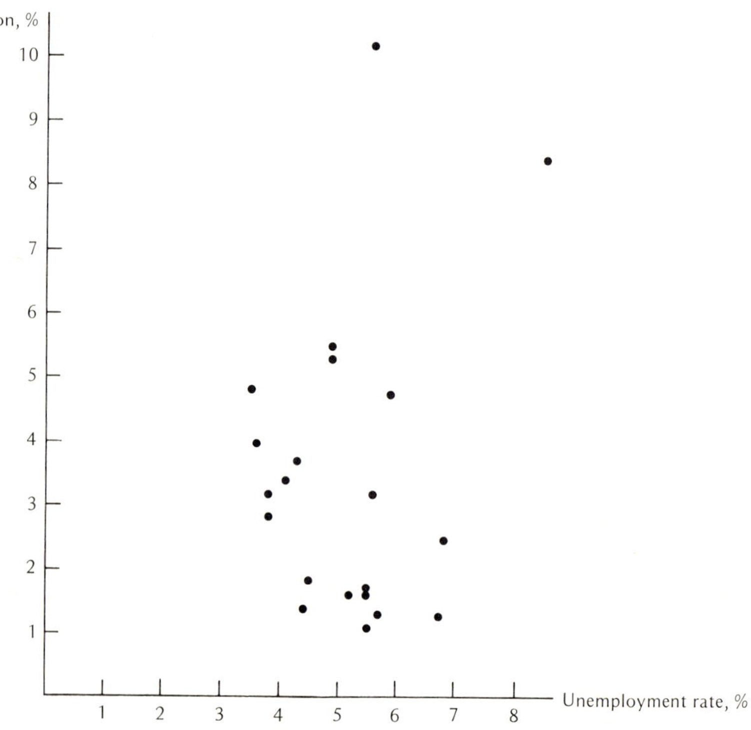

rate of unemployment and would seem to conform to the Phillips curve concept. However, Figure 14.2 displays inflation and unemployment data for the 1955–1975 period. The scatter of points in this case does not show a clear inverse relationship between unemployment and inflation. Rather, the data seem to be randomly scattered over the diagram.

A number of reasons may be advanced to explain the rather random scatter of points over the longer 1955–1975 period. First, improvements in labor productivity that permit higher wage payments without concurrent increases in product prices were not taken into consideration. Second, changes in the structure of industry and in the labor market may alter their response to changes in output demand. Finally, there are factors associated with the behavior of workers and of firms which lead to the long-run equilibrium view.

The Long-Run Equilibrium View

The long-run equilibrium view assumes that markets can be closely approximated by the model of perfect competition. In that model firms maximize profits by equating labor's marginal product to the real wage rate. Given the *principle of diminishing marginal product* (sometimes called the *law of diminishing returns*), employers will hire more labor when the real wage rate falls, and they will hire less labor when the real wage rate increases. Thus in the face of an increasing real wage rate, employment will fall and unemployment will increase. The reverse occurs when the real wage rate declines.

On the other side of the labor market, workers will supply more labor when the real wage rate increases, and they will supply less labor when the real wage rate decreases. Both workers and employers base their decisions on their perceptions of the real wage rate. In other words, workers know what the nominal wage rate is, but can only make a guess about what the actual price level is. Thus their perception of the real wage rate may or may not conform to reality. A similar argument applies to the employer, although it may be argued that the employer's perceptions are more likely to be in accord with reality than those of the employee. This is so because employers generally have more access to information about market prices than employees. To put it another way, both employees and employers are aware of what the nominal wage rate is. However, employers are more aware of general changes in demand that affect the market price of products because they sell products in fairly large markets. The employee, however, suffers from economic myopia and is not privy to the same type of information that is available to the employer.

Abstracting from changes in productivity, employees will continue to supply a given quantity of labor only if they believe the real wage rate is not changing. Thus if prices are rising at some given rate, they will want their nominal wage rate to rise at the same rate. For example, an employee who believes that prices are rising at a 6 percent annual rate will want the nominal wage rate to increase at a 6 percent annual rate if he or she is to continue to supply the same amount of labor. However, the rate of inflation perceived by the employee may differ from the actual rate of inflation. If, in the case just cited, the actual rate of inflation is 5 percent rather than 6 percent, and if the employee, believing the rate of inflation to be 6 percent, obtains wage increases amounting to 6 percent, then the actual real wage rate will increase. Assuming that the employer knows both the actual wage rate and the actual price level, the employer will observe an increase in the real wage rate and will therefore reduce the amount of labor hired, thus increasing unemployment. Thus if employees' expected or perceived rate of inflation is greater than the actual rate of inflation, they will demand nominal wage rate increases in excess of the actual rate of inflation, and the real wage rate will increase. This will be accompanied by a decrease in employment and an increase in unemployment. On the other hand, if the expected or perceived rate of inflation is less than the actual rate of inflation, employees will demand wage increases that are less than the actual rate of inflation. The real wage rate will therefore fall, and employers will expand employment, thus reducing unemployment.

This type of analysis means that unemployment can only be decreased if employees are caught by surprise. If the policy makers engage in policies that increase the rate of inflation above levels that employees expect, the result will be a fall in unemployment. However, sooner or later, as employees acquire information, they will recognize that prices are rising at a faster rate than they originally expected. They will therefore demand still higher wage increases to compensate for the purchasing power lost and to cover future anticipated rates of inflation. When this occurs, the real wage rate once again rises, and unemployment increases. In the face of an expansionary fiscal or monetary policy, we may observe first a decrease in unemployment as employees are caught by surprise and then an increase in unemployment as they begin to catch up. All this takes place as the rate of inflation steadily increases.

Once inflation reaches a critically high level, it becomes of major concern to the policy maker, and contractionary policies may be set in motion. However, such contractionary policies which tend to reduce the rate of inflation would once again catch employees by surprise. This time, however, employees will overestimate the rate of inflation, expecting previous high rates to prevail. The wage increases they will ask for will be in excess of the actual rate of inflation. Thus the real wage rate will increase, and employers will continue to cut back on the amount of labor hired, thus increasing unemployment. For a time we will face a situation of falling rates of inflation and increasing unemployment. Assuming that the contractionary policy persists, sooner or later employees will have acquired sufficient information for their perceptions of inflation to conform more closely with reality. This coupled with a high level of unemployment will cause them to ask for wage increases that are somewhat less than the increase in prices. Under this condition the real wage rate begins to fall, employers begin to hire more labor, and unemployment declines.

This pattern describes four distinct phases in the relationship between

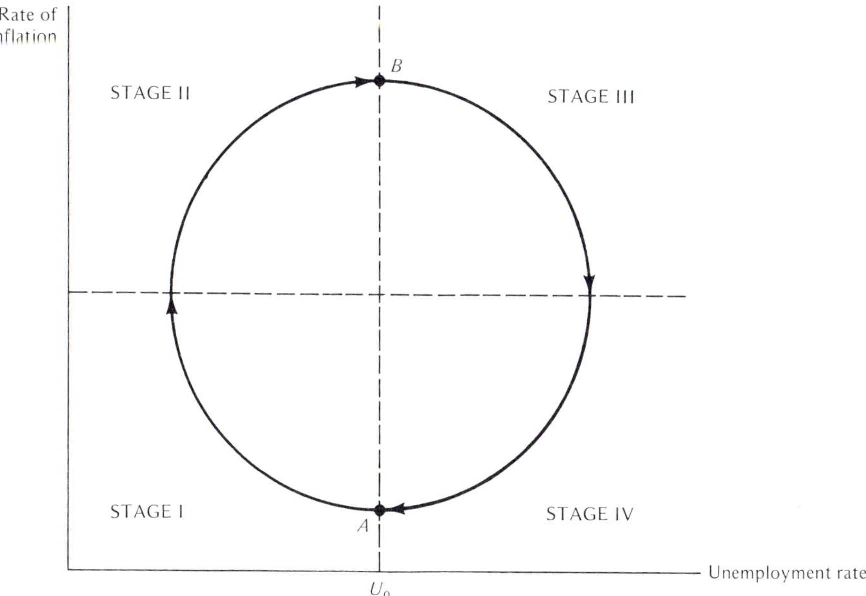

Figure 14.3

The unemployment-inflation cycle.

unemployment and inflation.* These phases are shown in Figure 14.3. Suppose the economy were to begin at point A in the diagram, which corresponds to a rate of unemployment (U_o) that is considered unacceptable by the policy makers. They therefore initiate an expansionary policy which tends to increase the rate of inflation faster than workers expect. As long as workers demand wage increases that are less than the actual rate of inflation, the real wage rate declines, and the rate of unemployment falls. This occurs throughout Stage I in the diagram. After some point workers recognize that prices are rising faster than they expected, and they begin to compensate for this by asking for larger wage increases. During this period, Stage II, wage increases exceed the actual rate of inflation, and unemployment increases. If the expansionary policy were maintained, the cycle might stop at point B. At point B, the nominal wage rate increases at the same rate as prices, and the real wage rate is the same as it was at point A. With the same real wage rate, unemployment remains the same as at point A. The only difference between point A and point B is the higher rate of inflation.

However, it is likely that policy makers will consider the rate of inflation at Point B to be excessive. They may even reach that conclusion before Point B is

---

*For a more detailed analysis see S. A. Morley, *The Economics of Inflation* (Hinsdale, Ill.: The Dryden Press Inc., 1971).

reached. Thus they initiate a contractionary policy which eventually begins to diminish the rate of inflation. In the early stages of the contractionary policy, wage increases will be commensurate with the old rate of inflation, which employees expected would continue. Thus the real wage rate once again begins to increase, and unemployment rises throughout Stage III. Finally, when employees' perceptions are brought into alignment with reality, wage increases are less than price increases as employees become willing to accept cuts in their real wages in order to increase their employment prospects. Thus during Stage IV the real wage rate declines and unemployment also declines.

The analysis implies that the trade-off between unemployment and inflation is a short-run phenomenon which is evident only in Stages I and III of the cycle. Regardless of the policy stance taken, eventually perceptions about price increases will be brought into conformity with reality and adjustments in wages will be made, so that the rate of unemployment returns to the "natural" rate of unemployment shown as U_0 in the diagram.* This theory offers an alternative explanation to the unemployment-inflation relationship that is proposed by the Phillips curve. An application of this theory is shown in Figures 14.4 and 14.5.

In the first figure both monetary and fiscal policy were decidedly expansionary in the years from 1965 to early 1969. Throughout those years the rate of inflation steadily increased and unemployment fell. From late 1969 through 1972 both fiscal and monetary policy were somewhat more contractionary than during the earlier years. Given some lag time between the change in poli-

---

*See M. Friedman, "The Role of Monetary Policy," *American Economic Review*, March 1968, pp. 1–17.

Figure 14.4

The unemployment-inflation cycle: 1965–1972. (*Source: Economic Report of the President,* 1975.) Inflation rate is the percentage change in the GNP deflator.

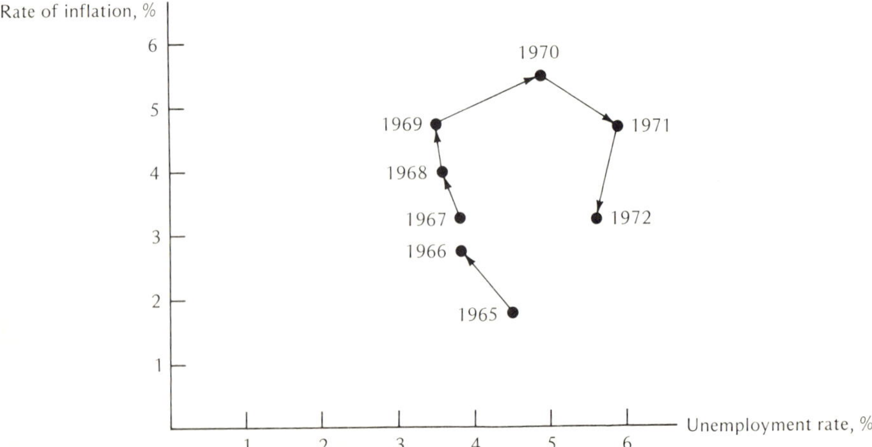

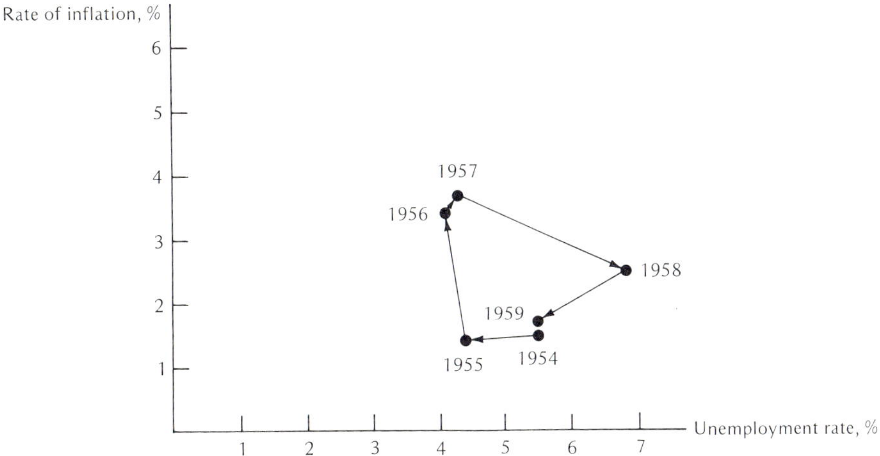

Figure 14.5

The unemployment-inflation cycle: 1954–1959. (*Source: Economic Report of the President,* 1975.) Inflation rate is the percentage change in the GNP deflator.

cy and its effect, the rate of inflation increased in 1970, but by a smaller relative amount than it had in the earlier years. By this time employees were active in catching up with previous inflation, and the economy entered Stage II with a rise in unemployment. Stage III was entered in 1971, with the rate of inflation falling in response to the contractionary policies and the rate of unemployment continuing to increase. Finally, the rate of inflation continued to fall into 1972, but by this time unemployment was so high that wage demands no longer exceeded the rate of inflation, and unemployment once again began to decline.

A similar pattern emerges for the 1954–1959 period, shown in Figure 14.5. The years 1954 through 1956 make up Stage I, with 1957, 1958, and 1959 marking Stages II, III, and IV, respectively. Again both fiscal and monetary policy were more expansionary in the first three years than they were in the last three years.

Both the long-run equilibrium view and the trade-off view suffer from defects.* We have already seen that the trade-off view does not consistently fit all the observations made during the 1955–1975 period. On the other hand, the long-run equilibrium view provides no a priori reason for establishing a particular rate of unemployment as the natural unemployment rate. The natural unemployment rate is a consequence of frictions and imperfections in the labor and product markets. It is due to monopoly elements and monopsonistic elements as well as to government restrictions on wage and price movements

---

*Elements of both views are presented by O. Eckstein and R. Brinner, *The Inflation Process in the United States,* Joint Economic Committee (U.S. Government Printing Office, 1972).

and labor mobility. What the natural unemployment rate is cannot be established in advance, but adherents of the long-run equilibrium view believe that it falls somewhere between 5 and 6 percent of the labor force. These views have contrasting implications for the conduct of monetary policy.

14.4 THE POLICY IMPLICATIONS

The trade-off view presents the policy makers with a dilemma. They must choose low unemployment and high inflation or low inflation and high unemployment, or some compromise in between that is not likely to be acceptable to all parties. If the long-run equilibrium view is accepted by the policy makers, the choice narrows to only one possibility.* The policy makers are unable, in the long run, to permanently influence the rate of unemployment, and they must therefore decide only on the long-run inflation rate. An implication of the long-run equilibrium view is that in order for unemployment to be held below the natural rate, inflation must increase without limit. In other words, the actual rate of inflation must be increased fast enough to be one step ahead of the perceptions of employees. This can be seen in the 1966–1967 period, when an increase in the rate of inflation from 2.8 percent to 3.2 percent only succeeded in maintaining the rate of unemployment at 3.8 percent. Again, in the 1968–1969 period, an increase in the rate of inflation from 4 percent to 4.8 percent resulted in a minor decrease in unemployment from 3.6 to 3.5 percent. Because of this implication for accelerating inflation, the long-run equilibrium view has also been called the *accelerationist view*.

While the accelerationist view implies that any rate of inflation, even zero, in the long run is consistent with the natural rate of unemployment, the natural rate of unemployment itself may be too high to be politically acceptable. Thus the policy makers may be forced to continually switch between expansionist and contractionist policies in an attempt to satisfy both those who prefer low inflation and those who prefer low unemployment.

We noted earlier that unanticipated inflation distorts more than just wage and price relationships. If policies are changed sharply for whatever reason, anticipations will continually tend to lag behind actual changes in prices. The detrimental effects of inflation discussed earlier as well as fluctuations in employment will then occur. However, if information systems were improved and policy changes were made more slowly so that all wages, incomes, and interest rates could adjust to anticipated inflation, many of the distortions discussed in this chapter would disappear. Unfortunately, the analysis of this chapter applies only to the domestic economy. Wages, incomes, and interest rates domestically may respond to changes in anticipated inflation, but distor-

---

*As a contrast, see Friedman, *op. cit.*; and J. Tobin, "Inflation and Unemployment," *American Economic Review*, March 1972, pp. 1–18.

tions will still develop in the economy because the United States engages in trade relationships with other countries. But those problems are deferred to the next chapter.

SUMMARY NOTES

1. Inflation (deflation) is a rise (fall) in the general price level as measured by a given price index.
2. Unexpected inflation may redistribute income and wealth between those on fixed and those on variable incomes and between creditors and debtors.
3. Inflation is the result of excess output demand in the aggregate. Sustained excess output demand requires continual increases in the money supply.
4. Unemployment results in lower levels of aggregate income, saving, and wealth than otherwise would be the case.
5. Unemployment and inflation may vary inversely in a relationship known as the Phillips curve. The relationship expresses the trade-off view.
6. The natural rate of unemployment is consistent with any rate of inflation in the long-run equilibrium view.
7. In the long-run equilibrium view the actual rate of unemployment deviates from the natural rate when the actual rate of inflation deviates from the expected rate of inflation.

DISCUSSION QUESTIONS

1. Increasing oil prices have been blamed for recent inflation. What conditions are necessary to make rising oil prices the sole cause of inflation?
2. Suppose a friend wanted to borrow $100 from you for one year. You want a 4 percent return on your money. A TV newscaster has just reported that inflation is expected to reach 7 percent during the coming year. What interest rate will you charge your friend? Why?
3. Now place yourself in your friend's shoes. How will he or she react to your interest charge? Do your answers suggest any relationships between inflation and interest rates?
4. Are people on Social Security hurt by inflation? Why or why not?
5. Are you employed or unemployed? Why are you going to school? Suppose the government ordered the salaries of everyone with a B.A. or B.S. to be cut in half effective tomorrow. What would you do? Can you now deduce some general principles about why some people may become unemployed voluntarily?
6. Examine unemployment and inflation data for the years 1973–1976. Do the data conform more to the trade-off view or to the long-run equilibrium view?

POLICY GOALS: FOREIGN

In the last few years considerable public attention has been focused on oil imports, tariffs, "wheat deals," and the weakening of the dollar. However, concern over the trade and financial relationships between countries is not confined to recent history. Interest in international economic relationships developed concurrently with national states. Governmental intervention in international relationships has evolved from attempts to maximize export surpluses, as was prevalent during the mercantilist period, to attempts to promote free international trade, as was the case in the United Kingdom in the mid-nineteenth century, to today's mixture of restriction and free trade. Policy makers must be concerned with international economic events because those events influence or constrain the pursuit of domestic policy objectives. Often it appears that policies designed to achieve balance of payments equilibrium or exchange-rate stability are in conflict with policies designed to reduce unemployment. Monetary policy has been a key element in attempts to attack both international problems and the domestic objectives of low inflation and relatively full employment. Thus, in this chapter, we will briefly examine the international system. We will also examine economic theory as it bears on adjustments in the balance of payments and examine the policy objectives of balance of payments equilibrium and exchange-rate stability.

15.1 THE INTERNATIONAL SYSTEM

People and institutions exchange goods, services, and financial assets across international boundaries for the same reasons that they exchange those items within the domestic economy. The reasons are grounded in the profit-maximizing behavior of business firms and the utility-maximizing behavior of individuals. For example, an individual in the United States may buy a Japanese automobile because she feels that she can get a greater amount of satisfaction from the Japanese automobile than she could obtain by spending the same number of dollars on a United States–produced automobile. Japanese automobile manufacturers are willing to sell their products in the United States because it is profitable to do so. American tourists spend dollars overseas because they obtain satisfaction from goods and services that cannot be obtained domestically, such as visiting the Tower of London or the Taj Mahal. Financial assets move across international boundaries for the same reasons. For example, given his relative preferences for risk and return, an English investor may prefer to buy U.S. Treasury bills rather than domestic (English) financial assets.

This is not to say that exchanges of goods, services, and financial assets are made whenever the preferences of business firms and individuals dictate. Almost all countries place restrictions on the types and amounts of foreign assets, goods, and services, including factor inputs, that can be brought into the domestic economy. Some countries place restrictions on the amount of the domestic currency that can be exported to pay for foreign-produced goods and services. Sometimes the restrictions take the form of *quotas* on the physical numbers of particular kinds of goods that can be imported. At other times, the restrictions take the form of *tariffs,* or taxes on the imported goods. Moreover, regardless of the preferences of individuals who wish to engage in trade, their abilities to engage in trade are constrained by their incomes and resource endowments.

The net flows of goods and services that cross international boundaries are, therefore, subject not only to the preferences and resources of the parties engaging in trade, but to the various restrictions that are placed upon trade by the governments involved. The measurement of such flows is accomplished through the balance of payments accounting system.*

Measuring Trade: The Balance of Payments Account

The intent of the balance of payments account is to measure the value of the flows (in units of domestic currency) of all goods and services and financial instruments traded between the domestic economy and the rest of the world for a

---

*This is not the place to go into the pure theory of international trade. The interested reader might consult C. P. Kindleberger, *International Economics* (Homewood, Ill.: Irwin, 1974). However, to some extent, we will integrate balance of payments concepts into one of our models in the next section.

Table 15.1
The United States Balance of Payments, 1973–1975
(In billions of dollars)

	1973	1974	1975
Current account			
Exports	$71.4	$ 98.3	$107.1
Imports	−70.4	−103.6	−98.1
Merchandise trade balance	1.0	−5.3	9.0
Military transactions (net)	−2.3	−2.1	−0.8
Net investment income			
Private	8.2	13.2	9.4
U.S. government	−3.0	−3.1	−3.4
Net travel and transportation	−2.8	−2.7	−2.0
Other services (net)	3.2	3.8	4.2
Balance on goods and services	4.1	3.8	16.4
Unilateral transfers	−3.8	−7.2	−4.6
Current account balance	.3	−3.4	11.8
Long-term capital (net)			
Private	.1	−8.4	−8.7
U. S. government	−1.4	1.1	−1.7
Basic balance	−1.0	−10.7	1.4
Nonliquid short-term private capital (net)	−4.2	−12.9	−2.8
Errors and omissions	−2.4	4.6	4.5
Net liquidity balance	−7.6	−19.0	3.1
Liquid private capital (net)	2.3	10.7	−5.6
Official reserve transactions balance	−5.3	−8.3	−2.5
Balancing items			
Changes in liabilities to foreign official agencies (net)	5.1	9.7	3.1
Changes in U.S. official reserve assets (net)	.2	−1.4	−0.6
	5.3	8.3	2.5

Source: Federal Reserve Bulletin, various issues.

given period of time. The various transactions may be grouped in a variety of different ways. Table 15.1 shows the groupings conventionally employed in the United States. The table is headed with a current account which generally captures the net transactions in goods and services between the United States and the rest of the world. It also includes transfer payments which are not part of current output, but which become part of the current incomes of individuals, firms, and government agencies domestically or in the rest of the world. One example would be a pension paid by a United States corporation to a retired executive living in Paris.

Within the current account, the *merchandise trade balance* shows the excess of nonmilitary goods exported from the United States to the rest of the

world over imports into the United States.* Net exports of military goods is
shown as a separate item. For example, in 1974 residents of the United States
imported $5.3 billion worth of nonmilitary goods above and beyond the goods
exported from the United States. There was a net outflow of military goods of
$2.1 billion. Interest and dividend earnings on financial assets formed part of
the current income of the individuals holding those assets. In 1974, there was a
net inflow of $13.2 billion on privately held financial assets and a net outflow
of $3.1 billion of interest earnings on United States government securities held
by foreigners. Expenditures on travel, transportation, and other services also influence the current incomes of individuals. Residents of the United States spent
$2.7 billion more on travel and transportation in other countries than the resi-
dents of those countries spent in the United States. On the other hand, there
was a net inflow of $3.8 billion on other types of services. The sum of these
items is the *balance on goods and services,* which represents the difference between foreign expenditures on currently produced United States goods and services and United States expenditures on currently produced foreign goods and
services. Unilateral transfers, which in 1974 amounted to a $7.2 billion
outflow from the United States, are added to the balance on goods and services
to obtain the *current account balance* ($ −3.4 billion in 1974).†

In addition to the transactions that influence the current flow of income and
expenditure, transactions involving financial assets are also made. Long-term
capital flows (involving assets which will not mature in the current year)
amounted to a net outflow of $7.3 billion in 1974. These long-term flows are
added to the current account balance to arrive at the *basic balance.* The basic
balance is supposed to show the net flow of all those items that respond to fundamental economic conditions in the United States and the rest of the world.

Short-term capital flows, which are supposed to be capricious and not
related to underlying economic conditions, are then added. In addition, many
transactions go unrecorded and yet involve flows across international boundaries. These are included in errors and omissions. When added to the basic balance, the nonliquid short-term private capital flows and errors and omissions
resulted in a *net liquidity balance* of −$19.0 billion in 1974. Finally, the net
transfer of liquid private capital is added to the net liquidity balance to arrive at
the *official reserve transactions balance,* which is what we often think of when
we refer to the balance of payments.

Settlement of the balance is made through changes in liabilities to foreign official agencies (such as the International Monetary Fund and foreign central
banks) and through changes in United States official reserve assets (such as

---

*All figures are in nominal rather than real terms because the balance of payments measures total dollar (price
times quantity) flows rather than quantities alone.

†More extensive interpretation and criticism of the various balances may be found in R. M. Stern, *The Balance of Payments* (Chicago: Aldine, 1973), chap. 1; and D. S. Kemp, "Balance of Payments Concepts—What Do
They Really Mean?" *Review,* Federal Reserve Bank of St. Louis, July 1975, pp. 14–23.

gold and special drawing rights). Items making up the official reserve transactions balance are *above-the-line* items, and the balancing items are *below-the-line* items. With the line drawn at the official reserve transactions balance, all private transactions are recorded above the line, and the items below the line include only official or governmental transactions. However, the line could be drawn anywhere in the balance of payments account. For example, if the line was drawn at the balance on goods and services, then such items as unilateral transfers and long-term private capital flows would become balancing items, used to settle the balance that results from above-the-line items such as exports, imports, and net investment income.

Where one draws the line depends upon one's theoretical conception of the forces that influence the balance of payments and of the forces that result in adjustment to balance of payments disequilibrium. A little later in this chapter we will consider some of the ideas that bear on the adjustment process.

Interest in the balance of payments cannot be separated from interest in the exchange media that are used to facilitate the various transactions contained in the balance of payments. Therefore we will now take a brief look at the foreign exchange market.

Media of Exchange: The Foreign Exchange Market

Exchange in the domestic economy is facilitated because all transactions are stated in a single unit of account. In the United States the unit of account is the dollar, and all prices and volumes of trade are stated in terms of dollars. However, this is not the case in international transactions. Different nations have different monetary systems. Each monetary system has its own unit of account in which prices and transactions are measured. For example, in the United Kingdom prices are measured in *pounds;* in France they are measured in *francs;* in Italy they are measured in *lira.* An American resident who wishes to purchase an automobile in the United Kingdom that costs £2,000 must make payment in pounds or its equivalent. The equivalent would be the number of units of a foreign currency (say the dollar) that is equivalent to £2,000 at the going exchange rate. Thus in the international market, there are two transactions for every one in the domestic economy. A United States resident who wishes to buy an automobile in the United States pays dollars for the automobile. If that resident wishes to buy a car in the United Kingdom, he or she pays dollars for pounds and then pounds for the automobile. Thus the markets for foreign goods are accompanied by markets for foreign exchange.

The *exchange rate,* which is the price of foreign currencies in terms of the domestic currency (or vice versa), provides a bridge which enables us to compare the prices of foreign-produced goods with those goods produced domestically. For example, suppose the identical camera costs $250 in the United States and £150 in the United Kingdom. A direct comparison of the prices cannot be made. However, if we also know that £1 can be purchased for $2.40, then £150 can be purchased for $360. Thus the camera costs $250 in the United States and $360 in the United Kingdom. The repercussions of this discrepancy between domestic and foreign prices for the identical good will be discussed in the next section. For now, we wish only to note that a market exists for foreign exchange; the market determines the price of foreign currencies in terms of the domestic currency, and these prices or exchange rates can be used to make comparisons between prices of goods in different countries. Exchange rates for several countries for the years 1971–1975 are shown in Table 15.2. Note that the rates are not constant over time. They fluctuate as market forces and international agreements change.

Although trading centers for currencies may be located in important financial centers, such as London, New York, and Tokyo, speedy worldwide communications systems make it possible to talk about a foreign exchange market that is worldwide. Information about prices and orders for various currencies can be transmitted almost instantaneously to far-flung centers. Such rapid communication makes it possible for exchange rates to be consistent around the world. Inconsistency among exchange rates opens the opportunity for profit taking. For example, if £1 is worth $2.40 and DM1 (Deutsche mark) is worth $0.40, then £1 should be the equivalent of DM6. Thus, $2.40 will buy £1 which can be traded for DM6, which can be exchanged for $2.40. Suppose that in some trading center £1 sells for DM10. It would then be possible for individuals to buy £1 with $2.40, sell the £1 for DM10, and then sell the DM10 in another trading center for $4. The profit on each original pound purchased would be $1.60. This profit cannot be sustained because individuals, in attempting to take advantage of this profitable opportunity, would raise the dollar price of the pound or lower the Deutsche mark price of the pound or lower the dollar price of the Deutsche mark or some combination of those changes. Thus arbitrage communicated on a worldwide basis causes exchange rates to move in directions that make them consistent with one another.

Table 15.2
Selected Foreign Exchange Rates
(United States cents per unit of foreign currency)

Country	1971	1972	1973	1974	1975
Belgium (franc)	2.06	2.27	2.58	2.57	2.72
Canada (dollar)	99.02	100.94	99.98	102.26	98.29
France (franc)	18.15	19.83	22.54	20.81	23.35
Germany (Deutsche mark)	28.77	31.36	37.76	38.72	40.72
Italy (lira)	.16	.17	.17	.15	.15
Japan (yen)	.29	.33	.37	.34	.33
Switzerland (franc)	24.33	26.19	31.70	33.69	38.74
United Kingdom (pound)	244.42	250.08	245.10	234.03	222.16

Source: Federal Reserve Bulletin.

Like a number of other assets and commodities, currencies can be bought and sold at present (spot market), or contracts can be made to purchase or sell them at specified exchange rates at some point in the future (forward market). A forward market exists for currencies because exchange rates are not fixed for all time. Underlying economic forces may cause a particular currency to appreciate or depreciate relative to other currencies as time passes. The forward market permits trading to take place with respect to future expected exchange rates as well as with respect to current exchange rates. For example, suppose an American automobile dealer contracts to purchase a certain number of English automobiles one year in the future. Further suppose that the contracted price per automobile is specified in pounds. Now suppose that the automobile dealer expects the dollar to depreciate relative to the pound over the course of the coming year. In other words, if the exchange rate is $2.40 per pound at present, the dealer expects the exchange rate to be higher at some point in the future. If he acquires pounds one year in the future, he expects to have to pay more in dollars for the English automobiles than he would pay if the exchange rate remained $2.40. The existence of the forward market permits him to *hedge* against possible depreciation of the dollar by entering into a contract to purchase the number of pounds required at a specified exchange rate one year in the future. Thus he may contract to purchase the required number of pounds at some point in the future at $2.40 per pound. If the price goes to $2.50, for example, he has avoided a loss.

Hedging takes place when people attempt to protect themselves from future variations in exchange rates. *Speculation* takes place when individuals attempt to profit by expected changes in exchange rates. For example, suppose an individual expects the exchange rate between pounds and dollars to increase from $2.40 to $2.60 at some point in the future. If this individual can find someone who does not share her expectations, she can contract in the forward market to purchase a specified number of pounds at $2.40 each at some point in the future. She can then turn around and sell those pounds at $2.60 if the pound appreciates the way she expects. If her expectations are fulfilled, she will have earned $0.20 per pound. Of course, there is always the possibility that the dollar might appreciate relative to the pound, so that the exchange rate might drop below $2.40. If this occurs, the speculator will lose. Thus, some people hedge in order to avoid risk, and others speculate in order to take advantage of risk.

It should be clear that the foreign exchange markets play an important role in international finance. Later in this chapter we will see how adjustments in exchange rates can act as an equilibrating mechanism to resolve balance of payments disequilibria. In fact, exchange-rate variations are so important in the world of international trade that international agreements have been made to regulate the extent to which currency prices can fluctuate against one another. The most important of these was the Bretton Woods agreement, which created the International Monetary Fund.

The International Monetary Fund

Although demand and supply conditions for foreign exchange are constantly changing in response to changes in the underlying economic forces in various countries, exchange rates have not always been completely free to reflect changes in supply and demand. During the post-World War II period, exchange rates were either fixed or permitted to vary only within very narrow limits. The value of the dollar, for example, was fixed in terms of gold. One dollar was worth one-thirty-fifth of an ounce of gold. Some other currencies were fixed in terms of dollars. Most of the post-World War II arrangements about exchange rates were created by the Bretton Woods Agreement.*

Toward the end of World War II, representatives of the British and American governments met to attempt to formulate a system of international exchange that would end the chaos brought about by the Depression of the 1930s and World War II. Finally they, along with the representatives of 42 other nations, met at Bretton Woods, New Hampshire, in July 1944. The end product of these deliberations was the Bretton Woods Agreement, which established the International Monetary Fund (IMF) and the International Bank for Reconstruction and Development, now known as the World Bank. The purpose of the IMF was to deal with international currencies, exchange rates, and balance of payments policies. The World Bank was established to raise capital for development purposes.

While the World Bank can play an important role in the financing of economic development, our concern in monetary economics is primarily with the International Monetary Fund. The IMF is, in reality, a pool of international currencies. Members of the IMF may obtain international reserves in the form of member currencies, such as the dollar, in exchange for their own currencies, subject to certain limitations. Since 1962 the IMF itself has been empowered to borrow from the so-called Group of Ten, consisting of Belgium, the United Kingdom, Canada, France, West Germany, Italy, Japan, Sweden, the Netherlands, and the United States. By virtue of their relatively strong position in international trade and finance, the countries comprised in the Group of Ten exert a strong influence on the policies implemented by the IMF.

Ever since its creation, the IMF has conducted its policies with certain objectives in mind. The IMF has argued for exchange-rate stability. In the IMF's view, exchange rates between different currencies should fluctuate only within very narrow limits. Adjustments to exchange rates should be made only in response to long-term balance of payments disequilibrium. Thus the IMF has provided international reserves for those countries experiencing temporary balance of payments difficulties. The provision of reserves on a temporary basis should

---

*See W. M. Scammell, *International Trade and Payments* (New York: St. Martin's, 1974), chap. 21; and R. W. Stevens, *A Primer on the Dollar in the World Economy* (New York: Random House, 1972), chap. 11 for a more detailed history and evaluation.

permit countries with temporary difficulties to weather the storm without recourse to exchange-rate devaluation or revaluation. In order to facilitate adjustment to changes in economic conditions, the IMF has also advocated the loosening of restrictions on free trade.

In pursuing these objectives, the IMF has not been completely successful. The principle of fixed exchange rates, subject to long-term adjustments, was breached in a number of instances during the post-World War II period. For example, France devalued its currency in 1948 and established an exchange-rate system which was not approved by the IMF. In 1950, Canada went to freely flexible exchange rates and maintained that system until 1962. Flexible exchange rates were contrary to the wishes of the IMF. Finally, in the early 1970s, several countries, including the United States, adopted flexible exchange rates. Not only were exchange rates made flexible, but the United States devalued the dollar in terms of gold and suspended convertibility of the dollar into gold. Thus, the long-term policies of the IMF collapsed under pressures over which it could have little or no control.

However, the IMF has been responsible for innovations that should serve to promote world trade. The most important of these is the introduction of special drawing rights (SDRs). Prior to the establishment of the SDR, international payment was made with gold or with certain key currencies such as the United States dollar and the English pound. However, an expanding volume of world trade requires an expanding stock of an international medium of exchange to finance the growing volume of international transactions. Given the existence of fixed exchange rates and the needs of domestic economic policies, it was not possible to rely upon growth in either the stock of gold or key currencies to finance the growing volume of world trade. In an effort to increase international liquidity, the membership of the International Monetary Fund ratified the SDR system in 1969.

In effect, the special drawing right system permits the IMF to use its own credit to create money in the same way that the Federal Reserve System uses its credit to create bank reserves. Previously, members of the IMF could obtain international reserves by depositing their own currencies with the IMF. Now the IMF creates an account for its members (called an SDR allocation). No deposit of currencies is required. The account is like a checking account which may be drawn upon to obtain currencies that are usable in world trade. SDR allocations may be expanded by the IMF as the needs of world trade dictate. Often called *paper gold,* the SDR is the first fiat money issued by an international agency.

Eurodollars

No discussion of international institutions would be complete without a brief description of the Eurodollar market. Eurodollars are bank balances denominated in dollars on the books of a bank outside the United States. Actually

Eurodollar (sometimes Eurocurrency) is a generic term that is used to denote bank balances of any currency located in a bank outside the country of that currency's origin. However, United States dollars dominate the Eurodollar market.

One important effect of the Eurodollar market is to make world liquidity greater than it would be if dollars were not deposited in foreign banks.* The major reason for this is that banks within the United States are subject to fractional reserve requirements on time deposits, whereas banks holding Eurodollars have no such requirement. Dollars may be withdrawn from time deposits in United States banks and placed in time deposits in banks in foreign countries (foreign banks or foreign branches of United States banks). The "Eurobanks" will then use those dollars to make loans or buy bonds denominated in dollars. If all the proceeds of the loans ultimately find their way back into deposits in the Eurobanks and if the Eurobanks themselves do not wish to keep any reserves behind their time deposits, the potential expansion of Eurodollar balances is infinite. However, it is likely that Eurobanks will wish to keep some minimal level of reserves, and it is also likely that not all the proceeds of Euroloans or Eurobonds will find their way back into the Eurobanks. Nevertheless, because the desired reserve levels are likely to be less than those required for domestic banks, the potential expansion in the world money supply is greater as a result of the Euromarket than it would be if the same deposits were held in United States banks.

A major impetus to the creation of Eurodollar balances has been provided by Regulation Q, which sets maximum interest rates payable on time deposits in the United States. The Eurobanks are not subject to such interest-rate ceilings. When world interest rates rise above the Regulation Q ceiling, funds are withdrawn from time deposits in the United States and placed in time deposits in foreign banks. Thus the Eurodollar market provides an opportunity for individuals and firms to obtain a higher rate of return on time deposits than is permitted by the Federal Reserve System. While many individuals in policy-making circles are concerned with the flow of dollars from United States banks to the Eurodollar market, such concern is easily alleviated. Removal of the interest-rate ceilings imposed by Regulation Q will permit domestic banks to pay interest rates that are comparable to foreign interest rates. This should stem or perhaps even reverse the flow of Eurodollars.

In this section we have hinted at various forces that affect the flow of goods, services, and financial assets between countries. It is now time to examine some of the underlying theories of adjustment in the balance of payments.

---

*See M. Friedman, "The Eurodollar Market: Some First Principles," *Review,* Federal Reserve Bank of St. Louis, July 1971, pp. 16–24, reprinted from the *Morgan Guaranty Survey,* October 1969, pp. 4–14, for a detailed analysis of the Eurodollar market. Also see F. H. Klopstock, "Money Creation in the Euro-Dollar Market: A Note on Professor Friedman's Views," *Monthly Review,* Federal Reserve Bank of New York, January 1970, pp. 12–15.

15.2 BALANCE OF PAYMENTS THEORY

The balance of payments is of interest to us because alterations in the balance affect the level of economic activity. In this section we shall see how changes in the components of the balance of payments affect the domestic economy and how adjustments can be made to resolve disequilibrium in the balance of payments.*

Relationships between the Balance of Payments and Domestic Economic Activity

In an earlier chapter we defined output demand as the sum of all expenditures on currently produced goods and services. These expenditures were classified as expenditures by the household sector on consumer goods, expenditures by the business sector on capital goods, and expenditures by the government sector on public goods. That definition is suitable for a closed economy in which no international trade takes place. However, in an open economy, some of the expenditures by the business and household sectors may be for foreign-produced goods. Moreover, residents of other countries purchase currently produced goods and services in the United States product market. Thus, output demand in the United States product market would have to exclude imports of goods and services from other countries and add exports of goods and services to other countries. This is accomplished by adding the balance on goods and services to the previous definition of output demand. Thus output demand consists of consumption, capital investment, and government expenditures, plus the balance on goods and services (often called *net exports* for short).

In the context of the IS-LM model, changes in net exports will shift the IS curve. An exogenous increase in exports or an exogenous decrease in imports will constitute an increase in domestic output demand and thus shift the IS curve to the right. An exogenous decrease in exports or an exogenous increase in imports will constitute a decrease in domestic output demand and therefore shift the IS curve to the left. Thus all other things being equal, an increase in net exports should result in an increase in the level of domestic economic activity, while a decrease in net exports will have the opposite result.

However, other components of the balance of payments in addition to changes in net exports influence the level of output demand. For example, suppose net exports is constant and there is an increase in long-term capital outflows from the United States. This outflow of dollars must be offset by some change in one of the balancing items. Certain of the balancing items are components of the domestic monetary base. For example, if an increase in the balance of payments deficit which is due to an increase in long-term capital

---

*For a review of the literature, see A. O. Krueger, "Balance of Payments Theory," *Journal of Economic Literature,* March 1969, pp. 1–26.

outflows is settled by a reduction in the domestic gold stock, the monetary base will fall. This will have the effect of shifting the LM curve to the left. In fact, since the balancing items enter into the determination of the monetary base, a change in any component of the balance of payments which is not offset by an equal and opposite change in another component will have monetary effects that result in shifts in the LM curve. We will discuss some examples at the end of this section.

Shifts in the IS curve due to changes in net exports and/or shifts in the LM curve due to changes in the balancing items will alter the domestic levels of income and interest rates. In addition, domestic prices may also be affected. Changes in these variables will in turn influence domestic levels of consumption and capital investment and may also influence imports and the flows of capital between the United States and other countries. Generally we assume that imports are influenced by the domestic level of income and by domestic prices relative to foreign prices. Like domestic consumption expenditures, expenditures on imported goods should vary directly with the level of income. Given the level of income, an increase in the price of domestic goods relative to foreign goods should increase the level of imports as people seek to buy the relatively less expensive goods. Exports, on the other hand, should vary inversely with the price of domestic goods relative to foreign goods. If United States prices rise relative to prices around the rest of the world, fewer goods will be purchased from the United States.

Long- and short-term capital flows should be influenced by relative interest rates. In seeking to purchase financial assets, investors will look for the highest rate of return given a particular level of risk. If domestic interest rates fall relative to foreign interest rates, domestic investors will buy relatively more foreign financial assets. Foreigners, on the other hand, will buy relatively fewer United States financial assets. Thus the net outflow of capital from the United States will increase.

Changes in foreign exchange rates can be viewed in the same way as changes in relative prices. For example, an increase in the price of English pounds in terms of dollars (for example, from \$2.40 to \$2.50) has the same effect as a reduction in the domestic price of goods and services or an increase in the foreign price of goods and services. Thus, balance of payments changes lead to shifts in the IS and/or LM schedules, which result in changes in income, interest rates, prices, and possibly exchange rates, which in turn have repercussions on the components of the balance of payments. We will now consider some of those adjustments in isolation.

Response to Balance of Payments Disequilibrium

More time has been devoted to examining the influence of relative prices on the balance of payments than to perhaps any other adjustment mechanism. In recent years, attention has focused on exchange-rate adjustment as a means of adjusting relative prices. We have already indicated that an increase in the price of foreign exchange relative to dollars produces the same effect as a decrease in domestic prices relative to foreign prices. Prior to the 1970s, most exchange rates in the world were more or less fixed under the rules of the International Monetary Fund. Countries with persistent or long-term balance of payments deficits would naturally ask about the effect of devaluation of their domestic currencies on the balance of payments, e.g., "Will devaluation reduce the balance of payments deficit?" The analysis has focused primarily on the balance on goods and services component.

Suppose a particular country has an excess of imports over exports, so that the balance on goods and services, or net exports, is in deficit. Suppose also that the country concerned would like to reduce the deficit or convert it into a surplus. Finally, suppose that exchange rates are fixed and subject to change by governmental decree only. If the price of foreign currency, in terms of the domestic currency, is increased (the domestic currency is *devalued*), this should produce the same effect as a reduction in domestic prices relative to foreign prices or an increase in foreign prices relative to domestic prices. Our first reaction to this might be that this will reduce imports of foreign goods and increase exports of domestic goods, thus improving the balance of trade.

However, this may not be the case. The balance of trade is the difference between the *total monetary value* (price times quantity) of goods exported and the *total monetary value* of goods imported. It is not the difference between the *quantity* of goods exported and the *quantity* of goods imported. Whether an increase in the price of foreign goods will decrease total expenditures on imports depends on the price elasticity of the demand for imported goods. If the demand for imported goods is price-elastic, an increase in the price of imported goods will reduce the total expenditures on those imported goods.

Moreover, whether a decrease in the price of domestic goods will increase the total expenditures by foreigners on domestic goods depends on the price elasticity of foreign demand for domestic goods. If the foreign demand for domestic goods is price-elastic, a decrease in the price of domestic goods will result in an increase in the total expenditures on domestic goods by foreigners. Thus if both demands are price-elastic, the devaluation will increase total expenditures on domestic goods and decrease total expenditures on imported goods, thus unambiguously improving the balance on goods and services.

However, such a condition is more restrictive than necessary.* The demand elasticities may be such that the devaluation increases the value of both exports and imports. As long as the increase in exports exceeds the increase in imports, net exports will be improved. Similarly, a devaluation may result in a decrease in both exports and imports. In this case, as long as the decrease in imports is

---

*A rigorous demonstration is unnecessary for our purposes here. The interested reader should consult Stern, *op. cit.,* chap. 2.

greater than the decrease in exports, net exports will be improved. The empirical evidence on the elasticities is somewhat mixed. However, the most recent work seems to indicate that the elasticities are large enough to make devaluation a viable means of improving the balance of trade.*

An analysis of the effects of changing prices is only one approach to balance of payments adjustment. Since alterations in the balance of payments are likely to exert an influence on the domestic level of income, some approaches have paid attention to the way in which net exports respond to changes in the level of economic activity. In the illustration cited above, devaluation was assumed to alter relative prices, and this produced effects on both imports and exports. However, devaluation, by changing imports and exports, may also change the level of income in the domestic economy. This in turn will influence the level of imports if we assume that imports are a function of income. For example, suppose we have a situation in which a devaluation takes place. Moreover, suppose that in the absence of other changes this would result in an increase in exports and a decrease in imports. In order to isolate the effect of the export change alone, let us also assume that a tariff reduction is introduced in the amount necessary to offset the effect of the devaluation on imports.

The initial effect is an increase in the balance of trade due to an increase in exports. However, assuming that the domestic economy is at a less than full-employment equilibrium, the increase in exports will increase domestic output demand. This will result in a higher equilibrium level of income in the domestic economy. The higher level of income in the economy has the effect of increasing imports of foreign goods. Whether the increase in imports of foreign goods is less than, equal to, or greater than the initial increase in exports is something that cannot be determined a priori.

The problem is illustrated in Figure 15.1. The upper half of the diagram shows the conventional IS and LM curves in real terms, as in earlier chapters. In the lower half of the diagram, (nominal) exports (X') and (nominal) imports (Z') are plotted as a function of output.† Imports are shown as an increasing function of the level of domestic output, and exports are shown as invariant with respect to the domestic level of output. The initial output level is y_0. At that output level, given export curve X', net exports is $X' - Z_0$. Since Z_0 is greater than X', there is a trade deficit.

The combined devaluation and tariff reduction increases exports, as shown by a shift in the export function from X' to X''. This increase in exports shifts the IS' curve to IS''. The new equilibrium occurs at a higher level of domestic output, y_1. At the higher level of domestic output, imports will be greater than

---

*See Stern, *op. cit.*, pp. 148–149; and United States International Trade Commission, *Foreign Trade Elasticities for Twenty Industries*, publication 738, Washington, D.C., August 1975.

†Notice that to plot nominal exports and nominal imports against output (real income), we are holding the domestic price level and the price of imported goods constant. Changes in those prices will shift the curves.

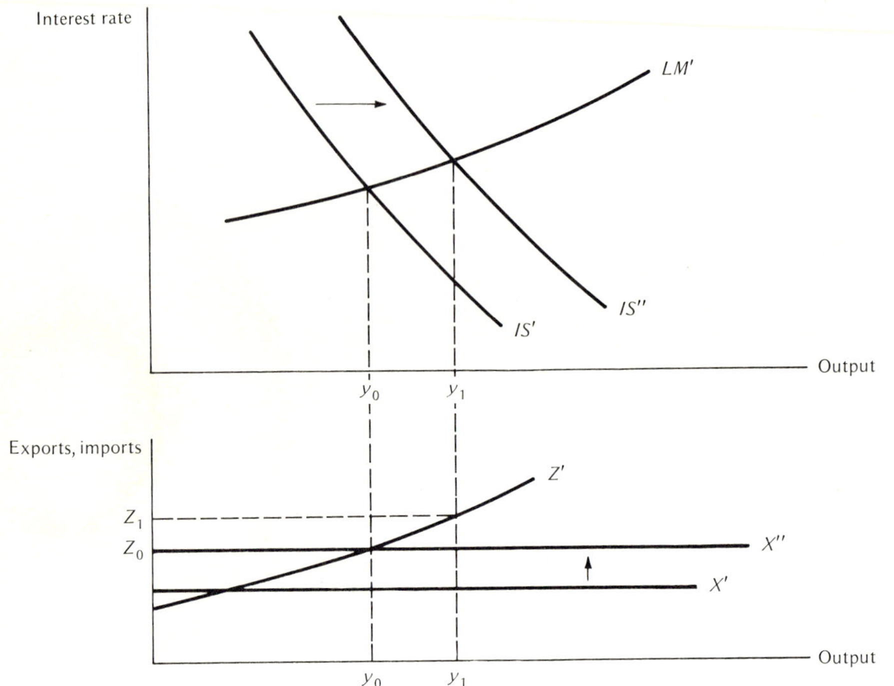

Figure 15.1

Net exports and income adjustment.

before. In the example shown, imports rise to Z_1, which is greater than X''. Thus there is still a trade deficit, but it is smaller than the initial one. Whether the new equilibrium will result in a larger or smaller balance of trade depends on the slope of the LM curve and the responsiveness of imports to changes in income. For example, had the LM' curve been vertical at y_0, the deficit would have been eliminated. Moreover, in this example we have ignored the effect of the change in the interest rate on the various capital flows. Changes in the various capital flows coupled with whatever change takes place in the balance on goods and services will alter the overall balance of payments. If that doesn't make matters complex enough, settlement of the alteration in the balance of payments will produce effects on the monetary base, which in turn will result in shifts in the LM curve. Thus the repercussions are quite extensive and involve changes in prices, income, interest rates, and their feedback effects on net exports and capital flows.

One approach toward the balance of payments which attempts to consider the overall effects on the balance on goods and services and capital flows is the monetary view of the balance of payments, which we consider next.

The Monetary View of the Balance of Payments

The monetary view of the balance of payments does not single out either net exports or capital flows as the object of analysis.* Rather, it treats decisions with respect to imports, exports, and capital flows as following from a general portfolio or wealth adjustment approach similar to the approaches discussed in an earlier chapter. Adjustments in the components of the balance of payments take place when there is a discrepancy between the quantity of money demanded and the quantity of money supplied. If, for example, there is an excess supply of money, individuals and business firms will attempt to resolve that excess by purchasing a wide range of goods, services, real assets, and financial assets. Moreover, the goods and assets they purchase will consist of both domestic and foreign goods and assets. Put another way, an excess supply of money will be distributed over domestic goods and services, domestic real assets, domestic financial assets, foreign goods and services, foreign real assets, and foreign financial assets. The precise distribution will depend on relative prices and yields of the various goods and assets.

In the monetary view, changes in the balance of payments only occur to the extent that factors inducing such changes influence either the demand for money or the supply of money. For example, an increase in the monetary base reduces the balance of payments surplus (increases a deficit) only because it creates an excess supply of money, part of which is used to purchase foreign goods and financial assets. In earlier chapters, we discussed how various exogenous or policy changes might affect the money supply and how various real changes in the economy might affect both money demand and money supply. These changes, by altering money demand relative to money supply, will result in balance of payments changes that will be reflected in changes in the balance of payments deficit or surplus.

In order to highlight these effects, the monetary view defines the balance of payments in such a way that the only items that appear below the line are those that affect the domestic monetary base and therefore the money supply. Such items would include United States holdings of gold and reserve assets and foreign deposits with the Federal Reserve System (liabilities to foreign agencies). These become the balancing items that not only are used to settle international accounts but also influence the magnitude of the monetary base.

Under the monetary view there can be no such thing as a persistent balance of payments deficit. Adjustment is automatic unless it is hampered by restrictions on trade or by policies of the monetary authority. For example, suppose there is an excess of money supply over money demand in the domestic

---

*For a review, see D. S. Kemp, "A Monetary View of the Balance of Payments," *Review,* Federal Reserve Bank of St. Louis, April 1975, pp. 14 – 22; and H. G. Johnson, "The Monetary Approach to Balance of Payments Theory," *Further Essays in Monetary Economics* (Cambridge Mass.: Harvard, 1973), pp. 229–249.

economy. Individuals will attempt to rid themselves of the excess supply by purchasing domestic and foreign goods, capital, and financial assets. This results in a balance of payments deficit. The deficit is balanced by an outflow of gold and other reserves, which reduces the monetary base and the money supply. Also, the initial excess supply disbursed for domestic goods and financial assets raises domestic prices and incomes and lowers interest rates. This increases money demand. With money demand increasing and money supply falling, equilibrium in the money market will be restored (the excess supply is eliminated). Further, the flow of expenditure on foreign goods and assets induced by the excess money supply is eliminated when the excess money supply is eliminated. The balance of payments returns to equilibrium. In short, the balance of payments merely reflects flow adjustment to stock disequilibrium in the money market. If exchange rates are flexible, adjustments in relative prices, income, and interest rates need not take place. Consequently adjustment to equilibrium will be faster.

Whatever the adjustments that take place, it is clear that balance of payments changes exert influences on the domestic economy. For this reason, the balance of payments and its resolution has become an object of monetary policy. In order to summarize the preceding ideas and arguments in an overall framework, we will now integrate the balance of payments into the IS-LM framework and experiment with a couple of changes.

IS, LM, and External Equilibrium

The conditions for external, or balance of payments, equilibrium can be integrated easily into the IS-LM model.* In order to keep things manageable, we assume that the balance of payments consists of only two parts, net exports (the balance on goods and services) and net capital outflows. Net exports, again, is the difference between exports X and imports Z. Net capital outflows KN is the difference between capital outflows KO and capital inflows KI. Balance of payments equilibrium occurs when net exports (an inflow of dollars) is just equal to net capital outflows (an outflow of dollars), or in other words when

$$X - Z = KN$$

Now consider each component in turn. According to our earlier discussions, exports should vary inversely with the price of domestic goods relative to foreign goods, given the exchange rate (the price of foreign currency in terms of dollars). Imports should vary directly with the price of domestic goods relative

---

*The title of this part was borrowed from D. Wrightsman, "IS, LM and External Equilibrium: A Graphical Analysis," *American Economic Review*, March 1970, pp. 203–208. Also see R. A. Mundell, "The International Disequilibrium System," *Kyklos*, 1961, pp. 154–172.

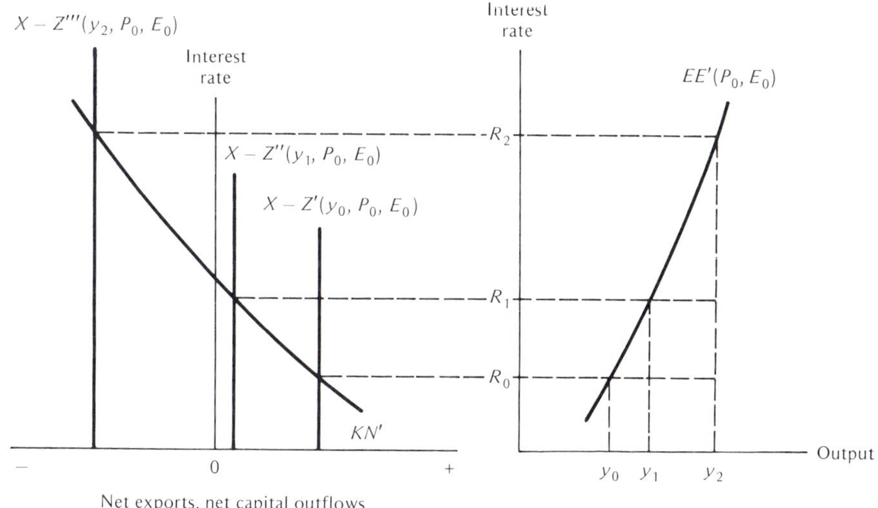

Figure 15.2

Derivation of the external equilibrium curve.

to foreign goods and directly with domestic output, given the exchange rate. This implies that net exports will vary inversely with the price of domestic goods relative to foreign goods and inversely with domestic output, given the exchange rate.

Capital outflows will vary inversely with the domestic interest rate, given foreign interest rates, and capital inflows will vary directly with the domestic interest rate. Therefore net capital outflows will vary inversely with the domestic interest rate, given foreign interest rates.

These relationships are shown in the left side of Figure 15.2. The KN' curve is drawn downward-sloping against the (domestic) interest rate. It is drawn for a given set of foreign interest rates which we will assume are constant throughout our analysis. The $X - Z$ curve is vertical because, by assumption, X and Z are not influenced by the interest rate. However, three curves are drawn, one for each of three output levels, where $y_0 < y_1 < y_2$. Each curve is drawn for a given domestic price level P_0 and exchange rate E_0. The foreign price level is assumed to be constant throughout our analysis and is not shown.

Equilibrium in the balance of payments occurs where the $X - Z$ and KN curves intersect. Given the three $X - Z$ curves, three interest rates are consistent with equilibrium. These are projected into the right-hand panel and, together with the corresponding output levels, describe interest rate–output combinations that are consistent with balance of payments equilibrium. The locus of such combinations is the external equilibrium or EE curve. The curve shown in the figure is drawn for a given price level P_0 and exchange rate E_0. A higher price level implies lower net exports for any given output level and exchange rate. This means a higher interest rate is required to lower net capital outflows correspondingly and restore external equilibrium. Thus an increase (decrease) in P shifts the EE curve to the left (right).

A higher exchange rate means that foreign currencies cost more dollars per unit. This raises the cost of foreign goods for United States residents and lowers the cost of United States goods for foreign residents. Thus a higher exchange rate increases net exports by increasing exports and decreasing imports. Higher net exports requires a lower interest rate to raise net capital outflows and restore external equilibrium, for any given output level and price level. Thus an increase (decrease) in E shifts the EE curve to the right (left).

The area to the right of the EE curve implies a balance of payments deficit because the level of output is too high (and imports too great) for equilibrium at any given interest rate. The area to the left of the EE curve therefore implies a balance of payments surplus.

In Figure 15.3 we have superimposed the EE curve over the IS-LM diagram. The three curves can now be used to analyze both internal and external equilibrium. Two points should be remembered from our earlier discussions. First, an increase (decrease) in net exports will shift the IS curve to the right (left). Note that this applies to changes in net exports due to changes in the price level or the exchange rate which are not shown on the IS-LM diagram. Changes in net exports that result from output-induced changes in imports result in move-

Figure 15.3

Effect of an increase in the monetary base on internal and external equilibrium.

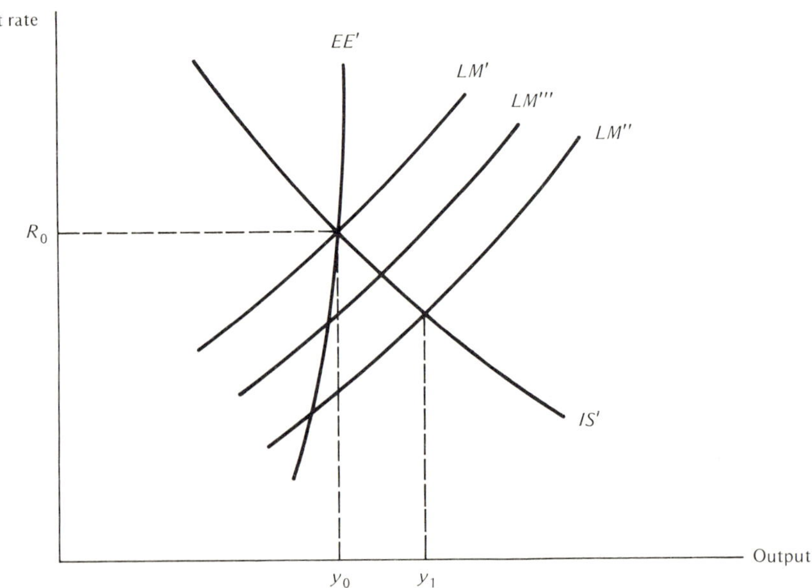

ments *along* the IS curve. Second, settlement of external disequilibrium, through changes in foreign deposits with the Fed or in the gold stock, will change the monetary base and shift the LM curve. Now consider two examples using the IS-LM-EE diagram.

Case 1: Suppose we are in internal and external equilibrium, as shown by the intersection of the IS', LM', and EE' curves in Figure 15.3. Assume we have a fixed exchange rate. Now suppose that the Fed, unhappy with the rate of unemployment, increases the monetary base. This shifts the LM' curve to LM'' and tends to increase output toward y_1 and reduce the interest rate. This reduces net exports and increases net capital outflows, and the balance of payments becomes a deficit.

The important result of this is that the deficit is settled by an increase in foreign deposits with the Fed or a reduction in the gold stock. The settlement reduces the monetary base and shifts the LM curve back, from LM'' toward LM'''.

However, note that full equilibrium cannot be restored at the intersection of IS' and LM'''. This is because at that intersection the deficit continues, and settlement continues to reduce the monetary base. Thus, the LM curve continues to shift leftward. Indeed, final equilibrium is restored at the intersection of the EE', IS', and LM' curves. The expansionary monetary policy has accomplished nothing more than a change in the composition of the monetary base.

Case 2: Starting from the same initial equilibrium as in Case 1, suppose that instead of an increase in the monetary base, there is an increase in real government expenditures. The changes are shown in Figure 15.4.

The increase in real government spending shifts the IS curve from IS' to IS''. This tends to raise output toward y_1 and to create an external deficit. The external deficit leads to a reduction in the monetary base and a leftward shift in the LM schedule. Final equilibrium occurs at the intersection of EE', LM'', and IS''. The net effect is that output is increased. Thus, fiscal policy succeeds where monetary policy failed.

The overall framework discussed above should be kept in mind when reading the following sections and chapters.

15.3 THE BALANCE OF PAYMENTS AS AN OBJECTIVE OF MONETARY POLICY

Balance of payments issues have long been a concern of policy makers. The reason is fairly straightforward. A persistent balance of payments deficit means that there will be an outflow of reserves from the country experiencing the deficit. The outflow of reserves may take the form of reductions in the domestic country's holdings of gold or of key currencies that are widely used to carry out

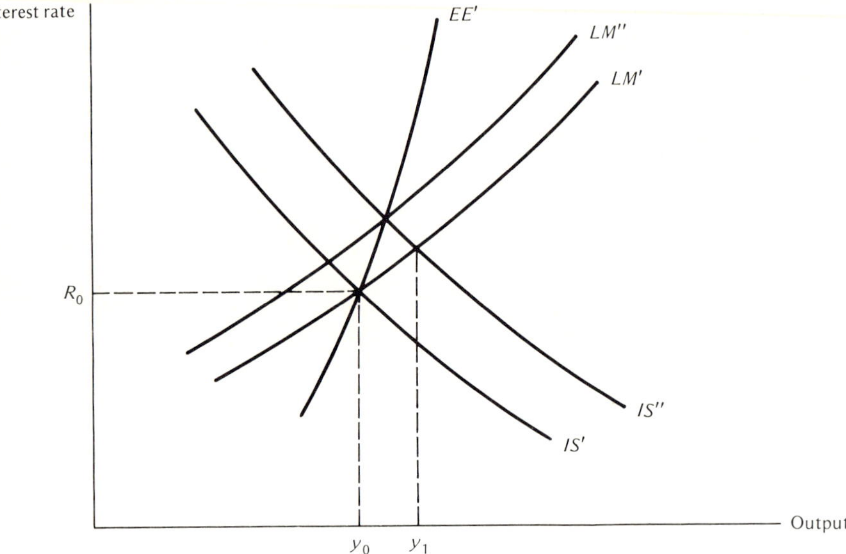

Figure 15.4
Effect of an increase in real government expenditures on internal and external equilibrium.

international exchange. As the deficit and the consequent outflow of reserves continue, the international liquidity position of the country is gradually diminished.

For many years, gold was the major international reserve. While gold has been diminishing in importance, it still accounts for over 80 percent of the United States' stock of international reserves (compared with 100 percent at the end of World War II). Table 15.3 shows the diminution in the United States gold stock from 1960 to 1975 in the face of persistent balance of payments deficits.

Nations that lack sufficient international reserves, and therefore the international means of payment, may be seriously hampered in their trade with other nations. In particular, imports of important goods may have to be foregone if the means for payment does not exist. It is not surprising, therefore, that nations become concerned when their balance of payments assumes a deficit position.

Various means have been used from time to time to resolve balance of payments disequilibrium. Given that components of the balance of payments respond to changes in income, prices, and interest rates, monetary policy may be used to manage the level of output demand. If this is used, improvements in the balance of payments may require reductions in the domestic level of income or increases in domestic interest rates or changes in relative price levels. However, we have just seen how once and for all changes in monetary policy may be frustrated.

In addition to policies that work through market pressures, various non-market measures also influence the balance of payments. Import quotas and tariffs have the effect of raising the price of imports and, therefore, reducing the level of imports. Quotas and tariffs also have multiple uses. In fact, quotas and tariffs have often been used not to alter the balance of payments, but to protect domestic industry from foreign competition. For example, quotas on oil imports were used for years to encourage the exploration for and development of domestic oil reserves.

From the time of the inception of the International Monetary Fund to the early 1970s, fixed exchange rates were the rule and flexible exchange rates were the exception. In a world of fixed exchange rates, improvements in the balance of payments may be accomplished through devaluation. We have already pointed out how this is tantamount to an increase in the price of imported goods and a decrease in the price of domestic goods. Given the current level of capital flows, the resulting improvement in the balance on goods and services will improve the overall balance of payments. In the past, however, nations have resorted to devaluation rather infrequently. There are two major reasons for this. First, it does no good to devalue if all the other countries with whom one trades also devalue their currencies. When that occurs, relative currency prices remain unchanged, and no effect is produced on net exports. Second, devaluation is often interpreted as evidence of domestic economic weakness. Since governments in the post-World War II era have taken the re-

Table 15.3
United States Balance of Payments and United States Monetary Gold Stock, 1960–1975

(In millions of dollars)

Year	Balance of Payments*	Gold Stock
1960	$−3,403	$17,804
1961	−1,348	16,947
1962	−2,650	16,057
1963	−1,934	15,596
1964	−1,534	15,471
1965	−1,290	13,806
1966	219	13,235
1967	−3,418	12,065
1968	1,641	10,892
1969	2,739	11,859
1970	−9,839	11,072
1971	−29,753	10,206
1972	−10,354	10,487
1973	−5,308	11,652
1974	−8,374	11,652
1975	−2,463	11,599

*Official reserve transaction balance.

Sources: *Economic Report of the President,* 1975; and the *Federal Reserve Bulletin,* various issues.

sponsibility for managing the level of domestic economic activity, any evidence of domestic economic weakness can be interpreted as evidence of political failure. Thus devaluation is a hard pill to swallow for any politician.

Another option, rarely followed, involves a do-nothing policy. If the monetary view is correct, balance of payments disequilibria result from money-market disequilibria and will eventually resolve themselves through monetary changes that affect the domestic economy, as we described in the previous section. On the other hand, actions of the Federal Reserve may sustain a balance of payments disequilibrium. Domestic constraints may require the Fed to offset reductions in the monetary base. This may be accomplished through open market operations (purchases). If the monetary base is not permitted to adjust, the balance of payments disequilibrium will continue. We will pursue this issue further when we consider constraints on monetary policy in the next chapter.

Finally, there is the option of flexible exchange rates, which was adopted by many countries in the 1970s. With flexible exchange rates, external equilibrium is automatic. However, the required fluctuations in the rates may engender uncertainty, and therefore many are opposed to flexible rates. We consider this next.

15.4   EXCHANGE-RATE STABILITY OR "PROTECTING THE DOLLAR"

Long-term growth in world trade is important because it promotes higher levels of welfare for the participants in such trade. All other things being equal, steady, stable growth is to be preferred to erratic or uncertain growth. It is widely assumed that stable exchange rates are necessary for stability in world trade. Uncertain or unstable exchange rates impose risks on the participants in trading contracts, especially forward contracts. For example, it is risky to engage in a contract to import a particular quantity of goods at a specified foreign price if one does not have any idea what the exchange rate will be when delivery and payment is to take place.

We have already noted the IMF's concern with exchange-rate stability. Central banks have also acted to stabilize exchange rates. Toward that end, in 1962, the Federal Reserve began operations in the foreign exchange markets to smooth out exchange-rate fluctuations while long-term policies had a chance to correct fundamental balance of payments disequilibrium.

Whether exchange rates should be pegged in this manner or be made completely flexible is another question.* Advocates of fixed exchange rates argue

---

*See M. Friedman, "The Case for Flexible Exchange Rates," in M. Friedman, *Essays in Positive Economics* (Chicago: The University of Chicago Press, 1953), pp. 157–203; or H. G. Johnson, "The Case for Flexible Exchange Rates, 1969," *Review,* Federal Reserve Bank of St. Louis, June 1969, pp. 12–24; and H. C. Wallich, "In Defense of Fixed Exchange Rates," in L. S. Ritter (ed.), *Money and Economic Activity,* 3d ed. (Boston: Houghton Mifflin, 1967), pp. 442–445; or "Why Fixed Rates?" *Social Science Quarterly,* June 1973, pp. 146–151.

that they reduce uncertainty and risk and are conducive to expanded trade. Moreover, they argue that exchange-rate fluctuations provide the opportunity for speculation, which may tend to intensify the fluctuations.

Advocates of flexible rates argue that the existence of a forward market greatly diminishes the uncertainty and risk associated with rate fluctuations. Risk avoiders can use the forward market to hedge against expected fluctuations in exchange rates. Our earlier illustration with the American dealer buying English automobiles is an example of how hedging can be used to remove uncertainty.

Counterarguments to the speculation issue are more difficult to marshal in view of the limited experience with flexible exchange rates in the post-World War II period. However, some observers argue that recent speculation is the result of attempts to maintain fixed exchange rates in the face of pressure for change. For example, in the late 1960s there was considerable evidence that the United States dollar was overvalued in terms of gold (or gold was undervalued in terms of the dollar). Yet the United States persisted in pegging the price of gold at $35 per ounce. Speculators, gambling on devaluation (an increase in the dollar price of gold), bought gold with dollars, thus raising the free market price of gold and placing "pressure on the dollar." Finally, in 1971, the United States suspended convertibility of the dollar into gold and allowed the official price of gold to rise.

Some observers argued that speculation fueled the "crisis" that resulted in devaluation of the dollar. Others argue that the crisis occurred because the value of the dollar was not permitted to change by small amounts over a longer period of time. Had that approach been taken, speculation would not have been associated with such dramatic changes.

SUMMARY NOTES

1. The balance of payments account measures the flows of goods, services, and financial assets between one country and the rest of the world.
2. Subcategories in the balance of payments include the merchandise trade balance, the balance on goods and services, the current account balance, the basic balance, the net liquidity balance, and the official reserve transactions balance.
3. The foreign exchange market is a market for currencies. The exchange rate is the price of one currency in terms of another.
4. The International Monetary Fund was established to deal with exchange-rate and balance of payments policies. The IMF issues its own money, called special drawing rights.
5. Balance of payments adjustment may take place through price, income, interest-rate, and exchange-rate changes.
6. In the monetary view, balance of payments disequilibrium is a flow adjustment to stock disequilibrium in the domestic money market. Settlement of

balance of payments deficits or surpluses implies changes in the domestic monetary base.

7. The conditions for external equilibrium may be incorporated into the IS-LM model. Payments settlement shifts the LM curve, and exogenous changes in net exports shift the IS curve. The EE curve shows interest-rate–output combinations that are consistent with balance of payments equilibrium.

8. Policy has traditionally been directed toward attaining balance of payments equilibrium and exchange-rate stability.

DISCUSSION QUESTIONS

1. Flexible exchange rates are supposed to imply balance of payments equilibrium. Check United States balance of payments figures for 1973 to 1976. Does equilibrium prevail? If not, can you suggest some explanation?

2. The examples in the chapter that integrate the EE curve into the IS-LM model ignore changes in the domestic price level. Use the full output market model of Chapter 10 to analyze the Case 1 and Case 2 changes discussed in the chapter.

3. Can the EE curve be integrated into the LB-LM model also? What factors would affect the LB curve?

4. Obtain the exchange rates between the United States dollar and Swiss francs, Deutsche marks, and Canadian dollars for the years 1972–1976 and 1952–1956. Which period shows the greater stability? Why?

5. Using the IS-LM-EE model, analyze the effect of an increase in the monetary base when exchange rates are flexible. Compare your result with Case 1 in the chapter. Do the same for an increase in government spending and compare the result with Case 2.

6. Use the IS-LM-EE model to show that an expansionary monetary policy will perpetuate a balance of payments deficit if exchange rates are fixed and the Fed uses open market operations to exactly offset changes in any other component of the monetary base.

POLICY CONSTRAINTS

While it is relatively easy to identify the objectives or goals of economic policy, the structure and organization of the economy itself may preclude the easy accomplishment of all goals simultaneously. According to the discussion of the previous two chapters, we should like to have, if at all possible, full employment, price stability, balance of payments equilibrium, and exchange-rate stability. However, the structure of economic relationships may present barriers to the attainment of these objectives. For example, the interaction of the various units in the economy may imply trade-off relationships between the various goals of policy. We have already seen, in Chapter 14, that under certain conditions there may be a trade-off between the objectives of price stability and full employment. Moreover, depending on the behavior of business firms and organized labor, output supply may not respond in the ways the policy makers anticipate. For example, attempts to expand total demand in the economy may not elicit an increase in total supply.

Not only may the behavioral characteristics of different sectors in the economy constrain monetary policy actions, but the economy's institutional arrangements may also act as constraints. For example, certain actions of the Treasury, as it implements fiscal policy, have monetary implications. For any given period in time these may be in conflict with the desired activities of the Federal Reserve System. Financial institutions other than banks create problems for monetary control. Moreover, the political activities of both the executive and legislative branches of the government may place constraints on the actions of Federal Reserve officials.

In this chapter we will examine a number of these constraints and the ways in which they interfere with the policy-making actions of the Federal Reserve System. When we have done so, we will be in a better position to understand the problems involved in the actual policy-making process, which we will discuss in the following chapter. We begin here by considering the constraints imposed by certain trade-offs in the economic structure.

16.1 TRADE-OFFS IN THE ECONOMIC STRUCTURE

The trade-off problem was already introduced in Chapter 14 in connection with our discussion of inflation and unemployment. We discussed foreign objectives in Chapter 15, and there may be trade-off problems between the attainment of those objectives and the domestic objectives of low inflation and low unemployment. In this section we will consider those two types of trade-offs, beginning with the trade-off between inflation and unemployment.

Inflation versus Unemployment

According to the assumptions of the traditional Phillips curve, there is a long-run trade-off between the rate of inflation and the rate of unemployment. It is not possible to drive the economy to low levels of unemployment without increasing the rate of inflation, and vice versa. Thus the Phillips curve, in this view, provides a "menu of choice" for the policy maker. The best of all possible worlds is not attainable, and thus the policy maker must select the best compromise. However, the best compromise may change from time to time as the preferences of society change. The public at large will tolerate neither extreme inflation nor extreme unemployment for any sustained period of time. Such extremes are likely to lead to a rejection of the party in power and its replacement by the opposition. Moreover, few members of the public are likely to believe that either unemployment or inflation can be reduced to zero. Thus it may be possible to ascertain the maximum rates of unemployment and inflation that will be tolerable to the public for any sustained period, and also the rates of unemployment and inflation the public would desire if their preferences were given free sway.

This places bounds on the operational range of the Phillips curve, as shown in Figure 16.1. A conventional Phillips curve is drawn in the figure, along with lines indicating the maximum and desired rates of inflation and unemployment. Any tendency of the economy to exceed these bounds for any reasonable length of time would cause the electorate to exert severe pressures on elected officials to reverse the trend. Thus the freedom of the policy maker is limited to the segment *AB* of the Phillips curve. That segment, reflecting as it does a consensus of opinion of the electorate, has been called the *consensual trap.**

Policy makers may repeatedly reverse their policies in an attempt to avoid exceeding the maximum allowable rates of inflation and unemployment while at the same time attempting to proceed toward the desired levels. Thus for a time policy may drive us to lower rates of unemployment and higher rates of inflation until the maximum allowable rate of inflation is approached. At this

---

*The origin of this is J. Adams, "The Phillips Curve, a 'Consensual Trap' and National Income," *Western Economic Journal*, March 1968, pp. 145–149.

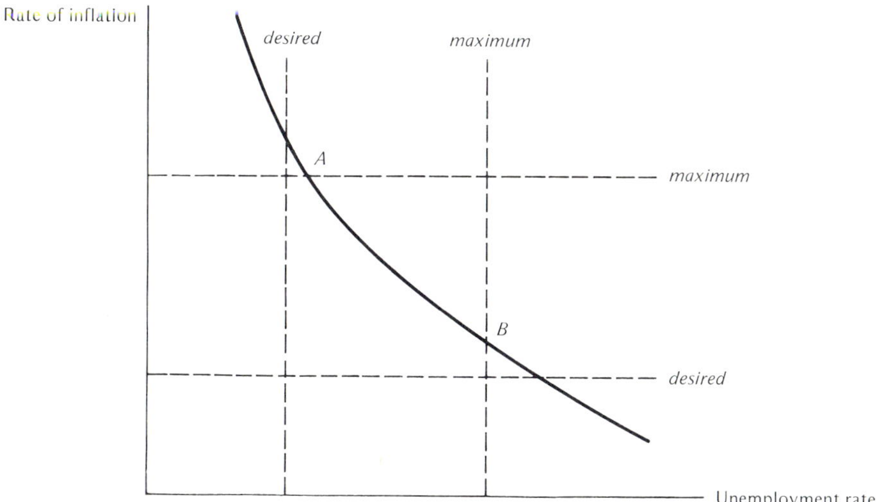

Figure 16.1

The consensual trap.

point, sufficient pressure develops to cause policy to be sharply reversed. The economy then proceeds toward higher rates of unemployment and lower rates of inflation until the maximum rate of unemployment is approached. At that point, the pressures again cause a sharp reversal of policy, and so on. A real example of this idea is President Ford's characterization of "double-digit inflation" as Public Enemy Number One in 1974, followed by a downgrading of inflation as unemployment approached 9 percent of the labor force in 1975. We will have occasion to examine similar reversals in policy in Chapter 19.

Under the accelerationist long-run equilibrium view of the Phillips curve discussed in Chapter 14, the conflict between the goals of inflation and unemployment ends. If any apparent trade-off is indeed a short-run, rather than a long-run, phenomenon, monetary policy can concentrate on management of output demand with a view toward fighting inflation alone. In this view, the natural rate of unemployment cannot be changed by demand management, and any rate of inflation is consistent with the natural rate of unemployment. The task of monetary policy would then be to reduce the rate of inflation to as close to zero as possible. Unemployment, on the other hand, would be attacked by means other than the management of output demand. Imperfect flows of information, discrimination, and imperfect labor mobility are factors that make the natural rate of unemployment what it is. Structural policies that would improve information flows, reduce discrimination, and improve job mobility would be appropriate to reduce the natural rate of unemployment. If accepted, the long-run equilibrium view would, therefore, make the demand policy planning process somewhat easier, but more structural policy decisions would have to be made.

Foreign versus Domestic Goals

Conflicts may exist not only between domestic goals, but between domestic and foreign goals as well. If the Phillips curve accurately describes the domestic trade-off and if we live in a world of fixed exchange rates, attempts to correct domestic problems may aggravate balance of payments problems. For example, suppose the domestic goal is to reduce the rate of unemployment through expansive monetary policy. If the Phillips curve is valid, this will be accompanied by an increase in the domestic rate of inflation. An increase in the domestic rate of inflation means that domestic prices will rise relative to foreign prices. Assuming that exporters and importers respond to relative prices and assuming that exchange rates are fixed, an increase in domestic prices relative to foreign prices should increase imports of foreign goods and decrease exports of domestic goods. This will worsen net exports and therefore the balance of payments.

The price effect is not the only influence on the balance of payments process. The same domestic policy that seeks to reduce the rate of unemployment will raise the level of domestic income. Given that the marginal propensity to import out of income is positive, this will also tend to increase imports of foreign goods. Now these problems are of no concern if the balance of payments disequilibrium happens to be a surplus. Attempts to reduce unemployment in this case will be accompanied by a reduction in the balance of payments surplus *toward* balance of payments equilibrium. The problem arises when the country faces high unemployment and a balance of payments deficit. In that case attempts to reduce unemployment will make the balance of payments deficit worse.

Unfortunately, this was the case for the United States in the early 1960s. Table 16.1 shows unemployment rates and components of the balance of payments for the years 1960 through 1964. Throughout the period, unemployment was over 5 percent and considered to be unacceptably high. The overall balance of payments was in deficit throughout the period even though the cur-

Table 16.1
Unemployment and Balance of Payments Components, 1960–1964

Year	Unemployment Rate	Current Account Balance*	Balance of Payments†
1960	5.5%	$1.80 billion	$−3.40 billion
1961	6.7	3.07	−1.35
1962	5.5	2.46	−2.65
1963	5.7	3.20	−1.93
1964	5.2	5.78	−1.53

*Balance on goods and services plus unilateral transfers.
†Official reserve transactions balance.
Source: Economic Report of the President, 1974.

rent account balance was a surplus. This was because the net outflow of private capital far exceeded the current account balance.

Now if we assume that private capital flows are responsive to interest rates, a solution to the problem suggests itself. Expansive policies, which would reduce the unemployment rate and raise prices and income, would reduce the current account balance toward, not away from, equilibrium. Thus there is no conflict there. The key for the early 1960s was to reverse the flow of private capital, in particular short-term private capital, so that the net capital outflow would not more than offset the current account balance. This was attempted after making two fundamental assumptions. First, it was assumed that the primary determinant of domestic investment expenditures was the long-term interest rate, and further, that a major determinant of short-term private capital flows was the short-term interest rate. Second, it was assumed that it was possible to change the relationship between domestic long-term and short-term interest rates. Thus policy was directed toward lowering the long-term interest rate to stimulate domestic recovery and raising the short-term interest rate to inhibit the net capital outflow. This policy, known as "Operation Twist," was implemented by changing the relative holdings of long- and short-term securities by the Federal Reserve System. The Fed would buy long-term securities and sell short-term securities (or simply buy relatively more long-term securities than short-term securities), which would have the effect of raising the prices and lowering the yields on long-term instruments and lowering the prices and raising the yields on short-term instruments. Of course, the procedure requires that the assumptions of the segmentationist hypothesis, which we discussed in Chapter 10, be essentially correct. In other words, it was necessary to assume that the actions of the Federal Reserve would not induce offsetting reactions on the part of the private sector. Evidence on the success of the policy is somewhat mixed, and the policy was ultimately discarded by 1965 as the buildup of the Vietnam war created new issues.*

The monetary view of the balance of payments provides a somewhat different perspective on the relationships between domestic and foreign objectives. As we pointed out in the previous chapter, the monetary view makes very little distinction among the various components of the balance of payments. Rather it assumes that the balance of payments changes in response to disequilibrium in the domestic money market. In other words, the balance of payments is a flow that is used to adjust the stock of money demanded to the stock of money supplied.

The lines of causation in the monetary view are somewhat different from the lines of causation in the traditional view. In the traditional view, changes in prices, income, and interest rates result in changes in the various components

---

*For a survey of the evidence, see J. B. Michaelsen, *The Term Structure of Interest Rates* (New York: Intext, 1973), chap. 7.

of the balance of payments. For example, if domestic policy actions result in a rise in the domestic price level and a rise in the domestic level of income, imports will increase and exports will decrease. If there is an increase in domestic short-term interest rates, capital outflows will decrease and capital inflows will increase.

By contrast, the monetary view starts with disequilibrium in the money market. If there is an excess of money supply over money demand, individuals will attempt to resolve the excess by purchasing foreign goods, services, and financial assets. In other words, an excess money supply is spread over all the components of the balance of payments. The resulting flows of goods, services, and financial assets between countries create balance of payments disequilibrium that leads to changes in foreign and domestic money supplies and ultimately to changes in prices, incomes, and interest rates.

In the monetary view, the effects of changes in domestic monetary policy differ depending on whether fixed exhange rates exist or not.* If fixed exchange rates are the rule, adjustment takes place through the various flows of the balance of payments. For example, suppose the Federal Reserve System engages in an expansionary monetary policy with a view toward reducing the domestic level of unemployment. Suppose the policy involves an increase in the monetary base through open market purchases of government securities, which increases the money supply relative to money demand. The excess money supply is disbursed for foreign and domestic goods, services, and financial assets. Put another way, given domestic and foreign prices and the existence of fixed exchange rates, there is now an excess demand for foreign goods and services and financial assets. Since exchange rates cannot adjust to eliminate this excess demand, increased purchases of foreign goods, services, and financial assets are made. Thus we have an increase in imports of goods and services and an increased outflow of private capital, and a balance of payments deficit develops in the domestic country.

The deficit is settled by a transfer of international reserves from the domestic country to the foreign countries. This reduces the domestic monetary base and consequently the money supply, and increases the monetary bases and money supplies of various foreign countries. The result is a partial offset to the domestic expansionary monetary policy and a weakening of Federal Reserve System control over the domestic monetary base. The increase in the monetary base of various foreign countries forces the central banks in those countries to engage in offsetting actions if they do not wish to pursue an expansionary monetary policy. If offsetting actions are not taken, the monetary bases of those countries will increase, thus putting expansionary pressure on the domestic economies of those foreign countries. Countries that are at, or close to, full employment will

---

*See the analysis in D. S. Kemp, "A Monetary View of the Balance of Payments," *Review*, Federal Reserve Bank of St. Louis, April 1975, pp. 14–22.

experience inflationary pressures as a result of United States domestic policy, and countries that are presently experiencing unemploymeent will be the beneficiaries of United States domestic policy.

However, the results are quite different if exchange rates are flexible. Any excess demand for foreign goods, services, and financial assets resulting from an excess domestic money supply will be resolved by adjustments in the exchange rates. Thus the expansionary domestic policy does not result in changes in the flows in the balance of payments and does not disturb the balance of payments equilibrium. Moreover, in a world of flexible exchange rates, the domestic monetary authority is able to maintain a tighter control over the domestic money supply. Finally, inflationary pressures are not transmitted from country to country.

Thus the possibility of conflict between foreign and domestic goals depends on one's view of the balance of payments mechanism. Given fixed exchange rates, the traditional view implies that changes in domestic policy could permanently aggravate balance of payments disequilibrium. Under the monetary view, with fixed exchange rates, changes in domestic policy temporarily result in balance of payments disequilibrium. In both cases flexible exchange rates effectively break the conflict between foreign and domestic goals.

16.2 PROBLEMS WITH SUPPLY RESPONSE

The object of a particular monetary policy stance may be to reduce unemployment. However, the effect of this policy on output and unemployment depends on the actions of firms and labor. Those actions may be beyond the control of the policy maker. A conventional approach assumes that output supply is fairly elastic at existing price levels if the economy is characterized by high unemployment. The chain of causation can be summarized as follows: The Federal Reserve engages in open market purchases of government securities, which increases the monetary base and the money supply. This leads to a reduction in interest rates, which stimulates private expenditures on real capital. Firms that produce capital goods experience a reduction in inventories below their desired levels. Given the existence of unemployment, those firms hire more labor at current wage rates in order to increase the rate of output. Thus unemployment falls and output increases.

However, this implicitly assumes that the marginal product of labor does not decrease as more labor is hired. If more labor cannot be hired without running into diminishing returns, then marginal costs will rise as output expands even if wage rates are constant. This means that producers will not expand output unless prices also rise. Moreover, depending on the industry involved, the elasticity of output supply with respect to the price level may be low, so that it would take a substantial increase in the price level to induce a small increase in output and therefore a small decrease in unemployment. This problem results from the technology of production and is beyond the control of the policy maker. Under such conditions, an expansionary monetary policy might result in significantly higher prices before there is much change in the rate of unemployment.*

Even if aggregate output supply is fairly elastic with respect to the price level, the response of supply may be rather slow. The actions of producers and the suppliers of labor may depend more on their expectations or perceptions about wages and prices than on the actual levels of wages and prices. We dealt somewhat with this issue in Chapter 14. While this problem is not solved by conventional attempts to manage output demand, the policy makers can provide corrective action by improving the flows of information about prices and wages so that the perceptions of firms and workers conform more closely to reality.

All this implies that the effect of policy on unemployment and inflation will not be instantaneous. Policy changes may operate only with a long lag. It may take a year or two before an expansionary policy produces any significant impact on the rate of unemployment. To make matters worse, the lags may be somewhat asymmetrical. For example, an expansionary policy may tend to increase the rate of inflation before it reduces the rate of unemployment. A contractionary policy may raise the rate of unemployment before it reduces the rate of inflation. Some hint of the lags involved is provided by Figure 16.2. From 1960 to 1965, the growth rate of the monetary base steadily increased, and this was accompanied by a fairly steady decline in the rate of unemployment together with a stable and low rate of inflation. In 1966, the Federal Reserve sharply reduced the growth rate in the monetary base. The previous decline in the rate of unemployment halted, and the rate of unemployment held at 3.8 percent of the labor force in both 1966 and 1967. However, the rate of inflation continued to rise in both 1966 and 1967.

Before the contractionary policy of 1966 had any chance to affect the rate of inflation, the growth rate in the monetary base was increased sharply to a level considerably above that in 1965. This high growth rate in the monetary base continued through 1968. This was accompanied by some slight decrease in the rate of unemployment and a fairly sharp increase in the rate of inflation. In 1969 the Federal Reserve sharply contracted the growth rate in the monetary base again, as it had done in 1966. However, in 1969 the growth rate in the monetary base was even less than it was in 1966. The impact on unemployment appeared to be fairly swift, as unemployment rose sharply in 1970 and again in 1971. The rate of inflation, on the other hand, continued to rise in 1970 and did not begin to decline until 1971, two years after the contractionary policy took effect. By then high growth rates in the monetary base had been resumed, and these persisted from 1971 through 1974. The rate of infla-

---

*Even during the expansion phase from 1933 to 1937, when unemployment ranged between 24.9 and 14.3 percent of the labor force, prices rose by an average of 3.3 percent per year, measured by the GNP deflator.

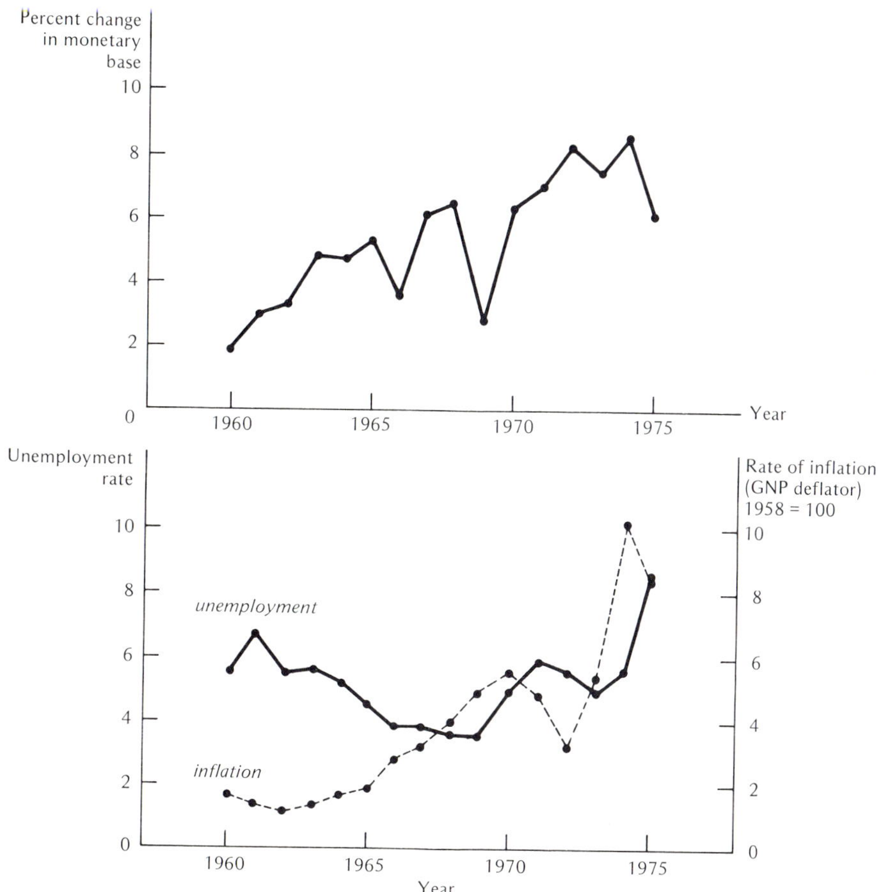

Figure 16.2

Growth rate of the monetary base, the rate of unemployment, and the rate of inflation, 1960–1975.

tion, which had declined from 1971 to 1972, increased sharply in 1973 and almost doubled in 1974.

Thus the turning points in monetary policy do not coincide with turning points in either the rate of inflation or the rate of unemployment. Some lags can be discerned from the figure, but the lags are variable, or not of the same length at all periods of time. Such lag response must be taken into account if the Federal Reserve is to plan its policy over any reasonable period of time.

16.3 CONFLICTS BETWEEN FISCAL AND MONETARY POLICY

Fiscal and monetary policy, though independently formulated, are not necessarily independent in their effects on the economy. The Federal Reserve System, when it formulates monetary policy, must consider the financial effects of fiscal policy. Changes in government expenditures or taxes may result in changes in the federal deficit, which must be financed by increased or decreased borrowing in the financial markets. Treasury operations to finance a deficit in turn induce changes in interest rates on government bonds. As buyers of financial assets, acting on their preferences, shift between government securities and private securities, the interest-rate changes filter through the rest of the financial markets, resulting in changes in interest rates on private securities as well. For example, should there be a substantial increase in government expenditures without a concomitant increase in taxes, a large deficit will be incurred. To finance the deficit, the Treasury will have to issue government bonds and other securities and attempt to sell those in the financial markets. Their attempt to do this will depress prices on government securities and raise the interest rates. As financial-market investors buy government securities to take advantage of the higher interest rates, they will sell private securities, whose prices in turn will fall and whose interest rates will therefore rise. Thus the impact of an increased government deficit due to a fiscal policy change will result in higher interest rates throughout the financial markets.

This increase in interest rates may be inconsistent with the Federal Reserve's view of what interest rates should be. In order to prevent interest rates from rising to undesirable levels, the Federal Reserve may feel compelled to purchase quantities of government securities. Prior to 1951, the Fed was virtually compelled to engage in open market purchases of government securities to the extent necessary to keep market interest rates at very low levels. In 1951, an accord was reached between the Treasury and the Federal Reserve which released the Federal Reserve from the requirement that it support government securities prices.

However, since 1951, the Federal Reserve has not been completely oblivious to Treasury financing operations. In 1953, the then Chairman of the Board, William McChesney Martin, enunciated what has become known as the Fed's "even keel" policy.* According to this policy, the Fed would maintain a hands-off or neutral policy during periods of heavy Treasury financing operations. This would ensure that monetary policy operations would not jeopardize the success of Treasury financing. The policy has persisted, so that even at the present time the directives issued by the Federal Open Market Committee contain a clause which requires the manager of the system's open market account to consider Treasury financing operations when carrying out the monetary policy directive.

The even keel policy may result in a more expansionary policy than otherwise would be the case. For example, consider the changes in Figure 16.3. The diagram contains the standard IS and LM curves. Suppose the initial

---

*W. McC. Martin, Jr., "The Transition to Free Markets," *Federal Reserve Bulletin*, April 1953, pp. 330–335.

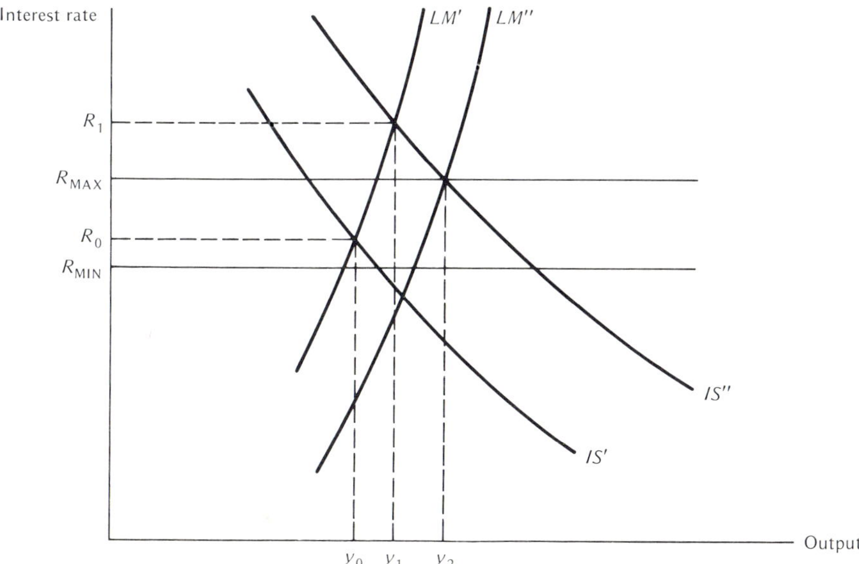

Figure 16.3
Federal Reserve accommodation of fiscal policy.

equilibrium, shown by the intersection of the *IS'* and *LM'* curves, is at interest rate R_0 and real income y_0. Now suppose that there is a substantial increase in government expenditures with no increase in taxes. The IS curve shifts to the right to *IS"*. Normally the Treasury operations required to finance the resulting deficit would raise the interest rate to R_1. However, suppose the Federal Reserve's stabilization objectives require the interest rate to be somewhere in the range between R_{max} and R_{min}. Interest rate R_1 is outside of that range, and therefore the Fed must take compensatory action to keep the interest rate from rising to that level. It can do this by engaging in open market operations which increase the monetary base, shifting the LM curve to *LM"*. In this way the interest rate is kept from rising above the maximum allowable level.

Unfortunately, this may produce adverse effects in other areas. If such a policy is followed, real income will rise not from y_0 to y_1, but from y_0 to y_2. The larger increase in real income may generate inflationary pressures that were not anticipated by the initial fiscal policy action. Thus attempts to keep an expansive fiscal policy from generating undesirably high interest rates result in both fiscal and monetary policy that are more expansionary than either group of policy makers planned.

In recent years, federal deficits have risen to fairly high levels. In the five years ending in June 1975, the federal deficit totaled more than $100 billion. This exceeds any previous five-year period since the end of World War II. Some writers have in fact argued that the rapid growth in the monetary base and the money supply during recent years is directly attributable to large federal deficits and the even keel policy of the Federal Reserve.*

The alternative to the even keel policy is for the Fed to specify its objectives in terms of the monetary base or the money supply and let interest rates go where they may. Whether interest rates or monetary aggregates such as the monetary base and the money supply make better targets of policy is something we defer to the next chapter. However, if the even keel policy is maintained and if federal deficits continue to grow as they have in the recent past, monetary policy will be increasingly cast in an accommodating role and will lose the independence granted to it by the structure of the Federal Reserve System. Thus not only may monetary policy be constrained in the results it hopes to achieve, as we indicated in the previous sections of this chapter, but its actions may also be constrained.

The even keel constraint is an institutional constraint that results from the particular structure of fiscal and monetary authorities that exists in the United States. However, institutional features of the private sector also create problems for Federal Reserve action.

16.4 THE INFLUENCE OF FINANCIAL INTERMEDIARIES

Earlier chapters indicated that financial intermediaries as well as the monetary and fiscal authorities play an important role in the economy. Their existence raises questions about the ability of financial intermediaries to offset the changes in output and the interest rate desired by the monetary and fiscal authorities.† In this section we will examine the extent to which financial intermediation and disintermediation inhibits or constrains the effectiveness of monetary policy. Financial intermediaries perform a service to the economy, but a case for additional government controls may be made if the intermediaries have the means to substantially offset the desired effects on the economy of monetary or fiscal policy *and* if the monetary and fiscal authorities currently lack the means to offset any undesirable effects.

Financial intermediaries are business firms that attempt to maximize profits within the constraints imposed by various regulatory agencies, including the Fed, which regulates member banks, states, which regulate state banks, and the Federal Home Loan Bank, which regulates saving and loan associations. Financial intermediaries will intermediate until their rate of return or the market interest rate just equals their rate of marginal cost (hereafter called the *cost rate*).

---

*For example, see D. R. Francis, "How and Why Fiscal Actions Matter to a Monetarist," *Review*, Federal Reserve Bank of St. Louis, May 1974, pp. 2–7; and S. R. Roesch, "The Monetary-Fiscal Mix through Mid-1976," *Review*, Federal Reserve Bank of St. Louis, August 1975, pp. 2–7.

†See *Report of the Committee on the Working of the Monetary System (The Radcliffe Report)* (London: H. M. Stationery Office, 1959). Also see K. Brunner, "The Role of Money and Monetary Policy," *Review*, Federal Reserve Bank of St. Louis, July 1968, pp. 9–24.

The cost rate includes the deposit rate and other rates of marginal cost such as the costs of processing and accounting for deposits.

If the interest rate exceeds the cost rate, financial intermediaries will increase their cost rate by increasing the deposit rate, thus increasing deposits and the supply of loans until the interest rate decreases by enough to make it equal to the cost rate, thus maximizing profits. Hence, financial *intermediation* occurs.

If the cost rate exceeds the interest rate, financial intermediaries will decrease their cost rate by decreasing the deposit rate until the interest rate increases by enough to make it equal to the cost rate, thus maximizing profits. Hence, financial *disintermediation* occurs.

In raising their deposit rates, financial intermediaries may run into the barriers imposed by Regulation Q and other ceiling rates. Should market interest rates exceed ceiling deposit rates, substantial financial disintermediation will occur in the absence of overt action by financial intermediaries. We will consider an example of this shortly.

Financial intermediation is only one way by which the interest rate (and level of output) can be changed.* Monetary and fiscal policies can change the interest rate (and level of output) as well. To determine whether financial institutions can offset changes in the interest rate (and level of output) brought about by monetary and fiscal policies, we must examine the profit-maximizing response of financial intermediaries to such changes.

Consider the case in which the interest rate decreases due to either expansionary monetary policy or contractionary fiscal policy. Financial intermediaries will then reduce their cost rate by decreasing the deposit rate, and as a result financial disintermediation occurs until the interest rate rises to equal the cost rate. Since disintermediation causes the interest rate to rise (and the level of income to fall), it reinforces contractionary fiscal policy but partially offsets expansionary monetary policy.

Although the fiscal authority must be aware of the effects of financial disintermediation if it wishes to compensate for it when formulating contractionary fiscal policy, financial disintermediation does not offset the impact of contractionary fiscal policy. And although financial intermediation can *partially* offset expansionary monetary policy, it cannot *totally* offset it.

Figure 16.4 illustrates our point using the LB-LM model. The *LB'* and *LM'* schedules determine the initial equilibrium values of the interest rate R_3 and level of output y_1. Expansionary monetary policy (an increase in the monetary base) shifts the LM schedule to *LM''*, and the interest rate falls to R_1 as output increases to y_3. The decrease in the interest rate prompts financial intermediaries to decrease the deposit rate because the old cost rate now exceeds the new interest rate. As a result, the LM schedule shifts to *LM'''*.

---

*At this stage it might be helpful to review Chapter 10.

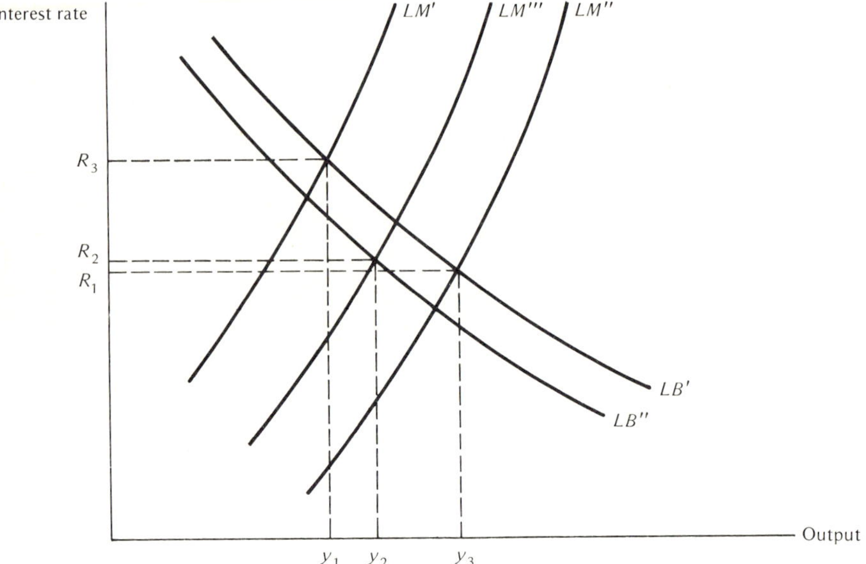

Figure 16.4

Financial disintermediation and expansionary monetary policy.

Changes in the deposit rate, and the additional money balances generated by the increase in the monetary base, also shift the LB schedule. However, the changes are opposite in effect. The decrease in the deposit rate tends to shift the LB schedule to the right, while the increase in additional money balances tends to shift the LB schedule to the left. The net effect is actually ambiguous. However, Figure 16.4 is drawn under the assumption that the latter effect dominates, so that the LB schedule shifts leftward from LB' to LB''. The interest rate rises to R_2 as output decreases to y_2. However, the interest rate will not increase to its original level, R_3. If it did, financial intermediaries would increase the deposit rate because the interest rate would then exceed the cost rate. This would tend to shift the LM curve to the right and the LB curve to the left, which would prevent the interest rate from rising to R_3. Thus, financial disintermediation partially offsets expansionary monetary policy, but does not completely offset it.

Moreover, the Federal Reserve, because it has effective control over the monetary base, can offset any undesirable changes in output and the interest rate that result from financial disintermediation. Therefore, in this case there is no need for additional controls to protect the effectiveness of monetary policy. The constraint on Fed policy lies in the fact that the Fed must be aware of the extent and effects of financial disintermediation. If the Fed is aware of the impact of financial disintermediation (as well as the impact of the concurrent policies of other policy makers) and the impact of its own policies, it is in a good position to realize desired changes in the interest rate and level of output.

When the interest rate increases due to either contractionary monetary policy or expansionary fiscal policy, financial intermediaries increase their cost rate by increasing the deposit rate, and financial intermediation occurs until the interest rate falls to equal the cost rate. We assume that the deposit rate is not at its legal ceiling, so that it can, in fact, be raised. If it cannot, the problem of intermediation does not arise. Since intermediation causes the interest rate to fall (and income to increase), it reinforces expansionary fiscal policy but partially offsets contractionary monetary policy.

Again, the fiscal authority must be aware of the effect of financial intermediation so that it can act accordingly when planning expansionary policy. Although financial intermediation partially offsets contractionary monetary policy, it cannot completely offset contractionary monetary policy.

Figure 16.5 indicates this point. The LB' and LM' schedules determine the initial equilibrium values of the interest rate R_1 and level of output y_3. Contractionary monetary policy (a decrease in the monetary base) shifts the LM schedule to LM'', and the interest rate rises to R_3 as output falls to y_1. The increase in the interest rate prompts financial intermediaries to increase the deposit rate because the interest rate exceeds the cost rate. The LM schedule shifts to LM'''. The decrease in additional money balances tends to shift the LB schedule to the right, while the increase in the deposit rate tends to shift the LB schedule to the left. While the net effect is ambiguous, Figure 16.5 assumes that the former effect dominates, so that the LB schedule shifts rightward from LB' to LB''. The interest rate falls to R_2 and output increases to y_2. The interest rate will not

Figure 16.5

Financial intermediation and contractionary monetary policy.

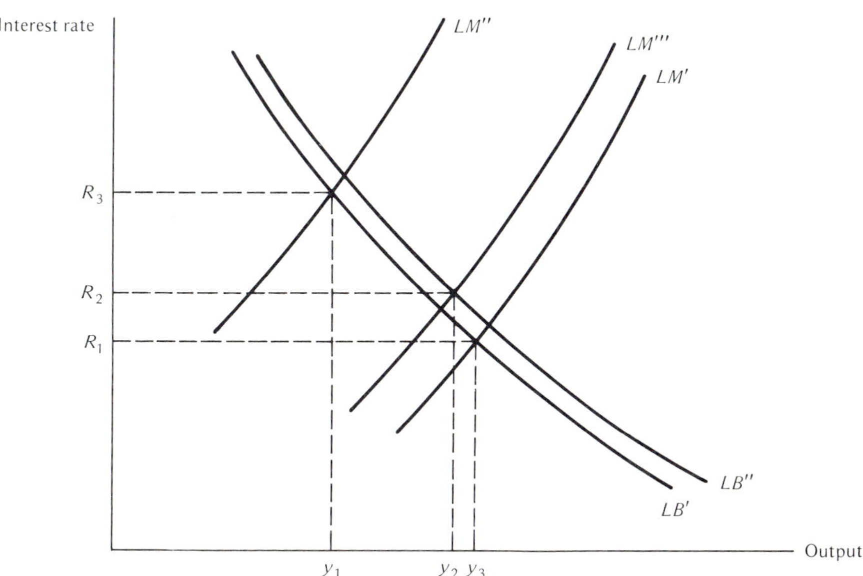

decrease to its original level, R_1. If it did, financial intermediaries would decrease the deposit rate because the cost rate would exceed the interest rate. These changes would reverse the fall in the interest rate. Thus, financial intermediation partially offsets contractionary monetary policy as long as financial institutions can raise the deposit rate, but it cannot completely offset contractionary monetary policy.

Again, we must mention that the power to partially offset contractionary monetary policy (and to reinforce expansionary fiscal policy) is limited by the ceilings which are set on the time and savings deposit rates of financial intermediaries.*

Banks are unable to raise their deposit rate above the limit set by the Fed's Regulation Q. Maximum deposit rates are set on the deposits of nonbank financial institutions as well. For example, the Federal Home Loan Bank sets the deposit-rate ceiling on the deposit liabilities of saving and loan associations.

When the interest rate rose faster than the deposit rate in the United States in 1966, 1969, and the early 1970s because of monetary restraint, inflation, and a lack of fiscal restraint, financial intermediaries were unable to increase the deposit rate fast enough (because of deposit-rate ceilings) to keep pace with increases in the interest rate. As a result, depositors withdrew funds from financial intermediaries and lent those funds directly to final borrowers in the loanable funds market. Thus, financial intermediaries were caught in a "credit crunch."

Table 16.2 illustrates the changes that took place during the past eleven years. Compare the first and fourth columns in the table. In 1965 private nonfinancial investors held $8.02 in time deposits for every $1.00 in short-term United States government securities. At that time the yield on short-term government securities was less than the ceiling rates on time deposits. As market rates rose relative to ceiling rates (deposit rates) in 1966, disintermediation occurred, and investors held only $7.54 in time deposits for every $1.00 of government securities. The pattern was reversed in 1967. Similar changes occur in the rest of the period covered by the table. Throughout the period, whenever market rates rise (fall) relative to ceiling rates, disintermediation (intermediation) takes place as investors alter their portfolios to take advantage of the relatively higher yield.

Now, financial intermediaries may prefer not to raise deposit rates.† If deposit rates are at their ceilings, of course financial institutions cannot raise them. However, even before ceiling rates are reached, it may not be profitable to raise deposit rates. Most of the assets of nonbank financial intermediaries are long-term. Only a small portion are short-term, and they are held primarily for

---

*See J. Tobin, "Deposit Interest Rate Ceilings as a Monetary Control," *Journal of Money, Credit and Banking,* February 1970, pp. 4–14.

†See S. M. Goldfeld and D. M. Jaffee, "The Determinants of Deposit-Rate Setting by Savings and Loan Associations," *Journal of Finance,* June 1970, pp. 615–632.

Table 16.2
Interest Rates and Relative Holdings of Financial Assets by the Private Nonfinancial Sector, 1965–1975

Year	Ratio of Time Deposits to Government Securities*	Treasury Bill Rate	Interest Rates	
			Regulation Q†	Spread‡
1965	8.02	3.95%	4.00%	−0.05
1966	7.54	4.88	4.00	0.88
1967	9.33	4.32	4.00	0.32
1968	8.61	5.34	4.00	1.34
1969	6.19	6.68	4.00	2.68
1970	8.50	6.46	4.50	1.96
1971	13.15	4.35	4.50	−0.15
1972	14.54	4.07	4.50	−0.43
1973	13.47	7.04	5.00	2.04
1974	12.81	7.88	5.00	2.88
1975	13.97	5.84	5.00	0.84

*Time deposits at banks and thrift institutions divided by short-term marketable United States government debt. Holdings are for the private nonfinancial sector.

†Ceiling rate on ordinary savings accounts.

‡Treasury bill rate minus Regulation Q ceiling.

Source: Economic Report of the President, 1975; and Federal Reserve Bulletin, various issues.

liquidity purposes. A rapidly increasing interest rate means that the rate of return is weighted by lower yields on past asset purchases. But if deposit rates are increased (and the increase is applied to all deposits, not just new ones), the cost of holding funds may exceed the returns. Thus, it may not be profitable to raise deposit rates, even in the absence of ceilings. Our analysis in this section made no allowance for asset holdings of different maturities. A more advanced analysis of portfolio management would have to take this into account.

Overall, financial institutions are clearly limited in their ability to offset the impacts of monetary and fiscal policies. Profit-maximizing behavior, deposit-rate ceilings, and the ability of the monetary and fiscal authorities to offset any undesirable effects of financial intermediation appear to protect the effectiveness of monetary and fiscal policies sufficiently. Nevertheless, precise monetary control requires that the Federal Reserve recognize, and be prepared to correct for, the effects of financial intermediation.

16.5 CONSTRAINTS IMPOSED BY POLITICAL ACTION

Congress originally created the Federal Reserve System as an independent monetary authority, free from political influence. This is a lofty ideal not always workable in practice. We indicated in Section 16.3 that the actions of the fiscal authorities, through their effect on the economy, may compel the Federal

Reserve to act in ways that are contrary to its own intentions. However, more direct political influence has also been used in recent years.

The Federal Reserve System is the creation of Congress, and Congress, of course, has every right to modify or amend the way in which the Federal Reserve operates. Moreover, the power of Congress to regulate monetary policy is embodied in Article I, Section 8 of the United States Constitution. From time to time Congress has modified the structure of the Federal Reserve System and assigned specific responsibilities to the Board of Governors. In 1975, the Congress took a direct hand in specifying the kind of monetary policy that should be followed by the Fed. In March of that year, the Congress passed House Concurrent Resolution 133, which requested the Board of Governors and the Federal Open Market Committee:

> (1). to pursue policies in the first half of 1975 so as to encourage lower, long term interest rates and expansion in the monetary and credit aggregates appropriate to facilitating prompt, economic recovery and (2). to maintain long run growth of the monetary and credit aggregates commensurate with the economy's long run potential to increase production so as to promote effectively the goals of maximum employment, stable prices and moderate long term interest rates.*

The resolution also requires the Board of Governors to consult with Congress at semiannual hearings before the Committee on Banking, Housing, and Urban Affairs of the Senate and the Committee on Banking, Currency, and Housing of the House of Representatives about the Board of Governors' and the Federal Open Market Committee's objectives and plans with respect to the changes in monetary and credit aggregates in the upcoming 12 months. The Board of Governors is permitted to deviate from its projections should change in economic conditions warrant.

In the first hearings on House Concurrent Resolution 133, held in April and May of 1975, Arthur Burns, Chairman of the Board of Governors, specified the target for the Federal Reserve as follows: For the 12-month period ending March 1976, the Board and the Federal Open Market Committee planned to increase the money supply narrowly defined (M_1) between 5 and $7^1/_2$ percent. Various broader measures of money were specified to grow at somewhat higher rates.† During the first nine months of this policy, the money supply narrowly defined grew at a 5.3 percent annual rate, which was within the range specified by Chairman Burns.

Thus the resolution produces two very important changes in the conduct of monetary policy in the United States. First, Congress will now directly influence the specific target growth rates for the money supply. Second, the target

---

*See Committee on Banking, Housing and Urban Affairs, *First Meeting on the Conduct of Monetary Policy,* U.S. Senate, 1975, p. 3.

†*Ibid.,* p. 172.

growth rates are announced in advance. This is a departure from previous practice, under which the minutes of Federal Open Market Committee meetings were not made public for three months after the fact. Just how these provisions will affect monetary policy is something we will speculate on in the last chapter.

While House Concurrent Resolution 133 is a monumental change in the relationship between Congress and the Federal Reserve System, other changes have also been introduced. For example, in September 1975 Senate Bill 2285 was introduced by Senator William Proxmire and referred to the Committee on Banking, Housing, and Urban Affairs. Among other things, this bill would require the Senate to confirm the appointment of the Chairman of the Board of Governors and the Presidents of the District Federal Reserve Banks. Presently the Senate confirms only the appointments of the members of the Board of Governors. The President of the United States appoints the Chairman of the Board of Governors without Senate confirmation, and the Board appoints the Presidents of the District Federal Reserve Banks, again without confirmation by either the House or the Senate. Should S.2285 become law, the Senate would be able to confirm not only the members of the Board of Governors but all members of the Federal Open Market Committee, since the Presidents of the District Reserve Banks serve on the Federal Open Market Committee on a rotating basis. Moreover, it is generally acknowledged that the Chairman of the Board exerts considerable influence on the deliberations of both the Board and the Federal Open Market Committee. Confirmation by the Senate would provide some congressional influence on the deliberations of the Board and the Federal Open Market Committee.

The effect of legislation such as that contained in the two bills just discussed is to reduce the independence of the Federal Reserve and make possible closer coordination of fiscal and monetary policy.* How such a system will work in the future is open to conjecture.

The reader may conclude from the material contained in this chapter that the Federal Reserve System has become so constrained that it can no longer effectively implement monetary policy. However, this overstates the case, and the Federal Reserve does formulate and implement monetary policy. The mechanics of this are discussed in the next chapter.

SUMMARY NOTES

1. The success of policy making is constrained by structural and institutional factors.

---

*Federal Reserve independence is often the subject of some discussion. For example, see the essays in J. Prager (ed.), *Monetary Economics: Controversies in Theory and Policy* (New York: Random House, 1971), pp. 100–122.

2. Structural constraints include conflicts between inflation and unemployment goals and between foreign and domestic goals.
3. Efforts to reduce unemployment are inhibited by the extent to which output supply responds to changes in output demand.
4. Institutional constraints include conflicts between fiscal and monetary policy and the influence of nonbank financial intermediaries.
5. Recent political actions by the House and Senate have restricted the scope of Federal Reserve discretion.

DISCUSSION QUESTIONS

1. Consider the competing theories of the trade-off between inflation and unemployment and of the balance of payments. Which set of theories presents the most difficult choice for the Fed? Which presents the easiest?
2. If you were Chairman of the Board of Governors and wanted to avoid ulcers, would you prefer fixed or flexible exchange rates? Why?
3. The federal budget for the fiscal year ending September 30, 1977, may contain a $45 billion deficit. If the entire deficit is to be financed with new money, by how much must the monetary base increase?
4. If the deficit in question 3 is fully financed by new money, by what percent will the money supply increase? Compare this with recent years. Would you consider the increase to be relatively expansionary or contractionary?
5. Outline some arguments, pro and con, on the statement, "The Federal Reserve should be more closely controlled by Congress."

POLICY IMPLEMENTATION FOR ECONOMIC STABILITY

In the previous three chapters we examined the goals of policy and the environmental constraints within which the Federal Reserve must operate. But before policy can be successfully implemented, even within these constraints, a number of questions must be answered. How should we measure policy? That is, how will we know whether policy is becoming expansionary or contractionary? What financial variables should the Federal Reserve seek to control? Given that some policy is implemented, what are the actual mechanics of policy formulation? How do we know what the Fed is actually doing? What alternative policies might be followed? These questions have been the source of confusion and controversy among economists and policy makers alike. We cannot hope in this brief chapter to resolve the issues that divide economists and policy makers, but at least we can shed some light on the questions. We will begin by considering the ways in which policy might be measured.

17.1 SELECTING AN INDICATOR OF POLICY

Two terms are often used interchangeably in the policy literature. We often speak of *indicators* of policy and *targets* of policy. To avoid confusion, it may be appropriate to define each at the outset. A policy *indicator* should measure the pressure or thrust of policy on the economy.* An indicator of monetary policy should inform the observer whether policy has become easy or has tightened. In other words, the indicator should tell us whether the Federal Reserve is pursuing an expansionary policy or a contractionary policy. On the other hand, a policy *target* is a variable that the policy maker attempts to control. We usually distinguish between two types of targets. The *ultimate targets* of policy are those variables that measure the performance of the economy, such as the rate of inflation and the rate of unemployment. For example, the ultimate target variable may be the unemployment rate, and the objective of policy may be to reduce that unemployment rate to 4 percent of the labor force.

Now the Federal Reserve cannot control unemployment or inflation directly. Since it cannot, it specifies goals with respect to an *intermediate target*. The intermediate target is generally some financial variable on which the Fed is assumed to exert a fairly significant influence. The money supply might be an intermediate target. If it is assumed that there is some kind of stable relationship between the money supply and the ultimate targets of unemployment and inflation, the Federal Reserve can specify its objectives in terms of the intermediate target. For example, the intermediate objective might be to make the money supply grow at a 4 percent annual rate under the assumption that that growth rate in the money supply will lead to the desired values for the ultimate targets. The Federal Reserve influences the intermediate target by adjusting the *instruments* of policy. An *instrument* of policy is a variable over which the Federal Reserve has total and exclusive control. These instruments include the required reserve ratio, the discount rate, margin requirements, maximum interest rates payable on time deposits at commercial banks (Regulation Q ceilings), and open market operations. Changes in these instruments produce changes in an intermediate target such as the money supply through the process that we discussed in Chapter 6. In this section we will examine possible indicators of policy. Targets will be discussed in the next section along with the mechanics of policy formulation.

Various types of indicators have been suggested by monetary economists. Generally the type of indicator proposed reflects the economist's view about the way in which the economy operates. For example, monetarists tend to suggest that various monetary aggregates such as the money supply or the monetary base be used as indicators of monetary policy. Keynesians tend to prefer interest rates or other indicators of money-market conditions such as free

---

*See K. Brunner and A. H. Meltzer, ''The Nature of the Policy Problem,'' in K. Brunner (ed.), *Targets and Indicators of Monetary Policy* (San Francisco: Chandler, 1969), pp. 1–26.

reserves. Unborrowed reserves is another possible indicator which was used in the econometric models discussed in Chapter 12.

A proper indicator of monetary policy should have a number of desirable characteristics. For example, the indicator should always provide consistent information about the effect of policy on the economy. It would not do for an increase in the value of an indicator to indicate an expansionary policy at one time and a contractionary policy at another time.

Since the indicator is supposed to describe the effect of policy on the economy, it is not appropriate for the indicator to be an endogenous variable. That is, the indicator should determine conditions in the economy, not be determined by them. If the value of the indicator is jointly determined along with other variables in the economy, we will not know whether a change in the indicator is a result of a policy change or a result of changes in conditions in the economy.

Obviously if the indicator is to measure the thrust of policy on the economy, it must be responsive to Federal Reserve actions. In fact it would be preferable if the indicator responded only to Federal Reserve actions and not to actions of the fiscal authorities. Otherwise we would be measuring both fiscal and monetary policy with the same indicator.

The possible indicators mentioned above may be evaluated against these criteria. Consider the first criterion. Is the indicator consistent with respect to direction of change in the economy? On the basis of the models used thus far in this book, we would have to answer "no" for the interest rate. Whether we employ the IS-LM model or the LB-LM model, an increase in the interest rate may be the consequence of either a contractionary monetary policy or an expansionary fiscal policy. Thus changes in the interest rate alone cannot tell us whether monetary policy has become expansionary or contractionary.

Free reserves suffers from the same deficiency. When this is used as an indicator of monetary policy, a reduction in free reserves is interpreted as a tightening of policy and an increase in free reserves as an easing of policy. That is, if the Federal Reserve withdraws reserves from the banking system through open market sales of government securities, total reserves and therefore excess reserves of the banking system should fall. Banks, feeling the pressure to maintain their reserve position, resort to increased borrowing from the Federal Reserve System. Thus excess reserves decrease and member bank borrowing increases. The effect of both these changes is to decrease the level of free reserves. However, we have already discovered in Chapter 6 that free reserves responds to endogenous elements in the model. For example, should market interest rates increase, banks will wish to reduce their levels of excess reserves and therefore reduce their levels of free reserves. Moreover, if market interest rates increase and such increases are not accompanied by increases in the discount rate, banks will both reduce their excess reserves and increase their borrowings from the Federal Reserve System. Thus it would appear from the resulting decrease in free reserves that the Federal Reserve has been tightening up on monetary policy even though the initial increase in the interest rate was the consequence of an expansionary fiscal policy.

Both the interest rate and free reserves are endogenous variables, but both can be influenced by the Federal Reserve. However, the extent of Fed control over the interest rate and free reserves is not clear.

Monetary aggregates such as the money supply and the monetary base are less subject to problems of this nature. Again, we have already noted that the money supply is an endogenous variable in the system. For example, suppose the fiscal authorities engage in a contractionary fiscal policy. According to the IS-LM model or the LB-LM model, the interest rate will fall. This will result in a reduction in the equilibrium money stock. Such a reduction would appear to be the result of a contractionary monetary policy even though the Federal Reserve may have taken no action at all. However, the empirical evidence cited in Chapter 6 on the interest sensitivity of the money supply indicates that while the interest rate exerts a significant influence on the money supply, it does not exert a very large influence. Thus significant changes in the money supply would be due primarily to monetary policy changes rather than to influences of the economy.

The same argument applies to the monetary base. We saw in Chapter 5 that the Federal Reserve exerts a dominant, but not exclusive, influence on the monetary base. The Fed could, if it wished to, offset external influences on the base through open market operations. However, the fact that the Fed has the ability to offset other changes in the base does not mean that it has made those offsets in the past or will make them in the future. Nevertheless, the bulk of the change in the base over the last 15 years has been due to changes in the Fed's holdings of government securities. This can be seen in the data contained in Table 17.1. The table lists changes in the base from 1960 to 1975 and corresponding changes in the Fed's holdings of government securities. The last column of the table lists the ratio of changes in Fed holdings of government securities to changes in the monetary base. In other words, the last column of the table indicates the percent of the change in the monetary base that is accounted for by open market operations. Where the ratio is greater than 1, changes in other sources of the base offset, to some extent, Federal Reserve open market operations. Where the ratio is less than 1, changes in other sources reinforced Federal Reserve open market operations. However, for the period as a whole the change in the monetary base is almost exactly equal to the change in the Federal Reserve's holdings of government securities, the average ratio being 1.08.

Regardless of the relative merits and demerits of the various indicators, no one single indicator seems to be able to forecast what will happen to the economy in each year. For example, consider the data contained in Table 17.2. The table contains growth rates for the money supply, the monetary base, and gross national product for the years 1971 through 1975. A long-term interest rate is also shown, as is the level of free reserves. Note that from 1971 to 1972,

Table 17.1
Changes in the Monetary Base and Federal Reserve Holdings of Government Securities, 1960–1975

| | *Changes in:* | | |
Year	Monetary Base	F.R.S. Portfolio	Ratio
1960	$0.5 billion	$0.2 billion	0.40
1961	1.4	1.9	1.35
1962	0.9	1.4	1.55
1963	2.6	3.2	1.23
1964	2.7	3.4	1.26
1965	3.9	3.7	0.95
1966	3.1	2.9	0.93
1967	3.6	5.1	1.42
1968	4.9	3.7	0.75
1969	3.5	5.0	1.43
1970	4.3	4.1	0.95
1971	5.5	7.5	1.36
1972	4.4	1.9	0.43
1973	8.4	8.7	1.03
1974	8.0	6.9	0.86
1975	3.9	5.4	1.38
Average	1.08		

Sources: Economic Report of the President, 1975; and *Federal Reserve Bulletin,* various issues.

the growth rates of the money supply and the monetary base increased. This would indicate an easing of monetary policy. The interest rate fell slightly, which would also indicate an easing of policy. On the other hand, free reserves declined, which would indicate a tightening of policy. Aggregate demand as measured by gross national product increased its growth rate from 1971 to 1972. Thus the money supply, the monetary base, and the interest rate correctly forecast the direction of the change in GNP, but free reserves did not.

However, as we move across the table to 1975 and compare the predictions of the various indicators with the actual changes that took place in the GNP,

Table 17.2
Performance of Selected Indicators, 1971–1975

	1971	1972	1973	1974	1975
Money supply (% change)	6.2	8.7	6.1	4.7	4.2
Monetary base (% change)	7.1	8.2	7.5	8.6	6.8
Interest rate (Corporate Aaa)	7.39	7.21	7.44	8.57	8.82
Free reserves ($, million)	58	−830	−1,036	−364	372
GNP (% change)	8.0	9.4	11.8	7.9	6.5

Source: Economic Report of the President, 1976.

we are forced to the conclusion that no one single indicator correctly forecasts the change in GNP for each year. Several problems do intervene. First, the table ignores any lags in effect between changes in a policy indicator and the ultimate change in gross national product. Second, the sample size is too small and may be unrepresentative. These two problems would be accounted for if we took a longer-term view which allowed for lags in the effect of policy. In addition, a third problem is that we have not accounted for the effects of changes in fiscal policy. We will consider some studies that deal with these issues shortly, after we consider two alternative indicators of monetary policy.

Perhaps the major complaint about the indicators discussed so far is that they are subject to influences other than monetary policy influences. The interest rate is affected by fiscal policy as well as monetary policy, and the money supply is influenced by fiscal policy through its effect on the interest rate. Two indicators have been developed that purport to eliminate influences other than monetary policy influences. One of these is the *neutralized money stock*, developed by Patric Hendershott. The other is the *monetary full-employment interest rate*, developed by Dennis Starleaf and James Stephenson.* The neutralized money stock is constructed by first determining through statistical analysis the effect of influences other than monetary policy on the money supply. These influences are then subtracted from the money stock to arrive at a concept that is responsive only to monetary policy. In terms of the money supply model developed in Chapters 5 and 6, this would involve correcting the money multiplier for the influence of interest rates and income.

The monetary full-employment interest rate is an interest rate concept that responds only to changes in monetary policy. It is calculated, in effect, by substituting the full-employment level of income into the LM curve and solving for the interest rate. This is done in Figure 17.1. The figure shows an LM curve and a curve representing the full-employment level of income (at y_F). The monetary full-employment interest rate is determined by the intersection of these two lines. Changes in the monetary full-employment interest rate occur only when the LM curve shifts. A shift in the IS curve (not shown) does not change the intersection of the LM curve with the full-employment line and therefore does not change the monetary full-employment interest rate. Note that as monetary policy becomes restrictive, the LM curve shifts to the left, and the monetary full-employment rate increases. Thus an increase in this concept indicates a tightening of monetary policy, and a reduction indicates an easing of monetary policy.

Various indicators have been compared in statistical tests in an attempt to determine which indicator best reflects the influence of monetary policy on the

---

*See P. Hendershott, *The Neutralized Money Stock* (Homewood, Ill.: Irwin, 1968); and D. Starleaf and J. Stephenson, "A Suggested Solution to the Monetary Indicator Problem: The Monetary Full Employment Interest Rate," *Journal of Finance*, September 1969, pp. 623–641.

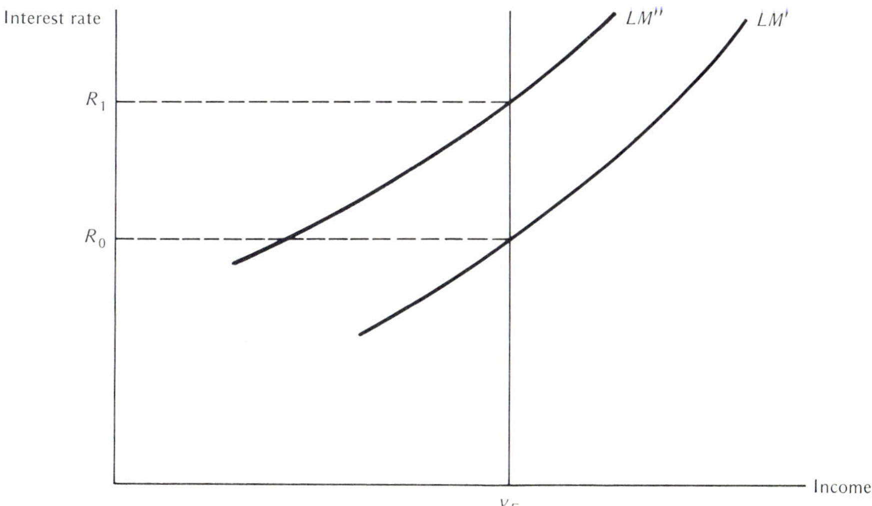

Figure 17.1

The monetary full-employment interest rate.

economy. Although the literature is fairly extensive, a couple of results can be cited. One early study by Richard Zecher attempted to compare the relative success of the money supply and interest rates as indicators of monetary policy.* This was done in the context of four econometric models, including versions of two of the models we discussed in Chapter 12. The tests are rather complex, but the general conclusion is that the money supply is usually a true indicator of monetary policy, and the interest rate is usually a false indicator of monetary policy.

Another study, using one of the equations from the St. Louis econometric model discussed in Chapter 12, was conducted by Michael Keran.† Keran considered the effect of fiscal and monetary influences on gross national product using different indicators of monetary policy. Three indicators of monetary policy were used: the level of interest rates, changes in interest rates, and the money supply. Keran's conclusion was that the money supply was a superior indicator of monetary policy. The tests employed data from the United States, Canada, Germany, Japan, South Africa, and the United Kingdom.

A fairly comprehensive study was done by J. Ernest Tanner.‡ This study compared the indicator qualities of the monetary base, the money supply, the

---

*R. Zecher, "Implications of Four Econometric Models for the Indicators Issue," *American Economic Review*, May 1970, pp. 47–54.

†M. W. Keran, "Selecting a Monetary Indicator—Evidence from the United States and Other Developed Countries," *Review*, Federal Reserve Bank of St. Louis, September 1970, pp. 8–19.

‡J. E. Tanner, "Indicators of Monetary Policy: An Evaluation of Five," Banca Nazionale del Lavoro, *Quarterly Review*, December 1972, pp. 413–427.

market rate of interest, the monetary full-employment interest rate, and the neutralized money stock. The object was to examine the thrust of these indicators on gross national product. First, however, the influence of fiscal policy on gross national product was removed. The residual changes in GNP were then used to evaluate the different monetary policy indicators. Tanner's conclusions place the monetary base at the top of the list, with the money supply running a close second. Market interest rates finished last, and the neutralized money stock and the monetary full-employment interest rate finish in the middle. Tests were also conducted by Tanner with free reserves, but the results are similar to those obtained with the market interest rate.

The debate over indicators is not over, nor is it likely to be over for some time to come. Generally, monetarists still prefer to use some monetary aggregate such as the money supply or the monetary base as the indicator of monetary policy. Keynesians, on the other hand, generally prefer interest rates or other measures of money-market conditions. But even if we were to decide on the proper indicator of monetary policy, we would still have to determine the proper intermediate target of monetary policy. In other words, we may decide what variable best measures the effect of monetary policy on the economy, but we still have to decide what variable the Federal Reserve is to attempt to control. We consider this issue in the next section.

17.2 POLICY FORMULATION AND POLICY TARGETS

Any discussion of policy targets cannot be separated from the process of policy formulation. Thus in this section we will first discuss the mechanics of policy formulation and in that connection deal with the issue of targets of monetary policy.

Current Policy Formulation

The techniques of policy formulation evolved over the years as the Federal Reserve developed sophistication in the policy-making process. The process discussed here is the process currently used by the Federal Open Market Committee.* Earlier methods are discussed in the last chapter.

The process of policy formulation begins with forecasts of economic events extending one to two years in the future. These forecasts are made several times a year by the staff of the Board of Governors. Initially two types of forecasts are made: a *judgmental* forecast and an *econometric* forecast. That is, forecasts are prepared by the Fed's staff using the best judgment of the staff members. Addi-

---

*See R. E. Lombra and R. G. Torto, "The Strategy of Monetary Policy," *Economic Review*, Federal Reserve Bank of Richmond, September/October 1975, pp. 3–14; and W. Poole, "The Making of Monetary Policy: Description and Analysis," *Economic Inquiry*, June 1975, pp. 253–265.

tionally an econometric forecast is made using a variation of the Fed-MIT-Penn model, which we discussed in an earlier chapter. The two forecasts are then compared and differences reconciled. The result is a *consensus* forecast for different assumed growth rates in the money supply, narrowly defined.

These forecasts provide the members of the Federal Open Market Committee with the projected effects on economic activity of different growth rates in the money supply. Given desired values for the ultimate targets, such as unemployment and inflation, the staff can then select the growth rate in the money supply that is consistent with the attainment of those goals. Once this is done, the level of the Federal Funds rate that is consistent with the desired growth rate in the money supply is specified. The underlying assumption is that open market operations conducted by the Manager of the System Open Market Account will influence the Federal Funds rate, and changes in the Federal Funds rate will in turn influence the growth rate of the money supply. Moreover, it is assumed that there is a relatively stable relationship between open market operations, the Federal Funds rate, and the growth rate of the money supply.

Since it is recognized that it is not likely that the intermediate target values can be exactly attained, a range of tolerance is specified for both the Federal Funds rate and the growth rate in the money supply. In other words, the Manager of the System Open Market Account is instructed to maintain the Federal Funds rate and the growth rate of the money supply within certain bounds. The following is an illustration of the type of directive that results.

> Specifically the members agreed that growth in M_1 and M_2 over the July-August period at annual rates within ranges of tolerance of 3 to $5^1/_2$ percent and 8 to 10 percent respectively would be acceptable. Such growth rates were thought likely to involve growth in reserves available to support private non-bank deposits (RPD's) within a range of -2 to $+^1/_2$ percent. The members agreed that in the period until the next meeting the weekly average Federal funds rate might be expected to vary in an orderly fashion within a range of $5^1/_2$ to $6^3/_4$ percent depending on the behavior of the monetary aggregates. The members also concluded that in the conduct of operations, account should be taken of the forthcoming Treasury financing and of developments in domestic and international financial markets.*

The ranges for the targets are revised from time to time as economic conditions warrant. Table 17.3 lists the target ranges for bimonthly periods during 1974 for the Federal Funds rate and the growth rate in the money supply.† The actual money supply growth rates and the actual ranges for the Federal Funds rate are also shown in the table. Judged by the ability to keep the Federal Funds rate within the targeted range, monetary policy must be considered

---

*"Record of Policy Actions of the Federal Open Market Committee," *Federal Reserve Bulletin,* September 1975, p. 584.

†While RPDs are often mentioned, they are apparently of minor importance. See Lombra and Torto, *op. cit.,* p. 8.

Table 17.3
Targeted and Actual Values for the Federal Funds Rate and Rate of Change in the Money Supply, January 1974–January 1975

Control Period	Money Supply Range*		Federal Funds Rate %	
	Target	Actual	Target	Actual
Jan.—Feb. 1974	3.0—6.0	4.7	8.75—10.0	8.93—9.47
Feb.—Mar.	6.5—9.5	11.8	8.25—9.5	8.82—9.33
Mar.—Apr.	5.5—8.5	9.6	9.00—10.5	9.61—10.36
Apr.—May	3.0—7.0	6.5	9.75—11.25	10.78—11.46
May—June	3.0—7.0	6.3	11.00—11.75	11.45—11.85
June—July	3.5—7.5	4.8	11.25—13.0	11.97—13.55
July—Aug.	2.0—6.0	2.1	11.50—13.0	12.02—12.60
Aug.—Sept.	4.75—6.75	1.5	11.50—12.5	11.48—11.84
Sept.—Oct.	3.0—6.0	2.6	10.25—12.0	10.11—11.41
Oct.—Nov.	4.75—7.25	5.3	9.00—10.5	9.34—9.81
Nov.—Dec.	6.5—9.5	4.5	8.50—10.0	8.72—9.46
Dec.—Jan. 1975	5.0—7.0	−3.4	7.13—9.0	7.17—8.45

*Percentage change at annual rate.
Source: Lombra and Torto, *op. cit.,* p. 10.

pretty much on target. Most of the time (67 percent) the actual Federal Funds rate falls within the specified range. When it falls outside the range, it only falls out by a small amount. On the other hand, consider the performance with respect to the money supply growth target. Half the time the actual money stock growth rate fell outside the targeted range. And often when it fell outside the range, it fell outside the range by a considerable degree. Figure 17.2 indicates that this should not be all that surprising. The top half of the figure shows the demand for the monetary base plotted against the interest rate. The demand for the base is a composite of banks' demand for total reserves (to satisfy required and desired excess reserves) and the nonbank public's demand for currency. Both of these are assumed to vary inversely with the interest rate, and therefore the demand for the total base varies inversely with the interest rate.

The supply of the base is assumed to be exogenous and invariant with respect to the interest rate. Following our discussion of the term structure of interest rates in an earlier chapter, we might assume that there is a stable relationship between the Federal Funds rate and the market interest rate. Thus we can plot on the vertical axis in the upper half of the diagram maximum and minimum interest rates that correspond to the upper and lower bounds of the Federal Funds rate as specified by the Federal Open Market Committee. The lower half of the diagram shows the relationship between the monetary base and the money supply. Under the assumption that throughout all this the money multiplier is constant, the money supply is proportional to the monetary base. The desired maximum and minimum money supplies are plotted on the vertical axis.

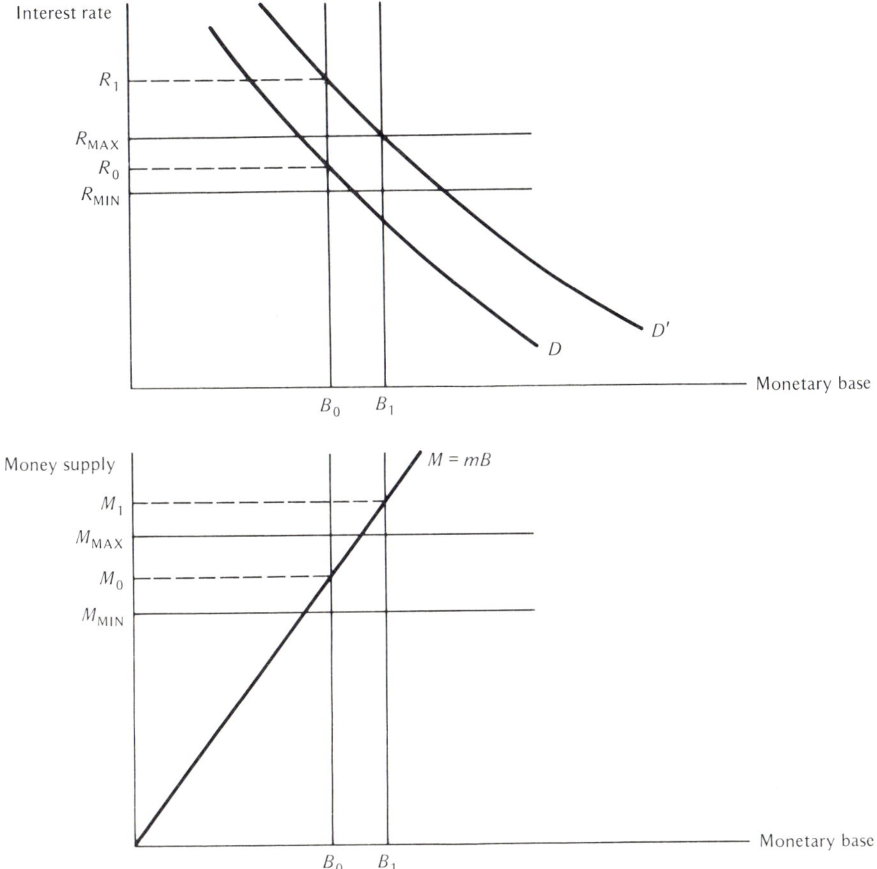

Figure 17.2
Demand for and supply of the monetary base and money supply determination.

Initially the base is equal to B_0. The market rate is R_0, and this corresponds to money supply M_0. Now suppose there is an unexpected increase in the demand for the base such that the demand curve shifts from D to D'.* If the monetary base were to remain unchanged, the market interest rate would rise above the upper limit to R_1. On the other hand, the money supply would remain within its specified range. However, if the Federal Reserve is more concerned about maintaining the interest rate within its bounds than it is about keeping the money supply within its bounds, it will engage in open market purchases of government securities which will shift the base from B_0 to B_1. This permits the interest rate to rise, but to rise no higher than R_{max}. However, if the Fed does

---

*This might be a random change unrelated to the state of the economy.

this, the money supply will be increased from M_0 to M_1, which is outside the targeted range. Thus attempts to maintain the interest rate within its targeted range in the face of shifts in the demand curve will force the money supply outside of its targeted range. On the other hand, had the money supply been kept within its targeted range, the interest rate would have gone outside of the targeted range.

Put another way, a stable relationship between the Federal Funds rate and the money supply requires a stable demand curve for the monetary base. This is not likely to occur, since changes in prices and income, which are always occurring, will cause the demand for the base to increase or decrease.

The lack of a close relationship between the Federal Funds rate and the growth rate in the money supply is further emphasized by the data shown in Figure 17.3. The points in the diagram represent combinations of the Federal Funds rate and the growth rate in the money supply for the various months of 1975. Inspection of the diagram indicates that there does not appear to be any systematic relationship between the two variables.

Figure 17.3

Growth rate of M_1 and the Federal Funds rate, February 1975–December 1975.

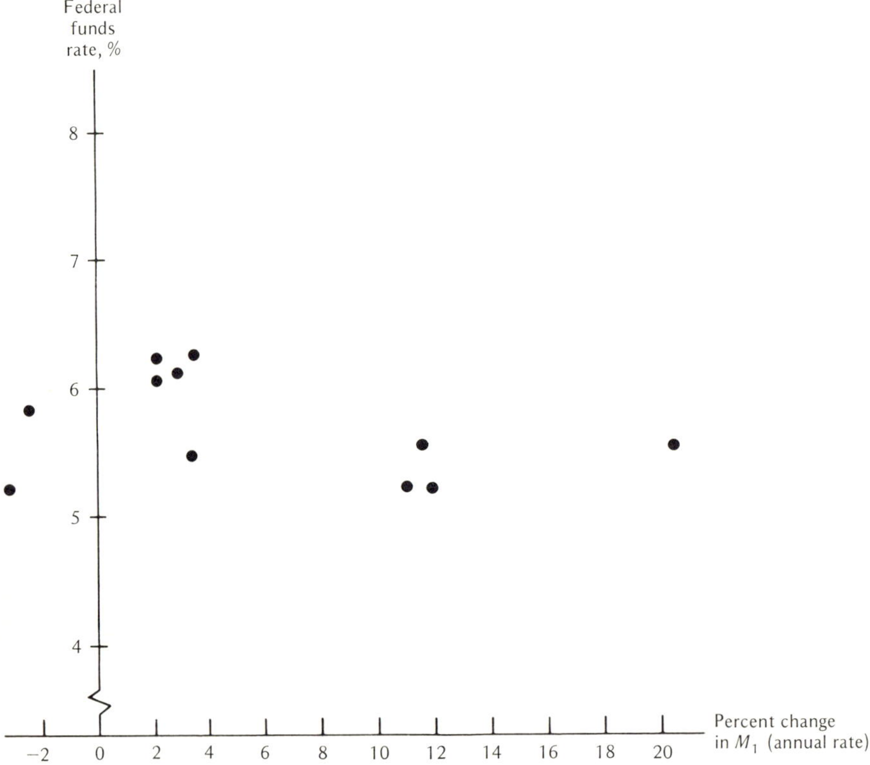

The current mechanics of policy formulation require the Federal Reserve to select intermediate targets and to engage in open market operations in an attempt to reach those targets. The targets, however, may be incompatible, as we have just seen. This, of course, raises the issue of what is the most appropriate intermediate target of policy.

Selecting the Policy Target

Perhaps we should again point out that in this discussion we are talking about intermediate targets of policy.* We assume that the ultimate targets of policy are unemployment, inflation, and so on. Recent policy making by the Federal Open Market Committee has focused on the two intermediate targets just discussed (the Federal Funds rate and the money supply narrowly defined). In the past, indicators of money-market conditions such as interest rates and free reserves have also been used.

Before speculating on the proper target of policy, we first must specify the criteria that a good target should possess. There are two general criteria which we should consider here. First, an intermediate target should be controllable by the Federal Reserve. In other words, the Fed should be able to determine the value of the target within a fairly narrow range over a reasonable period of time. Second, the linkages between the intermediate target or targets and the ultimate targets or goals of policy should be fairly close and predictable. That is, a given change in the target should consistently produce the same change in the ultimate goals.

Unfortunately, the structure of the economy may be such that if we select a target over which the Fed has tight control, the linkage betweeen that target and the ultimate targets or goals may be weak. On the other hand, if we select a target with close linkages to the rest of the economy, that may be a target over which the Fed has only weak control. Consider the following chain of causation, which is implicit in the IS-LM and LB-LM models. In those models, changes in the monetary base are initiated by the Federal Reserve. This leads to changes in the money supply, and then to changes in the interest rate, and then to changes in investment, and ultimately to changes in gross national product. The chain is summarized below.

$$\Delta \text{ monetary base} \rightarrow \Delta \text{ money supply} \rightarrow \Delta \text{ interest rate}$$
$$\rightarrow \Delta \text{ investment} \rightarrow \Delta \text{ income (GNP)}$$

Now it is clear from our earlier discussion that the Federal Reserve has fairly

---

*For some interesting reading on the whole subject, see *Controlling Monetary Aggregates* (Boston: Federal Reserve Bank of Boston, 1969); and *Controlling Monetary Aggregates II; The Implementation* (Boston: Federal Reserve Bank of Boston, 1972).

close, if not absolute, control over the monetary base. However, we also discovered, from our discussion of money supply theory, that the link between the base and the money supply is not completely under the control of the Fed. In fact the link, embodied in the multiplier, is subject to influences, such as the interest rate and income, over which the Fed has only indirect control. This raises the possibility that changes in the multiplier, in response to changes in monetary policy, may frustrate or offset the actions of the policy itself. For example, suppose the Federal Reserve engages in open market purchases of government securities. This directly increases the monetary base, but in the process also tends to lower interest rates. Interest rates fall because as the Fed buys more and more government securities, the prices of those securities are bid upward, and the yields therefore fall. We learned in Chapter 6 that the multiplier and the interest rate will vary directly. Consequently, the multiplier will also decrease in response to the decrease in the interest rate. Now if the monetary base is increasing and the multiplier is falling, what will be the net change in the money supply? The answer is not clear on a priori grounds. The empirical evidence does indicate that the sensitivity of the multiplier to the interest rate is low enough so that while there will be some offset to an increase (or a decrease) in the monetary base, the offset is not sufficient to frustrate the intentions of the Federal Reserve.*

However, this discussion should serve to highlight the essentials of the problem. If the Federal Reserve uses the monetary base as an intermediate target, the first criterion is satisfied; specifically, the Fed does have very tight control over the monetary base. The second criterion may not be well satisfied if there are great slippages between changes in the monetary base and changes in the money supply. On the other hand, if the Fed selects the money supply, for example, as an intermediate target, the link between it and the ultimate goal of changes in gross national product may be tighter. However, the Fed may not be able to exert close control over the money supply because of the slippages between the monetary base and the money supply itself.

Recent policy seems to have settled on the idea that there is a close relationship between the Federal Funds rate and the money supply. Thus, the System's Open Market Manager is assumed to exert substantial control over the Federal Funds rate, and a stable relationship is assumed to exist between the Federal Funds rate and the money supply. However, the data presented in the previous two sections would seem to cast some doubt on this.† Discussions of

---

*See R. Weintraub, "The Stock of Money, Interest Rates and the Business Cycle, 1952–1964, "*Western Economic Journal,* June 1967, pp. 257–270; and W. R. Hosek, "Determinants of the Money Multiplier " *Quarterly Review of Economics and Business,* Summer, 1970, pp. 37–46.

†However, see P. Meek,"Nonborrowed Reserves or the Federal Funds Rate as Desk Targets—Is There a Difference?" *New England Economic Review,* March/April 1975, pp. 31–47; and J. L. Pierce and T. D. Thomson, "Some Issues in Controlling the Stock of Money," in *Controlling Monetary Aggregates II: The Implementation* (Boston: Federal Reserve Bank of Boston, 1972), pp. 115–136.

the problem have centered around the Keynesian preoccupation with interest rates and the monetarists' preoccupation with monetary aggregates, especially the money supply. Monetarists contend that the Federal Reserve should use the money supply as its intermediate target because it has fairly tight control over the money supply. Moreover, they also contend that there is a very close and predictable relationship between the money supply and gross national product. Keynesians, on the other hand, contend that the Fed's control over the money supply is relatively weak, but that the Fed in fact has tight control over interest rates. Moreover, the Keynesian view of the world is that there is a closer relationship between interest rates and the ultimate goals of policy than between the money supply and the ultimate goals of policy.

This discussion may sound strangely familiar to the reader. Similar arguments were made about the proper indicator of monetary policy. Indeed, some writers collapse the two issues into one. Some monetarists argue that the money supply is the best indicator of the effect of policy on the economy. Further, the Federal Reserve exerts close control over the money supply. Consequently the best indicator and the best target are the same variable namely, the money supply. Many Keynesians would make a similar argument, but they would replace the money supply with the interest rate as the best indicator and target of policy. In the meantime, the Federal Reserve, while being buffeted by external opinions, has experimented with different targets and indicators of policy. Such experimentation is consistent with the Fed's quasi-independent structure. However, this raises a question about the extent to which the Fed should be permitted to exercise its own discretion in the conduct of monetary policy.

17.3 ALTERNATIVE POLICIES OR RULES VERSUS DISCRETION

Throughout this chapter and indeed throughout this book, we have assumed that the Fed has been conducting, and will continue to conduct, *discretionary* policy. In conducting such policy, the Federal Reserve specifies its own goals, makes its own economic forecasts, and formulates and implements its own policy. The alternative to discretionary policy is for the Fed to follow some policy specified by an external agency such as Congress or Milton Friedman. In this chapter we will take a brief look at recent discretionary policy and then consider the issues involved in the "rules versus discretion" controversy. The last chapter of the book will contain a more detailed review of past Federal Reserve actions.

Discretionary Monetary Policy

The major domestic goals of policy during the post-World War II period were to combat inflation and unemployment. A quick look at the data may serve to indicate the extent to which the Federal Reserve eased up on monetary policy

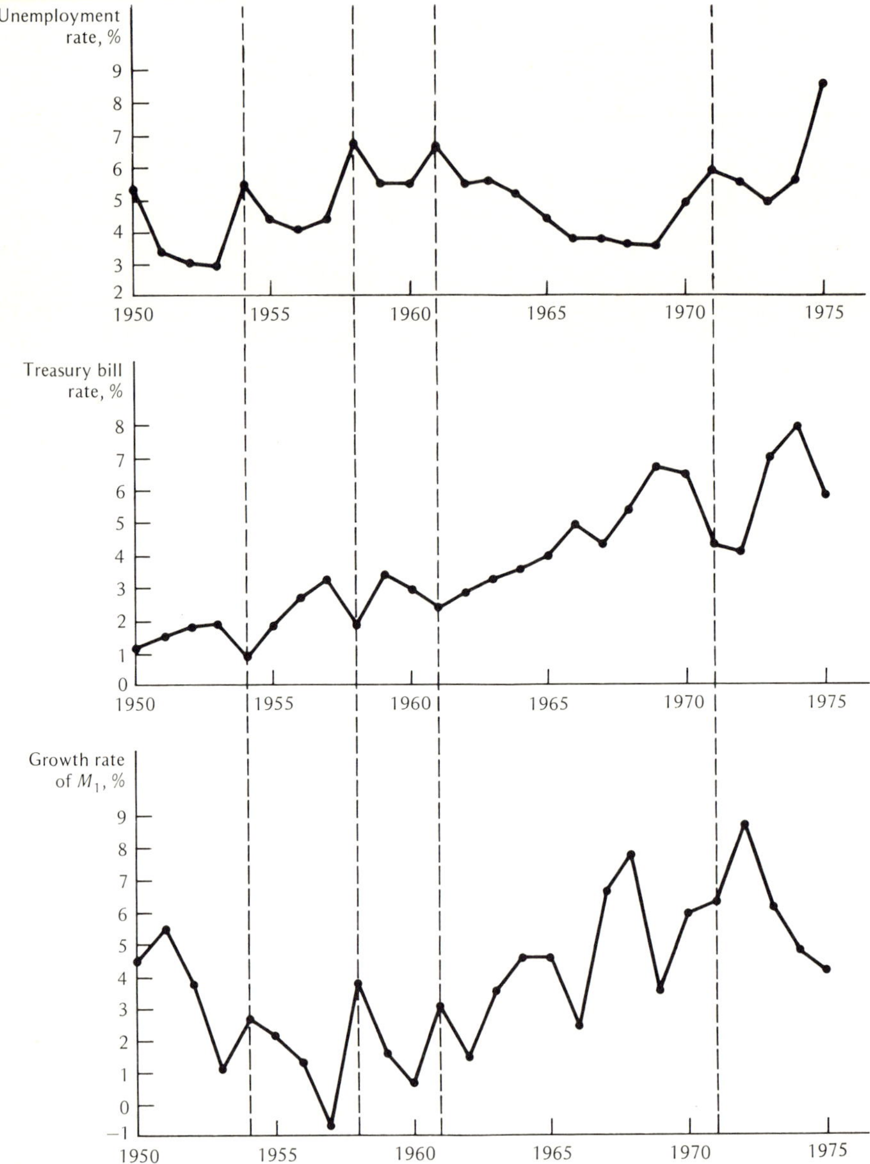

Figure 17.4

Unemployment rate, interest rate, and money supply growth rate, 1950–1975.

during periods of high unemployment and tightened up during periods of low unemployment. Figure 17.4 contains three charts, showing the unemployment rate and two monetary policy indicators for the years 1950 through 1975. As indicators of monetary policy, the charts display a short-term interest rate and the growth rate of the money supply. Remember that Keynesians would interpret an easy money policy as a reduction in the interest rate and a tight policy as an increase in the interest rate. Monetarists, on the other hand, view an increase in the growth rate of the money supply as indicating an easing of policy and a decrease in the growth rate of the money supply as indicating a tightening of policy. The peak unemployment rates (trough in the business cycle) are identified by dashed lines running vertically through the three charts in Figure 17.4.

Whether one is a Keynesian or a monetarist, it seems as though the Fed reacted sharply to increases in unemployment by easing up on monetary policy. In the four peak unemployment periods, the interest rate was reduced and the growth rate of the money supply was increased. Moreover, in most cases, as the unemployment rate fell, the interest rate was gradually increased and the growth rate of the money supply gradually decreased.

However, there are exceptions. For example, notice the period between the peak unemployment of 1961 and the peak unemployment of 1971. During most of this period, from 1961 through 1969, the unemployment rate steadily decreased. Concurrent with that decrease in the unemployment rate, inflationary pressures gradually developed. According to the interest-rate indicator, the Fed responded to this by a gradual tightening of monetary policy, for the interest rate rose throughout most of that period. On the other hand, the growth rate in the money supply indicates a perverse behavior. Although there are some fluctuations in the growth rate of the money supply during this period of time, the trend is upward. That is, over this period of time the growth rate in the money supply was gradually increased. This would indicate an easing of policy rather than a tightening.

This raises the problem of cause and effect. When we look at charts such as those contained in Figure 17.4, are we observing the reaction of the monetary authorities to changes in the unemployment rate, or are we observing the response of unemployment to changes in monetary policy? Comparing the interest-rate pattern with the unemployment-rate pattern, Keynesians are likely to assert the former. Monetarists, on the other hand, are likely to assert the latter. For example, monetarists might argue that the reason for the increase in unemployment in 1954, 1958, and 1961 was the gradual tightening of monetary policy in the years immediately preceding those peaks. Notice that in the years prior to those peaks in unemployment, the growth rate in the money supply is steadily reduced. On the other hand, the monetarists would interpret the continual decline in the unemployment rate from 1961 to 1969 as a consequence of the steadily increasing growth rate in the money supply over that same period of time.

Some researchers have attempted to avoid this problem in examining the behavior of the Federal Reserve by specifying behavioral relationships between the ultimate goals of policy and Fed reactions. In other words, if the Fed is to accomplish the goals of the Employment Act of 1946 and other goals, then it must react to the economic environment by adjusting its own instruments of policy. It should be possible, then, to specify a "reaction function" that relates the Fed's instruments of policy to the ultimate economic objectives in the same way that demand curves for consumers show their reaction, adjusting quantities purchased as a response to changes in such variables as prices and income.

The results of these studies generally indicate that the Federal Reserve, in exercising its discretion, did react to changes in unemployment and inflation in the way in which we should expect.* However, these same studies also indicate that the Fed's reaction to changes in the economic environment was not consistent throughout the post-World War II period. This has two causes. First, the importance attached to each goal by the Federal Reserve may change over time. During one period, low unemployment may be considered relatively more important than low inflation, and during another period, the reverse may occur. Second, the Fed's view of the structure of the economy, which shows the ways in which monetary policy affects the rest of the economy, may change. For example, as new research becomes available, estimates of the quantitative impact of changes in the money supply on prices must be revised. However, the importance of these studies lies in the fact that they generally demonstrate that the Federal Reserve has not been pursuing a random policy, but rather has attempted to achieve the generally accepted objectives of economic stabilization.

The fact that weights do shift between goals and the fact that the economic structure is not completely known with certainty pose a question for the use of discretionary policy. If our knowledge is so incomplete and our preferences shift from time to time, will not policy be unsuccessful quite frequently? Put another way, the Fed may fully intend to achieve certain objectives, but if its knowledge of the structure of the economy is erroneous, or if lag times are great, attempts to achieve those objectives may do more harm than good. Consequently some economists have objected to the use of discretionary policy as a practical matter and have instead suggested that the Federal Reserve follow an automatic rule for behavior.

Rules as Alternatives to Discretion

The objective of rules of policy is to eliminate or at least reduce the range of choice for Federal Reserve action. If a rule is followed, the Fed is not given the opportunity to specify its own goals, but instead must operate on an intermediate target specified by Congress or whoever else makes up the rule. The simplest and most popular rule is that the Federal Reserve act to cause the

---

*For example, see T. Havrilesky, "A Test of Monetary Policy Action," *Journal of Political Economy*, June 1967, pp. 299–304; W. R. Hosek, "Is the Money Supply a Target of the Federal Reserve?" *Economic and Business Bulletin*, Winter 1972, pp. 14–20; and J. Christian, "A Further Analysis of the Objectives of Monetary Policy," *Journal of Finance*, June 1968, pp. 669–678.

money supply to grow at a constant rate month in and month out, year in and year out. A hypothetical rule might be that the Federal Reserve act to cause the money supply narrowly defined to grow at an annual rate of 4 percent. This rate would be approximately equal to the long-term growth trend in real output in the United States economy.*

The rationale for such a rule must be seen in the context of previous discussions of various issues, including the natural rate of unemployment, the monetary view of the balance of payments with flexible exchange rates, and the stability of money supply and money demand. If the natural rate of unemployment is a valid concept, the Federal Reserve can do nothing about the equilibrium rate of unemployment and must eliminate that as one of its objectives. If the monetary view of the balance of payments with flexible exchange rates is valid, balance of payments equilibrium will be automatic and can be removed from the objectives of monetary policy. This also applies to any attempt on the part of the monetary authority to stabilize exchange rates. Finally, if the money demand and money supply functions are relatively stable, then velocity (the ratio of gross national product to the money supply) will also be stable, or at least predictable.

These three considerations reduce the goals of monetary policy to one, namely, price stability. If unemployment settles at the natural rate, then the growth in output will be determined by technology and growth in the resource base and will be out of the control of the Federal Reserve. If velocity is stable and approximately constant, then a growth rate in the money supply equal to the growth rate in real income implies that the rate of inflation will be approximately zero. Adjustments can be made if it is determined that there is a long-term secular trend in velocity. For example, if velocity can be assumed to be increasing at an annual rate of 1 percent and if output is growing at an annual rate of 4 percent, then a money supply growth rate of 3 percent would ensure price stability over the long run.

The proposal for such a rule encounters considerable opposition. First, the concept of the natural rate of unemployment is not universally accepted. Consequently, price stability is not perceived as the only goal of monetary policy. The same argument applies to the balance of payments. Second, the goals of society may change from time to time. Each change of goals may imply a different monetary policy strategy. If Federal Reserve actions are to reflect the preferences of society, the Fed must be free to exercise its discretion. The rule, of course, may be changed from time to time, but this substitutes discretionary action of Congress for discretionary action of the Federal Reserve, and the intent of the rule is to eliminate, or at least severely reduce, all discretionary action in the conduct of monetary policy.

---

*See H. Simons, "Rules vs. Authorities in Monetary Policy," *Journal of Political Economy*, February 1936, pp. 1–30; and M. Friedman, *A Program for Monetary Stability* (New York: Fordham University Press, 1960).

Third, even if price stability were the only objective of policy, the opponents of the rule argue, there is no necessary or stable linkage between changes in the money supply and changes in prices. This is so because the structure of the economy is constantly changing, and the quantitative linkages between the money supply and prices will therefore also change. Thus the growth rate in the money supply that would yield price stability changes from time to time as the economic structure changes. Fourth, the imposition of a rule implies that the monetary authorities are subject to a defective learning process. Surely, it is argued, we can learn from our past mistakes and our past successes so that over time, as knowledge becomes more perfect, monetary policy can be conducted on a discretionary basis which would be superior to any simple rule.

Not all the discussion of rules versus discretion has taken an "on the one hand this, but on the other hand that" tone. Some empirical testing has been done in an attempt to compare the relative performance of past discretionary policy with performance had a rule been followed instead. However, the researchers who have engaged in such studies arrive at contradictory results.[*]

Advocates of the rule are still in the minority, although that minority may be growing. In 1968, in a survey of 71 economists drawn from the academic, banking, and government communities, about 31 indicated that they preferred a rule or some modified rule to discretionary policy.[†]

Although the number of economists preferring a rule may constitute a minority, the pressures exerted by them seem to have been sufficient to cause the Congress to pass House Concurrent Resolution 133 in 1975. You will recall from the previous chapter that that resolution requires the Federal Reserve to follow a modified type of rule. Specifically, the Federal Reserve is to cause the stock of money to grow at a rate consistent with the long-term growth rate in real output in the economy. However, the rule is not completely automatic because nothing in House Concurrent Resolution 133 would require the Federal Reserve to follow the rule under any and all circumstances. Thus the policy that we are likely to observe over the next few years involves a combination of rules and discretion. Whether the results will be preferable to pure discretion is something we cannot yet answer.

SUMMARY NOTES

1. An indicator of policy measures the thrust of policy on the economy. A target is a variable the policy maker seeks to control. Instruments are under the exclusive control of the policy maker.

---

[*]For example, see M. Bronfenbrenner, "Statistical Tests of Rival Monetary Rules," *Journal of Political Economy*, February 1961, pp. 1–14; F. Modigliani, "Some Empirical Tests of Monetary Management and of Rules vs. Discretion," *Journal of Political Economy*, April 1964, pp. 211–245; and L. R. McPheters and M. B. Redman, "Rule, Semirule, and Discretion during Two Decades of Monetary Policy," *Quarterly Review of Economics and Business*, Spring 1975, pp. 53–64.

[†]Committee on Banking and Currency, *Compendium on Monetary Policy Guidelines and Federal Reserve Structure*, U.S. House of Representatives, 1968.

2. Possible indicators include interest rates, the money supply, unborrowed reserves, the monetary base, free reserves, the neutralized money stock, and the monetary full-employment interest rate.

3. In formulating policy, the Fed uses econometric and judgmental forecasts to specify target ranges for the Federal Funds rate and the money supply.

4. Monetarists tend to prefer a rule to guide policy, while Keynesians tend to prefer discretionary policy.

DISCUSSION QUESTIONS

1. In an earlier chapter we pointed out that James Tobin preferred, as an indicator, the yield on existing capital. What problems keep this from becoming a target or indicator of policy?

2. What difficulties might interfere with the use of the neutralized money stock or the monetary full-employment interest rate as an indicator and target of policy?

3. From general impressions received from the newspapers and TV, what does the general public believe is *the* target and indicator of policy?

4. Should politics enter into the formulation of monetary policy? Why or why not?

5. Evaluate the statement, "A monetary rule is inappropriate because there are no simple solutions to complex problems."

6. Why do many monetarists prefer a monetary rule?

POLICY EVALUATION

In the previous chapters, we discussed the nature of domestic and foreign policy goals; the constraints imposed upon the policy maker by the economic structure, institutions, and political actions; and problems in measuring policy. We also briefly examined the mechanics of policy formulation, including a consideration of alternatives to discretionary policy. Having considered all that, it is now appropriate to ask whether monetary policy works; that is, can monetary policy be used to manage output demand, and if so, how much effect does it have on output demand, especially in comparison with fiscal policy? We should also consider whether monetary policy is discriminatory in its effect on the economy. In other words, do policy actions benefit or hinder some groups in the economy more than others? In this chapter we will consider these issues, including some of the empirical evidence that bears on the effectiveness of fiscal and monetary policy. As a starting point, we will summarize the various transmission mechanisms of policy that are contained in the various models used in this book.

10.1 POLICY TRANSMISSION MECHANISMS

The models discussed in earlier chapters contain a variety of routes through which monetary policy may affect the economy.* However, much of the discussion was concerned with short-run effects, whereas the total effect of a policy change may only be felt after a longer period of time. Consequently in the following discussion, we shall distinguish between short-run or first-round effects and long-run or full effects.

First-Round Effects

Monetary policy changes may work through means other than the interest rate and may include relative price effects, direct wealth effects, and interest- and price-induced wealth effects. For example, suppose the Federal Reserve increases the monetary base by purchasing government securities from private commercial banks. Both the initial purchase of government securities and the subsequent increase in the money supply tend to reduce the interest rate. A falling interest rate in turn stimulates increased expenditures on new capital goods (investment) and possibly also stimulates increased real consumer spending. If the model used contains three assets, like the Brunner and Meltzer and Tobin models, the expansionary monetary policy will also tend to increase the price of existing capital and further stimulate expenditures on new capital goods.

Depending on the definition of real wealth used in the model, there may or may not be any direct wealth effects. If privately held real wealth is calculated by netting out private assets and private liabilities, the increase in the monetary base described above will not constitute a direct increase in the stock of privately held wealth. This is because the increase in the monetary base held by the private sector is exactly offset by a decrease in the private sector's holdings of United States government securities. On the other hand, if privately held real wealth is defined to include the total money supply, then the policy will have increased the stock of privately held wealth through the deposit expansion process. To the extent that such an increase in real wealth stimulates real consumption expenditures, this will reinforce the expansionary effects of the reduction in the interest rate.

Regardless of how real wealth is defined, the fall in the interest rate will produce wealth effects as described in Chapter 10. A decrease in the interest rate will increase real wealth. To the extent that an increase in the monetary base increases the price level, further indirect wealth effects are produced. As we pointed out in Chapter 10, an increase in the price level will reduce real wealth, increase real saving, and reduce real consumption. This should tend to increase real capital investment expenditures.

---

*For a detailed survey, see R. W. Spencer, "Channels of Monetary Influence: A Survey," *Review,* Federal Reserve Bank of St. Louis, November 1974, pp. 8–26.

These first-round effects are shown in Figure 18.1. The monetary base–money supply–interest rate–capital investment–output path is the simplest, and it is that path that is contained in the simple IS-LM and LB-LM models.

Since we will want to compare the relative effectiveness of fiscal and monetary policy in a later section of this chapter, we should at this time also consider the transmission mechanism for fiscal policy. Fiscal policy operates through the same channels described for monetary policy, with one addition. Fiscal policy also may have direct spending effects. For example, suppose the fiscal impulse is an increase in real government expenditures, with real net taxes and the monetary base held constant. Such an increase in government spending directly affects output demand in the output market. However, since the increased spending must be financed by selling government bonds (real net taxes and the monetary base have not been changed), interest-rate effects will also be evidenced. Specifically, an increase in real government expenditures, and the consequent increase in the deficit, will result in an increase in the interest rate. This should tend to retard private real capital investment expenditures and offset, to some extent, the effects of the increased government expenditures. Increased real government expenditures without increases in real net taxes also produce direct real wealth effects. As the government sells bonds to the private sector in order to obtain the funds to carry out increased expenditures, the real wealth holdings of the private sector increase. This may in turn induce an increase in real consumption expenditures. However, the direct real wealth effect is partly offset by a reduction in real wealth induced by the increase in the market interest rate and in the price level. These changes are summarized in Figure 18.2.

However, these initial impulses are not sufficient to tell us the full story of the effect of either fiscal or monetary policy on output and prices. In order to get the long-run picture, we need to consider the feedback effects from changes in output, prices, and real wealth to money demand and money supply.

Figure 18.1

First-round effects of an increase in the monetary base.

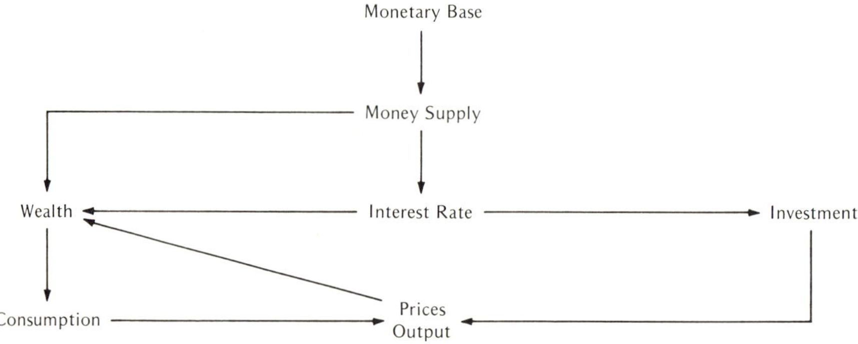

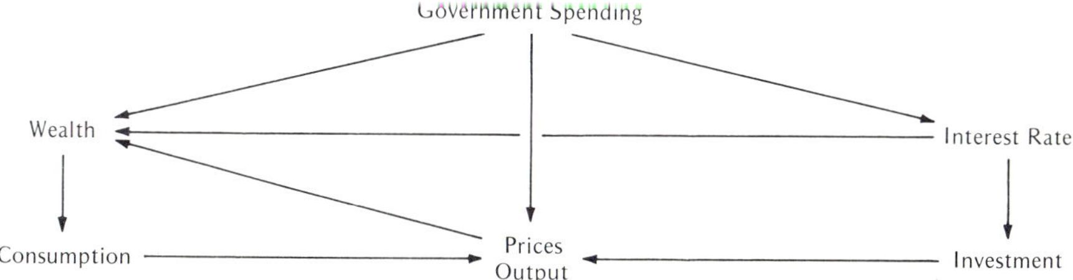

Figure 18.2

First-round effects of an increase in government spending.

Long-Run or Full Effects

The initial changes in monetary or fiscal policy may produce changes in output, real wealth, and prices that feed back to the financial sector and modify the first-round effects of policy. For example, both an expansionary monetary policy and an expansionary fiscal policy should tend to increase the level of output. In turn, an increase in output feeds back to the money market by increasing money demand. This means that in the case of an expansionary monetary policy, the interest rate does not fall as far as it would if there were no feedback, and in the case of an expansionary fiscal policy, the interest rate rises higher than it would otherwise. In both cases the feedback from the output change partially offsets the first-round effects. A change in the price level feeds back to money demand in the same way that a change in output does.

The IS-LM and LB-LM models already take account of the effect of output and price changes on money demand. The feedback effect from output and the price level to money demand is built into the structure of the LM curve.

However, real wealth effects are not built into the structure of these simple models. Yet, if real wealth is a significant channel through which policy operates, this is a critical omission. The omission is especially visible when we consider fiscal policy. If real wealth is to be considered, it belongs in both the consumption function and the money demand equation, according to our discussion of earlier chapters. Now the increase in government expenditures described earlier produces a deficit that must be financed in the present and subsequent periods. The financing, we may assume, is accomplished by borrowing from the private sector. This increases the private sector's holdings of United States government securities and so increases privately held real wealth. The first-round effect of this increase in real wealth is to increase real consumption expenditures, which reinforces the expansionary fiscal policy. However, the increase in real wealth also increases money demand, and this tends to offset the expansionary fiscal policy. Moreover, if real net taxes are held constant and there is no change in the monetary base, the deficit resulting from the increase in real government expenditures will continue into succeeding periods. This means that the government must sell additional government securities to the private sector in future periods as well as the current period.

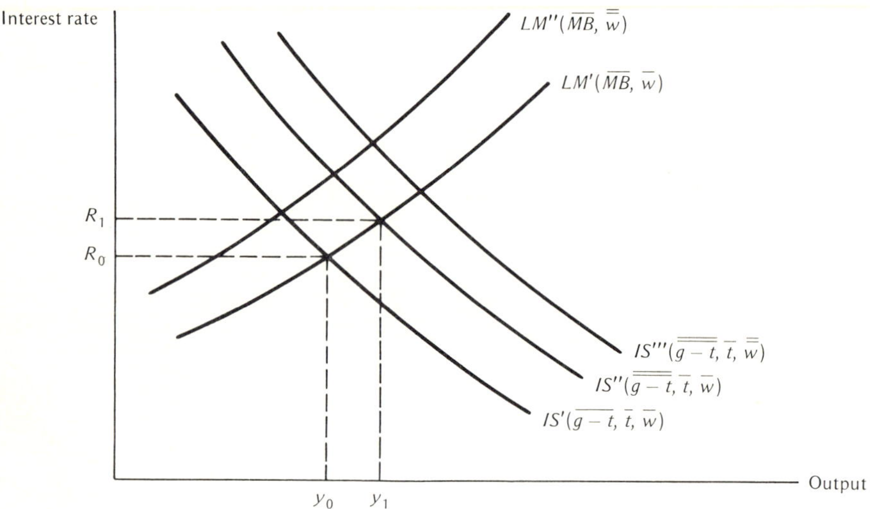

Figure 18.3

First-round and subsequent effects of an increase in government expenditures.

Thus the stock of real wealth held by the private sector continuously increases. This continues to stimulate real consumption expenditures while at the same time increasing the demand for money. The net effect of these changes on output is ambiguous. This is illustrated in Figure 18.3.

In the diagram are drawn the conventional IS and LM curves, but with one modification. Real wealth has been introduced into the model through its effect on real consumption expenditures and through its effect on money demand. Real consumption will vary directly with real wealth, and money demand will vary directly with real wealth. For purposes of this illustration, real wealth might be defined as consisting of liabilities of the government sector (in real terms) held by the private sector and the existing stock of real capital. Liabilities of the government sector include the monetary base and the stock of government securities held by the private sector. Also, only direct wealth effects are considered here. The initial equilibrium is shown as R_0 and output y_0.*

Now suppose there is a permanent increase in real government expenditures with no increase in real net taxes and no change in the monetary base. This shifts the *IS'* curve to the right, to *IS"*. The interest rate rises to R_1, and output rises to y_1. This is the end of the story in the standard IS-LM model. But, with real wealth effects added to consumption and money demand, the process is not complete. The initial changes are only first-round effects. The real deficit increase from $\overline{g-t}$ to $\overline{\overline{g-t}}$ that resulted from the increase in real gov-

---

*In order to focus on the changes in the IS and LM curves, we ignore the output market diagram. Consideration of this is left to an exercise at the end of the chapter.

ernment expenditures was financed by selling securities to the private sector. Thus the stock of privately held real wealth increases (from $\overline{w}$ to $\overline{\overline{w}}$), increasing real consumption and shifting the IS schedule further to the right, to IS'''. This same increase in the stock of privately held real wealth shifts the LM curve to the left because it has the effect of increasing money demand. Clearly the effect of these combined changes is to raise the interest rate still further. However, the net effect on output cannot be known unless we know the relative magnitude of the shifts in the two curves. The story is still not over. As long as real government expenditures continue at their new higher level and as long as real net taxes are not increased, the increased real deficit will continue. As it continues it must be financed by an ever-increasing stock of government securities held by the private sector. Thus private real wealth continually increases, shifting the IS curve to the right and the LM curve to the left.

As long as *any* deficit continues, the model will be in disequilibrium. However, this may be resolved by the introduction of an income tax. If, instead of maintaining a constant level of real net taxes, we permit taxes to vary directly with income, then any increase in income (through price or output) reduces the deficit by raising total tax receipts. Conversely, any decrease in income increases the deficit by reducing tax receipts. Now if the IS schedule shifts to the right faster than the LM schedule shifts to the left, output will steadily rise, taxes will steadily increase, and the deficit will gradually be reduced until it is eliminated. At that point, no further changes take place. On the other hand, if the LM curve shifts to the left faster than the IS curve shifts to the right, income will fall. Under these conditions, tax receipts will steadily decline, and the deficit will become *larger*. This means that the curves will continue to shift, and equilibrium will not be restored.*

The inclusion of the real wealth effects discussed above means that explicit consideration must be given to the way in which privately held real wealth varies in the face of government fiscal operations. Some writers accomplish this by including a government budget constraint in the model.† The budget constraint simply states that government expenditures must be equal to the sum of government revenues from whatever source, including borrowing. By focusing on the sources of government revenues, we can readily observe the effects on the stock of privately held wealth and therefore deduce the consequences for consumer expenditures and for money demand. In any event, the inclusion of real wealth effects in the IS-LM model provides us with conclusions different from those obtained using the standard model without real wealth effects. Put another way, the relative effects of fiscal and monetary policy are dependent

---

*For a detailed treatment, see A. S. Blinder and R. L. Solow, "Does Fiscal Policy Matter," *Journal of Public Economics*, November 1973, pp. 319–337.

†See C. F. Christ, "A Simple Macroeconomic Model with a Government Budget Restraint," *Journal of Political Economy*, January/February 1968, pp. 53–67. Also see W. L. Silber, "Fiscal Policy in IS-LM Analysis: A Correction," *Journal of Money, Credit and Banking*, November 1970, pp. 461–472.

on the specifications in the model used by the investigator. Different specifications will yield different results. Since not all economists operate with a single model in mind, it is not surprising that monetarists and Keynesians arrive at different conclusions about the relative effects of fiscal and monetary policy on output and prices.

18.2 THE KEYNESIAN-MONETARIST CONTROVERSY

In terms of the simple IS-LM model, disagreement between monetarists and Keynesians about the relative effects of fiscal and monetary policy depends on the assumptions made about the slopes of the IS and LM curves. However, the controversy involves considerably more than just that. The disagreement reflects different fundamental assumptions about the basic structure of the economy. For example, monetarists are more inclined to argue that the private sector is best characterized by the model of perfect competition. This enables them to concentrate on aggregate monetary effects in a search for solutions to the problem of inflation. Keynesians, on the other hand, tend to accept the existence of monopolistic elements in the economy that do not respond to market forces in the same way that firms under conditions of perfect competition do. Thus some Keynesians will more readily accept the use of wage and price controls to combat inflation that they believe originated in monopolistic price-fixing practices.

This same view of the structure of the economy leads Keynesians to conclude that, at least in some sectors, prices and nominal wage rates may experience short-run rigidity. Where there are rigidities in certain industries but not in others, policies designed to manage output demand with an intent to reduce overall inflation may result in distortions and misallocations of resources unless selective wage and price controls are used to restore equity. Contrary to this view, monetarists are likely to conclude that wages and prices are, for all practical purposes, flexible. This conclusion follows from the assumption of perfect competition. But even where perfect competition is not assumed, the monetarists would argue that slight monopoly elements are not free from pressures of the marketplace.

As long as competition is relatively free and as long as prices and wages are relatively flexible, monetarists will tend to conclude that the long-run tendency of the economy is toward relatively full employment. Unemployment under such circumstances is assumed to be frictional and voluntary. Keynesians, on the other hand, attribute unemployment to deficiencies in output demand that must be compensated for by governmental action. Unemployment, which occurs as a result of deficient output demand, is treated as involuntary unemployment.

Starting with a model of perfect competition and operating under the assumption that prices and wages are flexible, the monetarist concludes that the tendency of the private sector is to move toward a stable equilibrium. In other words, the structure of the private sector makes it inherently stable. The policy implication of this is that the government, through its fiscal and monetary policies, should avoid engaging in actions that would interfere with this tendency toward stability. Indeed some monetarists would go so far as to argue that virtually all the past fluctuations in the economy can be traced to governmental interference. Keynesians, citing the experience of the nineteenth and twentieth centuries up through the 1930s, tend to argue that the private sector is inherently unstable. Thus the need for governmental intervention in order to stabilize the economy is apparent. While many Keynesians would agree that government countercyclical policy has been less than completely successful in the post-World War II period, very few dispute the reason for its existence.

The link between monetary policy actions and the rest of the economy depends critically on the nature of money demand. If, as monetarists contend, money demand is a stable function of a few variables, changes in the monetary base and the money supply initiated by the Federal Reserve will produce predictable effects on nominal income (price times output). Moreover, such effects are, in the monetarists' view, generally not dependent on the interest elasticity of money demand. In other words, it is not necessary for an increase in the money supply to result in a significant decrease in the interest rate in order for monetary changes to affect the rest of the economy. This is because monetarists assume that money is a substitute for both financial assets and real assets. Moreover, the substitution relationships between money and real assets are closer than those between money and financial assets. Consequently, an increase in the money supply will generate increased expenditures on existing real assets, bidding their prices up and inducing expenditures on currently produced goods. The interest rate on financial assets may change very little under such circumstances.

On the other hand, Keynesians tend to view money as a very close substitute for financial assets—so close, in fact, that it takes great increases in the supply of money to induce even very small reductions in the interest rate. Since the linkage, in a Keynesian world, between monetary policy and the economy is through interest-rate and real capital investment changes, monetary policy is viewed as producing a relatively weak effect on the rest of the economy. Moreover, Keynesians would also argue that the money demand function is likely to be relatively unstable. Thus monetary policy changes will not produce predictable effects on nominal income or its price and output components.

Given the variety of assumptions and conditions specified by both groups, monetarists are likely to conclude that neither fiscal nor monetary policy can produce lasting changes in output and employment. Indeed in the monetarists' view, monetary changes will have a permanent effect only on prices. Fiscal policy is incapable of doing even that because changes in real government expenditures or in real net taxes will result in offsetting changes in private real expenditures, so that fiscal policy is incapable of producing permanent changes in the level of output demand, but only changes the allocation of resources.

Keynesians, on the other hand, place great value on the use of fiscal policy as a tool for permanently altering output and the level of employment. Monetary policy is likely to produce weak effects and asymmetrical effects. That is, if monetary policy is successful at all, it will be successful in fighting inflation. It is much less successful in fighting unemployment. The reason is, according to the Keynesians, that while it may be possible to provide the private sector with a greater money supply, the policy makers cannot force the private sector to convert that increased money supply into an increased flow of expenditures. This belief is often summarized in such statements as, "You can pull on a string, but you can't push on it," and, "You can lead a horse to water, but you can't make him drink."

At this point, the reader may be inclined to give up and ask, "How on earth are the policy makers to decide on policy if they can't get agreement from their economic advisors?" The disagreement does, in fact, make policy making more difficult. However, disagreement is not unique to economists. When medical doctors agree on the usefulness of vitamin C in fighting the common cold and when astronomers agree on the origin of the universe, Keynesians and monetarists will embrace a common theory and viewpoint. Until that utopian day arrives, continued analysis of both points of view is called for. In recent years, such analysis has taken the form of empirical tests to determine whether fiscal or monetary policy produces the greater impact on nominal income.

18.3   RELATIVE EFFECT OF FISCAL AND MONETARY POLICY ON AGGREGATE NOMINAL INCOME

Since economic variables can be measured and since we have modern statistical and econometric tools together with high-speed computers, it seems reasonable that one way to resolve the dispute between the Keynesians and the monetarists would be to construct models of the economy and test to see which policy produces the greatest impact. However, the issues are not quite that simple. We already noted in the previous section that the answer to the relative effectiveness question depends crucially on the economic structure assumed by the investigator. The analytical and descriptive power of an econometric model is only as good as the ideas that went into its construction. Nevertheless some tests have been run with econometric models to establish whether or not fiscal policy is more powerful than monetary policy.

Generally two approaches have been used. In the first approach, a large-scale structural model is designed and estimated. Such a model might be similar to the models discussed in an earlier chapter, such as the Brookings model and the Wharton model. Once the model has been estimated, simulations can be made under alternative assumptions. In a simulation, one exogenous variable or policy variable is changed by a specified amount, and then the computer simulates the effect on the endogenous variables of the model. For example, we might increase government expenditures by $1 billion, holding tax rates and the money supply constant, and see what impact this produces on an endogenous variable such as nominal income.

The second approach makes use of reduced-form equations. The reduced-form equation is supposed to be a single equation derived from all the structural equations. As we pointed out in our chapter on econometric models, the reduced-form equation expresses one endogenous variable as a function of all the exogenous variables in the model. The St. Louis model, which we discussed earlier, makes use of reduced-form equations. The advantage of the reduced-form approach is that not all the channels of policy need be specified. However, one must be certain that all the relevant exogenous variables are included in the equation. The structural model has the advantage of ensuring that the appropriate exogenous variables are accounted for. However, it has the disadvantage of being in error if significant channels of policy are left out of the model.

The relative advantages and disadvantages of structural and reduced-form models is an issue in itself, and we shall not deal with it here. In this section, we will simply report on the results of three models. Representing the large-scale structural models will be the Federal Reserve-MIT-Penn (FMP) model, which contains perhaps the most extensive structure of the channels of monetary policy of any of the large-scale structural models.* The St. Louis model is representative of reduced-form equations in the extreme. In the reduced-form equation for nominal gross national product, only two exogenous variables appear, the money supply and high-employment government expenditures.† As a kind of compromise between the two, we will also show the results of a reduced-form model that is more extensively specified than the St. Louis model. This model was constructed by Carl Christ in order to examine the relative effects of fiscal and monetary policy over a longer period of time than that covered by either the FMP model or the St. Louis model. The Christ model specifies the nature of the exogenous variables more carefully than the St. Louis model, but it is not a full-blown structural model like the FMP model. Moreover, the Christ model uses annual data, whereas the St. Louis and FMP models use quarterly data.‡

Table 18.1 shows the multiplier effect of a change in government spending on nominal gross national product. The effects are based on model estimates that cover roughly the same period of time for each of the models, namely, the post-World War II period. We should note here that some econometric models

---

*The policy channels are described by F. Modigliani, "Monetary Policy and Consumption," in *Consumer Spending and Monetary Policy: The Linkages* (Boston: Federal Reserve Bank of Boston, 1971).

†The estimates here are from K. M. Carlson, "The St. Louis Equation and Monthly Data," *Review*, Federal Reserve Bank of St. Louis, January 1975, pp. 14–17. The original model is in L. C. Andersen and K. M. Carlson, "A Monetarist Model for Economic Stabilization," *Review*, Federal Reserve Bank of St. Louis, April 1970, pp. 7–25.

‡C. F. Christ, "Monetary and Fiscal Influences on U.S. Money Income, 1891–1970," *Journal of Money, Credit and Banking*, February 1973, pp. 279–300.

Table 18.1
Multiplier Effect of a Change in Government Spending on Nominal GNP

Multiplier after:	St. Louis Model	FMP Model	Christ Model
Initial quarter	0.51	1.1	n.a.
Two quarters	0.77	1.5	n.a.
Three quarters	0.71	2.1	n.a.
Four quarters	0.58	2.6	3.6
Eight quarters	0.61	4.7	3.6
Twelve quarters	0.61	5.4	3.6

Source: Carlson, *op. cit.;* Modigliani, *op. cit.;* Christ, "Monetary and Fiscal Influences," *op. cit.*

forecast output y, the price level P, and nominal income Py. In this they are comparable to our output market model developed in Chapter 10. However, the central equation of the St. Louis model is stated in nominal terms. Nominal income is measured by nominal gross national product. In order to make the comparisons below, we report the effects of fiscal and monetary policy on nominal GNP and ignore the distribution of these changes between P and y.

The St. Louis model, a monetarist model, is, as might be expected, the least favorable toward fiscal policy. Notice that as time passes, the multiplier in the St. Louis model initially increases, then decreases as crowding out of private expenditures takes place. The full effect shows that GNP rises by less than the increase in government expenditures. In other words, a $1 billion increase in government expenditures will result in a $610 million increase in gross national product.

The FMP model is more favorable to fiscal policy. An increase in government expenditures starts producing a multiple impact on GNP in the first quarter. The effect rises gradually until by the end of three years a $1 billion increase in government expenditures would have increased GNP by $5.4 billion. In the Christ model, as in the St. Louis model, virtually the full effect of fiscal policy takes place within one year. However, the Christ model is closer to the FMP model in impact than to the St. Louis model. The full impact of the $1 billion increase in government spending increases GNP by $3.6 billion.

On the other hand, referring to Table 18.2, note that the Christ model and the St. Louis model agree fairly closely on the full effects of an increase in the money supply. In both cases, an increase in the money supply of $1 billion results in a $5.6 billion increase in nominal GNP after two years. However, the full effect is reached somewhat more quickly in the St. Louis model. Almost all the full effect takes place in the first year in the St. Louis model, while less than half the full effect takes place in the first year in the Christ model. All three models tend to agree on the effect of an increase in the money supply after two years. The multiplier in the FMP model is slightly lower than in the other two, but not by a great deal.

Table 18.2
Multiplier Effect of a Change in the Money Supply on Nominal GNP

Multiplier after:	St. Louis Model	FMP Model	Christ Model
Initial quarter	1.16	0.8	n.a.
Two quarters	2.72	1.3	n.a.
Three quarters	4.15	2.0	n.a.
Four quarters	5.15	2.5	2.1
Eight quarters	5.63	5.3	5.6
Twelve quarters	5.63	10.5	5.6

Source: Carlson, *op. cit.;* Modigliani, *op. cit.;* Christ, "Monetary and Fiscal Influences," *op. cit.*

However, the FMP model incorporates channels of monetary policy that operate with extremely long lags, but that produce very powerful effects. In particular, monetary policy produces a long-term effect on expenditures through its effect on price expectations. When this is taken into account, a $1 billion increase in the money supply results in a $10.5 billion increase in nominal GNP by the end of three years. If the price expectation effect is eliminated, the FMP results for the full effect are similar to the St. Louis and Christ results. We should point out that the potency of fiscal policy is also diminished in the FMP model when the price expectations effect is eliminated. In that case, the government expenditure multiplier reaches a peak of about 2.7 after six quarters and then declines thereafter. The value of the government expenditure multiplier after three years is only about 1.4.

Both the St. Louis and FMP models (without price expectation effects) indicate some crowding out of fiscal policy effects as time progresses. This can be seen by the fact that the multipliers reach a peak in early rounds, then diminish as the full effects of the increase in government expenditures become felt. The Christ model, on the other hand, makes no distinction between first-round and full effects of fiscal policy.

The FMP model exhibits another characteristic not allowed for in the other two models. Monetary policy has an asymmetric effect in the FMP model. That is, the multiplier effects for expansionary monetary policy are different from those for contractionary monetary policy. While the full-effect multipliers (after three years) for both expansionary and contractionary policy are close, the shorter-run effects are larger for a contractionary policy than for an expansionary policy. In other words, the model implies that the effect of monetary policy is much quicker when a contractionary policy is pursued than when an expansionary policy is pursued. This may give some credence to the string and horse and water analogies mentioned in the previous section. In any case, whether one adheres to a monetarist model such as the St. Louis model or a Keynesian model such as the FMP model, it is clear that monetary factors exert a powerful influence on the rest of the economy.

The effects of policy considered here are aggregate effects. The relationships observed were between total gross national product and monetary and fiscal variables. Regardless of whether the effect of monetary policy is weak or powerful, some writers have argued against using monetary policy because of its alleged discriminatory effects on the economy. We will examine this issue next.

18.4 THE INCIDENCE OF MONETARY POLICY

Certain tools of monetary policy exert uneven influences on the economy because of their very nature. For example, Regulation Q ceilings exert an influence over time deposits at commercial banks. If the ceilings are raised, the flow of funds into time deposits at commercial banks should increase. If the ceilings are lowered, the reverse should happen. Thus the flow of funds into commercial banks relative to other financial institutions may be altered by adjustments in the Regulation Q ceiling rates. However, economists have also been interested in determining whether general monetary policy is discriminatory in that it affects different groups in different ways. For example, will a contractionary policy designed to reduce the money supply through open market sales of government securities or through increases in reserve requirements hurt some groups in the economy more than others?

It is clear that the actions used to change the money supply may produce discriminatory effects at the outset. For example, if the Federal Reserve engages in open market operations, the prices and yields of government securities will be altered. This alters the market value of government securities held by business firms, individuals, and banks in the private sector. This effect occurs apart from and in addition to the effects produced by the resulting change in the money supply. Changes in reserve requirements will also produce effects other than those that result from changes in the money supply. For example, if the Federal Reserve lowers required reserve ratios, banks will be able to shift from assets that earn no interest (deposits at the Federal Reserve Bank) to assets that do earn interest (such as United States government securities). This will tend to increase the total profits of member banks.

In any case, the resulting changes in the money supply will produce changes in interest rates, which may have an uneven influence over different sectors of society. Put another way, the expenditures of different groups within the economy may have different interest elasticities which reflect differences in preferences among the groups. If a contractionary monetary policy is designed to retard private expenditures, those groups whose expenditures are most interest-elastic will bear the brunt of the contraction. While there are many questions that could be asked about the differential effects of monetary policy or the incidence of monetary policy, we will deal with three in this section. First, is residential housing or plant and equipment expenditure more sensitive to monetary policy? Second, are large business firms more sensitive to changes in monetary policy than small business firms? Third, are state and local government expenditures more sensitive to monetary policy than expenditures by the private sector?

Policy Impact on Housing versus Plant and Equipment Expenditure

One point that is made to argue that residential housing is more sensitive to monetary policy than plant and equipment expenditure involves the effects of interest-rate ceilings at commercial banks and other savings institutions. Consider a contractionary monetary policy which raises market interest rates. As market interest rates rise relative to ceiling rates on time and savings accounts, disintermediation takes place as depositors withdraw funds from these institutions and instead buy Treasury securities and other instruments that fully reflect the rising market rate of interest. Since thrift institutions are a major source of funds for residential construction, a shortage of funds develops in the housing industry. The result is that residential construction falls sharply. On the other hand, business firms can obtain funds if they are willing to pay the higher market interest rates. Both residential construction and plant and equipment expenditures fall, but residential construction falls by a relatively greater amount.

One study by Norman Bowsher and Lionel Kalish disputes this thesis.* On the basis of their work, Bowsher and Kalish conclude that contractionary monetary policy doesn't hurt the housing industry any more than other industries in general. They do conclude that inflation significantly hurts the housing industry. These results are supported by a study by Leonall Andersen.† Andersen estimated the interest elasticities of different types of expenditures. The elasticity estimates range from −0.17 to −0.26 for plant and equipment expenditures. The interest elasticity of residential construction was found to be −0.29. While residential construction is slightly more responsive to interest-rate changes than plant and equipment expenditures, the differences are not very great.

These results conflict with the results of a study by Sherman Maisel.‡ Maisel confined his analysis to the period of the 1966 "credit crunch." After examining the flows of funds, for 1965, 1966, and early 1967, into various financial institutions and after examining the borrowings and expenditures of various

---

*N. W. Bowsher and L. Kalish, "Does Monetary Expansion Discriminate against Housing?" *Review*, Federal Reserve Bank of St. Louis, June 1968, pp. 5–12. Also see the papers in *Housing and Monetary Policy* (Boston: Federal Reserve Bank of Boston, 1970).

†L. C. Andersen, "The Incidence of Monetary and Fiscal Measures on the Structure of Output," *Review of Economics and Statistics*, August 1964, pp. 260–268.

‡S. J. Maisel, "The Effect of Monetary Policy on Expenditures in Specific Sectors of the Economy," Speech at the Fifth Annual Conference of University Professors sponsored by the American Bankers Association, New York, Long Island University, Sept. 7, 1967. Reprinted in W. E. Gibson and G. G. Kaufman (eds.), *Monetary Economics: Readings on Current Issues* (New York: McGraw-Hill, 1971).

groups over the same period of time, he concluded that the major impact of a contractionary monetary policy is felt in the housing industry. Plant and equipment expenditures by business firms are also affected, but not to the same extent. On the basis of his own earlier studies of housing starts and expenditures, Maisel concluded that the average interest elasticity is about −0.56. After taking account of this and the effective credit availability, Maisel concluded that monetary variables account for about 42 percent of changes in housing starts. The interest elasticity obtained by Maisel is considerably higher than that obtained by Andersen and substantially higher than estimated interest elasticities for plant and equipment expenditures.

Policy Impact on State and Local Government Expenditures

The state and local governments are placed in a position similar to that of private borrowers. When they raise funds through borrowing, they must enter the financial markets and compete with private borrowers and the federal government for existing funds. State and local governments cannot rely on their own central banks to accommodate their borrowing in the way that the Federal Reserve System sometimes accommodates borrowing by the federal government. On the other hand, state and local governments generally have the power to tax to back up their demands for loanable funds. The taxing power is an alternative to borrowing as well as a source of funds for repayment of debt. The private sector doesn't have this option. Consequently, one might expect state and local borrowing to be somewhat less interest-elastic than private borrowing. This is confirmed by Andersen, who obtains an interest elasticity coefficient of −0.06 for state and local construction.* A study by Paul McGouldrick and John E. Petersen reached a similar conclusion.† McGouldrick and Petersen examined the effects of the 1966 credit crunch on state and local borrowing during that period. They concluded that, in general, state and local borrowing was not much affected by the contractionary monetary policy. However, some qualifications are necessary. First, not all state and local units reacted the same way. Generally small governmental units had to curtail their borrowing more than large governmental units. Second, borrowing was not curtailed in a significant way in the short run because many governmental units had large stocks of liquid assets that could be sold in order to obtain funds. Thus a long-term policy of monetary restraint might significantly affect state and local borrowing when the stock of liquid assets was finally sold off. Third, the 1966–1967 period saw a large increase in the amount of federal aid to state and local governments. Thus some units were able to maintain their levels of borrowing

---

*Andersen, "The Incidence . . . ," *op. cit.*

†P. F. McGouldrick and J. E. Petersen, "Monetary Restraint and Borrowing and Capital Spending by State and Local Governments in 1966," *Federal Reserve Bulletin,* July 1968, pp. 552–581 and December 1968, pp. 953–982.

because of inflows of federal funds. This was especially true when the aid came in the form of matching funds. In other words, the local government unit could obtain the federal aid only if it supplied some of its own funds. Rather than lose the federal funds, many state and local units maintained their level of borrowing even in the face of rising interest rates. Overall it would appear that monetary policy does not produce very large changes in state and local government expenditures, at least in the short run.

Policy Impact on Large versus Small Business Firms

The last question that concerns us here is the impact of monetary policy on small business firms relative to large business firms. Generally it may be argued that large business firms will be less sensitive to monetary policy changes than small business firms, because large business firms have greater internal liquidity than small business firms. In other words, the large firm, to the extent that it earns more total profits than the small firm, may have built up large stocks of liquid assets, such as government securities, from retained earnings. Should monetary policy become restrictive and interest rates rise, the large firm may not react by curtailing its capital investment expenditures because it can use the proceeds of the sale of these highly liquid assets rather than the proceeds of borrowing. Small firms, lacking such internal liquidity, are forced to pay the higher market interest rates or curtail their investment expenditures. Of course, this conclusion requires that the large firms not treat the market rate of interest as the relevant opportunity cost of using internal funds. Put another way, the opportunity cost of using internal funds is the market interest rate that could have been obtained by lending those funds out to someone else instead of using them to buy capital goods. If large firms do, in fact, ignore the opportunity cost, then they may behave in the way hypothesized above.

The evidence on this point is mixed. A study by George Bach and C. J. Huizenga concludes that monetary policy does not produce significant differential effects on small and large borrowers. However, results on this issue are not conclusive. A subsequent study by Deane Carson reached conclusions that were the opposite of those reached by Bach and Huizenga.*

Overall, we must conclude that monetary policy does produce an important impact on the economy. Further, the impact may be felt unevenly by different sectors in the economy. Whether this is more or less desirable than the use of selective policy controls or the use of fiscal policy, which is inherently selective, is a subjective question that cannot be adequately answered here.

---

*See G. L. Bach and C. J. Huizenga, "The Differential Effects of Tight Money," *American Economic Review,* March 1961, pp. 52–80; and D. Carson, *The Effect of Tight Money on Small Business Financing,* Small Business Management Research Report, 1962.

SUMMARY NOTES

1. Monetary and fiscal policies work through interest-rate, relative price, wealth, and direct spending channels.
2. The short- and long-run effects of deficit spending depend in great part on the nature of direct and indirect wealth effects.
3. Monetarists and Keynesians differ in their views about the extent of perfect competition in the economy, about wage and price flexibility, about the stability of the private sector, about the stability of money demand, and about the substitutability of money and other assets.
4. Both monetarist and Keynesian econometric models assign an important role to monetary policy. However, some monetarist models downgrade the importance of fiscal policy.
5. The evidence is mixed on the differential impact of monetary policy on residential construction versus business capital investment, the impact of policy on small versus large firms, and the impact of policy on state and local government expenditures.

DISCUSSION QUESTIONS

1. Analyze the first-round and full effects of an increase in the real government deficit, using the full output market model developed in Chapter 10.
2. The discussion in Section 18.1 ignored the indirect wealth effects of changes in the interest rate and in the price level. How would consideration of these variables alter the conclusions reached there?
3. As the market interest rate rises, what happens to the size of interest payments on *old* government debt; on *new* government debt? Assuming that some debt is constantly maturing and therefore must be refinanced, what happens to total interest paid on the government debt as the interest rate rises over time?
4. Define interest paid on the government debt as part of total government expenditures. In view of your answer to question 3, what changes do you want to make in your answer to question 2?

HISTORY OF FEDERAL RESERVE POLICY

Throughout the bulk of this book, whether our discussions dealt with theory or institutions, we dealt with contemporary problems and policies. Yet monetary policy under more or less its present structure has been in operation for many years. The insights gained from our analysis of monetary factors in the economy can be used to evaluate past monetary policy as well as to make recommendations and assessments about contemporary policy. The purpose of this chapter is to examine the history of United States monetary policy during the twentieth century using the general theoretical framework developed throughout the book.

In order to sort out the issues, we will borrow a framework for examination from another field in economics. In order to evaluate the role of various forms of industry in the economy, economists who examine *industrial organization and public policy* are interested in three characteristics: *structure, conduct,* and *performance.*

In the study of industrial organization, the standard for structure is the model of perfect competition. When they examine the structure of industry, economists draw comparisons with the ideal structure of perfect competition. In other words, the analyst who examines, for example, the automobile industry will compare such structural characteristics as number of firms and homogeneity of product in the automobile industry with the ideal that would prevail if the industry were perfectly competitive.

In examining monetary policy, we have an implicit ideal. While we did not specify the characteristics of that ideal, much of our earlier discussion implicitly assumed that there was a monetary authority that could establish goals for policy. We assumed that the monetary authority had whatever tools were necessary to achieve the objectives it had established for itself. In examining the structure of the policy-making apparatus for a given historical period, we will look at the types of tools available to the policy maker, we will examine the external constraints that prevent the policy maker from carrying out its own objectives, and we will examine internal influences within the policy apparatus that preclude the formulation of consistent policies. Now we have already done this to some extent with respect to the contemporary structure of the Federal Reserve System. However, the existing structure has not always prevailed, since the Federal Reserve was placed into operation in 1914. Some tools that were available to the Fed in the past are not available now, and many of the tools that are available now were not available in the past. Moreover, the external pressures from both the Congress and the public and the structure of financial institutions have also changed.

Returning to our industrial organization example, economists compare the behavior or *conduct* of firms in a particular industry under consideration with the hypothetical behavior of firms under conditions of perfect competition. For example, under conditions of perfect competition, firms are supposed to act in certain ways with respect to establishing their own output and price level. The price and output behavior of a firm in a particular industry under consideration can be compared with that hypothetical ideal. In our examination of monetary policy, we will be interested in comparing the actual conduct of the Federal Reserve with the hypothetical conduct that would have prevailed had the Fed actively pursued the generally accepted goals of economic policy, given the structure within which it had to operate. In other words we might ask, given a generally desired goal of full employment, given the institutional structure within which the Fed had to operate, and further, given the economic models that describe the way in which policy affects the economy, did the Fed conduct its operations in such a way as to be consistent with the attainment of the goal of full employment? Of course, since the inception of the Federal Reserve System, the goals of policy have changed from time to time. Consequently we will have to be careful to compare the Fed's conduct with the objectives that prevailed at that time, not with the objectives that we think should prevail at present.

Finally, returning to our example drawn from the field of industrial organization, economists, when they examine an industry, look not only at the structure of the industry and the conduct of firms within the industry, but also at the *performance* of firms within the industry. Again the standard is the model of perfect competition. Under that model prices are supposed to be flexible, efficiency is supposed to prevail, and the pressure of competition is supposed to generate a respectable amount of technological output. One reason for examining performance is that it may enable us to live with a second best alternative. For example, the structure of a particular industry and the conduct of the firms in that industry may not conform to the perfectly competitive model. However, if the performance is as desirable as that which could hypothetically be obtained from the perfectly competitive model, we may be inclined to say "so what?" about structure and conduct. Similarly the performance of monetary policy is measured in terms of the degree to which the desired objectives of policy were achieved. If full employment was a goal of policy, we might ask whether full employment was in fact achieved. If price stability was the objective, we might ask whether price stability was achieved. Some economists in fact do take the view that regardless of the criticisms that may be levied at the structure of the Federal Reserve System or the conduct of the Board of Governors and the Federal Open Market Committee, the results were in many cases relatively full employment with reasonable price stability. Consequently, it may be argued that criticism of structure and conduct is mere nit picking. Thus performance is an important dimension in any overall assessment of monetary policy.

There is one important qualification that we shall have to keep in mind throughout most of our discussion. The Federal Reserve's influence on the economy is not exclusive. Whatever happens in the way of employment and price change depends at least in part on the conduct of fiscal policy. Thus the Fed's conduct may be in complete accord with the desired objectives, but a contrary fiscal policy may have made those objectives unattainable. Of course, the reverse may also happen. Now how much allowance one wants to make in a discussion for the effect of fiscal policy on performance depends on one's view of the relative effects of fiscal and monetary policy on the objectives of policy. A monetarist may be inclined to discount the role of fiscal policy and argue that the performance of the economy has been almost solely due to the conduct of monetary policy. A Keynesian, of course, might draw the opposite conclusion. However, you will have to draw your own conclusions based upon the empirical evidence on the relative effects of fiscal and monetary policy which we reported on in the previous chapter.

In any case the next four sections will employ the structure, conduct, performance, and framework to evaluate the conduct of monetary policy in the past.

19.1 PRE-ACCORD MONETARY POLICY

In the year 1951 a landmark change in the policy system in the United States took place. Prior to 1951 the Federal Reserve was in its formative stages. It had an uncertain structure, and from World War II to 1951, it was forced into the role of accommodating fiscal policy. In 1951 the Treasury and the Federal Reserve reached an agreement which established a more centralized and truly independent Federal Reserve System with a structure close to the structure that exists today. The difference in structure is in fact so striking that we will separate the decades following 1951 from those that preceded it.

During the earlier period, from 1914 to 1951, the major events that dominate were the Great Depression and World War II. Our examination of the Federal Reserve during the pre-Accord period is confined to these two events.

The Great Depression

It is quite likely that no economic event of the twentieth century traumatized the American people as much as the Depression that took place during the 1930s. The years preceding the collapse were characterized by extensive stock market speculation, declining farm prices, and credit expansion. In October 1929 the collapse of the stock market signaled the onset of a contraction in output, prices, and employment. Figure 19.1 diagrams the changes in unemployment, output, and prices from the start of the collapse in 1929 to the trough of the Depression in 1933. The unemployment rate increased nearly eightfold, from 3.2 percent of the labor force to 24.9 percent. Prices declined by over 22 percent, and output measured in 1958 prices declined from $203.6 billion to $141.5 billion, a decrease of 31 percent.

The specter of one out of every four workers being unemployed made it clear that the single most important goal of policy was to reduce unemployment. In terms of the theoretical models we have employed in this book, the policy implications were clear. What was necessary in terms of either the IS-LM model or the LB-LM model was to shift the LM curve to the right by a significant degree. Had we been called upon to provide advice, we might have suggested reductions in the required reserve ratios on time and demand deposits or reductions in the discount rate or extensive open market purchases of government securities or some combination of these changes.

However the structure was not completely conducive to the recommendations we might make operating from a position of hindsight. First, the Federal Reserve System was largely decentralized in authority. Indeed this was one of the intentions of the Federal Reserve Act. Fear of centralized monetary control was very real among the American public. The Federal Reserve Act was a compromise which provided for a sort of central bank, but without the concentrated control that central banks in other countries had. There was no formal Federal Open Market Committee which had sole jurisdiction over open market

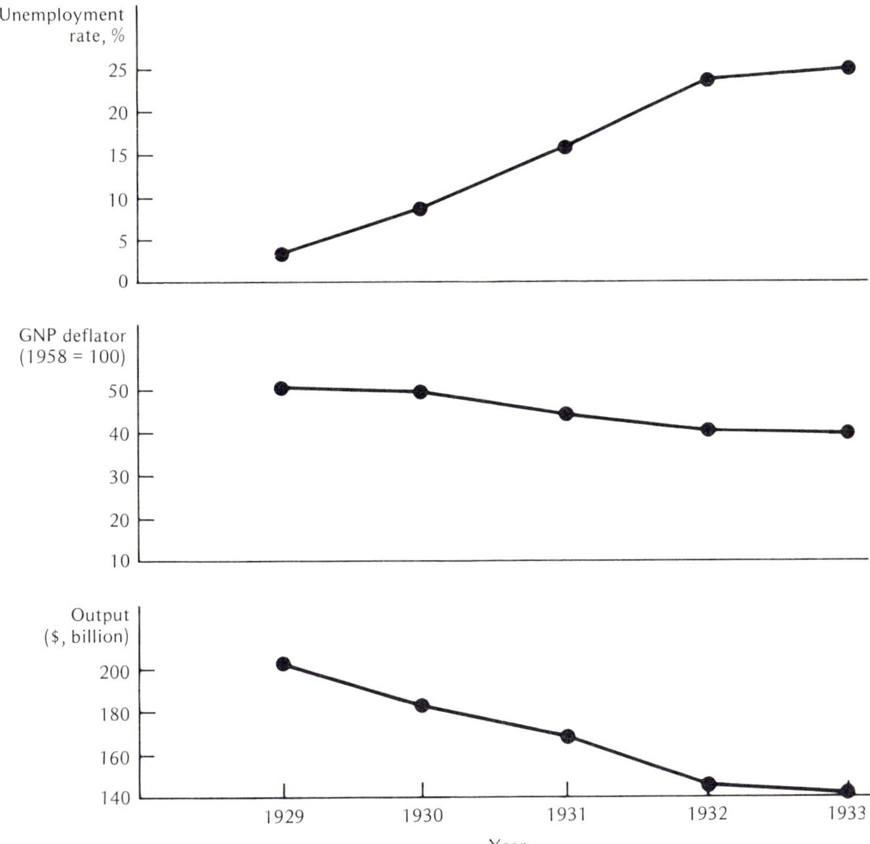

Figure 19.1

Unemployment, price level, and output, 1929–1933.

operations. Instead, open market operations were conducted by the individual Federal Reserve Banks. The original Federal Reserve Act did not provide for coordination of open market operations. However, some informal coordination (that is, not provided for by law) was provided for by agreements reached in 1923. Nevertheless, an authoritative Federal Open Market Committee did not exist.*

Not only were open market operations as a tool of policy uncertain, but the Federal Reserve did not have the authority to adjust required reserve ratios. These ratios were established by Congress and were not open to adjustment by the Board of Governors, as they are today. The only one of the three major tools

---

*The power conflicts between the Board of Governors, the Open Market Investment Committee, and the Reserve banks make interesting reading. See Committee on Banking and Currency, *Federal Reserve Structure and the Development of Monetary Policy, 1915–1935,* U.S. House of Representatives, 1971.

that was explicitly granted to the Fed was the discount rate. Thus during the period from 1929 to 1933, the Federal Reserve could have aggressively lowered the discount rate, it could not adjust the required reserve ratios, and it had the potential, but not the clear mandate, to engage in aggressive open market operations.

Federal Reserve conduct during the period is somewhat mixed. The Fed did engage in open market purchases of government securities over the period, and for most of the period it did lower the discount rate. Despite these actions, the money supply fell from $26.4 billion in 1929 to $19.8 billion in 1933, a 25 percent reduction. A careful analysis of the determinants of the money supply should indicate why.

The money supply framework developed in earlier chapters will help us dissect the changes that led to the massive reduction in the money supply. First, the currency ratio doubled in the 1929–1933 period, increasing from 0.16 to 0.32. Much of this was largely prompted by fear of bank failure. During that period of time there was no Federal Deposit Insurance Corporation to insure demand deposits at commercial banks as there is today. Consequently depositors ran the risk of losing all their funds in the case of bank failure. Their concern was justified, because large numbers of banks failed as the Depression progressed. Consequently, people found it safer to shift their money holdings from demand deposits to currency.

The excess reserve ratio also increased dramatically, from 0.002 to 0.051 during the 1929 to 1933 period. This increase can be largely explained by decreases in the market rate of interest over that period of time. Remember that in Chapter 6 we discussed some of the determinants of the ratios that compose the base money multiplier. Market interest rates and the Federal Reserve discount rate figured prominently in the determination of the excess reserve ratio. Confirmation of this relationship can be seen in Figure 19.2. On the vertical axis of the figure is plotted the ratio of the market interest rate (measured by the Treasury bill rate) to the Federal Reserve's discount rate. An increase in this ratio due to either an increase in the market interest rate or a fall in the discount rate should, according to our discussion in Chapter 6, lead to a decrease in the excess reserve ratio. Conversely, a reduction in the ratio of market interest rate to discount rate should result in an increase in the excess reserve ratio. Data points for the years 1931 to 1941 are plotted in the diagram. Note that the scatter of points clearly describes a downward-sloping relationship consistent with the ideas we developed in Chapter 6. Now, in fact, from 1929 to 1933 market interest rates did fall faster than the discount rate. This, according to our theory, should have led to an increase in the desired, and consequently actual, excess reserve ratio held by banks. We have just seen that the actual excess reserve ratio did in fact increase very sharply.

Both an increase in the currency ratio and an increase in the excess reserve ratio should lead to a reduction in the base money multiplier. This was partly offset by a fall in the time deposit ratio from approximately 0.9 to 0.7. This fall resulted from the fall in income. Recall from Chapter 6 that time deposits are

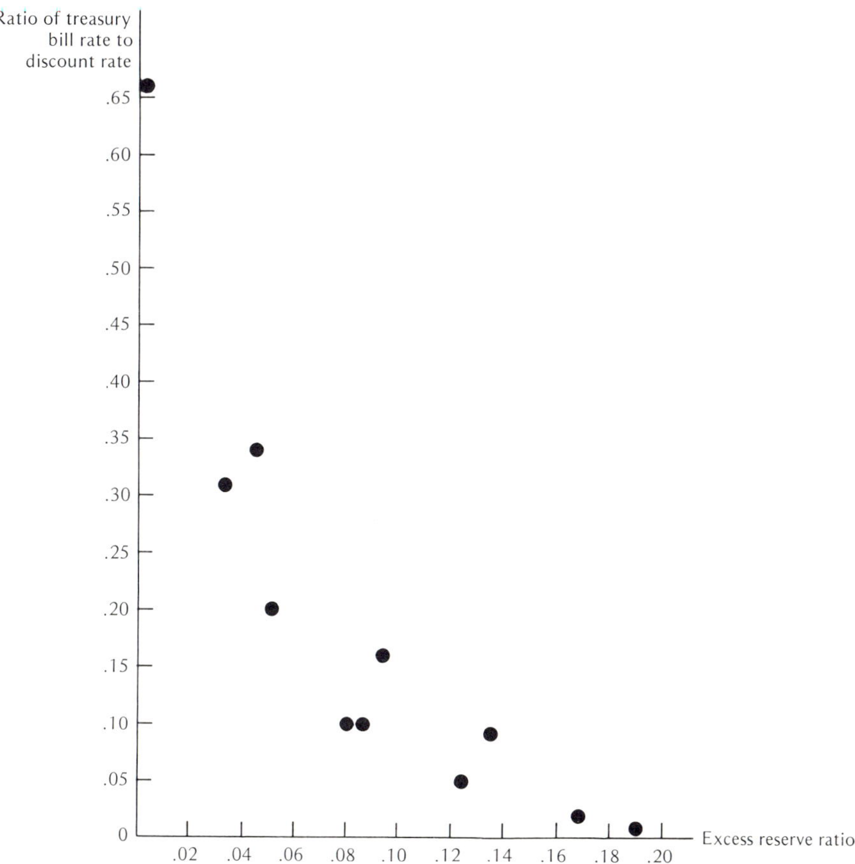

Figure 19.2

Relationship between the excess reserve ratio and the Treasury Bill rate relative to the discount rate, 1931–1941.

more income-elastic than demand deposits. Overall the base money multiplier fell from 4.47 to 2.64 during the 1929–1933 period. In the face of this very significant reduction in the base money multiplier, the money supply that prevailed in 1929 could have been maintained in 1933 had the monetary base increased from its $6 billion value in 1929 to $10 billion in 1933. On net over the period, the Federal Reserve did engage in open market purchases, so that its holdings of United States government securities increased by $2 billion, from $0.4 billion to $2.4 billion. Not only was this increase in Fed holdings of government securities insufficient to increase the base by enough to maintain a constant money supply, but gold outflows offset part of open market purchases, so that the base increased to only $7.5 billion. This was $2.5 billion less than the base required to maintain a constant money supply. Thus throughout the period, open market purchases were inadequate to offset other factors.

To compound the problem, the Federal Reserve increased the discount rate in 1931 after lowering it from its high level in 1929. The intent of this was to retard or reverse gold outflows from the United States. However, this also had the effect of discouraging member bank borrowing. In view of the decrease in the base money multiplier and consequently in the money supply, the policy was inappropriate, and it was shortly reversed by the Fed. The Fed continued to lower the discount rate after 1931 until by 1933 it was half of what it was in 1929.

In view of the massive decline in the money supply, it is not surprising that the economy continued to decline right up until 1933. Put another way, given a set of policies that could not or did not prevent a 25 percent reduction in the money supply, it is not surprising that unemployment increased, output fell, and prices fell. The models we have employed in this book would have predicted those results. Thus the economy performed the way we should expect given the policies that were followed.

However beginning with 1933, significant structural changes were made that permitted a more aggressive monetary policy. The Federal Deposit Insurance Corporation (FDIC) was established on a temporary basis by the Banking Act of 1933. The Banking Act of 1935 made the FDIC permanent. If fear of loss due to bank failure made the currency ratio increase dramatically from 1929 to 1933, the establishment of the FDIC should have brought a halt to that increase. In fact, not only did that occur, but the currency ratio reversed itself and declined toward its pre-Depression levels. From its peak of 0.32 in 1933, the currency ratio declined to 0.22 over the next two years. For the rest of the decade it fluctuated slightly between 0.21 and 0.23.

On the other hand, the excess reserve ratio continued to rise through 1935, largely in response to falling interest rates. Interest rates did rise in 1936 and 1937, and during those years the excess reserve ratio fell. However, after 1937, interest rates continued to decline and the excess reserve ratio rose. Strangely enough, the time deposit ratio fluctuated, but along a downward trend. This occurred in the face of rising income. Such behavior would not have been predicted on the basis of our Chapter 6 discussions. The net effect of the changes in the currency ratio, the time deposit ratio, and the excess reserve ratio was that the reduction in the base money multiplier continued, but at a substantially slower rate than from 1929 to 1933. In the four-year period from 1929 to 1933, the base money multiplier fell by 41 percent. In the four year period from 1933 to 1937, the multiplier fell by only 11 percent.

While the establishment of the FDIC through the Banking Acts of 1933 and 1935 stabilized the currency ratio, the Banking Act of 1935 broadened the powers of the Federal Reserve System. That act enabled the Federal Reserve to set required reserve ratios. The act also formally established the Federal Open Market Committee and centralized open market operations in the New York Federal Reserve Bank under the control of the FOMC. The act also broadened the basis upon which member banks could borrow at the Fed's discount window. On the other hand, the Banking Act of 1935 made it clear that discounting by member banks was a privilege, not a right. In other words, it firmly established the right of the Federal Reserve to turn away a member bank when it sought to borrow. Thus the Fed could control the interest rate at which borrowing took place and the quantity.

Overall then, structural changes enacted by Congress broadened the policy tools that could be employed by the Federal Reserve. Currency drains from the banking system stabilized, although the excess reserve ratio continued to increase and the time deposit ratio continued to decline. Overall the money multiplier continued to decline slightly. An increase in the money supply from its low point in 1933 would have required an increase in the monetary base large enough to offset the declining multiplier. To give you some idea of the magnitudes involved, in 1933 the base was $7.5 billion. In order to increase the money supply in 1937 to the level that had prevailed in 1929, the base would have had to be increased to $11.3 billion.

While the actual monetary base increased to a level higher than necessary to achieve a money supply equivalent to that in 1929, this increase was not due to vigorous open market purchases by the Federal Reserve. Rather, the Fed permitted gold inflows to increase the base without engaging in any offsetting open market operations. By 1937 the money supply stood at $29.7 billion, nearly $3 billion higher than the amount that prevailed in 1929. However, the increase in the money supply would have been greater had not the Fed raised required reserve ratios sharply in 1936 and 1937. From mid-1936 to mid-1937, required reserve ratios were doubled. For example, at Central Reserve City Banks the required reserve ratio on demand deposits was raised from 13 percent to 26 percent.

The purpose of the increase in reserve requirements was to absorb unnecessary excess or redundant reserves.* The Fed apparently believed that tighter control over monetary aggregates could be exercised if the cushion provided by excess reserves was eliminated. However, the increase in the required reserve ratio did not change bank preferences. We have already seen that bank preferences are largely responsive to interest rates. Market rates relative to the Fed's discount rate did in fact increase in 1937. This induced banks to accept the reduction in their excess reserves, and they reduced their excess reserve ratio from 0.08 to 0.04. However, by 1938, market interest rates had declined relative to the discount rate, and banks once again increased their excess reserve ratios to still higher levels, higher than those that had prevailed in 1936. One other consequence of the increase in the required reserve ratios was that the multiplier was reduced by 8.5 percent from 1936 to 1937. In spite of an increase in the monetary base, this resulted in a reduction in the money supply

---

*See Board of Governors of the Federal Reserve System, *The Federal Reserve System: Purposes and Functions* (Washington, D.C.: 1963), p. 53.

from $31 billion to $29.7 billion, a 4 percent decrease in one year. The increase in the excess reserve ratio in 1938 and thereafter continued to reduce the base money multiplier, but this was more than offset by substantial increases in the monetary base. The net effect was that after 1937 the money supply began to increase again.

Overall, from 1933 to 1937 monetary policy was expansionary. A contractionary increase in the required reserve ratio did take place in 1937, but afterward the expansionary policy was continued. The economy performed as might be expected under such circumstances. Unemployment fell from 24.9 percent of the labor force in 1933 to 14.3 percent in 1937. Over the same period of time, output rose 44 percent and prices rose 13 percent. The contractionary policy in 1937 did produce an effect, for in 1938 unemployment rose once again, to 19 percent. In 1938 output also fell by 5 percent and prices fell 1.3 percent.

While we are primarily concerned with the conduct and performance of monetary policy, the performance picture would not be complete without some reference, however brief, to the conduct of fiscal policy. Generally throughout the period, fiscal policy moved in directions similar to those of monetary policy. From 1929 to 1933, while the money supply was contracting, total government expenditures on goods and services also declined from $8.5 billion in 1929 to $8 billion in 1933. After 1933 and throughout the rest of the decade, government expenditures increased substantially. It should be pointed out that any contraction in fiscal policy was not the result of restrictive federal policies. Federal government expenditures on goods and services increased throughout the entire period. From 1929 to 1933, however, state and local expenditures decreased by more than the increase in federal expenditures, so that total government expenditures declined. After 1933, both federal and state and local expenditures increased. Tax receipts, which were largely income-related, declined with the fall in income from 1929 to 1933 and then rose thereafter.

From 1933 through the end of the decade, the overall reduction in the unemployment rate and the increases in output and prices were consistent with the stance taken by both fiscal and monetary policy. However, before recovery was completely achieved, the nation entered World War II, and the goals of monetary policy had to change.

World War II

By the time the nation entered World War II, the structure of the Federal Reserve contained most of the policy tools available to the modern-day Federal Reserve System. Open market operations were centralized and coordinated under the Federal Open Market Committee. Moreover, the Open Market Committee had had sufficient experience with open market operations to be able to use open market policy as a vigorous tool. The Federal Reserve was also able to control required reserve ratios and the discount rate. As the war progressed, the problem of unemployment was forced into the background. Both military conscription and significant increases in production reduced the unemployment rate to 1929 levels and below. The major requirement for the country was to maximize output. Toward this end, the goals of monetary policy were reduced to one—support the war effort.

Supporting the war effort meant creating conditions which would enable the federal government to obtain the funds it needed for military expenditures easily and cheaply. Substantial monetary expansion was necessary to provide sufficient loanable funds to finance federal expenditures. As an indication of the necessary expansion, consider the following calculations. From 1941 to 1945, output increased by 35 percent, and the price level rose by 26 percent. According to some of the empirical evidence cited in Chapter 7, both the output and the price elasticity of money demand seemed to be equal to 1. Consequently, given those increases in output and prices, money demand would have risen by about 61 percent. Without an equivalent increase in the money supply, a shortage of loanable funds would have developed, and rising interest rates would have interfered with the war financing.

The Federal Reserve did conduct its activities with a view toward assisting the war effort. Shortly after Pearl Harbor, the Board of Governors promised support for federal government financing of military expenditures. In their March and April 1942 meetings, the Federal Open Market Committee adopted a policy of pegging United States government bond prices. In order to accomplish this objective, the Fed increased its holdings of United States government securities by over 1000 percent from 1941 to 1945. This was the dominant source of increase in the monetary base from $22.1 billion in 1941 to $42.4 billion in 1945, a 92 percent increase.

In addition to vigorous open market purchases, the Fed also lowered required reserve ratios early in the war. For example, at Central Reserve City Banks the required reserve ratio on demand deposits was lowered from 26 percent to 20 percent. By itself this would have tended to increase the base money multiplier. However, offsetting factors occurred. For example, the currency ratio rose from 0.25 to 0.35 over the war period. On the other hand the excess reserve ratio, continuing to respond to declining interest rates, fell from 0.86 in 1941 to 0.19 in 1945. Finally, the time deposit ratio increased from 0.40 to 0.62 over the period, which was consistent with the upward trend in income. Thus increases in the currency and time deposit ratios tended to decrease the multiplier, while reductions in the excess reserve ratio and the required reserve ratios tended to increase the multiplier. The net effect of these changes was to increase the multiplier slightly, from 2.20 to 2.41. The combined effect of the increase in the monetary base and the increase in the base money multiplier was to increase the money supply by 111 percent from 1941 to 1945. Thus the actions of the Federal Reserve were completely consistent with the need to provide massive increases in the money supply.

In terms of the objective of maintaining low interest rates on government securities, the policy pursued by the Fed performed well. Interest rates on government securities were kept low and in fact declined slightly on long-term securities during the war period. Thus it was possible for the federal government to finance $200 billion of war debt at low interest cost. On the other hand, the increase in the money supply was over three times as great as the increase in output during the war period. This should have created great pressures on prices. Since fiscal policy was by definition expansionary and monetary policy was designed to accommodate fiscal policy, the problem of dealing with inflationary pressure was left to price and wage controls and nonprice rationing of scarce commodities. Many commodities, including various food items and gasoline, were allocated through the use of ration coupons. This together with the wage and price controls kept the increase in prices down to 26 percent over the four-year period from 1941 to 1945. Once price controls were removed after the war, the pressures of rapid monetary expansion were released, and prices rose 33 percent in the three years following the war—significantly more than the price increase in the four years during the war.

After World War II until the time of the Korean war, monetary increases were more modest. In the five years after World War II, the money supply increased by slightly more than 8 percent. During this period of time, the monetary base was virtually stable. Although the Federal Reserve did reduce its holdings of United States government securities by about $3.4 billion, this was approximately offset by inflows of gold and reductions in Treasury deposits with the Fed. Consequently the entire increase in the money supply during the post-World War II period up until 1950 was due to an increase in the base money multiplier from 2.41 to 2.62. As a consequence of this only modest monetary expansion, interest rates on government securities did tend to rise somewhat. However, by 1950 the pressures of Korean war financing once again called for accommodation by the Federal Reserve System. Such accommodation interfered with the Fed's independent pursuit of the objectives of the Employment Act of 1946. Reconciliation was necessary, and this was expressed in an accord between the Treasury and the Federal Reserve in March of 1951. The agreement changed the complexion of monetary policy.

19.2 MONETARY POLICY IN THE 1950s

During the 1930s and 1940s, the Federal Reserve either was armed with inadequate tools of policy or had its goals specified by outside agencies. Beginning with the 1951 accord, the Federal Reserve was empowered to pursue an independent monetary policy equipped with modern policy instruments. To be sure, official policy was specified in the Employment Act of 1946. However, the act is broad enough to allow a variety of interpretations. Thus the goal of "maximum employment" might mean full employment as defined by the

Board of Governors. "Maximum purchasing power" might be interpreted as price stability. In any event, the Fed was able to engage in open market operations to achieve its goals subject only to its self-imposed "even keel" policy. Moreover, adjustments in required reserve ratios and in the discount rate could be used to supplement open market operations.

Not only was the monetary authority more powerful and more independent than before, but the prevailing view of economic theory had changed since the mid-1930s. During the 1950s Keynesian economics came to dominate academic circles. In the absence of war and its aftermath, the 1950s offered the first real opportunity to test whether Keynesian economics was an appropriate framework for planning stabilization policy. On the other hand, while Keynesian economics may have achieved a large following among academic economists, the economists of the Eisenhower administration did not in general advocate the use of fiscal tools for stabilization purposes. In fact, in the face of increased unemployment in 1954, the Federal government reduced its expenditures on goods and services by $10 billion.

Actions of the private sector, insofar as they affect the base money multiplier, did not create difficulties for Federal Reserve policy. The currency ratio during the period did not display erratic behavior, but declined slightly, from approximately 0.27 in 1952 to 0.25 by 1960. The excess reserve ratio was also relatively stable, fluctuating between 0.004 and 0.007. The time deposit ratio, on the other hand, did change, but the change was along a stable secular trend. This ratio rose slowly and steadily from approximately 0.4 in 1952 to 0.6 in 1960. In the absence of any changes in required reserve ratios, the trends in the currency, excess reserve, and time deposit ratios would have implied a steady but slow fall in the base money multiplier, which could have been easily offset through open market operations. Thus changes in the multiplier posed no unexpected problems for control of the money supply.

In the conduct of policy, the intention of the Fed was to be reactive rather than proactive. In other words, the Fed would not attempt to prevent economic fluctuations, but rather would attempt to reduce their severity by implementing the appropriate policies as changes in the economic climate occurred. The policy was described by the Fed as "leaning against the prevailing wind." In practical terms this would mean that the Fed would tighten policy as unemployment decreased and inflationary pressures developed and ease up on policy as unemployment increased and inflationary pressures subsided.

Table 19.1 lists some figures that bear on the Fed's conduct during the 1952–1960 period. The first column lists the unemployment rate, which we might use as a measure of the "prevailing wind." That is, as unemployment increases, the Fed should ease its policy, and as unemployment decreases, the Fed should tighten its policy. The second column shows the annual percentage change in the money supply. Notice that as unemployment decreased from 1952 to 1953, the Fed reduced the growth rate in the money supply. When

Table 19.1
The Unemployment Rate and Selected Policy Variables, 1952–1960

				Annual Percentage Change in		
Year	Unemployment Rate	M_1	Monetary Base	Required Reserve Ratio*	Discount Rate
1952	3.0%	3.8	4.5	24%	1.75%
1953	2.9	1.1	−1.9	23	1.99
1954	5.5	2.7	−1.9	21	1.60
1955	4.4	2.2	0.6	20	1.89
1956	4.1	1.3	1.5	20	2.77
1957	4.3	−0.7	0.0	20	3.12
1958	6.8	3.8	−0.4	18.5	2.15
1959	5.5	1.6	0.6	18	3.36
1960	5.5	0.6	1.0	17.75	3.53

*Required reserve ratio on demand deposits.
Source: *Federal Reserve Bulletin,* various issues.

unemployment increased in 1954, the growth rate in the money supply was increased. With a lower level of unemployment in the years 1955 through 1957, the growth rate in the money supply was lower than it was in 1954. With an increase in unemployment again in 1958, the growth rate of the money supply was once again increased, and then reduced in 1959 and 1960 as unemployment fell. Thus it might seem at first glance as though the Fed was indeed leaning against the wind.

However, the third column, which shows the growth rate in the monetary base, casts some doubt on this conclusion. Notice that the growth rate of the monetary base was the same in 1953 and 1954 even though the unemployment rate was almost twice as high in 1954 as it was in 1953. Moreover in 1958, when the unemployment rate increased sharply, the growth rate in the monetary base was actually reduced still further. Thus the source of the percent changes in the money supply did not follow from changes in the monetary base induced through open market operations.

The fourth column, which shows the required reserve ratio on demand deposits, provides us with some clue to the source of changes in the growth in the money supply. Notice that throughout the period the required reserve ratio was steadily reduced. This reduction in the required reserve ratio more than offset the trend increase in the time deposit ratio, so that from 1952 to 1960 the base money multiplier increased from 2.63 to 2.99. There is some indication that the timing of reductions in the required reserve ratio coincided with increases in unemployment or high levels of unemployment. For example, during the years 1955 to 1957, unemployment was fairly steady at slightly more than 4 percent.

During that period, the required reserve ratio was held constant at 20 percent. Then in 1958, unemployment increased sharply, and the required reserve ratio was reduced by $1\frac{1}{2}$ percentage points. In 1959 and 1960, unemployment was slightly lower than in 1958, but still high by the standards of the 1950s. Consequently the required reserve ratio was steadily reduced in those years.

The last column in the table shows the Federal Reserve discount rate, which provides another clue to the Fed's countercyclical activities. Notice that the discount rate was increased as unemployment fell from 1952 to 1953, and then decreased as unemployment increased from 1953 to 1954. A similar pattern occurs in the rest of the years. Overall, then, it seems as though countercyclical policy was implemented primarily by changes in the discount rate and by the timing of reductions in the required reserve ratio rather than through open market operations.

Regardless of the policies followed, many observers feel that the performance of the economy during the 1950s was less than ideal. Indeed, certain actions of the Federal Reserve did not produce the effects one might expect from glancing at the figures in Table 19.1. For example, even though the discount rate was reduced in periods of increasing unemployment, the reductions were not adequate. Market interest rates fell by relatively greater amounts than the discount rate, so that in both 1954 and 1958 member bank borrowing actually decreased rather than increased. Thus the Fed apparently moved in the right direction, but with insufficient vigor. Given the lack of vigorous policy, the performance of the economy was erratic. The unemployment rate ranged from 2.9 percent in 1953 to 6.8 percent in 1958. The rate of inflation ranged from 0.9 percent in 1953 to 3.7 percent in 1957. Further, output growth was rather modest. In general, then, the period was characterized by fluctuations in economic activity and a rather modest rate of economic growth. It should be pointed out that fiscal policy was not very supportive either. Federal government expenditures actually decreased from 1953 through 1956. However, transfer payments were increased steadily throughout the period.

Nevertheless the Fed's policy of leaning against the wind may not have been the best approach. One reason for this is lags in effect of policy. If the Fed waits for a recession before engaging in antirecession activities, the impact of those policies may not be felt until the following upswing. Also, if anti-inflation policies are not implemented until inflation becomes severe, the effect of those policies may not be felt until the following recession. Thus leaning against the wind may intensify cyclical problems rather than moderate them. Moreover, the appropriate use of monetary policy was hampered by a general feeling among Keynesians that monetary policy, in the final analysis, didn't really matter. However, beginning with the election of President John F. Kennedy in 1960, significant changes occurred in official governmental attitudes toward policy. In particular, the election marks the ascendancy of Keynesian economics to the White House.

19.3   MONETARY POLICY IN THE 1960s

The Federal Reserve entered the 1960s equipped with essentially the same policy tools that it had in the 1950s. Minor structural modifications include the counting of vault cash as part of legal reserves beginning in late 1959 and a turnover of the job of system open market manager. In mid-1962, Robert W. Stone became the open market manager, replacing Robert G. Rouse. This may not appear to be significant until one recognizes that throughout most of its history the Federal Open Market Committee had issued directives to the system open market manager that were subject to varying interpretation. Thus a change of manager might imply a slightly different interpretation and consequently a slightly different policy.

However, in the early 1960s the dominant influence in the background was the policy stance of the Kennedy administration. During these years, the President's Council of Economic Advisors included such prominent Keynesians as James Tobin and Gardner Ackley, with Walter Heller as Chairman. The Council argued that the major concern should be the problem of unemployment. In the face of a growing labor force, higher rates of economic growth were necessary in order to reduce permanently the rate of unemployment. Inflation, in the Council's view, was relegated to the background and not considered to be much of a problem as long as the economy was at less than full employment. The Council argued for vigorous use of fiscal policy to stimulate the rate of growth in the economy. Monetary policy was cast in an accommodating role, if it had any role at all. In other words, fiscal policy was to take the lead in stimulating the economy, and monetary policy was to refrain from doing anything that would interfere with the success of the fiscal policy. The major specific fiscal policy recommendation was a reduction in tax rates to eliminate something the Council called "fiscal drag."

Fiscal drag is the consequence of a progressive income tax structure. As income levels rise higher and higher, marginal tax rates increase. Thus the constraints on spending imposed by taxes gradually increase automatically as the economy grows. This in itself, in the Keynesian view, retards economic growth. Consequently, the Council proposed that the entire tax structure be revised downward. The progressive features were to be retained, but the level of rates was to be reduced. Although proposed under the Kennedy administration, the tax cut was not finally passed until 1964 under the administration of Lyndon Johnson.

Accommodation implied that the Federal Reserve would have to increase the growth rate in the money supply to keep pace with increased growth rates in output. In order to accomplish this objective, the Fed had to be concerned with actions of the private sector, as those actions influenced the base money multiplier. However, those actions presented no particular difficulties. Both the excess reserve and currency ratios were relatively stable. Fluctuations in the excess reserve ratio ranged between 0.002 and 0.005, and the currency ratio fluctuations ranged between 0.25 and 0.28 during the 1961–1969 period. There was a steady upward trend in the time deposit ratio, from 0.69 in 1961 to 1.20 in 1969. This was an expected consequence of the steady upward trend in income. Reserve requirements were relatively constant throughout most of the period, so that the effect of private preferences was to reduce the base money multiplier from 2.99 in 1961 to 2.81 in 1969.

In addition to the problem of stimulating the growth rate in the economy, the United States was also running a significant balance of payments deficit. The Vietnam war dominated the latter half of the 1960s. War expenditures, coupled with the Great Society programs of President Johnson, placed heavy pressures upon the Federal Reserve System to provide adequate financing.

The Fed's conduct was generally in accord with fiscal objectives. The system engaged in substantial open market operations, increasing Federal Reserve holdings of United States government securities by 40.5 percent from 1961 to 1965 and by another 40.6 percent from 1965 to 1969. These increases were offset in part by outflows of gold. (The gold stock decreased by about $7 billion from 1961 to 1969.) Nevertheless the monetary base increased 18.4 percent from 1961 to 1965 and 26.3 percent from 1965 to 1969. These increases, together with the slight downward trend in the base money multiplier, resulted in an increase in the money supply of 15.2 percent from 1961 to 1965 and 21.8 percent from 1965 to 1969. These increases may be compared with a 13.2 percent increase in the money supply for the entire period from 1952 to 1960. Thus monetary stimulus was significantly greater in the 1960s than it was in the 1950s.

What may seem contrary to the rapid increase in the money supply was a steady increase in the discount rate from 3 percent in 1961 to nearly 6 percent in 1969. However, this is not as contradictory as it seems. While the discount rate doubled, many short-term market interest rates more than doubled. For example, the yield on three-month Treasury bills nearly tripled from 1961 to 1969. With market rates rising relative to the discount rate, we should expect a steady increase in member bank borrowing. In fact member bank borrowing did steadily increase, from $0.1 billion in 1961 to over $1.0 billion in 1969.* Federal Reserve increases in the discount rate were a reaction to rising market interest rates rather than the initiation of a new policy. In fact the most frequent reason used by the Fed to justify increases in the discount rate was to bring the discount rate into alignment with market rates. Had they not done this, member bank borrowing would have increased even more than it did.

Nevertheless such increases in the discount rate were sometimes interpreted by some observers as signals of impending tight money. For example, in

---

*The borrowed reserve ratio increased from 0.001 to 0.007. This would tend to increase the base money multiplier. See Chapters 5 and 6.

Table 19.2
Performance Comparisons, 1952–1960 and 1961–1969

Performance Measure	1952–1960	1961–1969
Average rate of unemployment	4.7%	4.7%
Average annual rate of output growth	2.9%	5.7%
Average annual rate of inflation	2.3%	2.8%

Source: *Economic Report of the President,* 1975.

December 1965 the Fed increased the discount rate from 4 to 4.5 percent. President Johnson was severely critical of this change, arguing that the Fed should have at least waited until the fiscal 1967 budget was released before implementing a tight money policy. However, many short-term market interest rates were already above 4 percent when the change was made.

During the first half of the 1960s, the Federal Reserve did make some attempts to cope with the balance of payments problem by changing the maturity structure of outstanding government debt. We have already discussed "operation twist" in an earlier chapter. Suffice it to say here that the evidence about its success is mixed, and the policy was terminated in 1965.

Aggressive fiscal policy together with supportive monetary policy yielded the desired performance. Unemployment declined steadily from 6.7 percent in 1961 to 3.5 percent in 1969. On the other hand, the annual rate of inflation increased steadily from 1.3 percent in 1961 to 4.8 percent in 1969. Output increased 45.9 percent over the entire period. Table 19.2 compares the performance of the unemployment rate, the rate of inflation, and the rate of output growth for the 1961–1969 period with the 1952–1960 period. While the average rates of unemployment are the same for the two periods, the trend was downward during the 1960s, while the unemployment rate fluctuated during the 1950s. The average annual rate of growth in output was almost twice as great in the 1960s as it was during the 1950s with an annual rate of inflation somewhat higher in the 1960s than in the 1950s. Moreover during the 1960s recessions were confined to a slight slowdown or "minirecession" in 1967. This was due in large part to a sharp slowdown in the growth rate of the money supply in 1966. The growth rate in the money supply was again sharply reduced in 1969, but the effects of this were not felt until 1970.

As successful as these policies seemed to be, they did set the stage for problems in the 1970s. The rate of inflation gradually accelerated until it became of major concern as the economy moved into the 1970s. Market interest rates rose steadily in the face of rapid monetary expansion. The latter phenomenon has engendered a new look at the relationship between monetary growth, rates of inflation, and interest rates. These ideas will prove to be of importance in the 1970s.

19.4 MONETARY POLICY IN THE 1970s

In terms of erratic performance, the 1970s look more like the 1950s than like the 1960s. Moreover, this performance is due in large part to the behavior of the policy makers. Consider the environment in which the Federal Reserve had to operate.

1. After several years of outspoken opposition to wage and price controls, President Richard Nixon froze wages and prices in August 1971.
2. For the first time since the 1930s, the United States decided, in 1971, to cease pegging the price of gold and went to flexible exchange rates.
3. After many long years the Vietnam war was brought to an unsuccessful conclusion.
4. In 1973 another Arab-Israeli war ignited a smouldering natural resource crisis. Suddenly the United States was faced with a severe oil shortage that signaled shortages in other resources.
5. In 1974, for the first time in United States history, a President resigned his office. Fiscal policy was uncertain and seemed to lack direction.
6. Throughout the period, federal deficits reached levels unseen since World War II.
7. Congress, as we reported in an earlier chapter, intensified pressures on the Federal Reserve.

In 1969 the economy reached its low point in unemployment. Because of inflationary pressures, the Fed sharply contracted the growth rate in the money supply. The effect was felt in 1970, and unemployment began to rise rapidly. In response, the Fed sharply reversed its 1969 stance. Table 19.3 summarizes the growth rates for the monetary base and the money supply. The federal deficit is also shown in the table.

Overall, from 1970 to 1974 the money supply grew 28.5 percent, which is significantly faster than in the 1965–1969 period cited in the preceding section.

Table 19.3
Selected Policy Variables, 1970–1975

	Annual Percentage Changes		
Year	**Money Supply**	**Monetary Base**	**Federal Deficit***
1970	6.0	5.8	$2.8 billion
1971	6.3	7.0	23.0
1972	8.7	5.4	23.2
1973	6.1	9.5	14.3
1974	4.7	8.2	3.4
1975	4.2	6.8	43.6

*Fiscal year basis.
Source: Federal Reserve Bulletin, various issues.

Table 19.4
Inflation and Unemployment, 1970–1975

Year	Rate of Inflation	Rate of Unemployment
1970	5.4%	4.9%
1971	4.5	5.9
1972	3.3	5.6
1973	5.6	4.9
1974	10.2	5.6
1975	8.4	8.5

Source: Federal Reserve Bulletin, various issues, and *Economic Report of the President,* 1975. The rate of inflation is the percent change in the GNP deflator (1958 = 100).

Thus the 1970s continue the acceleration in the money supply begun in the 1960s. The effects on unemployment and inflation are shown in Table 19.4. While the average rate of unemployment is higher in the 1970s than in the 1960s, so also is the rate of inflation. Moreover, the ranges for both variables are more extreme than they were in preceding decades. In fact, the most recent bout with unemployment began to raise the specter of the 1930s and must be held largely responsible for increased congressional pressures on the Federal Reserve.

What surprises many adherents of the Phillips curve is that the significantly higher rates of inflation in the 1970s are not accompanied by lower rates of unemployment. Another seeming curiosity is the fact that with historically high growth rates in the money supply, interest rates are not historically low, but high. A paradox? Not according to the monetarists.

Recall that according to the monetarists, price changes are closely related to changes in the money supply. If increased growth rates in the money supply give rise to inflationary expectations, both lenders and borrowers will make adjustments. Lenders will try to protect themselves by charging higher interest rates. Borrowers, expecting inflation to depreciate the value of the debt, will be willing to pay higher interest rates. Thus more rapid monetary growth, by generating increased inflationary expectations, results in higher market interest rates.

An alternative explanation is provided by the expanded federal borrowing that characterized the early 1970s. As a consequence of the deficits shown in Table 19.3 public debt held by the private sector increased by over $110 billion from the beginning of 1970 to the beginning of 1976. Without rising interest rates, the private sector might not have been induced to absorb such a large increase in the stock of public debt. Thus both monetarists and Keynesians may find the events of the 1970s consistent with their theories.

While the events of the 1970s (thus far) have created agony for policy makers, they have created new opportunities for testing existing and new economic theories. The results may permit more certain policy making in the 1980s. This of course, begs the question,"Should we employ stabilization policy at all?" The answer varies widely from economist to economist. From a practical standpoint, it is not certain whether we will ever develop the capability to conduct effective policy. The history of monetary policy is not one of unqualified success. Indeed, it is not clear that the 60 years of Federal Reserve activity resulted in an improvement in economic performance over that during the 60 years preceding the establishment of the Federal Reserve. Moreover, some economists argue that we will never gain sufficient expertise to manage, with a high degree of success, an economy as complex as that of the United States.

On the other hand, our understanding of the economy has improved a great deal over the past 60 years. Continued improvement may well make rational policy making possible. Thus the answer to the question "Can we manage the economy?" may be "Yes!" in the near future.

That still leaves the question,"Should we manage (or attempt to manage) the economy?" The answer to this question will reflect one's view of the proper role of government. In dealing with this issue, the economist has no more expertise than anyone else. The Employment Act of 1946 provided an answer of sorts. Yet the Act was passed in response to fears of a return of the Depression of the 1930s. Recent failures of policy have generated dissatisfaction with the role of government. Voices both inside and outside of government are questioning the role of government in the management of economic affairs. What the outcome of the current debate will be only time will tell.

SUMMARY NOTES

1. Monetary policy in the 1930s was characterized by a rapidly evolving structure and ample opportunity for the Fed to learn to use its policy tools.
2. During World War II monetary policy was subordinated to the war effort. The Fed was successful in keeping interest rates on government securities low.
3. The Federal Reserve–Treasury Accord of 1951 established the independence of the Fed from the need to support government bond prices.
4. During the 1950s the Fed tried to follow a policy of leaning against the prevailing wind.
5. Under the pressure of expansionary fiscal and monetary policy, unemployment steadily declined throughout most of the 1960s.
6. The 1970s introduced a problem not encountered before: high inflation, high unemployment, and high interest rates all at the same time.

DISCUSSION QUESTIONS

1. Examine data for the 1970s to see if the excess and borrowed reserve ratios respond to market interest rates and the discount rate as they did in the 1930s.
2. During the 1970s the growth rates of the money supply and the monetary base were different, implying changes in the base money multiplier. Examine data on the excess reserve, currency, and time deposit ratios to determine the source of changes in the multiplier.
3. Using whatever models and theories make sense to you, devise a policy strategy for the remainder of the 1970s.

APPENDIX

The end-of-chapter questions in the book are intended to provoke discussion and consideration of issues beyond those contained in the corresponding chapters. Some questions have answers, while others are open ended. Following are hints and/or answers for selected questions in the book.

CHAPTER 1

1. Ask yourself whether a transaction is completed when you use a credit card, money order, or traveler's check. When you use a credit card, are you transferring ownership over an asset or are you incurring a liability?

5. What can you do with a checking account or cash that you can't do with an ordinary savings account? Is that worth anything to you?

CHAPTER 2

2. Think of consumption as a means of adjusting one's actual stock of wealth to one's desired stock of wealth. Should we consider wealth as a determinant of consumption? What would be the direction of influence?

3. You should have answered false. Remember the concept of opportunity cost. What is the opportunity cost of using internal funds?

CHAPTER 3

2. Would you consider a NOW account to be a perfect substitute for a checking account at a commercial bank? Remember also the prohibition against the payment of interest on checking accounts.

CHAPTER 4

4. Equating the supply of and demand for loanable funds:

$$50 + 0.02y + 700R = gb - 300R$$

Given that $y = 1300$ and $gb = 100$,

$$50 + 0.02(1300) + 700R = 100 - 300R$$
$$R = 0.024 \text{ or } 2.4 \text{ percent}$$

$$\text{Quantity of loanable funds} = 100 - 300(0.024)$$
$$= 92.8$$

If y increases to 1400 from 1300, we have:

$$50 + 0.02(1400) + 700R = 100 - 300R$$
$$R = 0.022 \text{ or } 2.2 \text{ percent}$$

$$\text{Quantity of loanable funds} = 100 - 300(0.022)$$
$$= 93.4$$

CHAPTER 5

4. The currency, time deposit, excess reserve, and borrowed reserve ratios become zero, Thus,

$$m = \frac{1 + c}{r_T t + r_D + e - b + c}$$
$$= \frac{1 + 0}{0 + r_D + 0 - 0 + 0}$$
$$= \frac{1}{r_D}$$

CHAPTER 6

4. Ask yourself why banks hold excess reserves. Do they need more reserves than are necessary to pay off their deposit liabilities? Define the total amount of excess reserves desired in order that all deposit liabilities be settled. Substitute into the base money multiplier and simplify.

CHAPTER 7

3. The present value is

$$PV = \frac{\$10}{0.06} = \$166.67$$

The bond should be purchased. The effective yield is

$$^{10}/_{25} = 0.40 \text{ or } 40 \text{ percent}$$

6. Note that the rate of inflation can be considered to be the rate of return on commodities. As such it is a cost of holding money balances instead of commodities. If the rate of inflation increases, both asset and transaction money balances demanded will fall.

CHAPTER 8

3. For this question simply derive (graphically) two LM curves, one with fairly inelastic money demand and supply curves and one with fairly elastic money demand and supply curves.

4. Note how an increase in money demand affects the interest rate and how the change in the interest rate affects the portfolio decisions of banks and the nonbank public. Does the base money multiplier increase or decrease?

CHAPTER 9

2. Does an increase in real government spending directly or indirectly affect output demand? How about an increase in real net taxes? How does the magnitude of the marginal propensity to consume play a role?

CHAPTER 10

3. Note what effect on the interest rate an increase in the government deficit has when the monetary base is held constant, using the IS-LM model. Using the LB-LM model, consider an increase in real government net borrowing.

CHAPTER 11

1. Note that this change increases the private sector's holdings of bonds without any reduction in existing capital or money. Do you see why? What does this imply about total wealth held by the private sector? What is the net effect of the changes in government spending, wealth, and relative yields on output demand?

3. Think in terms of their uses as stores of value and of similarities in the services yielded by each asset.

CHAPTER 12

3. If properly answered, the first two questions should lead you to the conclusion that every model yields as many reduced-form equations as there are endogenous variables in the model. Moreover, each reduced-form equation contains all the exogenous variables and only one endogenous variable (the one explained by the equation).

CHAPTER 13

2. You first must define equitable. Does it mean that everyone should pay the same interest rate? Should interest rates reflect relative preferences among people? Should the banker's preferences play a role? Who should decide whether the borrower really "needs" the loan, the lender or the borrower?

CHAPTER 14

1. Note that if the demand for petroleum products is price-inelastic, an increase in price will increase total expenditures on petroleum products. What does this imply about expenditures on other goods and services, given the level of nominal income? What will permit an increase in nominal income?

5. For this question think in terms of costs and benefits at the margin. For example, what are the expected increases in the costs and benefits of an additional year of college?

CHAPTER 15

2. Note that changes in the domestic price level influence both the LM and IS curves. Does a change in the price level result in a shift in or a movement along the IS curve?

6. Notice that outflows of foreign reserves are now offset, so that the LM curve cannot shift leftward.

CHAPTER 16

3. Don't forget that the required change in the money supply will be a multiple of the change in the monetary base.

5. This question gets you into issues dealt with in "political economy." What is the proper role of government in a democracy? What does the Constitution say about the role of Congress in regulating money? Does the economic knowledge of the people, or their representatives, make any difference?

CHAPTER 17

1. Is the yield on existing capital an endogenous or exogenous variable? Can you think of a way to measure the yield on existing capital? What do corporate shares represent?

6. Think of the proper role of government in the economy as it might be defined by the "typical" monetarist. Is the role completely determined by considerations of economic stability?

CHAPTER 18

2. Note whether the changes in the interest rate and price level produce indirect wealth effects that offset or reinforce the direct wealth effect.

NAME INDEX

SUBJECT INDEX